The Uses of Terror
The Soviet Secret Police 1917–1970

THE USES OF TERROR

The Soviet Secret Police 1917–1970

BORIS LEVYTSKY

Translated by H. A. Piehler

COWARD, McCANN & GEOGHEGAN, INC.
NEW YORK

Printed in Great Britain

Contents

To

the memory of my parents and my brothers Myron and
Olezy, innocent victims of Stalin's Terror

Foreword
to the English Edition

T H E first edition of this work appeared under the title of *Vom Roten Terror zur Sozialistischen Gesetzlichkeit* (From the Red Terror to Socialist Legality), nearly ten years ago, even before Khrushchev and other Soviet leaders had for the first time, at the 22nd Party Congress in 1961, spoken openly and in detail concerning the blackest chapter in Soviet history, the crimes of Joseph Stalin. The second edition, with much additional material, was published under the title of *Die Rote Inquisition* and was followed by translation in French and Italian. The present edition, in English, includes the latest developments in the Soviet Union, down to the middle of 1970, the final chapter being based almost entirely on information derived direct from the Soviet Union itself—information that was illegally circulated there through the underground publications of the *Samisdat*.

The author has been studying internal Soviet problems for over twenty years and he uses sociological methods. His object was to determine and clarify the part played by terrorism in the Soviet system and Soviet society. The security service, as the instrument of terrorism, is intimately involved in every phase of Soviet history. Some critics may feel that the author's ascription of such a key role to the security service is overdone, but an attempt to confine an account of the Soviet system exclusively to its political and economic aspects would be a falsification of history, and that view is valid even down to the present day.

Many reviewers have paid the author the compliment of comparing this book to a thrilling crime novel. It is a fact that he found it essential to include many dramatic and exciting incidents in his account of the history of the Soviet Union and especially of its security service. But he has always been most anxious to avoid presenting a distorted picture, and on many occasions he found it quite impossible to describe the cruel facts without denouncing the despotic cynicism of the authorities responsible. Apart from providing the reader with reliable information and analyses of events, the author hopes that he is assisting in some small measure those progressive and courageous spirits in the Soviet Union who are striving for a better future all round and, in unimaginably difficult conditions and under the oppressive rule of a power-drunk reactionary establishment, are struggling for the realization of true legality and the defence of human dignity.

August 1970 B.L.

Chapter One

Lenin and the Terror

C A S T your mind back to the year 1917. Tsarist Russia no longer exists. In Petrograd (which was St Petersburg before the First World War and today is Leningrad) there has been a provisional government since February. The revolutionary ferment has permeated the country. The Bolsheviks, led by Lenin, are far from being the largest political party in Russia, but they know exactly what they want. In the late autumn of 1917 they resolved to seize power by an armed rising, and on 24 and 25 October (6 and 7 November)[1] they made themselves masters of Petrograd. Simultaneously came Lenin's summons 'To the Citizens of Russia', and the first Bolshevist government was created. Soon afterwards there was fighting in Moscow too, and on 2 November troops in sympathy with the Bolsheviks occupied the Kremlin. With Lenin's revolutionary slogan 'All Power to the Soviets!', i.e. the councils set up by the people, the Bolsheviks seized power throughout the country between the end of October 1917 and March 1918.

At that time the Bolsheviks were still a comparatively small group. In a population of about 140 million the party numbered a quarter of a million at the most. Thus there was only a single committed Bolshevik for every six hundred inhabitants. But even these figures do not give a true picture, for only a few party members had at that time any definitely Bolshevist political aims, and they were only thinly scattered over the whole country. In the great cities and industrial centres, of course, they had a strong backing, but only a few miles outside Moscow, for example, foreign journalists who asked the peasants 'Who is Lenin?' were told 'He is our Tsar'. The peasants had no knowledge of Communism or the struggle between the parties, but they had heard that Lenin[2] would give them the land. There were districts with a population of hundreds of thousands where a single Communist was a rarity. Nevertheless the October Revolution was a mass movement.

What forced Lenin and the leaders of the Bolsheviks, in such a situation, to create a security apparatus, a political police?

At this point a brief sociological reflection seems to be appropriate, for one of the most important social backgrounds of events in Russia is still overlooked by many historians and research workers. According to Karl Marx's teaching, the workers, the proletariat, are the primary instrument of social upheavals. Marx drew a clear distinction between the workers and those plebeian elements that he called the 'Lumpen Proletariat' (ragamuffin proletariat). According to Marx, the 'Lumpen Proletariat' had nothing to do with a real revolutionary change, with the struggle for a new historical development. It was more likely on the other hand to sabotage the success of the working classes, and could in fact completely nullify any such success.

When the workers go to the barricades, fight against the police and the army, and occupy government buildings, that is the natural course of a proletarian revolution. But what has it to do with revolution when the mob plunders the shops, sets fire to museums and churches, and wantonly destroys everything it can lay its hands on? In every society there are dregs in the form of antisocial people, Marx's 'Lumpen Proletariat', who are especially numerous in the transition to industrial development. Hitherto there has been no precise sociological analysis of the events of the Russian Revolution. Both elements—proletarian and plebeian—played decisive roles. Lenin was well aware of the difference between action by class-conscious workers and excesses committed by street mobs. But his strategic genius also envisaged the possibility of utilizing the destructive capacity of the 'Lumpen Proletariat' in the struggle against Tsarism and the Bolshevik seizure of power. The working class in the narrow sense was extremely weak in the Russia of those days.[3] So Lenin had to try to buttress the revolutionary struggle of class-conscious workers by making deliberate use of the mob.

Moral responsibility for the excesses of the masses—the murdering of landowners, the destruction of historic monuments and museums—must, of course, be borne by the Bolsheviks, who in 1917 deliberately included mob violence in their plans; however, the ensuing mob violence exceeded to a terrifying degree the violence that Lenin planned. The 'Lumpen Proletariat' eagerly adopted Lenin's slogan 'Rob the robbers!' and a wave of abominable crimes swept across Russia. Bandits calling themselves proletarians, Bolsheviks, or anarchists plundered and burnt, raped and murdered.

The struggle with political opponents was not the sole reason for setting up security organizations. An important part was played by the necessity for measures to combat increasing criminality and to restore elementary law and order. The combination of terror and the need to protect public order was possibly from the outset fatal to any hope of establishing an equitable code of justice. Anyone who tries to derive the origin of terror in the Soviet Union from Communist ideology should pay more attention to its actual development. Among the Bolsheviks the fear of 'counter-revolution' was widespread. Primarily, of course, the charge of counter-revolution was directed at political opponents, but banditry and criminal deeds were included in the condemnation.

For public safety in Petrograd the Military Revolutionary Committee was responsible. On 21 November (4 December) 1917, on the proposal of Dzerzhinsky,[4] a special commission was set up to deal with counter-revolution. This was the first security organ of the Bolsheviks, though only on a local and miniature scale. On 6(19) December 1917, at Lenin's proposal, a session of the Council of People's Commissars resolved that 'Comrade Dzerzhinsky be entrusted with the formation of a special commission to examine the possibilities of revolutionary measures to counter strikes and malevolent sabotage'. On the next day, i.e. on 7(20) December, Lenin proposed a decree to set up such a commission. He wrote to Dzerzhinsky: 'The bourgeoisie, the landowners, and the wealthy classes are making desperate efforts to undermine the Revolution.' This memorandum formed the basis for Dzerzhinsky's speech on the necessity of 'creating an organ of the dictatorship of the proletariat in order to protect the security of the Soviet Republic'. It was entitled 'Extraordinary Commission for the Struggle against Counter-Revolution, Speculation, and Sabotage'. In Russian, 'Vserosyskaya Chrezvuchaynaya Kommisya no Borbye s Kontrevolutzryey i Spekulyazyey Zabotazhem', abbreviated to VECHEKA.

All Soviet sources insist that this happened on the personal initiative of Lenin. He decided also that Dzerzhinsky should be the head of Vecheka, which was then and is now commonly known as the Cheka. Experienced Bolsheviks were appointed to the Board of the Vecheka. The most important were two Letts, Martin Yanovich Latsis (Sudrabs), a member of the Party since 1905, and Yakov Khristoforovich Peters, a member since 1904. Other members of the Board were: V. A. Avanezov (1903), G. I. Boky (1900), Vazily Vazilevich Fomin (1912), Mikhail Sergeyevich Kedrov (1901), Ivan Kzenofontovich Kzenofontov (1903), F. D. Medvedy (1907), V. R. Menzhinsky (1902), I. D. Chugurin (1902), Yosif Stanislavovich Unshlikht (1900), and S. G. Uralov (1914).

When Anarchists and other political opponents of the Bolsheviks took up arms against them and severe counter-measures seemed to be unavoidable, Lenin, who was wrapped up in the history of the French Revolution, asked: 'Is it impossible to find among us a Fouquier-Tinville, to tame our wild counter-revolutionaries?'[5] His glance fell on Felix Dzerzhinsky.

Felix Edmundovich Dzerzhinsky[6] was a strange person—a fanatical revolutionary, but quite different from all other revolutionary leaders of the time. They betrayed a hunger for power in their actions and attitude, but Dzerzhinsky was an ascetic. It is said that he had dreamy eyes like Don Quixote, and some compared his face to Christ's. His character was a mixture of severity, cruelty, and poetic sentimentality.

Like many other revolutionaries, Dzerzhinsky did not have a proletarian background. Born on 11 September 1877, in the district of Vilna, he was a scion of the minor Polish nobility. In 1894 he made his first acquaintance with Socialist literature, joined an illegal Socialist circle, and began a fanatical study of the works of Karl Marx. When in 1895 he joined the Lithuanian National Democratic Party at Vilna, he immediately became a member of the Left Wing and embarked on assiduous revolutionary activity among the artisans and craftsmen of Vilna, for there were no true proletarians or factory workers there. In 1896 he left high school of his own free will in order to become a provincial revolutionary. He was given the task of founding the first revolutionary groups in Kaunas. There he published an illegal newspaper in the Polish language, and became a correspondent for various Socialist periodicals in other parts of Poland. On 17 July 1897 he was arrested for the first time and kept in solitary confinement at Kaunas for a whole year.

In the Lithuanian and Polish workers' movement there arose about the turn of the century a passionate discussion as to whether the Polish and the Lithuanian Socialist parties should carry on an independent struggle for liberation from Tsarist Russia, or whether they should be merely branches of the Russian Social Democratic Workers' Party. Dzerzhinsky was already playing an outsider's part: He was working to degrade the Lithuanian and Polish Socialist parties into mere offshoots of the Russian Socialist movement and he stigmatized all opponents as 'Nationalists'. In his memoirs he expressed his consternation at the decision of the Lithuanian Social Democratic Party to act independently. In 1898 he was sent for three years to Nolinsk in the government of Vyatka. There he worked in a tobacco factory, but when he resumed his practice of preaching revolution among the workpeople, he was sent off to a village under police surveillance. In August 1899 he fled to Warsaw and helped to rebuild the Social Democratic Party, which had been scattered by the Russian gendarmerie. He was arrested again in 1900, and after several months' imprisonment in Warsaw Citadel he was sentenced to five years' banishment in Eastern Siberia. He escaped again in 1902, this time to Berlin, where he contacted Lenin's famous journal *Iskra* and at once joined him in the effort to build up a Marxist party. In this connection he organized the 4th Congress of the Social Democratic Parties of Poland and Lithuania, at which he advocated the union of the two parties with the Russian Social Democratic Workers' Party. This step, however, was never completely effected, as only a small group of members backed Dzerzhinsky, who both in Lithuania and in Poland was always a somewhat lonely figure. When in 1905 the first Russian revolution broke out, Dzerzhinsky was in Warsaw. He organized strikes in Warsaw, Lodz, and Czestochowa, and in the mining districts. Arrested in July 1905 but amnestied in October, he was soon afterwards found among the instigators of a strike in Silesia.

At the 4th Congress of the Russian Social Democratic Workers' Party at Stockholm in 1906 Dzerzhinsky came into personal contact with Lenin, Stalin, and Trotsky. In the quarrel with the

Mensheviks he was an unconditional supporter of Lenin's proposals. Arrested again the same year in Warsaw, he escaped in 1907, was re-arrested in 1908, and a year later sent to Siberia. When he succeeded in escaping once more, in November 1909, he visited Capri in order to restore his impaired health. He returned to Poland in 1911, but was soon re-arrested, and it was only the February revolution of 1917 that restored him to freedom. He at once joined the Party's preparations for revolt and as an experienced Leninist became a member of the Central Committee of the Russian Social Democratic Workers' Party.

These particulars of Dzerzhinsky's former career provide a good picture of his personality. Even in his youth he was looked upon by his own comrades as a renegade, for he had a fixed idea that the Polish people could only be liberated in company with the Russian proletariat. He hated the Polish Socialists who advocated an independent revolution even more than he hated the Russian Chauvinists. Lenin's ironical remark that among the non-Russian Communists there were more chauvinistic champions of a Greater Russia than among the Russian Communists themselves, applied to Dzerzhinsky as much as to Stalin.

All the Bolshevist leaders were in principle agreed that terror as a means to destroy the enemy and set up a dictatorship of the proletariat was essential. But Lenin said frequently that terror was not only unavoidable in the transition stage, but also had a positive role to play. The problem revealed the contradiction between Lenin the idealist and Lenin the revolutionary strategist and statesman. At one time he writes that 'In our ideals there is no place for the use of force against people'. The Communists were fighting for a society in which violence would be unnecessary. On the other hand, Lenin stated emphatically that enemies could never be forced to surrender by merely preaching to them. That was the teaching of history. Lenin was thinking of the Paris Commune of 1871. When the workers seized power on 18 March 1871, only one officer was killed and only one general wounded. But when the counter-revolution crushed the Paris Commune 30,000 Communards lost their lives. Lenin believed that the Commune failed merely because it had omitted to destroy its enemies when they were in its power. Lenin's basic attitude was that in principle Communists were against terror and violence, but without them they could not break the resistance of their implacable enemies. Lenin was in the habit of supplementing this opinion by a theory that the Bolsheviks' forceful measures were only a temporary phenomenon, and differed from similar measures taken in the past by the fact that they 'represented the will of the people' and gained their validity from the consent of the great majority of the people.[7]

Such views of Lenin's led him to chose Dzerzhinsky to be the Grand Inquisitor of the Revolution. On the one hand, Dzerzhinsky's fanaticism was a guarantee that he would show no pity towards the people's enemies; on the other hand, his ascetism and modesty were a promise that he would never misuse the powers of such an autocratic post.

In 1917 the Bolsheviks had formed a sort of coalition with the Left-Wing Social Revolutionaries, who loudly expressed their objection to the use of terror. The post of People's Commissar of Justice was occupied in the first government under Lenin by the Left-Wing Social Revolutionary I. Z. Shteynberg. Even in revolutionary conditions Shteynberg tried to build up a judiciary system, and he protested against all the arbitary acts of the Vecheka. Very often he ordered the release of people who had been arrested, and insisted that all such cases be discussed by the Council of People's Commissars. In order to keep quarrels to a minimum Commissar Shteynberg drafted the Vecheka statutes in such a way that the competence of the organization was strictly limited. Lenin welcomed his initiative and himself proposed several additions and amendments. Thus the first statute of the Soviet security organization came into being as a compromise between the Bolsheviks and the Left-Wing Social Revolutionaries. With the whole weight of his authority Lenin sought to enlarge the competence of the Vecheka. The most ticklish question was whether the Vecheka should carry out arrests on its own authority. The Left-Wing Social Revolutionaries demanded as a minimum, in order to retain a certain degree of law and order, that arrests should be made only with the knowledge of the People's Commissars of Justice and Home Affairs. Lenin succeeded in getting a resolution passed that the Vecheka could make its own decisions regarding arrests, but must notify the People's Commissar of Justice simultaneously. Should differences arise as a result of this regulation they were to be decided by the Council of People's Commissars.[8] Lenin laughed at objections to the enlargement of the Vecheka's powers, even when they came from his closest collaborators: 'How can one make a revolution without executions?' he replied to Kamenev when the latter, at that time one of Dzerzhinsky's closest friends, voted for the repeal of the death sentence for deserters from the front. When in 1918 discontent at the arbitrary actions of the Vecheka grew more and more vocal Lenin became its most prominent defender. On 7 November 1918 there was an assembly in Moscow and at the same time a concert for the Vecheka staff. Lenin used the opportunity to explain that he defended the Vecheka 'not only from our enemies, but also very often from our friends'. He tried to convince the public that one should not squabble over a few border-line cases, but should view the work of the Vecheka as a whole.[9]

Lenin's constant argument was that responsibility for the use of terror lay with the enemy. He tried to mollify and convince Shteynberg, the People's Commissar of Justice, with these words: 'We don't use the terror weapon in the style of the French Revolution, i.e. guillotine helpless people. I hope we shall never do so in the future, for we are in power.' Almost simultaneously Trotsky, one of Lenin's most popular colleagues, declared that it was the sabotage and unrest caused by the Bolsheviks' opponents that provoked the terror. He added: 'We are strong and have no need to go to extremes. Nevertheless everybody must realize that the people will not be patient indefinitely and will sweep away all obstacles in its path.'[10]

One episode in Lenin's life as politican and statesman had a considerable influence on his attitude towards the security organs. There is no mention of it in most of the books about the revolution in Russia, and so a few words about it are perhaps in place.

In the reference books published since Stalin's death there are complete lists of members of the Central Committee of the Communist Party. Among the committee members of the 4th Congress of the Russian Socialist Workers' Party (i.e. Bolshevik) in 1912 is R. V. Malinovsky, with the word *provocateur* in brackets after his name. In the history of illegal revolutionary movements it is far from rare that a *provocateur* is able to acquire a leading position inside a revolutionary group. But the fact that an agent of the Tsarist secret police could work himself into Lenin's innermost staff is unprecedented. Malinovsky was unmasked while abroad. Although he knew what awaited him on his return, he came back to Russia in 1918. He was arrested, tried with N. V. Krylenko as accuser, condemned, and shot. The incident became a matter of conscience for Lenin. There were several reasons for this. On the one hand, this close associate of Lenin's was responsible for the arrest of hundreds of revolutionaries. On the other, the Mensheviks were trying to discredit the general policy methods of Lenin and the Bolsheviks, basing their arguments on the Malinovsky case. From some of Lenin's statements it is clear that he was trying to look with different eyes on the secret methods hitherto employed by him. He admitted, for example, that Malinovsky might have done far more damage if the Party had confined itself to illegal measures. It sounds rather naive, coming from the mouth of a statesman and political strategist like Lenin, when he says that through the division into legal and illegal measures the *provocateur* Malinovsky found himself obliged to play also a positive role inasmuch as he had to disseminate Bolshevik ideas. 'With one hand Malinovsky sent dozens and dozens of the best Bolsheviks to forced labour and death, with the other he was compelled to create thousands of new Bolsheviks by educating them through the legal Press.'

Lenin was now faced with the problem of how to detect and nullify the machinations of possible *provocateurs* within the Party. We have no certainty that Lenin relied on the Vecheka alone; in fact it is clear from his writings that to protect the Party from the activities of traitors he took other steps, e.g. screening the background of Party members and constant purges in the Party. Still one must assume that in extreme cases he consulted Dzerzhinsky.

All this shows that Lenin was not only the creator of the Red Terror machine, but was also its 'regulator'. As the great strategist of the October Revolution he determined the ebb and flow of the Terror, e.g. when it was permissible for the Chekists to shoot enemies on the spot without a trial, and when on the other hand a strict observance of the laws was required of them, even a minor maltreatment of arrested persons entailing a loss of career. The other Communist leaders were in full agreement with Lenin's attitude on this question.

Immediately after its foundation the Cheka set up its head-quarters in Petrograd, but its statutes were not laid down until a year later, i.e. in November 1918. The Cheka was thereby set up as an organ of the Soviet Government, to work in close liaison with the People's Commissariats of Justice and Home Affairs. Its members were to be appointed by the government. They were allowed to maintain their own military units, which, however, were in no case to take over the authority of the militia.

The Cheka expanded in two directions, territorially and functionally. Cheka branches were established in all the Soviet republics, and, secondarily, Cheka units were set up in transport, industry, the army, etc. Dzerzhinsky succeeded in penetrating with his organization all spheres of life in Soviet Russia and the other Soviet republics. As early as 1918 the Chekists could boast: 'There is no region in our possession on which the Cheka has not its eagle eye.' The police organization in the Soviet Army and Fleet was of special importance; it was created in February 1919 and bore the name of 'Special Department'. It was even earlier, in 1918, that the Cheka began to develop a system of concentration camps.

The basis for this great expansion of the Cheka under Dzerzhinsky was the introduction of the 'Red Terror'. When the Cheka was founded the Bolshevik leaders under Lenin probably had no precise idea of what it would lead to. In the first days of Soviet power in Petrograd the Chekists were certainly busier with the extermination of looters and robbers than with fighting counter-revolutionaries. 'Immediately after the Revolution of 25 October 1917', wrote Lenin on one occasion, 'we did not even stop the bourgeois newspapers and of terror there was no trace. . . . It was not until the exploiters, i.e. the capitalists, began to increase their resistance that we retaliated by systematically suppressing them— a policy that culminated in Terror.'

Each revolution seems to be a separate case, but in such times all humane feelings—most of all, of course, in the security organs— are stifled. It may be that the Cheka developed into a blood-stained terror machine more quickly than even its creators wanted.

In September 1917 the Council of People's Commissars had drafted in very general terms the tasks allotted to the Cheka. These directives made no overt reference to arbitrary proceedings and terror, though they contained certain elastic formulas which could be interpreted according to wish or necessity. The three main tasks of the Cheka were expressed in the following terms:

1. All measures and actions of counter-revolutionaries and saboteurs anywhere in Russia—no matter from which direction they come—are to be suppressed and liquidated.
2. All saboteurs and counter-revolutionaries are to be handed over to be judged by the revolutionary tribunal, and directives to combat them are to be drafted.
3. Preliminary investigations are to be carried out only where necessary as preventive measures.

It is clear from this that in the beginning the Cheka was not entitled to pass sentences or carry out executions. The revolutionary tribunals[12] had nothing to do with the Cheka. They were special revolutionary courts which in accordance with the decree of the Council of the People's Commissars passed on 24 November 1917 had been set up in order to suppress 'counter-revolution and most dangerous crimes'. From the middle of 1918 onwards they were subject to the regional state organizations, i.e. the soviets. They were intended to be the beginning of a regular system of justice under the control of the appropriate authorities, and in 1922 they were finally dissolved. The Cheka had merely to investigate individual cases and then hand them over to the tribunals for judgement.

The definitive transformation of the Cheka, however, happened as early as 1918. The Bolsheviks were faced with overwhelming tasks. In the non-Russian areas of the former Tsarist Russia there were uprisings everywhere, inspired by nationalist sentiments. As whole regions began to fall away, the Bolsheviks in Petrograd and Moscow felt more and more insecure. The 'White Terror' of the anti-Communists found a more favourable soil than before. The coalition between the Bolsheviks and the Left-Wing Social Revolutionaries was approaching a crisis. The total collapse of the economy brought famine to the cities and opportunities to speculators. When Lenin on 1(14) January 1918 was returning from a conference, his car was shot at, although he was escorted by Red Guards. The car was damaged and the windshield shattered, but Lenin himself escaped unhurt. In spite of all the Cheka's efforts the attackers escaped and succeeded in joining the White Armies in the Don region. At the end of January the Council of People's Commissars adopted for the first time a threatening tone towards the food-speculators: 'We are helpless if we do not use terror and do not shoot speculators on the spot.' After the temporary breaking-off of peace negotiations with the Germans at Brest-Litovsk on 18 February 1918 the anti-Communist armies, with Anglo-French aid, increased their activities, and the situation in Russia grew more and more desperate. On 23 February the Vecheka published the following statement in *Pravda*: 'The Vecheka hitherto has always been tolerant in its struggle against the enemies of the people. But now, when the hydra of counter-revolution, encouraged by the treacherous attack of the Germans, grows bolder every day, and the world bourgeoisie is trying to crush the vanguard of international revolution, i.e. the Russian proletariat, the Vecheka sees no means of combating counter-revolutionaries, spies, speculators, thugs, roughs, saboteurs, and other parasites, except by mercilessly destroying them on the spot.' The various sections of the Cheka throughout the country were urged to ferret out the enemies of the revolution and render them harmless on the spot.

This was the first intimation to the Cheka that they were now allowed to shoot—and on the very next day the first shots rang out in Moscow. A man called Eboli was shot by the Moscow Chekists without trial because he was trying to blackmail someone who had forged papers. The Chekists long boasted that the shooting of 'Prince Eboli' (as he called himself) was an example of 'Chekist justice'. In previous months several White Guard organizations had been suppressed—e.g. the 'Association of Real Aid', the 'White Cross', the 'Black Point', and 'All for the Fatherland'—without their leaders suffering capital punishment. The Eboli case ushered in a new era. It was the first death sentence carried out by the Vecheka on its own responsibility. Previously death sentences had been carried out by other institutions, usually by the 'Revolutionary Tribunal'.

The Moscow Cheka was founded in February 1918. Its director was M. Y. Latsis, who at that time was Dzerzhinsky's right hand man and one of the most feared of the Chekists. On 10 March 1918 Dzerzhinsky transferred the headquarters of the Vecheka from Petrograd to Moscow, and a few days later, on the 18th, he began its first reorganization. He approached suitable party and state organizations with a request for the seconding of useful personnel for service in the Vecheka. On 18 April the 'Soviet Finnish Department' was affiliated to the Vecheka, which was then amalgamated with the 'Lettish Department', already existent in Moscow, and the two were formed into a military unit, which became the most reliable instrument of state security.

In April 1918 the Vecheka succeeded in accomplishing a task that was of vital importance for the restoration of public order in Moscow, viz. the destruction of the Anarchists. There has been no detailed research into the origin and growth of the Anarchist movement in the Moscow of the period, but Soviet sources agree with the few reports published in the West that it had changed from a political into a terrorist movement, and was rendering Moscow unsafe by brutal attacks, murders, and assassinations. In George F. Kennan's book *America and the Soviet Power* it is stated that the foreign diplomatic missions felt particularly threatened, and demanded that the Bolsheviks should take drastic measures against the Anarchists.

The Anarchists had organized a so-called 'Black Guard'. It appears that the Anarchist theoreticians were gradually losing their influence on the organization and that the Guards were practising 'anarchism' off their own bat. They installed themselves in houses of wealthy Russian families in Moscow's villa quarters and held parties which not seldom ended in orgies.

The resolutions passed by the Moscow authorities against the Anarchists proved ineffectual because they could only be carried out by force. The authorities tried to avoid open fighting in the streets of Moscow, for everybody knew that the 'Black Guard' were well armed and would fight to the last. Dzerzhinsky therefore had to prepare the action against the Anarchists with great care. In the night of 11–12 April their hiding places were stormed and searched by selected and well-armed Lettish troops of the Vecheka. The Black Guards put up a stubborn resistance and to crush them the Vecheka had to call in artillery. The machine-gun fire of the Anarchists caused severe losses among the Chekists.

Dzerzhinsky had invited several members of the French, British, and American diplomatic missions in Moscow to witness the action. In his book Kennan published an extract from a report by Bruce Lockhart, head of a special British mission to the Soviet

Union at the time. They went from house to house. The filth was indescribable. Broken bottles were scattered over the floor. Splendid ceilings were perforated with bullet-holes. Aubusson carpets were defiled with wine-stains and human excrement. Valuable paintings had been slashed. Dead men lay where they had fallen. Among them were officers in Guards' uniform, students, lads of twenty, and men who obviously belonged to the criminal classes and who had been let out of prison by the revolutionaries. In the luxurious drawing room of the Gracheva Palace some of the Anarchists were surprised in an orgy. The long dining table with the remains of a banquet had been overturned, and broken plates, glasses, and champagne bottles lay among a pool of blood and spilt wine. Face downwards on the floor lay a young woman. Peters turned her over. Her hair was loose. She had been shot in the neck, and her blood was clotted and purple. She was barely twenty years of age. Peters shrugged his shoulders, 'Prostitutka,' he said. 'Perhaps that was the best for her.'

Foreign observers in Moscow at the time were of the opinion that Dzerzhinsky's successful action against the Black Guards greatly strengthened the authority of the Bolsheviks in Moscow.

On 11–14 June 1918 the first conference of Cheka officials was held in Moscow. Sixty-six delegates from forty-three Cheka units passed a series of resolutions reorganizing the Vecheka. The chief theme of the conference was the campaign against speculation and corruption. The second question on the agenda was the establishment of a special force for the Cheka. The already existing 'military unit' of the Cheka was transformed into the 'Corps of the Vecheka Armed Forces'. This move was to prove of vital importance in view of the fact that the position of the Bolsheviks had badly deteriorated again during the summer of 1918 owing to their open conflict with the Left-Wing Socialist Revolutionaries.

During the coalition between the Bolsheviks and the Left-Wing Socialist Revolutionaries the latter held several posts in the Council of People's Commissars and other State organizations. There was also a Left-Wing Socialist Revolutionary, we know, at the head of the Commissariat of Justice. Through his influence, several of his party friends had been co-opted on the board of the Vecheka, and among them was a certain Popov, who commanded a Vecheka section in Moscow.

The Left-Wing Socialist Revolutionaries, after the Cheka had obtained permission to use firearms, realized that they themselves had to face an uncertain future. The Cheka consisted almost exclusively of Bolsheviks and, with few exceptions, had Bolshevik leaders. The Left-Wing Socialist Revolutionaries could foresee a speedy end to their coalition with the Bolsheviks, so they decided to alter their tactics. Their more radical elements resolved on direct action against the Bolsheviks, using all the terrorist methods.

There were various 'minor' attacks on both sides, until on 20 June 1918 the murder of W. Wolodarski gave the signal for open hostilities.

Wolodarski, son of a poor Jewish workman in Volhynia, had had quite a colourful political past. As a youth he joined the Jewish Socialist organization known as the 'Bund', which was detested by Lenin, and later he supported the anti-Lenin Menshevik wing of the Russian Social Democratic Workers' Party. He was several times arrested, beaten up, and deported. In 1915, on his return from exile in Siberia, he emigrated to the USA, where he attached himself to the American Workers' Movement. Back in Petrograd by 1917, he joined the Bolsheviks. He rose speedily in the Petrograd party organization and when the Bolsheviks assumed power he became Commissar of Propaganda and Agitation, besides being chief editor of the *Red Newspaper*. He was murdered by Sergeiyev, one of the Left-Wing Socialist Revolutionaries.

At once Lenin personally advocated a strengthening of terror measures in Petrograd. But the situation was quickly overshadowed by fresh events. The Left-Wing Socialist Revolutionaries were only a section of the Socialist Revolutionary Party, which had played an extremely important part in the Russian Revolution. In the summer of 1918 it gained the upper hand in many districts and was joined in June by the troops of the famous Czechoslovak Legion, who were already in conflict with the Bolshevik armies. It is easy to imagine that the feelings of the Socialist Revolutionaries were in sympathy with those of their Left Wing, which meanwhile had become more and more hostile to Lenin's policy. In these circumstances the Left-Wing Socialist Revolutionaries likewise resolved on direct action against Lenin and his party. At the 5th Congress of the Soviets they put forward a programme consisting of five points: (1) immediate abolition of forcible confiscation of grain from the peasants; (2) reform of the Red Army; (3) immediate abolition of the Cheka; (4) peace with the Czechoslovak Legion; (5) initiation of a partisan war against the German troops occupying the Ukraine and parts of South Russia.

The rebellion of the Left-Wing Socialist Revolutionaries met with strong sympathy from the rural population, and also from many officers of the Red Army. To Lenin's and Dzerzhinsky's dismay, some of the leading Cheka officers were undisguisedly cool in their attitude.

While the Soviet Congress was still discussing the programme outlined above, the Left-Wing Socialist Revolutionaries staged an open rebellion in Moscow. On 6 June 1918, at midday, the leaders of the revolt assembled in the building of the Vecheka. The sections subordinate to Popov, the Left-Wing Social Revolutionary, became the headquarters of the rebels. At the same time two young men drove up to the German embassy in Moscow. Their car waited in front of the house with its engine running, while they presented to the secretary of the Embassy an official document from the Vecheka which authorized them to negotiate with the German Ambassador. Their names were Yakov Blumkin and Nikolay Andreyev. They refused to deal with subordinate officials at the Embassy. When finally they were received by the German Ambassador, Count Mirbach, the two visitors drew their revolvers and shot him down. Mortally wounded, he fled into another room, and, to make sure, the assassins threw a hand-grenade after him.

The news of the murder of Count Mirbach electrified all Moscow. The identity of the assassins soon became known. The Bolshevik leaders, usually so self-confident, were filled with dismay. Lenin himself was less afraid of a success for the Left-Wing Socialist Revolutionaries than of the international complications that would be the inevitable result of an ambassador's murder. He commissioned Dzerzhinsky to conduct the inquiry himself. When Dzerzhinsky arrived at the embassy he was shown the letter from the Vecheka, which he immediately saw to be a forgery. In a storm of rage he rushed to the headquarters of the Cheka, but there he and his escort were disarmed and arrested by the rebellious Chekists.

The rebels acted with great confidence. They occupied many of the public buildings, including the Moscow telegraph office, which at that time was the most important communications centre in the city. Thence they sent out to all parts of Russia the news that they had taken over power in Moscow. The situation looked desperate for the Bolsheviks. Anti-Communist risings broke out in a whole series of towns: Yaroslavl, Vologda, Rebinsk, Murom, etc. The Vecheka, it is true, was aware that there were secret organizations in the ranks of the Red Army, most of which were agitating for the restoration of the Provisional Government. But the Bolsheviks' counter-measures proved insufficient. The rising of the Left-Wing Socialist Revolutionaries started a series of events which neither Lenin nor his party had foreseen. In the cities mentioned large units of the Red Army went over to the rebels. But the rising was eventually to be crushed and its organizers liquidated.

The Left-Wing Socialist Revolutionaries had declared war on the Germans on their own account, causing panic among Lenin and his close supporters. Lenin did all he could to unravel the complications, though later it became obvious that the dangers had been exaggerated. Immediately after the assassination of Count Mirbach many commanding officers in sympathy with the rebels gave their troops the order to march on Moscow, with the war cry of 'Then on to Berlin!' After their defeat many of the rebels sought to draw an advantage from their 'declaration of war'. In Yaroslavl, for example, there was a camp of 1,500 German prisoners who, in accordance with the treaty of Brest-Litovsk, were awaiting repatriation. When the rising broke out there, the Germans armed themselves. As soon as it was clear that the fate of the rebels was sealed, their leaders claimed that logically the former German prisoners of war should take them prisoners, as they had declared war on Germany. The German representative, Lieutenant Balk, signed an agreement to that effect and made fifty-three leaders of the Yaroslavl rising his 'prisoners of war'. The result was a serious dispute between the Germans and the Russian authorities; the former were disarmed and their 'prisoners of war' severely punished.[14]

In Moscow the Cheka very quickly crushed the revolt of the Left-Wing Socialist Revolutionaries. On 6 June they surrounded the Bolshoi Theatre, where the Soviets were in session, forced their way in, and arrested the whole Left-Wing Socialist Revolutionary faction. The most difficult problem was how to render harmless Popov's Chekists, who had occupied the Lubyanka prison. Peters solved it by a trick. He gave them an order to carry out a raid in a distant suburb of Moscow, to search for arms. The stratagem succeeded, for the rebels thought the order came from Popov and proceeded to the appointed spot. Meanwhile the Chekists who were loyal to the Bolsheviks stormed the Lubyanka, occupied the weakly defended Popov headquarters, and freed Dzerzhinsky. On the next night the rebels were driven out of the Central Telegraph Office. Many western historians talk of atrocities committed in connection with the murder of Count Mirbach. From the fact that the two assassins had entered the German embassy armed with credentials from the Vecheka, they deduced, avid for the sensational, that the wire-pullers in the murder were Dzerzhinsky and Lenin himself. They ignore the fact that at that time the Vecheka was not a homogeneous organization. Apart from the Left-Wing Socialist Revolutionaries there were many other parties that were discontented with the Bolsheviks. Popov himself fled from Moscow after the debacle. He later joined the Makhno units fighting against the Bolsheviks, fell into Red Army hands in 1921, was recognized, and shot.[15] The events of 6 and 7 June 1918 were an extra reason for finally bolshevizing the Vecheka. Not only the Left-Wing Socialist Revolutionaries but all other untrustworthy elements were purged.

No wonder that after the speedy crushing of the rebellion in Moscow the Cheka's importance automatically soared to unlimited heights. Shortly after his liberation Dzerzhinsky said to a Press conference: 'We exist on a basis of organized terror, which is an absolutely essential element in revolution. We counter the enemies of the Soviet Government with terror and extirpate the criminals on the spot. . . . The Cheka is not a court of justice. It is a defender of the Revolution, just like the Red Army. And just as the Red Army in the civil war cannot stop to see whether it is wronging individuals, and is obliged to pursue a single aim, i.e. the victory of the Revolution over the bourgeoisie—in the same way the Cheka is obliged to defend the Revolution and crush the enemy, even if its sword sometimes chances to strike the heads of innocent people.' In the middle of July the Bolsheviks commissioned a squad of Lettish Chekists to murder the Tsar and his family, in order to dispose of at least one of the 'complicated questions'.

The Left-Wing Socialist Revolutionaries, though defeated in

Moscow, saw no reason at all to abandon their struggle against the Bolsheviks. Their influence in the rural areas was still much greater than the Bolsheviks'. True, their organization was inferior, but they had just as many fanatical adherents ready at any time to give their lives for the victory of Revolutionary Socialism. The Cheka terror they answered with an unremitting counter-terror.

On 30 August 1918 a fresh impetus was given to Dzerzhinsky's Cheka. Socialist Revolutionary conspirators on that day made two attempts at assassination, one of which was successful, with dire consequences.

A student called Leonid Kannegiesser murdered M. Z. Uritsky, head of the Petrograd Cheka, and a woman tried to shoot Lenin in Moscow. As the latter was leaving a building she stopped him to ask some questions, then shot him three times at close quarters. Although one bullet passed through his neck and another smashed his collarbone, Lenin was not mortally wounded. The woman was seized by the bystanders. In the Lubyanka prison she stated: "My name is Fanya Kaplan. I shot Lenin today of my own accord. I will not say from whom I obtained the revolver, I have long had the intention of killing Lenin. In my eyes he has betrayed the Revolution. Because of my share in an attempt to kill a Tsarist official I was exiled to Akatoi, where I served eleven years' forced labour. After the Revolution I was freed. I was for the Constituent Assembly and I still am. My parents are in the United States, they emigrated there in 1911. I have four brothers and two sisters. They are all workers.'

The murder of Uritsky and the attempt on Lenin's life inaugurated that dreadful period which is known in the history of the Soviet Union as the 'Red Terror'. The All-Russian Central Executive Committee issued on the same day an appeal to the workers and peasants: 'Answer the White Terror with a Red Mass-Terror!' Zinoviev said to a soldiers' meeting: 'The bourgeoisie can kill a few people, but we can kill whole classes.'

On the following day, 1 September, Petrovsky, the People's Commissar of Internal Affairs, declared that all the soviets were told to order their Cheka organs and soldiers 'to shoot everyone without exception who had any connection with the White Army'. His order included the following words: 'Sentiment and slackness must be discarded. All Right-Wing Socialist Revolutionaries known to the authorities are to be arrested immediately. From the bourgeoisie and officer circles a considerable number of hostages should be selected. The slightest sign of resistance, the slightest move on the part of White Guard circles, must be ruthlessly crushed by mass executions.'

The Communist Press exhorted the workers 'to extirpate the bourgeoisie as quickly as possible', if they did not want to be themselves destroyed.

When the mass-shootings of innocent hostages and suspects were already in full swing in Petrograd and Moscow, the Council of People's Commissars issued on 5 September 1918 the famous decree 'Concerning the Red Terror', which authorized the Cheka to take 'class enemies' to concentration camps and shoot all those 'involved in White Guard organizations, conspiracies, and risings'. It further ordered that the names of all those who had been shot should be published, with the grounds for their execution. Finally, on 17 September, the Cheka was authorized to sentence and execute in 'cases of grave dereliction of duty'.

The introduction of the 'Red Terror' was a sign of desperation, a sign that the Bolsheviks were trying to maintain their power by any means at their disposal. Their edicts gave almost unbridled power to the Cheka. Lenin's situation once again was such that he could not dispense with the services of the mob. Therefore, the whole government propaganda was directed towards inciting the mob to take lawless action. Even before the 'Red Terror' was officially proclaimed the following appeared in *Pravda* on 4 August 1918: 'Workers and poor, take up arms, learn to shoot, prepare yourselves for a rising by the kulaks or the White Guards, take action against all who agitate against the Soviet Power, ten bullets for every man who raises a hand against it. . . . The rule of Capital will never be extinguished until the last capitalist, nobleman, Christian, and officer draws his last breath.'

A wave of utterly arbitrary murders, committed from the basest motives, swept through the country, and the victims of 'spontaneous action' included civil servants, engineers, factory managers, priests, and many others.

'Disciplined terror', on the other hand, was carried out by the Cheka itself. Immediately after the assassination of Uritsky five hundred hostages were shot in Petrograd. In revenge for the rising in Yaroslavl more than four hundred persons (according to official figures) were executed. The Soviet press reported mass arrests throughout the country, and the Cheka left its bloodstained tracks everywhere. Historians will never be able to calculate the exact number of the Cheka's victims. H. W. Chamberlin thinks that about 50,000 persons perished.[16] But others, who survived the Chekist hell, consider that figure much too low.

The Terror exercised by the Left-Wing Socialist Revolutionaries and the Cheka's counter-measures naturally had a great influence on the structure of the Cheka itself, and indeed on all Bolshevik policy at that period. For this reason it is necessary to speak first of the bloody measures taken by Lenin and Dzerzhinsky against the Left-Wing Socialist Revolutionaries. Nevertheless these were by no means the only opponents of the Bolsheviks. The forces in Russia with which the Bolsheviks had to contend were manifold. One can well believe Lenin when he wrote that they far outnumbered the Bolsheviks.

In the first half of the year 1918 the Russian Monarchists organized a resistance movement throughout the territory under Bolshevik control. There was a 'Right Centre' and later a 'National Centre', consisting of White Guard officers and active opponents of the Bolshevists. The 'Union for the Defence of the Fatherland and Freedom', partly consisting of 'progressive' Monarchists and Left-Wing Liberals, flourished especially among the middle classes and the young.

We can here mention only a few of the more important 'Rightist' organizations, for there were literally hundreds of them in 1918. The most dangerous factor for the Bolsheviks in the situation was the association of the 'Rightists' with the powerful anti-Communist armies. The secret organizations maintained close connections with such leaders as Kolchak, Denikin, and Yudenich. Their most important task was to create recruiting offices for the White Armies in the larger cities and industrial regions held by the Bolsheviks. The volunteer army, especially, commanded by the White generals Alekseyev, Kornilov, and Denikin was thus enabled with their assistance to draw a large number of recruits from all parts of Russia.

The destruction of these illegal security organizations was one of the most important special tasks of the Cheka, in which it acted with special ruthlessness. While the terror exercised on the Left-Wing Socialist Revolutionaries was unpopular, and opposed by many a Communist, the shootings after court martial, when the recruiting offices for the White Armies were unearthed, were approved by every Bolshevik.

Things became worse in 1918 when the Entente began to carry out their plans for intervention in Russia in favour of the White Armies. On 9 March 1918 two hundred British soldiers were landed in Murmansk, and were later joined there by American infantrymen. Japanese infantry landed at Vladivostok in April, followed by American military units. Reinforcements poured in, and in August 1918 Archangel was occupied by the White Armies with the help of British troops. The Czechoslovak Corps fought against the Bolsheviks, playing in general an extremely important role in the history of the period. It consisted of Czechs and Slovaks who had served in the Austrian Army and been taken prisoners of war by the Russians. The Soviet Government allowed them to march in military formation from Siberia and the Far East to Europe. But the Czechoslovak politicians Thomas Masaryk and Eduard Beneš put the Corps at the disposal of the Entente. Some 50,000 well-trained and armed Czechs and Slovaks thus occupied a long section of the Trans-Siberian railway, from Penza and Syzran to Irkutsk and Vladivostok. Everywhere their units appeared, the weak Bolshevik elements vanished.

In August 1918 the British occupied Baku and, coming from Persia, penetrated the Trans-Caucasian region.

Foreign intervention in the Russian civil war was a deadly threat to Bolshevik power. For not only did the White Armies obtain material aid from abroad, but their prestige among the civil population was visibly increased thereby. Worse still were the measures of imperial Germany, which at that time held the Ukraine, Belorussia, a part of Trans-Caucasia, the Crimea, and the whole of the Baltic provinces. The result was desperate shortages and famine in Bolshevik Russia. Over 40 per cent of all factories were brought to a standstill through lack of raw materials.

On 26 November 1918 the 2nd conference of Cheka officials was held in Moscow.[17] On the agenda were the questions of expanding Cheka activity in the army, co-operation with other state departments, the organization of the transport sections of the

Vecheka, and strengthening the campaign against the black market. The efforts of the Cheka to increase its influence in the Red Army met with stubborn resistance from Trotsky, Commander-in-Chief at the time. The Cheka then tried to show that there were spies and saboteurs among the leading officers on all fronts. For this purpose they set up a card index with information and reports concerning all field officers. Eventually a great many spies who had crept into leading positions in the Red Army were shot. On 1 January 1919 the military department of the Vecheka was replaced by a special department which from then onwards was solely responsible for all security arrangements within the Soviet armed forces.

Throughout 1919 the Soviet security authorities carried on a bitter struggle with illegal anti-Bolshevik organizations. One of the most dangerous conspiracies against the Bolshevik regime was the 'National Centre', which succeeded in creating an illegal army in the area occupied by the Bolsheviks. Its groups were formed not only in Petrograd and Moscow but even among the Red Army garrisons. When the Entente, in cooperation with the White Army, began their first large-scale offensive in the spring of 1919, Petrograd was seriously threatened by Yudenich's army. The units of the 'National Centre' and other illegal organizations were showing their strength. In June 1919 there was an anti-Bolshevik revolt in the fortress of Krasnaya Gorka which could only be crushed by the employment of large forces. There were similar more or less successful risings in Moscow and other Russian cities.

Whereas these risings were for the most part suppressed by Bolshevik units of the Red Army, the bloody annihilation of the 'National Centre' was the exclusive work of the Chekists. Here for the first time Dzerzhinsky made large-scale use of *agents provocateurs* as a means of defeating the enemy. Hundreds of Chekists and devoted Communists were infiltrated into the feverishly operating illegal organizations under the guise of White Guard officers and monarchists. Many of them even fought in anti-Bolshevik actions. Dzerzhinsky permitted this so as to be able to destroy the 'National Centre' at one swoop by the end of 1919. Lenin and later Soviet historians had the highest respect for Dzerzhinsky's services in this crisis. Certainly the destruction of the illegal organizations by the Cheka was a contribution towards the victory of Bolshevism in

Russia of no less importance than the fighting of the Red Army on the war fronts.

The Cheka produced a volume of evidence showing that there were close connections between foreign diplomats in Russia and the anti-Bolshevist conspirators. Many political circles, especially in France, Great Britain, and later in the USA, did much to help the Bolsheviks' opponents, although they acted in haphazard fashion with no well-conceived general plan. As far back as 21 December 1917 (1 January 1918) the Council of People's Commissars concerned itself with the 'counter-revolutionary activity of the French Mission'. The Cheka is said to have held proofs at the time that some of the members of the French Mission were involved in the attempt on Lenin's life. In April 1918 the Cheka published a report on the complicity of representatives of the USA, Great Britain, and France in the conspiracy of Derber, the Social Revolutionary, who created the 'Siberian Government' at Tomsk on 9 February 1918. In a note dated 25 April 1918 the Soviet Government demanded from the French, British, and American Governments the immediate recall of their diplomatic representatives at Vladivostok.

In the 'Diplomats Conspiracy', as Soviet writers call it, Robert H. Bruce Lockhart, head of the British special mission, played an important role. He is said to have been aided by a large number of collaborators in the Intelligence Service scattered around various parts of Russia. On his initiative several diplomatic missions in Moscow and St Petersburg decided to support the conspiracy of Savinkov and his 'Union for the Revival of Russia'. This developed into a minor struggle between Lockhart and the Cheka, in which the Chekists had to act with extraordinary skill if they were to thwart the conspirators' plans without thereby causing grave diplomatic complications.

After Russia had concluded peace with the Germans at Brest-Litovsk, most of the Entente's diplomatic representatives left Moscow for Vologda. Lockhart and his assistant Sydney Reilly stayed on in Moscow. The former was at this time without doubt the most dangerous wire-puller in the conspiracy, and the Cheka's efforts were concentrated on him. Chance came to their assistance. On 11 August the commanding officer of the 1st Light Artillery Division of the Lettish Brigade, a certain Y. P. Berzin, reported that a former Russian officer of his acquaintance had informed him of his contacts with the British Embassy in Moscow and that the British were showing special interest in the Lettish Brigade in Moscow. The Cheka authorized Berzin to assume the role of an *agent provocateur*. Three days later Lockhart received Berzin in his private apartment. Berzin informed him of anti-Soviet sentiments among the Lettish troops, and Lockhart urged him to foster the soldiers' disloyalty still further by acts of sabotage, e.g. by doctoring their rations, and by nationalistic propaganda. Berzin was given the cover-name of 'Constantine' and became Lockhart's chief agent. From then onwards Lockhart's schemes increased in audacity. 'Constantine' asked payment for his services, and the Cheka were amazed to hear that without hesitation Lockhart was paying Berzin two million roubles. Berzin stuffed the notes into a sack which he carried with some difficulty to the Hotel Metropole, where Sverdlov, Russian Governmental Chief at the time, had his office.

According to the official Soviet documents, to which we owe knowledge of the details of this affair, the following plan was worked out between Lockhart and 'Constantine'. Two Lettish regiments were to be transferred from Moscow to Vologda, where they would desert to the Entente's cause and assist an offensive of the Anglo-French forces from Archangel. The Lettish units left in Moscow were to arrest the members of the Russian Government. The only question was what to do with Lenin. Lockhart wanted to take him to Archangel, Reilly was for shooting him on the spot. They even envisaged a divine service to commemorate the fall of the Bolsheviks, and Tikhonov, the Metropolitan of the Russian Orthodox Church, had already been warned for the purpose.

Meanwhile Berzin went to Petrograd, for research into the activities of Lockhart's helpers—information which was later to prove very useful to the Cheka. Perhaps the affair would have developed further, had not Uritsky been assassinated on 30 August. The Vecheka now decided on immediate action against the diplomatic missions, regardless of the possibility of international complications. On 31 August Dzerzhinsky raided the British Embassy in Petrograd. At 5 p.m. the building was surrounded and a special detachment of the Cheka forced an entrance. The embassy administrator, Francis N. A. Cromie, shot one Chekist dead and severely wounded two others. He was shot down on the spot. According to the Soviet report, forty White Guards were arrested in the building. The British press later reported that all the members of the embassy had been arrested and taken first to the Cheka prison and later to the fortress of SS Peter and Paul, where they were confined in inhuman conditions.

On the following night Lockhart was arrested in Berzin's company. Released at first as a diplomat, he was later re-arrested. After a great show-trial Lockhart and some other diplomats were expelled from the country as 'enemies of Russia'; two of the accused, Kolomatiano and A. V. Friede, were sentenced to death by shooting, and eight others were acquitted.[18]

Another chapter in the story of the successful counter-espionage work of the Cheka deals with the destruction of the Polish military organization, the Polska Organisacja Wojskowa, abbreviated to POW. This was a revolutionary organization created by Pilsudski to fight against Tsarist Russia and was mostly composed of Polish Socialists. Pilsudski, who looked upon the Bolsheviks as inheritors of the Tsarist imperialist foreign policy, revived the POW in order to support the Ukrainian national movement under Petlyura and to obviate the danger of a Bolshevik invasion of Poland. The POW was a failure: it was discovered and shattered.

The Cheka, moreover, was able to chalk up another considerable victory over the Anarchists in the course of the year 1919. But this time not over Nihilists of the 'Black Guard' type, but over an underground movement which had set up an extensive illegal network of bases throughout Russia. By the end of 1919 the Cheka had succeeded in uncovering most of the Anarchists' meeting places. When they found a terrorist organization known as the 'All Russian Staff of Revolutionary Partisans' and began to carry out terrorist actions in Moscow and many other places, the Cheka was able to liquidate the whole movement. First in Moscow and Petrograd, then in the provinces. Its greatest success was the arrest of the most important Anarchist leader, Donat Cherebanov, who was later executed.

Cheka terrorism helped to secure the rations of the Bolshevik armies. As mentioned already, speculators were profiting by Russia's difficult economic position. Cheka activities, especially in the large cities, were mainly aimed in their direction. They carried out regular and successful raids against the black marketeers. In Petrograd alone, as a result of a single raid at the end of 1917, 300,000 pud (*c.* 100,000 cwt) of grain was confiscated. Similar raids in the provinces were directed against wealthy peasants. Many historians and specialists, when dealing with this period of wartime Communism, speak of a strictly centralized requisitioning system by which the cities and the civil service received their supplies. In reality, however, these requisitioning methods were more like organized raids on the rural population in order to obtain food by searching farms and other terrorist measures. This was another 'glorious chapter' in Cheka history.

One of the most significant happenings in this period was the creation of the 'special tribunals' of the Cheka. These notorious institutions were the occasion of serious differences of opinion among the Bolshevik leaders. They all agreed in principle on the 'Red Terror' because they saw in it the only possible means of maintaining the Bolshevik dictatorship in Russia. But opinions and convictions were divided concerning questions of competent authority and the efforts of certain circles to re-establish a 'socialist legality'.

On 2 November 1918 the Council of People's Commissars decided to add to the Cheka board representatives from the Commissariats of Justice and Internal Affairs. The purpose of this step was to put a light bridle on the hitherto almost uncontrollable activities of Dzerzhinsky and his organization. In the People's Commissariat of Justice there was a large accumulation of complaints of unjustified arrests by the Cheka. Among those arrested were not only members of the bourgeois classes, but also workers and Communists. Attempts were made to examine and check some of these cases from a wider angle, but Dzerzhinsky put up energetic resistance to any form of control over the Cheka organs. His views were expressly supported by Lenin, for at the time he was encouraging the ambitions of Dzerzhinsky, in whom he still had boundless confidence. To the demand that the Cheka should be controlled by the judicial authorities, Lenin's answer was: 'When I consider the activities of the Cheka and compare them with the attacks on it, I find the latter to be *petit bourgeois* considerations of no value.'[19]

The 'special tribunals' of the Cheka, nicknamed 'three-man troikas', became notorious as hellish machines which destroyed thousands of Soviet citizens. As these 'troikas' became more and more active in their rough treatment of 'suspicious' but mostly innocent persons, so the resistance to them among the Communists grew more vocal.

Certain circles, but certainly excluding Lenin himself, tried to subject the Cheka tribunals to some degree of control. At first they tried to subordinate each Cheka to its local soviet. The sharpest attacks, however, came from the People's Commissariat of Internal Affairs. On 18 October 1918 *Pravda* published an article by a leading civil servant, which referred to differences of opinion between the Cheka and the soviets. Many Communists asserted openly that the revolutionary slogan 'All power to the Soviets' had now become 'All power to the Cheka'.

As the Red Terror at that time was raging outside the Party itself, in which democratic conditions still prevailed to a certain extent, the People's Commissariat of Internal Affairs dared to address a question to the local soviets, asking them whether they favoured the subordination of the Cheka to the soviets or whether they wanted the Cheka to be entirely independent.

The principal target for the malcontents among the Communists was always the Cheka's 'troikas'. Many of the documents issued by the People's Commissariat of Internal Affairs referred to the unlawful character of the Cheka tribunals. The attacks against the Cheka finally reached their culmination at the end of 1918, when Krylenko, the People's Commissar of Justice, made himself the chief spokesman for the Cheka's opponents.

There is quite a simple answer to the question why the arbitrary power of the Cheka lasted so long, in spite of resistance among the Communists themselves. The long reign of the Cheka suited Lenin's policy, for he was opposed to all efforts of the Communists to establish 'socialist legality'. He is responsible for the fact that from 1918 to 1921 the Cheka was subject neither to law nor to higher authority.

In 1921 a leading member of the Cheka described its extra-legal position in the following terms: 'As the Cheka is not a judicial authority, its activities have the character of administrative acts. . . . It does not judge the enemy but strikes at him. . . . Its extreme sanction is death by shooting. . . . Next to that, detention in a concentration camp. . . . The third punishment is confiscation of property.... The Cheka's aim is that its measures should make such an impression on the people that the mere mention of its name will make everybody abandon any idea of sabotage, extortion, or conspiracy.'[20]

Nevertheless, the opposition to the Cheka, especially in Communist circles, grew in like proportion to the bloodthirsty outrages of Dzerzhinsky's organization. Moros, a contemporary witness, wrote in *Pravda* for 21 January 1919 that the Cheka was looked upon by many as unnecessary and even damaging to the Revolution. Among simple Russians it was usual to call a Chekist 'inquisitor' or 'persecutor', with the result that Latsis, a leading Chekist, openly complained: 'An atmosphere was created which stifled any wish to be employed in these essential organs of the State's power.' A steadily growing wall of fear, abhorrence, and contempt arose between the Chekists and the general public.

The result was a sociologically very interesting change within the Cheka itself. Initially its numbers were not very large. Official Soviet sources speak of 'not more than a hundred men'. But very quickly the organization grew and grew. At first the backbone of its troops consisted of the 'Lettish formations' which were largely manned by Russian Communists posted to them by the Party. Some of the sections are said to have been composed of former Hungarian prisoners of war. Others were Chinese, formerly employed as foreign workers in Russia, and these are said to have introduced the notorious Chinese tortures. In any case Chinese were frequently employed as guards, especially valuable because they had little knowledge of Russian.

The Cheka organization flourished and expanded under its master Dzerzhinsky—another reason for the discontent among the Communists. At the 7th Congress of the Soviets in December 1919, for instance, Martov protested against the irresistible expansion of the Cheka. According to Latsis, there were already in 1921 as many as 31,000 Chekists—an enormous organization in the circumstances. At that time the total personnel of the Ministry of Internal Affairs numbered only 2,823.

Divided from the general public by an impossible wall, the Cheka became more and more a privileged caste. The people's distrust was explained by the Chekists simply as 'a lack of political consciousness', and they regarded themselves more and more as 'the

Romantics of the bloody Terror'—the only 'real Communists' and 'true Revolutionaries'. The Cheka considered itself not as a tool of dictatorship, but as the real wielder of power, which needed to stop at nothing.

Such a development had once been feared by Lenin himself, and it was now the probable cause for his remarkable tactics as regards the Cheka. He omitted nothing that might strengthen the powers of the Cheka and enlarge its spheres of activity. But, as a strategist of genius, he saw the dangers that might arise from a rift between the Cheka and the masses, and therefore from time to time he ordered measures which might seem to curb the arbitrary powers of the Cheka. And these were not merely tactical gestures. Both Lenin and Dzerzhinsky were well aware how easily in those revolutionary times they could lose command of the Cheka. There is reason to think that the remarkable sporadic examples of legality, and even 'humanity', to be found in Cheka documents, were merely the products of Lenin's strategical genius.

For instance, the Board of the Cheka warned its organization in October 1919 against arresting people without concrete evidence of guilt. On 17 December 1919 an order was issued in the following terms: 'No one is to be arrested on the strength of a mere rumour, or on mere suspicion. . . . In all cases of petty offences no arrest is to be made, unless an attempt at escape is expected.' In a circular issued by the Board on 23 March 1920 the leaders of the Cheka organs in the provinces were even threatened with severe punishment if they made unjustified arrests. Among Cheka documents at the height of the Terror there is a strange memorandum addressed by Dzerzhinsky to the well-known Chekist Unshlikht: 'It is a thousand times better to err on the side of a liberal decision than to send a politically inactive person into exile, from which he will certainly return as an active enemy, mobilized against us by the mere fact of his condemnation.' At Lenin's personal intervention in 1919 an order was given that all organs of the Cheka should submit lists of arrested persons to the appropriate authorities.

Other documents of similar character might be mentioned, such as precise instructions for house searches and a strict prohibition of ill-treatment of arrested persons.[21]

But it was all on paper. The turn for the better in the Civil War, the defeat of the White Armies, caused a change in the Cheka atmosphere. The plenary assembly of the Central Committee of the Russian Communist Party (Bolshevik) made it plain that Soviet power was now so strong that any intensification of the 'Red Terror' was unnecessary.

In the summer of 1919 the Bolsheviks recruited 137,000 men, mostly from the factories in the area held by them, and thereby reinforced the army on the southern front. At the turn of the year they succeeded in crushing Denikin's army, which had been decisively weakened by the destruction of its illegal bases. The Red Army captured Rostov on the Don. The Soviet Government abolished the death sentence on the proposal of Lenin, 17 January 1920. At the session of the All Russian Central Executive Committee, 2 February 1920, Lenin explained: 'The Terror was forced upon us by the Entente's terrorism, when the world powers turned their military forces against us and shrank from nothing. We should not have held out for two days had we not reacted to the attacks of officers and White Guards, and that means Terror. . . . And when we had won a decisive victory, even before the end of the war, we abolished the death sentence. As soon as we captured Rostov. . . . We repeat that the use of violence was caused by the necessity to suppress exploiters, landowners, and capitalists. Once this task is completed, we shall relinquish all the special measures.'[22]

Typical of Lenin in this period were the motives which caused him suddenly to distrust the Vecheka and Dzerzhinsky. More than any other Bolshevik leader of the time he concerned himself with the economic development of the country. In both factories and civil service the Bolsheviks found themselves compelled to use former technical personnel of Tsarist Russia. These people were certainly no friends of Communism, but Lenin was convinced that they would, in certain conditions, serve the Soviet power loyally, and he valued their contributions highly. As these men found it necessary, in order to get the factories working, to challenge the rights of the technically ignorant soviets in the factories, they became targets for fanatical attacks and every kind of obstruction. When the Vecheka intervened and arrested some of these experts, Lenin's patience was exhausted. In his collected works one finds many documents in which he demanded the re-examination of cases already decided by Dzerzhinsky, sometimes even ordering the release of the prisoners. It would seem that it was in connection with these complicated questions that Lenin's first disappointments with Dzerzhinsky became noticeable. Some years later they grew until they formed a completely negative picture.

In 1921, by when the Bolshevik position in Russia was wholly secure, Lenin, addressing the 9th Congress of the Soviets, said: 'Our failures are sometimes the continuation of our virtues, and that is so in the case of the Cheka. It was heroic when it defended the Revolution against countless foreign enemies, when it was our most effective weapon against innumerable attacks. . . . But now, in present circumstances, it is necessary to restrict the institution to a purely political sphere. We say emphatically that it is time to reform the Cheka.'[23]

In country districts, however, Soviet power still failed to find firm footing. Memories of the war period and the Communists' brutal requisitioning policy were too fresh. In the southern Ukraine the Anarchists under Makhno's leadership were able to register certain successes, and the nationalist Basmachi movement in Central Asia was constantly growing stronger. Finally, in February 1921, the famous anti-Bolshevisk mutiny of the Kronstadt sailors broke out. Its war cry, 'For the Soviets without the Bolsheviks', elicited the best efforts of the masses, not from reactionary elements, not from the adherents of the old social order, but from a general public bent on revolution. No less dangerous were events in Karelia, where a rising of the local nationalists was supported by strong bands of Finnish freedom-fighters. From Poland Savinkov's armed units penetrated Belorussia, and the broken armies of the Ukrainian freedom-fighters under Simon Petlyura were reassembled abroad and sent back to the Ukraine through Poland and Rumania.

Until the outbreak of the Kronstadt mutiny there existed, according to Soviet sources, about fifty anti-Soviet rebel armies. The strongest of these had been formed in the government of Tambov under A. S. Antonov, who by 1921 had assembled an army of 50,000 men. It was led by a general staff and a political organization known as the 'Union of Peasant Labourers' (Soyus Trodovogo Krestyanstva). As soon as Antonov's unit occupied new territory a nationalist committee was formed there. Vecheka units were sent to combat the Antonov guerrillas. When they were beaten, they had to be replaced by regular units of the Red Army. According to official information a thousand Communists were killed by Antonov's army. The Central Committee discussed the situation on several occasions, and after the intervention of the security organs had proved fruitless a special commission of the All Russian Executive Committee was formed, with Antonov-Ovseyenko at its head. It was not until June 1921 that the well-known Soviet commander Uborevich succeeded in striking a decisive blow against the rebels.[24]

All these risings and anti-Communist movements were mercilessly crushed by the Bolsheviks. A new element in their actions can no longer be overlooked—a feeling of self-confidence and a conviction of their own superiority.

When in 1921 a great famine started in consequence of a drought, Russia was in a very difficult situation indeed. In the Volga region, in the southern Urals, and in parts of the Ukraine 27 million people were starving by the end of the year. Millions of people died of starvation and epidemics. Thousands left their homes and scattered over the country. In the summer and autumn of 1922 epidemics and cannibalism reached their worst pitch in the Volga region. The number of people who died of hunger and its effects in 1921 and 1922 is estimated at nearly 5 million. And some believe this figure to be much too low.

Communists throughout the world and also various non-Communist charitable organizations started campaigns for assistance. The Comintern formed the 'International Workers' Aid', the German branch of which, under Willi Münzenberg, issued a famous poster designed by Käthe Kollwitz, and collected for the hungry in Russia. Anatole France gave his Nobel prize. The call for help by Fridtjof Nansen, the Polar explorer, met with generous response all over the world, and Nansen was made an honorary member of the Moscow Soviet. But most assistance came from America. Here the leading organization was the American Relief Administration (ARA), which as long ago as 1919 had, in conjunction with the YMCA, worked out a plan for the relief of the hungry children in Russia. The situation was so grave that even the Patriarch of the Russian Orthodox Church was allowed to appeal to Christians throughout the world for aid for hungry children and women in Russia. In August 1921 the government of the Russian Socialist Soviet Republic made an agreement with the ARA regarding help for the famine-stricken. Without active help from abroad a still greater catastrophe could not have been avoided. According to contemporary reports, American aid was regarded by the Chekists with the deepest distrust. Employees of the ARA were arrested and accused of counter-revolutionary activity. The Soviets complained that certain foreign circles were trying to utilize the famine in order to increase political insecurity.

After the activity of the ARA in Russia had been cancelled, almost all the Russian employees of the ARA were exposed to persecution. Later, during the Stalin reign of terror, the mere fact of having worked for the ARA was sufficient to brand a person as a spy.

Of all the Soviet leaders Lenin was probably the best judge of the agricultural situation. With great anxiety he observed the quarrel between the Bolsheviks and the peasants, which had deteriorated into open combat. He longed to be the 'Little Father' of the Russian peasants, as he already was of the factory workers, and perhaps this sentiment was one of the reasons for Lenin's superiority over the Bolshevik leaders. When in 1921 there was a peasants' revolt in the government of Tambov, Lenin received a delegation of peasants from the region on 14 February and took a personal interest in the details of their grievances. The peasants asked him to stop the requisitioning of food, and Lenin actually tried to comply with their request. The peasants' rising soon convinced him that a new land policy was a crucial necessity for the Bolsheviks. At the 10th Congress of the RKP (Russian Communist Party) in March 1921, at Lenin's instigation, the 'New Economic Policy' (NEP) was announced. This was more than a mere strategic chessboard move, and it gave fresh strength to those elements in the Bolshevik leadership which were trying to bridle the activities of the Cheka.

When Lenin in 1921 openly demanded the reform of the Cheka, its reorganization was already taking place. At Dzerzhinsky's instigation various steps were taken, and these could be grouped under three headings: meticulous respect for the laws in the official measures of the Cheka; greater production in the economic sphere; and a change of method, i.e. from the blind rage of the Red Terror to perfected security measures.

The activities of the Cheka now had to follow certain legal rules, and the effect showed itself in two directions. First, the victory of Krylenko, the State Attorney, over Dzerzhinsky was obvious to all.

The organs of justice became ever bolder in their fight against the arbitrary power of the Cheka. The process, as we have seen, began early in 1919. In January of that year, in the provinces, the Cheka organs in the communal administrations or 'uyezds' were abolished and their powers transferred to the local militia. However, this was not a drastic change, for it was simultaneously resolved that 'political officers' should be posted to the militia commands, and these soon reverted to the Cheka domain. But in February 1919 an edict was issued whereby judgement was to be given by the revolutionary tribunals in cases which the Cheka had initiated.

The secondary development was in the Cheka itself. Dzerzhinsky demanded of his Chekists more and more frequently that they should conform to the laws. In June 1920 the Board of the Cheka issued an order entitled 'Concerning the Correct Treatment of Arrested Persons'. This directive recommended that persons arrested on account of minor offences should be released at once, and that only really guilty persons should be sent to labour camps and prisons. Workers and peasants guilty of petty offences against the law must be carefully distinguished from spies and bandits. The latter must still be severely punished, but as much toleration as possible must be shown towards the former group. To quote actual words: 'The general differentiation between persons according to their social background—kulak, ex-officer, landowner, etc. —had to be taken into account as long as Soviet power was weak. But now one must carefully investigate what offence had actually been committed, and whether an arrest is justified.' One of the orders issued to Chekists in the same year was to render in public assembly an account of their activities.

Much more important was the extension of Cheka activities to industry and transport. A first step in this direction was taken at the 4th Conference of Chekists from Transport and other departments on 3 February 1920.[25] Its importance is underlined by the fact that Lenin himself took part in the conference.

The shorthand report of Lenin's and Dzerzhinsky's speeches throws some light on the beginning of the 'reorganization' of the Cheka.

Lenin emphasized in his final speech that from the beginning—although capital punishment has been abolished in Russia—nobody had excluded the possibility of execution by shooting. He warned:

'Although the period of armed conflict on a major historical scale is nearing its close, we must in all circumstances remain in a state of readiness. The organs for the suppression of counter-revolution, i.e. the Cheka, are faced with a somewhat difficult task. On one side we must allow for the transition from war to peace, on the other we must always remain on our guard, for we do not know how quickly a real peace is attainable. . . . Retaining our readiness to fight, and without weakening the apparatus for the suppression of exploiters, we must find a new means of transition from war to peace, we must change our tactics as well as the form of our re-prisals.'

Lenin described the difficult situation in the country's economy, especially in transport, which was constantly in danger of complete collapse. In the task of purging the transport section of the economy 'the organs of the Cheka must be the instrument for implementing the centralized will of the proletariat, an instrument for the restora-tion of discipline such as we have successfully brought about in the Red Army'. Lenin pointed out that in transport the number of saboteurs and wasters was much larger than in other sectors. The Chekists must at all costs bring about an improvement in the organization of transport labour.

Dzerzhinsky formulated the new attitude to the use of terror even more precisely than Lenin: 'Counter-revolution and conspir-acy from within are no longer dangers for us. For that reason the weapon of terror, without which we should not have been able to survive when the bulk of our armed forces had to be sent to the front, is not necessary at the present time, because it is a weapon used by the proletariat only when it would be defenceless without it.'

A transport system that functioned without friction was a matter of life and death to the Soviet Union. The conference resolved that the best efforts of the Cheka should in future be centred on trans-port—supervisors must become organizers.

Of special significance were measures taken by Dzerzhinsky directed at a new sphere of work for the Cheka. He had outlined his proposals at the conference: 'As I have already said, the weapons of terror we can now dispense with. But what are still necessary, instead of terror, arrest, searches of houses and per-sons . . . are new methods by which, without razzias and terrorism,

we can maintain a constant watch on and nip in the bud our adversaries' conspiracies and hostile schemes.' Dzerzhinsky thought the
enemies of Soviet Russia, defeated in the field, would continue the
campaign clandestinely, sending spies into Russia with special
objectives, and trying to infiltrate them into Soviet institutions:
'Therefore the watch of the secret operational sections should be
concentrated on our economy, on supply and distribution, on transport and the like.'

The above speech heralded the end of the first chapter in the
history of the Soviet security organs, i.e. the Cheka period. It was
an era of 'Romantic Terror', and even the Chekist uniform was
attuned to the times: leather jacket and cartridge belt characterized
the Chekist. They shot thousands, and hundreds of Chekists fell in
the struggle. The Chekists were not a secret police; treachery and
the use of *agents provocateurs* were not unknown among them, but
by no means typical of their methods. Much that they had initiated
later remained unaltered—notably the training to blind devotion
and ruthlessness.

In anticipation, however, of the New Economic Policy, many
changes had to be made in the Cheka, among them the outward
appearance of its members: leather jackets gave way to bright blue
uniforms, resembling those formerly worn by the political sections
of the Tsarist gendarmerie.

'Romantic Terror' was a thing of the past, replaced by a stage in
the democratic developments of terrorist measures.

Chapter Two

GPU and OGPU

(I 9 2 2 – I 9 3 4)

AFTER victory in the civil war, Lenin again displayed his tactical skill. Whereas the leaders of the left wing of the Party were trying to spread their revolutionary ideas worldwide, without regard for the situation in their own country, Lenin understood that civil war within the Soviet community would only be ended when the Communists succeeded in regaining the peasants' confidence. The peasants hated the Communists not for their ideology, but because they had robbed and plundered them during the period of 'War Communism'. They had suffered worst under the notorious *prodrazvierstka*—the ruthless confiscation of foodstuffs for the use of the army and the factory workers. This method was now replaced by taxation, the peasants being allowed to sell their produce freely and openly. This was the first of a whole series of measures which finally figured in the history of the Soviet Union as the New Economic Policy—the NEP.

The driving force behind the NEP was Lenin. His authority over the Communists was so great that they agreed to a series of concessions to the peasants which amounted almost to a restoration of capitalist conditions. Private trade was permitted by a decree of the Council of People's Commissars dated 30 July 1921. Living conditions changed, as though touched by a magic wand. The peasants once again had a strong material incentive to increase their production, and their freedom to trade banished hunger and misery from the cities—to an extent that astounded even the Communist leaders.

The NEP, however, was not merely an economic move. Lenin's

effort to regain contact with all levels of the population was seriously meant. So the NEP was accompanied by miscellaneous measures in other spheres, all of which were aimed at the restoration of legality, and at putting the civil service back on the right lines. With the well-being of the population the authority of the State would grow.

Previously the police and civil authorities had acted according to their own ideas and in a completely arbitrary manner. Lenin wanted to strengthen the feeling of personal security among the Soviet citizens. He insisted that laws in all parts of the country should be uniformly applied without regard for the social origin or status of the individual. In May 1922 the State judicial system was organized on new principles. It was now to have the duty of seeing that the laws were observed not only by the citizens, but by government departments as well. At the same time a new criminal and civil code was promulgated, and the whole judicial system was basically reformed. In October 1922 land reform, already carried out, was legalized by the creation of a land law, and a labour law was issued simultaneously to regulate general working conditions.

These multifarious changes affected also the security organs. Unveiled terror was no longer tolerated. Lenin and the Central Committee commissioned Dzerzhinsky to create an 'orderly' out of an 'extraordinary' political State police. By decrees of 28 December 1921 and 6 February 1922 the Vecheka was renamed 'State Political Administration' (Gosudarstvennoye Politichezkoye Upravleniye) or GPU. Feliks Dzerzhinsky stayed its head. Some powers of the Vecheka were transferred to the law courts. The investigation procedure and the whole of the preliminary examination remained with the GPU, which was only to carry out an execution when the offender was caught red-handed. In all other cases judgement was the business of the criminal courts. As a guarantee of the legality of GPU measures, a GPU Board of Justice was set up, to act in close cooperation with the judicial authority.

On the ruins of the Russian Empire there first arose a number of independent states, comprising the Caucasian peoples, the Ukraine, Belorussia (White Russia), Lithuania, Latvia, and Estonia. But through the overwhelming power of the Red Army these sovereign states were destroyed and replaced by Soviet republics. Each had its own government and its own army. The only connecting link between them was the Communist Party, which was strictly subordinated to its central headquarters in Moscow. In many questions, it is true, the Communists in the non-Russian republics acted in cooperation with Russia, but they were in no way disposed to surrender their sovereignty. Stalin, the specialist in nationality questions, represented the view that all the regions in which Soviet power prevailed should form a unified State, in a framework that guaranteed the maximum possible autonomy to each group of people. This 'autonomous' tendency was denounced by Lenin as non-Russian chauvinism and firmly rejected. His theory was: 'No autonomy, but an alliance of united republics with equal rights and equal sovereignty.' On 27 September 1922 he proposed that the 'Russian Socialist Federative Soviet Republic' (RSFSR) should enter a union with the other Soviet republics, namely the 'Union of Socialist Soviet Republics' (USSR). In a memorandum he announced a life-and-death struggle with pan-Russian chauvinism. He demanded categorically ('Absolutely! Absolutely!') that in the new Union Government the presiding officials should take turns, so that the Head of the Soviet State should be at one time a Russian, at another a Ukrainian or a Georgian, etc. The discussion of this question aroused the most passionate arguments. But finally Lenin's authority and foresight won the day. On 30 December 1922 the agreement for the formation of the USSR was signed.

The new situation was naturally not devoid of consequences to the organization of the GPU. Side-by-side with the Communist Party the security organs throughout Soviet territory were strongly centralized. The Vecheka was controlled by two different bodies, namely its Moscow headquarters and the local authorities. The same was true for the GPU, but after the creation of the Soviet Union they were amalgamated into the 'United GPU' (Obyedinyonoroye GPU), renamed the OGPU. This new institution was not only formally the central headquarters of the security apparatus for the whole Soviet Union, but was given the status of a People's Commissariat and was thus directly responsible only to the Council of the People's Commissariats of the Soviet Union. In spite of this legal tie-up between the security organs and the State, a clear sign that from now on there must be more respect for legality, it was obvious to everyone that the OGPU would continue to be an instrument of Party policy and that the instructions of the Party would prevail.

Dzerzhinsky, entrusted with the reorganization of the security apparatus, retained Lenin's confidence, having realized that what was now wanted was no longer Chekist brutality but perfect functioning of the security machinery. A new line was gradually introduced: 'scientific methods' replaced beating-up and torture. Instead of a blind-with-rage destruction of the enemy, 'protective measures' began to come into fashion. The old Chekists with the traditions of 'Romantic Terror' were surprised to find the new measures so effective. Dzerzhinsky, too, did something to enhance the reputation of the OGPU personnel. He raised their wages, arranged for them to enjoy privileges with regard to food and other supplies, and saw to it that they made a more civilized impression. Formerly the Chekists had been despised and no decent man wanted to be a Chekist—but now there were ample numbers wanting to join the security service.

Under the NEP the law courts began to play a more important role. But until the end of the Stalin era there was no change in the double procedure. Side-by-side with the regular courts an administrative security authority persisted, and it was equipped with far-reaching powers for the punishment of offenders. So long as this practice lasted, there could be no question of a real restoration of legality. Various changes introduced in the NEP period must be evalued from the realistic angle of the times. The problem was never concerned with the abolition of the double procedure, but with the limits within which the powers of the security services could be kept. After the foundation of the OGPU the law of 6 February 1922 attempted to define more precisely what full powers should be assigned to the security officers. It granted rights of arrest, house search, and confiscation within forty-eight hours of the deed. After that, any such measures needed the written consent of the OGPU. The arrested person must be notified of the charge within two weeks, and after two months he must be either brought before the court or released. There was, however, a loophole in the law which allowed the security officers to apply to the highest department of the OGPU for the prisoner to be kept in solitary confinement, a measure which gave them a free hand in his treatment. The result was that only persons arrested by the OGPU for minor offences were actually brought before the courts. The decree of 16 October 1922 gave the OGPU greatly enlarged powers to send arrested persons into exile. Arrested persons who had already appeared once in court were liable to exile without further ado. The same decree also empowered the OGPU to shoot on the spot street-robbers and highwaymen caught in the act. Such cases did not need even a death sentence pronounced by the OGPU.

What was the character of the Soviet judicial system at this period? In 1922 a constitutional law established a uniform judicial system throughout the Soviet Union. Compared with the revolutionary tribunals, which lasted from the outbreak of the October Revolution until 1923, this signified some progress. True, the judicial system and the Cheka competed with each other, but not because the feeling for justice was stronger in the revolutionary tribunals. Some Soviet jurists even refused to recognize them as courts of justice at all. As in the case of the Vecheka, they were subject to no precise rules and regulations and acted solely in the interests of the Revolution. The decrees of 17 February and 12 April 1919 gave them unlimited powers of punishment. In 1920 the revolutionary tribunals were converted into special courts, which were finally abolished in 1922.[26]

The publication of the first regulations governing the courts brought a degree of clarity to jurisprudence. The courts were wholly dependent on the Party and State apparatus. Krylenko, the well-known Soviet jurist and former Minister of Justice, taught in his lectures in 1923: 'We regard the courts as class establishments, as a tool of governmental power, and we set them up to be an institution completely dominated by the vanguard of the working class. Our law courts are not official establishments independent of the Government. . . . Therefore, they can only be established in such a way that they are dependent on Soviet power and capable of being overruled by it.'[27]

The New Economic Policy (NEP) was intended only to be a comparatively short-term interlude in the development of the Soviet Union. The new and relaxed conditions automatically strengthened the position of the anti-Bolsheviks in the cities and on the land. Businessmen and peasants grew rich from trade in foodstuffs, textiles, and footwear (still in short supply). A new class of 'private capitalists' appeared, and only a year after the introduction of the NEP the Soviets were obliged to start a campaign against 'local capitalists'. The official reason given was that it was intended to use the improvement in the agricultural situation to help realize the plans for industrialization. The Russian *émigrés* and other anti-Communists abroad took heart and renewed their efforts. On 8 May 1923 Lord Curzon, the British Foreign Minister, sent an ultimatum demanding the immediate cessation of the Soviet's anti-British policy in the Middle East and the recall of Soviet diplomatic missions in Afghanistan and Persia. On 10 May 1923 the White Russian *émigré* Konradi in Lausanne assassinated the well-known Soviet diplomat V. V. Vorovsky. The defeat of the Conservatives in the British parliamentary elections in December 1923 and, later, the formation of a Leftish government in France under the Radical Socialist Édouard Herriot strengthened the international position of the Soviet Union considerably, but the threats to Soviet power by anti-Communist elements both at home and abroad were not thereby lessened.

This situation formed the background for the further enlargement of the OGPU. The security organs perfected their methods in their combat with the White Guard *émigré* organizations. Since 'the most interesting objectives', the White Guard headquarters, were in foreign countries, the result, from Dzerzhinsky's time onwards, was a feverish expansion of the foreign section of the OGPU, which gradually infiltrated its agents into all the anti-Communist organizations, especially in Poland and France.

At the same time the activities of the Soviet security organs on the economic sector were considerably expanded. It is no accident that Dzerzhinsky, in February 1924, was appointed chairman of the Supreme Economic Council (Russian abbreviation VZNK). The appointment was not only a recognition of Dzerzhinsky's energy and push, but also a sign that the Communists thought a combination of economic control and security police essential to the realization of their bold schemes for industry.

But gradually a fresh problem thrust itself into the foreground, a problem that refused to be shelved. Lenin's health worsened from day to day, and his approaching death gave rise to a struggle for power in the Party.

This was by no means a mere personal tug-of-war; what lay at stake was the realization of various political conceptions within the

Party. Trotsky, leader of the left wing, represented the idea of 'permanent Revolution'. He was convinced that Socialism could not be realized in Russia alone and his ambition was to extend the Revolution as speedily as possible to the industrialized lands of the West. A similar 'internationalistic' policy was advocated by Zinoviev and Kamenev, who, however, pursued a somewhat obscure and see-saw course between Trotsky and the Centre represented by Stalin. Stalin and his satellites Molotov and Kaganovich gradually began about then to develop the theory of 'Socialism in one country'. On the right wing of the Party were the advocates of a liberal policy towards the peasants. At their head were the brilliant publicist Bukharin and the trades union leader Tomsky.

While the struggle for the succession to Lenin raged within the Party, relations between Lenin and Stalin worsened daily. Stalin was obviously trying to isolate the sick Lenin from the Party and even from his immediate surroundings. Finally, in March 1923, Lenin broke off all personal relations with Stalin.

On 24 January 1924, at a time when the divisions within the Party were at their worst, Lenin died. His last will and testament ran as follows: [28]

'Since Comrade Stalin became Secretary-General he has gathered enormous powers into his own hands, and I am not sure that he always knows how to use them with the necessary caution. On the other hand Comrade Trotsky is distinguished not only by his extraordinary capabilities, as shown in his dispute with the Central Committee on the question of the People's Commissariat of Roads and Traffic, and he is certainly the best-qualified man in the present Central Committee. But he is inclined through excessive self-confidence to interest himself too deeply in the purely administrative side of things.

'These qualities of the two most capable leaders of the present Central Committee might, quite unexpectedly, lead to a split. If our Party cannot make arrangements to prevent this, the split might happen quite suddenly.

'I will not characterize more precisely the personal qualities of the other members of the Central Committee. I will only remind you that the October episode of Zinoviev and Kamenev is of course no chance happening, yet this should not be counted in their disfavour any more than Trotsky's "non-Bolshevism" should be counted against him.

'As regards the junior members of the Central Committee, I should like to say a few words about Pyatakov and Bukharin. They have to my mind the most capable brains among the younger members. In their respect, one must bear in mind that Bukharin is not only our most valuable theorist, and also the most important, and he might well be thought the best-loved man in the whole Party. His theoretical views can only with the greatest reservation be considered as fully Marxist, because he is too much of an academic. (He has never mastered the dialectic, and I think he has never quite understood it.)

'And now Pyatakov: a man with doubtless the best will in the world and with capabilities, but too much involved in administrative questions to be reliable in important political matters.

'Of course these estimates of character refer only to present conditions, with the presumption that these two clever and loyal workers will have no occasion to enlarge their experience and become less one-sided. 25 December 1922.

'P.S.   Stalin is too coarse, and this failing, quite tolerable among us Communists, is completely intolerable in the Secretary-General's office. I therefore propose to the comrades that they find some means of removing Stalin from that post and appointing another, differing from Stalin in no wise except superiority in some respects—more patient, more loyal, politer, more thoughtful towards the comrades, less moody, and so on. These qualities may seem of minor importance, but, to avoid a split in the Party and in view of the relations between Stalin and Trotsky, about which I have already written, I believe this is no trifling matter, or at least it is one which might become of decisive importance.   4 January 1923.

                                                    Lenin.'

Lenin, though a dictator, was devoid of vanity and of any inclination towards autocracy. In 1912, still in Lenin's lifetime, Yosif Vissarionovich Stalin had been chosen as Secretary-General of the Central Committee of the Communist Party of the Soviet Union. For Dzerzhinsky that meant at the time a certain degree of continuity in the connection between the security organs and the

Party, as it had existed under Lenin. Since the Cheka and later the OGPU were always subordinate to the Party, the man who controlled the Party was automatically in command of the security organs also. But Dzerzhinsky was one of the few Communist leaders who was precisely informed as to the relations between Lenin and Stalin, and he was acquainted with the terms of Lenin's testament. Nevertheless he helped to create the preconditions for the personal dictatorship of Stalin. As Lenin was reaching the end of his life, Dzerzhinsky was already Stalin's loyal and devoted adherent.

Dzerzhinsky's friendship with Stalin dated from the civil war years. At that time Stalin, who probably realized the power inherent in the secret police, had more or less forced his friendship on Dzerzhinsky. And there were other occasions when Lenin encouraged good relations between the two men. At the front the Bolsheviks were faced with appalling difficulties, and Lenin was always on the look-out for clever and resolute persons to take charge of weak sectors. That Stalin was a gifted organizer was already beyond question. Lenin sent him and Dzerzhinsky several times to dangerous points on the front. When, for example, Kolchak's army occupied Perm, and there was imminent danger of a junction between the anti-Bolshevik armies in Siberia and the Entente army that had landed in Archangel, he sent them to the eastern front on 3 January 1919 with full powers. It is said that the two men discovered a great White Guard conspiracy there, and several commanders of the 3rd Army on the eastern front were shot. Soon afterwards Dzerzhinsky and Stalin were posted together to Vyatka and later to Yaroslavl. It is hard to say what attitude Dzerzhinsky adopted during these events. For Stalin all these measures were merely a part of his great game against Trotsky, who as Commander-in-Chief of the Red Army was responsible also for the conspiracies unveiled by Stalin.[29] At that time Stalin was still the coadjutor of Dzerzhinsky, and mutual confidence between the two made rapid growth. On 3 May 1919 it had reached such a pitch that Dzerzhinsky proposed that the leader of the special department of the Vecheka should make a weekly report of his activities to the head office of the organization. As liaison officer between the organization office of the Central Committee and the leader of the Special Board of the OGPU he recommended Stalin.

The relations between Dzerzhinsky and Stalin were strengthened by their collaboration in the leadership on the south-western front during 1920. When the two men put in an appearance in Georgia in 1921 (where Stalin's agent Ordzhonikidze was already all-powerful), their friendship had reached a stage at which the two men conspired together and shamelessly profited by the fact that Lenin's health was deteriorating. Georgia's independence was recognized by treaty on 7 May 1920, at Lenin's demand. Stalin and Ordzhonikidze were against the treaty. By all possible means, especially through the contrivance of Bolshevik risings in Georgia itself, they sought to produce a new political situation. On 11 February 1921 detachments from the Red Army attacked independent Georgia on Stalin's orders, and in mid-June Stalin entered Tiflis as victor.

The cooling of relations between Lenin and Dzerzhinsky, already mentioned, now culminated in open conflict. The situation in Georgia became extremely precarious and, against Lenin's wishes, was inflamed by Stalin, Ordzhonikidze, and Dzerzhinsky. Stalin's representative at that time was Ordzhonikidze, and his quarrels with Mdivani led to actual fisticuffs in the sessions of the Central Committee of the Georgian Communist Party. On one occasion Ordzhonikidze boxed the ears of one of Mdivani's adherents.[30] When Lenin heard of this on his sickbed he was furious and made a great affair out of what the Party called the 'Georgian incident' (Gruzinski Intsident). There is much to show that Lenin insisted on the punishment of all concerned. On the other hand it is certain that Lenin was informed of the affair by Dzerzhinsky. The main cause of these quarrels has been mentioned. Stalin was for an 'autonomization' of the non-Russian republics, i.e. for their joining the Russian federation as autonomous units, while Lenin was for the establishment of a federative State, to which each republic would belong as a sovereign and independent unit. The Trans-Caucasian Communists with Ordzhonikidze and Kirov at their head succeeded in getting the Trans-Caucasian Party leadership to agree to Stalin's 'autonomization'. The Georgian Communists with Mdivani as their leader bitterly opposed this solution and a truly paradoxical situation arose: those Communists in Georgia who wanted to brand Stalin and Ordzhonikidze as 'nationalist deviators' and 'enemies' were Lenin's only allies in the Caucasus! From documents published after Lenin's death it is clear that

Dzerzhinsky was Stalin's close ally in these negotiations. What is more—he sent Lenin false reports about the situation in the Caucasus. Lenin reproached Dzerzhinsky and Stalin on several occasions with acting against the nationalities policy of the Party and with pan-Russian chauvinism.

'Of course Stalin and Dzerzhinsky must be made responsible for this pan-Russian campaign' was a note made by Lenin at the time.[31] On 6 March 1923 he wrote to the Georgian opposition: 'To Comrades Mdivani, Makharadze, and others (copies to Comrades Trotsky and Kamenev). Dear Comrades, In this affair I am entirely on your side. I am horrified at Ordzhonikidze's arrogance and Stalin's criminal alliance with him. I am preparing memoranda and a speech in your defence. With high regards, Lenin.'

And on the following day he wrote to Trotsky: 'Dear Comrade Trotsky, I ask you urgently to undertake the defence of the Georgian affair in the Central Committee of the Party. It is now being directed by Stalin and Dzerzhinsky, so that I cannot reckon upon impartiality. Quite the contrary in fact. . . .'[32]

Even before Lenin's death Dzerzhinsky involved the OGPU directly as Stalin's tool in internal Party disputes. After Lenin had quitted political life on account of his illness, Dzerzhinsky used the OGPU apparatus against a group of leading Party members, before a Party process had been opened against them. A group of Tatar Communists under the leadership of Sultan Galiyev and Uzbek Communists under Fayzul Khodzhayev engaged in a strong propaganda campaign for equal rights for the Turkish peoples in the Soviet Union. The friction between them and non-local emissaries developed into open conflict in the middle of 1923. At Stalin's request Dzerzhinsky simply had the malcontents arrested. It was not till June 1923 that the affair was formally considered in an enlarged full session of the Central Committee.[33] The action of the police, who for the first time had intervened in internal Party matters as the 'first instance', was severely criticized by several prominent Communists, including Zinoviev and Kamenev. Stalin, however, won his point, and the Central Committee approved his action after the event. Thereby he established a precedent which was to be of vast importance to his future career. Sultan Galiyev, as a 'National Communist', enjoyed little sympathy among the

Soviet leaders at the time. Stalin, a Georgian, had discovered how to appeal to the mass of Russian Communists.

Stalin's friendship with Dzerzhinsky did not prevent him from filling the OGPU with his own nominees. It is certain that Stalin's sinister intimate, Henry Yagoda, was also one of the closest collaborators of Dzerzhinsky. While Dzerzhinsky was responsible for the general activities of the OGPU, Yagoda was constructing in his shadow an OGPU apparatus consisting of devoted followers of Stalin and directing its efforts exclusively against Stalin's opponents.

These divisions in the Party helped Stalin and enabled him to realize more speedily his plans for a definitive showdown with the opposition. The 13th Party Conference of January 1924 was a masterpiece. Stalin had filled the Party apparatus beforehand with his followers and his plans were supported by Dzerzhinsky unconditionally. The 13th Party Congress of the Russian Communist Party (Bolshevik), the RKP (B), took place in May 1924. Stalin had made his Party bureaucrats into delegates, who without exception represented not the mass of the people but the apparatus now dominated by Stalin. Stalin's victory was complete. Trotsky was unable to make a single speech during the whole conference, for the Stalinists shouted him down and threatened to beat him up. Lenin's testament was naturally not disclosed to the delegates.

Dzerzhinsky was totally involved in the machinations of the General Secretary. Stalin's tactics were characteristic. As Dzerzhinsky's importance within his narrow circle was constantly growing, he tried to load him as far as possible with economic problems and to concentrate purely political questions in the hands of his own henchmen inside the security organs. Dzerzhinsky was a fanatical champion of a 'quick rise in industrial production' for the Soviet Union and he pursued this aim by strong measures, with no regard for human lives. In many publications about Dzerzhinsky that appeared in Stalin's lifetime it is stressed that he advocated 'strict labour discipline' and the introduction of 'one-man leadership' into industry. At the 14th Party Conference in April 1925 Dzerzhinsky came forward as a specialist in the metal industry. He gave a lecture on the possibility of further development in the industry and emphasized its importance for defence. Stalin approved Dzerzhinsky's proposals at this conference with a special tribute.

In December of the same year the 14th Party Congress passed all Stalin's plans for industry.

Trotsky, who had been Commissar of War since March 1918 and had won all the victories over the White generals, was removed from his post in April 1925. His successor was Mikhail Vasilyevich Frunze, an old revolutionary and military leader who had made his name in the civil war. He was only for a short time Commissar of War. He died in November 1925, during a stomach operation. Rumour had it that Frunze was a victim of a criminal action by Stalin's party. Trotsky at any rate said in his Stalin biography that Frunze had been dissuaded by his doctors from submitting himself to complete anaesthesia because his heart was weak. Stalin laid the question before a board of physicians. The doctors chosen by Stalin recommended complete anaesthesia and Frunze died.[54] It may have been chance, but it is certain that all the doctors who treated members of the Central Committee were attached to the GPU.

In 1926 Stalin delivered his first hard blows against the supporters of Trotsky and his other opponents. Dzerzhinsky again played a leading part in the conflict. Spurred on by Stalin, at the expanded plenary session of the Central Committee of the Communist Party on 20 July 1926, he delivered a speech against his former friends Kamenev, Pyatakov, and others. Two hours later Dzerzhinsky died of a stroke. V. R. Menzhinsky was named as his successor.

Viacheslav Rudolfovich Menzhinsky, born in 1874 as the son of a Petersburg teacher, was a jurist. He joined the revolutionary movement in 1895. In 1902 he joined the Russian Social Democratic Workers' Party, and after the 2nd Party Congress in 1903 he supported the Bolsheviks. Arrested in 1906, he later fled to Belgium and afterwards to Switzerland and France. He did not return to Russia until 1917, after which he worked in Communist soldiers' organizations. After the victory of the October Revolution he became People's Commissar of Finance. He broke the resistance of the Russian bankers and nationalized the banks. In 1918 he became Consul General of the Russian Federative Soviet Republic in Berlin, and finally in 1919 People's Commissar for the State Control of the Soviet Ukraine. After that he worked in the Cheka and was quickly advanced to the position of Dzerzhinsky's first deputy.

One of Menzhinsky's contemporaries, V. V. Fomin, a Chekist, says in his memoirs that Menzhinsky was very well educated and that his capacity for learning foreign languages almost amounted to genius. Although he was already fluent in twelve languages when posted to the Cheka, he learnt four Oriental languages in addition: Chinese, Japanese, Persian, and Turkish. He devoted his free time to study, and took a lively interest in literature, chemistry, astronomy, physics, and mathematics. Certainly he was a rare bird among the Chekists. The memoirs of former Chekists, published later, mention how many of them, used to rough talk, were astounded when Menzhinsky, instead of giving orders, asked them politely to carry out certain requirements. The verdict of Menzhinsky's contemporaries varies considerably. The Stalinist historians describe him as 'a fearless champion of the Bolshevist cause'.[35]

Trotsky, however, was of a different opinion and wrote about him: 'Menzhinsky is not a man, but the shadow of a man.' He was in every way the opposite of Dzerzhinsky, whose 'great moral power' impressed Trotsky even when Dzerzhinsky at the end of his career became Stalin's right-hand man. Trotsky writes that Stalin deliberately made the weak Menzhinsky head of the OGPU so that behind his back he could expedite his own plan of making the security organs into a blindly obedient instrument for the destruction of such Communists as opposed him. This statement of Trotsky's is probably true. Moreover official sources report that Menzhinsky's ill health kept him out of office for several months and that his first deputy, Yagoda, was the real head of the OGPU.

The security organizations were further enlarged under Menzhinsky. Their members were favoured even more than in Dzerzhinsky's time, well clothed, and provided with all manner of goods in special shops. The armed forces of the OGPU were greatly enlarged in connection with Stalin's measures against the peasants. The year 1928 brought the first wave of collectivization. Whereas the prisons and concentration camps hitherto had been used for the punishment of crime and for the 'political re-education' of the inmates, now for the first time the idea occurred to Stalin and his associates to make a 'national utilization' of the inmates' labour for the benefit of the national economy.

No sooner said than done. In 1930 a new administration was set up in the OGPU for the concentration camps, which had hitherto

been under the Ministry of Justice. This was the GULAG (Glavnoye Upravleniye Lagerey), the 'Chief Administration for corrective labour camps', and its head was Yagoda.[36] The Soviet
Union had made use of concentration camps since the beginning.
One of the most notorious was the penal colony of Solovki, on an
island in the Gulf of Onega in the White Sea. Originally a four-
teenth-century monastery, it was now the headquarters of a gigantic
prison camp. In the twenties the Communists tried to make Solovki
a model penal settlement. Hothouses, stables, and a tannery were
built, and experimental farms laid out. But when the number of
prisoners continued to grow, it was decided to put them to hard
labour, and that in the most unfavourable conditions. They mined
for coal or ore in primitive shafts, they built roads in the wilderness,
they felled the endless forests. Their living conditions were pitiable.
When in 1933 the famous Stalin-Byelomov Canal was dug to con-
nect the White Sea with the Baltic, Yagoda had to build special
camps for the project, so as to provide 'reinforcements' for the
labour. The workers were armed only with picks and shovels, with
no protection against the murderous climate. (The canal is frozen
over for more than six months in the year.) More than 100,000
prisoners died on the 150-mile section between the White Sea and
Lake Onega. This was, according to official Soviet sources, 'on the
initiative and under the direct management of Comrade Stalin'.[37]

Whence came the men in the concentration camps and labour
camps? At the beginning of the thirties Stalin's collectivization
plans for agriculture were carried through with blood and tears.
The structural change in agriculture, compulsory cooperation, had
always been in the Bolsheviks' programme, but in Lenin's opinion
two pre-conditions were essential. From the economic standpoint
he considered that the transition to large-scale agriculture could
only succeed when a well-developed industry could provide the
collective farms with sufficient machines and tractors. That alone
could make a transition to industrial methods in agricultural production profitable. Lenin's second condition was that the peasants'
cooperation must be voluntary. His view was that the peasants
would only consent to collectivization when convinced of the value
of such a step. He was a follower in this respect of Friedrich Engels,
according to whom peasants would only join a union 'voluntarily
and with an offer of mutual assistance'. When Stalin began his

collectivization neither condition was present—it was a compulsory measure which could only be carried out by terrorization.
In February 1930 the Central Executive Committee and the Council of the People's Commissars issued an instruction concerning
measures to be taken against the 'kulaks' or large farmers. They
were divided into three classes: the first were the counter-revolutionary kulaks, who were to be arrested and brought before the
courts. The second category kulaks were to be banished to far-
distant regions, while those of the third were to be turned out of
their holdings and resettled in the same area.[38]

Soviet documents, including those of the Khrushchev era, assert
that most kulaks were in the third category, but this statement is
contradicted by documents since published in the West. In the
Menshevik periodical *Sotsialistichesky Vestnik* (USA), S. Wollin
published in 1955 an instruction which had been issued to Party
organizations and the OGPU, justices and lawyers, from which it
appears that the number of prisoners in concentration camps and
labour colonies, arrested in consequence of the OGPU measures
against the peasants, amounted to no less than 800,000—more than
the GULAG had anticipated.[39] This instruction, as to the genuineness of which there is no doubt, consequently demanded a reduc-
tion in arrests and sentences to banishment. As a practical remedy
for the congestion a table was given showing the maximum number
of arrests that might be made annually in each area, so that by the
end of 1934 the total number of arrested peasants could be reduced
to 400,000.

The Stalinists launched the class war on the countryside with the
aim of liquidating the kulaks. Stalin and his assistants justified this
policy on the grounds that the kulaks were resisting Soviet rule and
that terrorists, saboteurs, and murderers were largely recruited
from among them. But anybody who has the slightest acquaintance
with conditions in the rural areas of Russia knows that the measures
taken against the kulaks were out of all proportion to their danger
to the State. The official reason put forward was merely to hide the
real motives. In the liquidation of the kulaks the Stalinists had the
same motives as those used by Stalin to justify his extermination
measures against his opponents in the Party. The threat from the
kulaks was exaggerated by Stalin in order to give free play to his
forced collectivization measures carried out by terror. The

Stalinists and many of today's Soviet writers declare that the hard blows of the OGPU would have in any case been specially directed at the kulaks because of their bitter resistance to collectivization. It is true that the peasants were driven to counter-terrorism, and the number of the officials that they murdered was very large. But that does not alter the fact that Stalin looked on collectivization not as an economic but as a political-administrative measure, the main object of which was to secure the grain crops for the city-dwellers. The OGPU was the most suitable tool for the purpose.

After Stalin's death several reports of what happened in this period were published, and they give a truly desperate picture. Here is an example in illustration. In March 1928 A. A. Andreyev, at that time secretary to the North Caucasian Agricultural Committee, who was later a faithful adherent of Stalin's and survived him, wrote as follows about the crop seizures in the Northern Caucasus: 'I believe that the only people to whom we ought to take off our hats, to whom we can pay real compliments, are the OGPU. . . . Without them we should have been lost and have had no grain. It is clear that the OGPU on the Party's orders produced more grain for us than all our collective farms.'[40]

Such documents were kept secret in Stalin's time, because they confirm what hundreds of eye-witnesses and Western reporters had said. A fig for all Communist theories! The political police stole the grain. That this action had nothing to do with crushing the kulaks' resistance is proved by many other facts, but the document we have quoted is enough. It states that in the course of the OGPU reprisals against the peasants in the first months of 1928 some 759 kulaks were arrested and punished, together with 1,535 middle-class and poor peasants. Similar reports came from all parts of the Soviet Union and even at that date there was a certain amount of opposition among the Stalinists themselves to Stalin and his methods. Stalin himself remained unmoved. As far back as the twenties the outlines of the new social order had grown clearer, and the powerful position of the political police, with a steady extension of their powers in the economic sphere, was one of the chief means of putting the system into effect. Stalin's contempt of the peasants as a social class in the community was already known in the civil war. 'The peasants will never willingly fight for Socialism' said Stalin as far back as the 8th Congress of the Russian Communist

Party in the year 1919.[41] When at the end of the twenties the kolkhozes or collective farms were to be 'bolshevized' (a favourite expression of Stalin's) economic factors were not so important for him as the extension of the control and supervisory power of the security apparatus in the rural areas. All difficulties in the kolkhozes were explained away by Stalin as the result of 'enemy activity'. 'Kulaks need not be looked for outside the kolkhozes,' he exclaimed, 'they are in the kolkhozes themselves.' In this way he encouraged the Party cadres to step up their reprisals against the peasants. The political departments in the countryside which were set up in the mid-twenties were more and more staffed with OGPU officials, and finally Stalin at the end of the twenties succeeded in persuading the Central Committee of the Party that the deputy leader of the political departments should be an OGPU man with full powers.[42]

Dzerzhinsky's death left Stalin free to convert the OGPU into his personal power tool. Under the pretext of fighting Trotskyism, one of the greatest mass-murders in human history began, destroying the whole generation of the original Bolsheviks and thousands of innocent people besides; as a prelude the Soviet security organs arranged a series of show-trials. Thereby not only would the real or imaginary opponents of Soviet power be destroyed, but also the 'rightness' of Stalin's theory be proved—that Socialism, incessantly spreading, must necessarily lead to a stepping-up of class warfare and the Reign of Terror.

Stalin's day of reckoning with an opposing group of industrial experts was handled promptly by the OGPU. In fulfilling this task the OGPU perfected the method which had been used in Dzerzhinsky's time: a mixture of fiction and truth. It was true that in those early years there were many determined opponents of Soviet power. The art lay in finding sore points and converting malcontents into instruments of Stalin's schemes. The first steps towards the industrialization of the country were marked by a series of failures. The causes were manifold, but objective inquiries put them down to lack of experience, technical methods, and personnel. The working classes were still very weak and untrained. The Stalinists decided to transfer the responsibility for these faults to some of the economic specialists. Former landowners and various experts from the old times, according to the grand-scale propaganda, were working closely with 'foreign capitalists' and imperialist

3—TUOT * *

intelligence organs. It was their fault that Stalin's plans for industry had not yet been fulfilled.

After 1930 the number of cases and trials increased. For instance, the OGPU unearthed a counter-revolutionary organization supposed to be active in the transport world. Its alleged leader was a Von Meck, of the family of Russian railway kings to which Nadezhda von Meck, Tchaikovsky's patroness, had belonged. In the precious metal (gold and platinum) industry a certain Palchinsky was arrested, who had been a leading politician in Kerensky's time. Both men were shot in 1930. The number of such trials grew from day to day, and the public were thus prepared for the theory invented by the security organs, that behind all these subversive associations there must be one great and powerful central organization. This was speedily disclosed in November 1930, in the shape of the 'Industry Party' (Prompartiya). Its leaders were said to be former leading Russian capitalists with headquarters in Paris and in touch with the French secret service. Their object was to overthrow the Soviet regime and restore capitalism in Russia. In Russia itself the chief figures were an engineer called Ramzin and a whole series of former factory-owners and well-known specialists. The OGPU asserted that the conspirators had succeeded in planting their men in various economic institutions, including the State Planning Commission (GOS Plan) and in forming illegal groups in all the industrial centres and important combines. The process against the 'Prompartiya' was by no means as well publicized as the Shakhty 'conspiracy' in the Donets Basin which had been discovered by the OGPU just previously.

At the beginning of 1928 several engineers and specialists in the Donets Basin had been arrested on charges of sabotage. *Pravda* of 10 March 1928 criticized the union officials severely: 'They confess that the engineers have been spreading their counter-revolutionary plots through the works and mines.' The Party organizations were subjected to still more harsh criticism for 'having shown quite extraordinary blindness' in the affair. The so called 'Shakhty trial' took place in Moscow and lasted from 18 May to 5 July 1928. Eleven of the accused were sentenced to death and thirty-four received sentences of from one to ten years. Four were acquitted, and three of the defendants were sentenced to three years each with probation. In order to demonstrate to foreign countries the 'humaneness' of Soviet justice, the court asked the Government of the Soviet Union to reduce the death sentence in the case of six defendants to 'another social protective measure'.[43] In the proceedings against the counter-revolutionary and espionage organization called 'Prompartiya', which lasted from 25 November to 7 December 1930, the Soviet leaders dispensed with any such theatrical humanitarianism.

The two prosecutions showed that OGPU tactics had become more refined. Elements from various opposition parties, suspected or potentially hostile, were alleged to have combined to form an 'illegal organization'. But the real organizer of the conspiracy was Stalin's secret police. For the OGPU itself had arranged to bring the various individuals into contact with each other and had created an organization which in its turn made contact with foreign countries. All these contacts were contrived by *agents provocateurs* of the OGPU, who saw to it that the communications functioned smoothly, until in the end the whole 'conspiracy' could be crushed at one blow. By these tactics the Communist Party, with the greatest possible psychological skill, was able to 'bring under one hat' all hostile or suspected elements and thus get rid of them with greater ease.

In the Shakhty case this procedure of the OGPU did not work perfectly. One must not forget that many OGPU officials were uneducated and had no idea of what conditions were like abroad. The chief defendant, Ramzin, for instance, admitted during the trial that he had been visited by two Russian capitalists, Ryabushinsky and Vishnegradsky, and received instructions from them to carry out counter-revolutionary acts. Actually, however, the two men in question had long been dead. Still worse blunders were made when giving evidence about 'contacts' with the French, Germans, and British. Western newspapers made jokes about them, but for the internal development of the Soviet Union they were of no importance. The OGPU learnt from its mistakes and improved its methods in the next stage of its organized destruction of Stalin's enemies.[44]

In order to rescue the credit of the OGPU after such blunders, the regime became more inventive. Fictitious stories about the excellent and infallible work of the secret police and the unscrupulousness of counter-revolutionary elements distracted the attention

of the general public. Here is an example: 'On 6 July, at 9.15 p.m.,
two White Guards who had arrived a week before from Paris, with
the help of the Rumanian spy service, threw a home-made bomb
into the room where permits to enter the offices of the State Political Administration (GPU) were issued. The explosion killed one
Red Guard and badly injured another. One of the criminals, a
former member of the Pages' Corps and a Wrangel officer, Georgy
Radkovich, thirty years of age, was killed while attempting to
escape. His accomplice, an *émigré* White Guard, was arrested near
the town of Podolsk in the government of Moscow, the organ of
the State Political Administration being zealously supported by the
peasants in the pursuit of the criminals.'[45] This item of news was
published throughout the Soviet press!

The amalgamation of opposing or suspected elements into
alleged 'organizations' proved to be another effective method of
liquidating 'enemies'. It was especially successful in the non-
Russian republics, as a weapon against the nationalist intelligentsia.
Everywhere the OGPU staged monster trials, the most impressive
of which was held at Kharkov in 1930 against the 'Association for
the Liberation of the Ukraine' (in Ukrainian, Spilka Vysvolennie
Ukrainy). There certainly existed members of the intelligentsia in
the Ukraine who were striving for more independence. With the
help of its *provocateurs*, a well-tried method, the OGPU arranged
for the suspects to contact each other and it created an organization
for them. Here, too, a web of truth and deceit was woven, impossible to disentangle. The OGPU asserted that the organization had
been in existence since 1926 and that it had been working, with the
support of nationalistic elements abroad (the Polish Government
and the Western powers), for the separation of the Ukraine from
the Soviet Union. The show-trial, blown-up and highly publicized,
ended in the sentencing of forty-five defendants to long terms of
imprisonment. The political aims of the trial were in complete
accord with Moscow's Ukraine policy. The purpose was to suppress
the Ukrainians' national aspirations and create an atmosphere for
their total elimination.

The illegal 'Menshevik Centre' was also ensnared by the Soviet
security organs. As the foreign department of the Russian Social
Democratic Workers' Party (i.e. the Mensheviks) later acknowledged, it did in fact try to carry on an illegal struggle with the

Bolsheviks after the October Revolution. For this purpose the 'Union Bureau of the Central Committee of the Russian Social Democratic Workers' Party' was founded, which was suppressed by the OGPU in 1931. At the end of February 1931 the trial of fourteen members of this centre was staged in Moscow. The Mensheviks wanted to fight the Bolsheviks by political methods only, but the security organs had seen to it that at the right moment evidence for 'espionage and diversional activity' was available. F. I. Dan, a Menshevik living in Paris, was stated to be a courier between the 'American capitalists' and the Menshevik centre in Moscow. The charge was that R. Abramovich, then Menshevik leader, living in the USA, had entered Soviet Russia illegally in the summer of 1928 and carried instructions to the 'Union Bureau' —a pure invention. All the accused were sentenced to long terms of imprisonment, for the security organs still shrank from shooting. The *Sotsialistichesky Vestnik* reported that three of the accused in the Menshevik trial were still alive in September 1954, in Kazakhstan.[46] Their case was exceptional, for when the war broke out in 1941 most of the surviving Menshevik leaders and Left-Wing Socialist Revolutionaries were liquidated by the special commandos of the security organs.

In May 1967, almost the sole survivor of the Mensheviks' trial, Mikhail Yakobovich, sent a letter to the State Attorney General of the USSR regarding the Mensheviks' trial in 1931. This shattering document was first published in the Soviet Union, and did not reach the West until the middle of 1969, where it was published or quoted from in various journals. Yakobovich describes the methods used by the security organs in fabricating the alleged Menshevik plot, how they 'manufactured' connections between the individual Russian Social Democrats, and had forced false admissions out of Yakobovich himself. Groman, too, one of the most prominent of the accused, described in detail various meetings with a leading Menshevik, Abramovich, who in fact at the time was living in the USA.

Lenin was doubtless a strategist of genius, who led Communism to victory in Russia. Stalin was no less an inventive genius when it was a question of securing his own personal success. By the show-trials he created an atmosphere which secured for him the agreement of all the leaders of the Communist Party to the further

expansion of the OGPU. That is probably also the reason why the
sentences in the Shakhty case and others of that time were so
'humane'. In many cases the defending counsel were brought in
from abroad and the proceedings broadcast direct from the court
room. Looking back, there is no doubt that all these manoeuvres
were intended to further the 'just' advancement of the security
organs and serve only one end, namely the gradual elimination of
Stalin's opponents in the Communist ranks.

Such elimination had already begun under Menzhinsky, the first
victim being Y. G. Blumkin at the end of 1920. He came from the
party of the Social Revolutionaries and as a sixteen-year-old fanatic
had thrown a bomb at the German ambassador in Moscow. Later
he went over to the Bolsheviks and served in the civil war. He
worked at first as military secretary to Trotsky and afterwards was
transferred to work in the OGPU. At no time did he disguise
the fact that his sympathies were with Trotsky. When in January
1929 Trotsky was banished from the Soviet Union, Blumkin visited
him in Constantinople and had several conversations with him.
Blumkin made no attempt to hide the contact from his superiors.
Menzhinsky and the head of the foreign department of the OGPU,
Trilisser, were informed of Blumkin's journey. But Stalin recommended Yagoda to get rid of Blumkin. He was treacherously shot,
and soon afterwards two other Trotskyists, Silov and Rabinovich,
were liquidated by Yagoda without any court hearing or party
inquiry.[47]

That was the beginning of the reprisals, for not even the OGPU
was reliable enough for Stalin. In order to use the security organs
in the internecine Party conflicts, the OGPU too must be purged
of suspect and unreliable elements. Stalin's opening shots therefore
were directed at Trotskyist Chekists.

Soon a fresh hunting-ground was found for the Soviet security
apparatus—international Communism, or, more precisely, the
Communist International or Comintern.[48] Between the OGPU and
the foreign Communist parties there had always been close relations. The Soviet Communists were deeply interested in the personnel of these parties. They were anxious to prevent enemies of
communism or *provocateurs* taking up leading positions in the
Comintern. For that reason, there were usually trusted collaborators with the Cheka or OGPU in the personnel department which

appointed to the principal posts in the apparatus of international Communism. Even in the earliest disputes between Russian Communists and foreign Communist parties, leading representatives of the security organs had been infiltrated. When the 'Polish Commission' in the Comintern was set up in 1926, two leading Chekists besides Stalin and Zinoviev were members, namely Dzerzhinsky and Unshlikht. The latter also played a decisive role in the 'Chinese Commission'.

Under Dzerzhinsky this bond between the Cheka or OGPU and international Communism was understandable to some extent. But what Stalin now ordered was entirely new: the OGPU was to carry out a purge of adverse elements in international Communism. Stalin and Yagoda were well aware that it was much easier to liquidate an opponent in the Soviet Union than to get rid of a particular person or group in a foreign country. Nevertheless they gave instructions that the clutches of the OGPU must stretch across the frontiers and that their laws must prevail in foreign countries also. At great expense foreign departments of the OGPU were set up in every country.

The splinter process among the Russian *émigrés* was by now almost complete: in nearly all the Russian *émigré* associations there were OGPU agents. The *provocateurs* changed their tactics from time to time. Sometimes they played the role of fanatical opponents of Bolshevism, at others they gave themselves out as friends of the Soviets. Among the nationalist-minded White Guard *émigrés* the latter disguise was effective. The Soviet agents encouraged the *émigrés* in their doubts as to whether anti-Communist activity would lead to the break-up of the Soviet Union, which after all was still a 'Russian state'. It was a trick which before, in 1922, had led to a mass-return of Russian *émigrés* to the Soviet Union. [The 'Zmienoviekhovskoye Movement' at that time had shattered the anti-Communist unity of the White *émigrés*. Among those who returned was the Russian writer Aleksey (not Leo) Tolstoy.]

The OGPU agents found themselves in their element among the demoralized, splintered, and mutually antagonistic White *émigrés*. Their special aim was to discredit the leaders of the *émigré* group in the eyes of the public and thereby to destroy the trust of other *émigrés* in the rightness of their policy.

Their boldest coup was with V. V. Shulgin, a representative of the chauvinistic, anti-semitic Russian circles among the *émigrés*. Before the war he had been the publisher and editor of the periodical *Kyevlyanin*, which had openly advocated Jewish pogroms at Kiev, the heart of the Ukraine, and decried the Ukrainians as a 'doubtful Russian tribe'. Shulgin, who was living in Paris in the thirties, was chosen by the OGPU as a victim. They provided for him connections with a 'monarchist' organization in Russia, and when the time was ripe brought him by a 'secret route' back into the Soviet Union. He was supplied by 'illegal' persons with the necessary papers, was able to travel almost everywhere, and was able to convince himself with his own eyes that there was 'nothing new' in the Soviet Union, the people were just as 'patriotic and Jew-hating' as ever. After some weeks Shulgin, again with the help of the 'illegals', returned home via Poland. *Three Capitals: a Journey through Red Russia* was the title of his memoirs. Scarcely had the book appeared than the Communists burst into roars of laughter and published a series of reports from which it was clear that for the whole time Shulgin had been the 'guest' of the OGPU and had only been allowed to see what was put before him. When Shulgin one Sunday in Moscow had expressed a desire to attend a religious service, one was immediately provided for him. The mass took place in a cellar according to traditional rites, and the pious Shulgin kissed the priest's hand repeatedly. But the priest was no other than Menzhinsky, deputy chief of the OGPU. The 'heroic exploit' of a White *émigré* became in a flash a worldwide scandal. Shulgin was compelled to write another book about his Russian journey, but his credibility was gone for ever.

The method became a theme with variations. After the Russian *émigrés*, the Ukrainians were the next victims of the special departments of the OGPU. Here too they fostered disputes among the *émigrés* and tried to infiltrate their ranks with *provocateurs*, who on every occasion displayed their 'patriotism' and 'profound anti-Communism'. In this way the OGPU contrived to produce results which were on a smaller scale but no less successful than the Shulgin affair.

By 1934 the activity of the Soviet security organs was growing more intense every day. It was more varied, more dramatic, and, as in the Shulgin case, more 'humorous'. For this Menzhinsky was no longer responsible, as he was very ill and was now merely the nominal head of OGPU. When he finally departed this life in May 1934 there were rumours that his death was not a natural one. The communiqué published by Stalin and his henchman Yagoda stated that Menzhinsky had fallen at his post—as a victim of the promoters of the 'anti-Soviet counter-revolutionary Right-Wing Trotskyist block'. Some years later, when Stalin brought his favourite Yagoda before the court and had him shot, with Trotskyists and other opponents, the question of Menzhinsky's death cropped up again. Stalin's enemies asserted that Yagoda had simply poisoned him.[49]

In any case Menzhinsky's death left the way open for a new type of Soviet security organization: Yagoda's NKVD, the precise sort of security organization which Stalin had always desired.

Chapter Three

The Chemist Yagoda
as Chief of the NKVD

A portrait

'W E have made some progress since the days of Caesar Borgia',
wrote Bayonov à propos Trotsky's banishment in February 1929.
'In those days one cleverly shook a powerful powder into a beaker
of Falernian, or one's enemy died immediately after he had eaten
an apple. Present-day methods are quite different, thanks to
scientific progress. Koch's bacilli, mixed with the food and
systematically administered, gradually produce galloping tuber-
culosis and a sudden but natural death.... I don't see why ...
Stalin should not have used this method, which so well suited his
habits and character.' Perhaps merely because Henry Yagoda was
not yet chief of the security organization.

Yagoda was in every way the exact opposite of Dzerzhinsky: the
latter with a 'revolutionary's pride' and a determination to strike
down the enemies of the Revolution; the former an intriguer who
laid treacherous snares for his opponents and got rid of them,
preferably with poison.

Henry Yagoda, born 1891, a Party member since 1907, came
from the textile city of Lodz. He was a chemist, like his father.
The story of his career is somewhat obscure. As a youth he is
said to have joined the Radical workers' movement in Poland and
later in Russia. In the civil war he commanded a unit in the Red
Army. It is certain that by 1920 he was a leading Chekist and
closely associated with Stalin. Trotsky asserted that Yagoda was
one of the Chekists in contact with the sick Lenin. When the
opposition spread a rumour in the thirties that somebody had

'hastened' Lenin's death, many people thought that was by no means impossible: Yagoda the chemist later showed that he was a virtuoso in the sphere of 'medical murder'.

Yagoda's methods aroused even the Chekists' disgust and contempt, and some of them of their own accord went so far as to study Yagoda's past life. They hoped thereby to spike his guns. In 1930 Yagoda's deputy, the old Bolshevik Trilisser, reported to Stalin the results of these investigations. He was able to prove that all the official biographies of Yagoda were false. Stalin's pleasure at the compromising document was great, but because he liked best to work with men whom he had in his power, this episode had no unpleasant consequences for Yagoda. Trilisser, however, who had hoped for promotion, fell into disgrace and was later shot.[50]

The OGPU is converted into the NKVD

After Menzhinsky's death Stalin turned the OGPU into the GUGB, the 'Chief Administration for State Security' (Glavnoye Upravleniye Gozundarstvennoye Bezopaznosti) and on 10 July 1934 he subordinated it to the Union Commissariat for Internal Affairs, the NKVD (Narkeomad Vnutrennith Del). The People's Commissar of the NKVD was Henry Yagoda. Today there is probably no historian, even in the Soviet Union, who would not agree that this step of Stalin's was of epoch-making importance in the history of the Soviet Union. Stalin shaped history according to his own ideas, but without creatures like Yagoda and other scoundrels in the secret police he would never have succeeded.

The reorganization of the security organization was an important step of Stalin's on his way to personal dictatorship. Formally it looked only as if the OGPU had been converted into a department of the People's Commissariat of Internal Affairs. But in reality the new 'Administration of State Security' thereby took into its grip the whole administrative area of the People's Commissariat. The NKVD, dominated by the security police, was now in charge of militia, frontier control, and all armed forces which were not directly part of the army and the fleet, and also of the forced labour camps and prisons, and all the fire brigades. The inter-Soviet pass system, introduced in 1932, guaranteed the complete control of the whole civil population. The security organs were now more powerful than ever.

Under Yagoda, as was to be expected from the first chief of the GULAG, the labour camps had a special role. Forced labour had been introduced as far back as 1918, when the Five-Year Plan was announced, and was an important and precisely planned factor in the realization of the economic aims of the Soviets. But the chemist Yagoda was the first to invent the organizational recipe for the wholesale use of convicts in the so-called 'Stalin Constructions' as part of the first Five-Year Plan. But he also found a means of making the forced labourers work in the worst conditions: each time he promised an amnesty in return for a rapid completion of the project. It is unnecessary to say that almost always he failed to keep his promise.

Yagoda demonstrated his methods on a grand scale for the first time in the digging of the Byelomov Canal, which we have already mentioned. He put 300,000 men to work on it, including the engineers, most of whom were convicts also. His promise of a complete and comprehensive amnesty induced the prisoners to finish the job as quickly as possible. In fact Yagoda freed 72,000 after the canal was finished. The rest were immediately loaded into goods wagons and sent off to work on new projects. Two of these 'Stalin Constructions' were of special economic importance: the Baikal-Amur Railway in the Far East and the Moscow-Volga Canal, which was begun in 1932. In the latter case, too, productivity was promoted by the hope of an amnesty. When the Canal was opened on 4 July 1937, 55,000 prisoners were amnestied, but most in any case were near the end of their sentences and for them the amnesty meant only the gift of a few days or weeks.

Stalin and his henchmen were very proud of the fact that their system of combining forced labour and economic development functioned with so little friction. He, Kaganovich, and Khrushchev (whose star was in the ascendant) often visited the works. To none of them did the thought occur that it hardly became Marxists and Socialists to create a new society with the help of slave labour. Forced labour was for the rising generation of Stalinists a natural element in the building of 'Socialism in one land'. There were convicts enough, for the Soviet Government had provided for unlimited reinforcements by its edict of 7 April 1930. By this two kinds of people could be sent to hard labour and concentration camps: firstly, those who had been sentenced by the courts to more than three years' imprisonment and, secondly, all those sent there by the security organs.

On 10 July 1934 the former OGPU's Board of Justice was abolished. In its place came the Special Boards (Ozoboye Zovezshchaniye) of the NKVD, which were empowered, in arbitrary and secret procedure, devoid of any form of legality, with not even a hearing for the accused, to order imprisonment, security restrictions, and resettlement.[51]

These Special Boards soon became the most tragic and detested instruments of terror in the Soviet Union. They were not comparable with the Vecheka of the civil war period or with war communism. Their most outstanding characteristics were pure arbitrariness and savagery. In many cases they were misused by criminals or half-criminals as mere instruments of revenge. The regular courts were helpless against their activities, for only the representative from the Public Prosecutor's office could appeal against the sentences of the Special Boards. But the Public Prosecutor's office, as reformed by Lenin personally for the maintenance of legality, had since been reorganized by Stalin for his own purposes. In June 1933 he set up the 'Office of the Public Prosecutor for the Soviet Union', at the head of which he placed his supporter A. Y. Vyshinsky. This office alone was empowered to control the activities of the security organs,[52] and Vyshinsky saw to it that Stalin's measures were never hampered by existing laws. That was not Stalin's only bureaucratic dodge. In January 1953 the expanded plenary session of the Central Committee and the Central Commission of the Communist Party of the Soviet Union (Bolshevik) had at Stalin's request resolved on purging the Party of its 'unreliable elements'. A commission for the purpose was set up on 29 April, and N. I. Yezhov was appointed by Stalin to its chairmanship. Yezhov proved himself of value and barely a year later was given the job of carrying out a comprehensive purge of the whole Party.

Stalinists v. Stalin

It was not until after Stalin's death, at a very late date, i.e. at the time of the 22nd Party Conference (1961), that something more became known about the situation among the pro-Stalin elements in the Party at the beginning of the thirties. Information on the subject was published, but scattered in various periodicals and memoirs. The following summary provides a picture of the situation at that time.

Stalin, in his struggle with the 'party enemies', Trotskyists, and other ideological theories of the twenties, was supported by a not inconsiderable number of Old Bolsheviks, military men who had fought in the civil war, professional revolutionaries, and even intellectuals and economists. Without the help of such prominent Bolsheviks as Kirov, Sergo Ordzhonikidze, and others, Stalin would never have won through. They agreed with the use of security organs and terrorization of opposing groups. But that was the crux on which opinions finally split. Most of the Stalinists were for 'limited' terror and watched its boundless expansion with growing concern. In the efforts of the security organs to hold a monopoly position in the community they saw a lessening of importance for the Party and themselves. A good example of what might happen could be seen in the events in the Caucasus. The chief of the security organs in Georgia, L. P. Beria, was chosen in November 1931 to be First Secretary of the Central Committee of the Communist Party of Georgia (Bolshevik). M. D. Bagirov was making a similar career for himself in the Azerbaidjan Soviet Socialist Republic. From 1921 to 1930 he was chief of the Azerbaidjan security organs and his treatment of all alleged 'enemies' was brutal. By 1932 he was Governing Chief of the whole Azerbaidjan Soviet Socialist Republic and by 1935 First Secretary of the Central Committee of the Communist Party of Azerbaidjan (Bolshevik) and Chief of the Party Organization in Baku, the capital of Azerbaidjan. Meanwhile Stalin had transferred to Moscow the most popular Caucasian party leaders and thus left the field clear for the Chekists in Trans-Caucasia. His policy of making the Party security organs supreme in all spheres became more and more obvious. From day to day discontent among the Stalinists grew more menacing, and there is much to show that at the beginning of the thirties a plan was being hatched in the party ranks for the legal removal of Stalin from his post of General Secretary. Various documents seem to justify the theory that the leaders of this opposition were Sergo Ordzhonikidze, once Stalin's most intimate associate, and Sergey Mironovich Kirov, the popular 'People's Tribune'.

What actually happened behind the scenes at the 17th Party Congress of the Communist Party of the Soviet Union (Bolshevik) in January 1934 has always been concealed by the Soviet party leaders and historians. Nevertheless the truth gradually seeped through. Bolsheviks who survived the Stalin terror have described the situation at the time, mostly by word of mouth but also in memoirs or newspaper articles. According to them, most of the delegates had made up their minds to depose Stalin at the 17th Party Congress from his post of General Secretary and replace him by Kirov. L. Shaumyan, the Old Bolshevik, son of the well-known writer Z. G. Shaumyan, who was shot by the British in 1918 with the Baku commissars, reported in *Pravda* for 7 February 1964 that many delegates to the 17th Party Congress were well aware that Stalin was abusing his position. Some of the delegates had come to the conclusion that Stalin should, if possible, be Stalin is said to have been informed of the feeling in the party: According to Shaumyan many party officials hoped for Kirov. 'He knew that the old Leninist section in the Party would strongly oppose any further strengthening of his position.'

Even the 2nd edition of the *History of the Communist Party of the Soviet Union*, which was published in 1962, confirms this version of the state of things.[53] The Italian journalist Giuseppe Boffa, who after Stalin's death paid several long visits to Moscow and is an expert on political conditions in the Soviet Union, confirms that the most varied rumours were circulating in Moscow concerning the 17th Party Congress, which to all appearance were based on statements made by former inmates of concentration camps. The most credible, according to Boffa, was that shortly before the 17th Congress the delegates were secretly asked to strike Stalin's name off the list of candidates. Boffa wrote: 'Many even assert that in fact he was not elected, but that at the last moment the number of members of the Central Committee was increased and that in this manner Stalin slipped into the list.'[54]

Much water will flow down the Volga before the Soviet party archives are released without restriction for general study. But one thing is certain: the large anti-Stalin groups of the twenties were defeated by the beginning of the thirties. Most of the opposition leaders had capitulated to Stalin; fanatical adversaries of Stalinism had been arrested and eliminated from political life. Of course there still survived here and there opposition groups that were orientated on the exiled Trotsky and conspired against the Stalinists. Thanks to new material, however, our previous views of the history of the Communist Party of the Soviet Union in the thirties must be fundamentally revised. The strongest brake on Stalin's progress towards despotic rule was not the Trotskyists and other 'Party enemies' but the Stalinist malcontents. And it was the latter that now received Stalin's hardest blows.

The Murder of Kirov

On 1 December 1934, in the Smolny at Leningrad, Lenin's revolutionary headquarters, Kirov was murdered. Sergey Mironovich Kirov, born in 1886, Party member since 1904, had always been one of Stalin's closest collaborators. He was one of the organizers of the Bolshevik movement in the Northern Caucasus and later in Trans-Caucasia. In May 1920 he was appointed ambassador of the Russian Soviet Federal Socialist Republic in independent Georgia. Shortly afterwards he marched into Georgia at the head of the 11th Army, which helped the Communists there to seize power by violent means. From 1923 onwards he was a member of the Central Committee of the Russian Communist Party (Bolshevik). In 1926 he became head of the Leningrad party organization. There he became prominent as a determined opponent of the Zinoviev group and the Trotskyists. His talent for organization and speechmaking won him the favour of the Stalinists. It was not by chance that the ovations of the delegates to the 17th Party Congress were less for Stalin than for him. And Kirov was certainly well aware of his own importance. But the documents now at our disposal show that he was careful to act on a strictly legal basis. We must not forget that, in spite of the personality cult that was already prevalent, the party was still a political organization in the early stages of Stalinism, i.e. the democracy of the party was restricted, but the Stalinists could at least discuss matters among themselves, make proposals, and even—as we know—make plans to depose Stalin. Thus it sometimes happened that Stalin's proposals were only accepted after argument. It is known that Kirov and others opposed Stalin on this or that question. Stalin presumably remembered it, but such occasional opposition was probably not the real motive for Kirov's murder—a deed which shook the world of the Old Bolsheviks. The facts of Kirov's death are now no longer a secret. Fairly exact accounts of its background and details are available.[55]

Stalin and Yagoda commissioned a certain Zaporozhets, an experienced OGPU agent, to bring about Kirov's death. Zaporozhets discovered that a young man named Nikolayev, who had been expelled from the Party, unjustly he thought, was plotting to murder the President of the Control Commission in Leningrad. Nikolayev was a fanatical and idealistic Communist, who believed that the murder would arouse the conscience of the Communists and bring about some action against the so-called 'degenerates', i.e. the party bureaucrats. Even Stalin himself, thought Nikolayev, would understand his motives. Zaporozhets convinced Nikolayev that his plans, though right in principle, would only be really successful if he murdered Kirov, a man who was well-known outside Leningrad. Nikolayev's first attempt failed, because the guards would not let him pass. Zaporozhets and his helpers consequently had recourse to various manoeuvres—complicated by the fact that the head of the Leningrad NKVD, Medvedy, was not in the plot. On 1 December 1934 all went according to plan. Nikolayev was given a pass and found Kirov's office unguarded. Kirov's personal guard was killed in an arranged motor accident on the following day, on the way to the inquiry, and thus was prevented from saying who had told him to stay away from his post on the day of the murder.

On the evening of the day of the murder the Secretary of the Central Executive Committee, Yenukidze, issued the following instructions on Stalin's orders:

1. The investigating authority is to expedite the cases of persons accused of terrorist actions.
2. The judicial authority is not to postpone, because of the possibility of an eventual reprieve, the carrying out of the death sentence for crimes of this nature, as the Presidium of the Central Executive Committee of the USSR will not accept such appeals.
3. The People's Commissariat of Internal Affairs (NKVD)

is to carry out the death sentence against criminals of the above category, immediately after the pronouncement of judgement.

The first official version of the Kirov assassination stated that agents 'from Poland and other western countries' smuggled into the Soviet Union had used Nikolayev as their tool. The report of the NKVD, published immediately after the murder, spoke of the discovery of 'a great White Guard terrorist organization'. On the evening of the murder, 1 December, seventy-one persons were arrested in Moscow and Leningrad, including Count Rumiantsev and Count Stroganov. On the very next day the investigations were closed and the documents handed over to the War Board of the Supreme Court. Simultaneously arrests were made in Belorussia and the Ukraine. In all 103 persons were shot in Moscow, Leningrad, Minsk, Kiev, and Kharkov, in many cases without trial. Among the victims were suspects whose names were on the 'black lists' of the NKVD, while others were merely by chance involved in the first wave of executions. In Moscow, for example, journalists discovered among those arrested the two brothers Krüger, sons of a German colonist, who when trying to escape to Germany had some months before been arrested at the frontier. They were sentenced to five years' imprisonment, but now they were fetched from their cells and shot as 'murderers of Kirov'. In Kiev the victims were mostly West Ukrainian Communists, writers, and other intellectuals, political refugees who had fled to the Soviet Ukraine years before.

The investigation of the murder was undertaken by Stalin and Yagoda personally, in order to cover the traces of the real murderers of Kirov. The leading officials of the Leningrad Cheka, with Medvedy at their head, were arrested at the same time and brought before the court. Strangely enough they received very light sentences; they were merely charged with neglect and lack of watchfulness. Apparently the Leningrad Chekists, who perhaps knew a part of the truth or might have formed correct suspicions regarding Kirov's death, were removed from involvement in the investigation and the preparations for the legal proceedings. The paternal punishment, however, was only a blind; two years later they were all liquidated without further trial.

With Nikolayev, however, who was arrested redhanded, there were difficulties. By chance he recognized Zaporozhets as the man who gave him the murder weapon. Stalin altered his tactics. The first allegation that Kirov had been murdered by White Guards and foreign agents was dropped.

On 22 December *Tass* published a statement regarding the arrest of fifteen members of the former Zinoviev group, who were alleged to have been responsible for Kirov's murder. Seven of the accused, said *Tass*, were because of lack of evidence merely handed over to the organs of the Ministry of Internal Affairs for administrative punishment. The list of arrests compromised only the names of prominent Communists, leaders in the civil war, and high civil servants. The best-known were Zinoviev, companion of Lenin, former member of the Central Committee and the Politbureau, former chairman of the Comintern; Kamenev, companion of Lenin, former member of the Central Committee and the Politbureau, and Deputy Chairman of the Council of the People's Commissars; Zalutsky, an Old Bolshevik, former Secretary of the Leningrad Party organization; Yevdokimov, an Old Bolshevik, former member of the Central Committee, one of the leaders of the Leningrad Communists; and finally, Safarov, companion of Lenin, former member of the Central Committee, responsible editor of the *Leningrad Pravda*. Safarov had travelled with Lenin in the famous railway journey through Germany to Russia. The official communiqué stated that investigation had shown that 'in the years 1933/34, in Leningrad, former members of the Zinoviev opposition had formed an illegal counter-revolutionary group of terrorists, led by the "Leningrad Centre". This group had set itself the task of murdering the leaders of the Communist Party. Comrade Kirov was to be the first victim. From the admissions of the members of the counter-revolutionary group it was evident that they were in contact with representatives of foreign capitalist states and had received money from them.'

Almost simultaneously there was published another account of the arrest of a group of Leningrad terrorists, who were said to have directly planned and carried out the Kirov murder, i.e. the above-mentioned 'Leningrad Centre'. Five of those arrested were students, eight were civil servants, one was an engineer. The chief accused were Nikolayev and a twenty-nine-year-old student named

Kotolynov, who in the charge (27 December) was named as ring-leader of the group. He was to have shot Kirov near his residence if Nikolayev's attempt had failed. In the trial, which was held on 28 and 29 December, only Nikolayev and three others pleaded guilty to the charges against them. All the rest maintained to the last that they were in no way implicated in the Kirov murder. The court condemned all the defendants to death by shooting, and the sentences were carried out immediately.

One might have expected that the Zinoviev group would play an important part in the proceedings, but neither in the charge sheet nor in the course of the trial was Zinoviev or Kamenev mentioned, although they had been arrested in connection with Kirov's death. Apparently neither Yagoda's security specialists nor Stalin's public prosecutors had been able to discover, much less 'prove', any connection between the two groups. So Yagoda's apparatus worked all the more feverishly on the preparations for the proceedings against the Zinoviev group, which had now grown to nineteen persons. Stalin's *History of the Communist Party of the Soviet Union (Bolshevik)* describes the event as follows: 'Soon afterwards an underground counter-revolutionary movement was discovered, known as the "Moscow Centre". The investigators and the proceedings revealed the shameful role played by Zinoviev, Kamenev, Yevdokimov, and other leaders of this organization in inspiring their followers with terrorist sentiments and in planning the murder of members of the Central Committee and the Soviet Government.

'The double-dealing and vileness of these people went so far that Zinoviev—one of the organizers and instigators of the murder of Comrade Kirov and the man who had pressed the murderer to carry out his wicked deed as quickly as possible—actually wrote a eulogy of Kirov after his death and demanded publication for it. The Zinoviev gang pleaded penitence before the court and thereby revealed their continued duplicity. They denied any connection with Trotsky. They denied the fact that like the Trotskyists they had sold themselves to the Fascist spies, they denied their own spying activity and sabotage. The Zinoviev gang denied before the court their connections with the Bukharin gang and the existence of a Trotskyist-Bukharinist band.'

Before the proceedings Yagoda had exercised such pressure on

Safarov that he succeeded in making him appear as crown witness for the prosecution. He admitted the existence of a counter-revolutionary group in which Zinoviev and Kamenev had played the leading parts. They were the moral instigators of Kirov's murder, and the others, 'who shrank from no criminal deeds in their conflict with Soviet power', were the immediate organizers of the murder.

Yagoda, however, did not succeed in extorting from Zinoviev and Kamenev a confession that they had organized the assassination. After long hesitation the Public Prosecutor during the proceedings of 15/16 January, 1935, had to declare himself satisfied with the statement of Lenin's old comrades that 'the activity of the former opposition under the compulsion of objective circumstances had furthered the degeneration of the criminals' (meaning Nikolayev) and that they thus bore a 'moral responsibility' for the murder of Kirov.

Zinoviev was condemned to ten years' imprisonment, Kamenev to five years, the others received sentences varying from three to ten years. The terms of the condemnation admitted that the investigations had produced no proof of a direct responsibility of the 'Moscow Centre' for the assassination of Kirov.

That the Kirov murder was not the work of Zinoviev and Kamenev, but vilely provoked by Stalin and Yagoda, was confirmed by Khrushchev at the 20th Congress of the Communist Party of the Soviet Union in February 1956. He hinted that Stalin was the organizer of the crime. Amid great excitement he said: 'It seems extraordinarily suspicious that the Chekist responsible for Kirov's security, when about to appear before the court on 2 December 1934, should have lost his life in a "traffic accident", in which nobody else was injured. After the Kirov murder the head officials of the Leningrad NKVD were given quite short terms of punishment, but in 1937 they were shot. It is to be supposed that their execution was a means of extinguishing all trace of the organizers of Kirov's assassination.'

Among the measures taken by Stalin to destroy the traces of Kirov's murderers the destruction of Kirov's assistants played an important part. In 1937 there disappeared into the dungeons of the security organs such well-known Communist leaders as M. S. Chudov, F. Y. Ugarov, P. P. Smorodin, N. P. Komarov, Ludmilla

K. Shaposhnikova, and B. P. Pozern. The reason for their liquidation was the same in every case: they were Kirov's closest friends.

Zinoviev and Kamenev were probably spared not for lack of
evidence but for other reasons. They were both still very popular
with the masses. Nobody in the Soviet Union would have straight-
away accepted the idea that they were spies, terrorists, and foreign
agents. Stalin knew that a sudden eradication of all the Old Bolsheviks would give the populace a severe shock. He had to prepare
the masses step by step for the coming Terror. He therefore
initiated a massive psychological campaign in the Press against
the murderers of Kirov and the men behind them, and tried to
bring to the boil the general hatred and indignation against the
'conspirators'.

The beginning of the Moscow trials

The liquidation of the Old Guard of Bolshevism continued. On
26 May 1935 the Soviet newspapers reported that the 'Association
of Old Bolsheviks' had been abolished. A commission, which included Malenkov, confiscated the records of the association and
'distributed its property among the museums and other State
institutions'. Only a few weeks later, on 25 June, another important
political organization of the Old Bolsheviks was abolished, namely
the 'Association of former Prisoners and Exiles'. Founded in 1921,
it ran a fund for mutual help and found suitable work for invalids
and the disabled. For Stalin, who was determined to eliminate the
entire generation of Old Bolsheviks, this association was an in-
convenient historical relic.

Yagoda's specialists worked day and night to reveal new conspiracies to the expectant masses. At Stalin's orders, they initiated,
with Vyshinsky, fresh proceedings against Zinoviev, Kamenev, and
other leading Bolsheviks. In the 'Moscow Centre' case they had
successfully laid on them the moral responsibility for Kirov's death.
Meanwhile, however, public opinion could be adequately prepared
for the condemnation of Lenin's old companions as murderers and
paid agents, provided the charge could be put in a sufficiently
convincing manner. For this purpose Yagoda built up a counter-
revolutionary opposition party which, however, every thinking man
must consider pure fantasy: a block formed of the Right and
Trotskyists. Stalin still looked upon Trotsky, though living abroad

for years, as his chief enemy, and he forged a series of documents to show that 'Judas Trotsky' was the head of 'this whole band of murderers and spies'.

Between 19 and 24 August 1956 the War Board of the Supreme Court of Justice of the USSR busied itself with the conspiracy of the 'Trotskyist-Zinoviev Terrorist Centre'. Stalin dared not allow the case to be tried by jury, for he could not trust the elected representatives of the people. The chairman of the board was V. V. Ulrich, a former member of the anti-espionage department of the Vecheka. The accused, who included Zinoviev, Kamenev, Y. N. Smirnov, Yevdokimov, Mrachkovsky, and Bakayev, were surrounded by armed guards. Opposite them, at a small table, sat the Public Prosecutor, Andrey Vyshinsky. Yagoda and his assistants were not present in court. They followed the proceedings through a loudspeaker in an adjoining room, where they were well supplied with food and drink. During the adjournments the defendants were kept in rooms adjoining the court; here they received final instructions from the public prosecutor about what they were to say and how they were to behave before the court.

Eye-witnesses report that the accused seemed less exhausted in court than they had been during the preliminary examinations. Apparently they had been allowed to get some sleep and eat their fill. The pressure which must have been put upon them before the trial can best be seen by a comparison of statements made in January 1935 with those made in August 1936, as published by Trotsky in the exiles' journal *Byulleteny Oppozitsii*:

January 1935	*August 1936*
Kamenev admitted that he had not been sufficiently active and energetic in combating the disintegration which was a result of the struggle against the Party and on the basis of which such a band of criminals (Nikolayev and others) could be formed and accomplish their misdeeds.	Vyshinsky: 'You admit therefore that such a strange plan (seizure of power with the aid of terror) existed among you?' Kamenev: 'Yes, this strange plan did exist.' Vyshinsky: 'The murder of Kirov was directly your work?' Kamenev: 'Yes.'

January 1935	*August 1936*

Bakayev admitted that among the Zinoviev supporters there was only malicious and hostile criticism of the Party's most important measures.

Vyshinsky: 'Did you receive instructions to organize the murder of Stalin's comrade?' Bakayev: 'Yes.' Vyshinsky: 'Did you take part in Kirov's murder?' Bakayev: 'Yes.'

Zinoviev: 'The Party is wholly right when it makes the former Zinoviev group, enemies of the Party, responsible in the question of the political responsibility for the murder that took place.'

Vyshinsky: 'Were you in this "centre", you, Kamenev, and others?' Zinoviev: 'Yes.' Vyshinsky: 'So you organized the murder of Kirov?' Zinoviev: 'Yes.' Vyshinsky: 'That means that you murdered Kirov?' Zinoviev: 'Yes.'

Yevdokimov: 'We should bear the responsibility because the poison that we have strewn around us in the last ten years favoured the commission of the crime.'

Vyshinsky: 'Do you admit that the murder of Kirov was planned with your assistance?' Yevdokimov: 'Yes, I admit it.'

This, the first of the three notorious 'Moscow trials', ended with the sentencing of all the accused to death. When the President of the Court read the verdicts, the defendant Lurie shouted in a penetrating voice: 'Long live the cause of Marx, Engels, Lenin, and Stalin!'

With the help of the special tribunals of the NKVD Yagoda, in the weeks following the first trial, slaughtered thousands of persons who for some reason or other seemed to be disloyal or might be among Stalin's possible opponents. Innumerable foreign Communists living in the Soviet Union were arrested. A large number of veterans of the Polish Communist Party were shot. The Terror in the Party was not confined to Russia. Yagoda considered that one of his important tasks was the strengthening of the security organs abroad, especially in Spain. (It was the period of the

Spanish civil war.) While Communists of all countries in their idealism came forward voluntarily to defend Republican Spain, Yagoda saw only that it was a favourable opportunity to get rid of undesirables, both foreign Communists and Soviet Communists. He instructed the foreign department of the NKVD to bring the whole of the Comintern activities in Spain under the control of the security organs. Yagoda himself was unable to complete the task—that was left to his successor.

The close friendship between Stalin and Yagoda, though cemented by complicity in crime, was not to last. Yagoda's successes gradually went to his head. He looked upon the NKVD and especially the powerful administration of state security as his personal domain, and he demanded absolute submission from his subordinates. When Stalin promised him an additional career in the Party centre, his megalomania knew no bounds. But this made him a rival in Stalin's ever-suspicious eyes. And there were other reasons for the cooling off of the once so warm friendship. That man is imperfect is shown even in Yagoda's 'perfect' technique. Practically no important affair can be carried out without a blunder or mistake, and among the Chekists there were some men who retained certain principles in the struggle against their opponents. Stalin had to obliterate the traces of the crimes he and Yagoda had committed together, and the last trace of all was Yagoda himself.

So gradually a new plan matured in Stalin's brain—the destruction of Yagoda. The man had murdered Trotskyists at Trotsky's orders! All his actions served only 'to mask his own criminal activities'. On 25 September 1936 Stalin and Zhdanov sent the following telegram to Moscow from Sochi, where they were on holiday: 'We consider it absolutely necessary and urgent to appoint Comrade Yezhov to be People's Commissar of Internal Affairs. Yagoda has definitely shown himself incapable of exposing the band of Trotskyists and Zinoviev people. The NKVD is four years behindhand in this respect. This opinion is shared by all Party officials and most of the NKVD staff.' Soon afterwards Yagoda was arrested.

This telegram contains one important statement, that the NKVD's work was limping four years behindhand. Four years—what does that mean? The answer is not difficult. It was just four years since the ferment among the Stalinists had begun. The old opposition had not been specially active during the interval. Stalin had often expressed his opinion as to what was the chief duty of the security organs. Yagoda had shown himself a master in liquidating the Old Bolsheviks. But for the carrying out of fresh tasks Stalin thought him quite incapable.

A part of Stalin's 'strategic genius' in the struggle for personal power was his faculty of getting rid of his closest supporters at the right time, so as to secure the continuity of his own plans, without having to pay the penalty for all that had happened in the meantime. These tactics demanded that Stalin should always be aiming at a 'new procedure' and 'new men'. Just as in Dzerzhinsky's time his successor Yagoda was growing up in the womb of the security organization, so Yezhov was making rapid advancement in the last years of Yagoda's service. When in February 1954 he was appointed head of the purging procedure, the most important branch of the Soviet security organization came under his management. The greatest purge in the history of the Soviet Union began with friendly cooperation between Yezhov and Yagoda. A year later, when Stalin had made up his mind to part with Yagoda, Yezhov was not only feared in the Party, he was an authority in the security organs.

The Yagoda period in the history of the Soviet security services and the Communist Party was precisely planned, and all that Stalin hoped to achieve with Yagoda's help was in fact attained. Briefly, Stalin needed 'proofs' that his opponents—Trotskyists, Bukharinists, and others including the Mensheviks, 'bourgeois nationalists', and syndicalists—were forming a conspiracy against Soviet power, that they had resolved, with the help of foreign capitalists, to destroy the constitution of the Soviet Union and 'restore capitalism in Russia', and that they were attempting to attain their aims by means of murder and terrorism. If this theory could be proved, thought Stalin, his reckoning with the opposition would be simpler. The Old Bolsheviks would no longer be regarded as Stalin's political opponents, but as enemies of the State and traitors. Nobody could have imagined that the people of the Soviet Union, unless they were mad, would credit a conspiracy between the Old Bolsheviks and foreign capitalists. With his forgeries, misrepresentations, treacherous assassinations, and use of *agents provoca-*

teurs, Stalin made the impossible possible, at least for internal consumption and for those elements in international Communism which were orientated on Stalin. Yagoda, his intimate friend, was clever enough to carry out Stalin's ambitions. The theory that all Stalin's opponents were enemies of the State and traitors was now 'justified'. That was the work of Stalin and Yagoda. Yezhov was to be entrusted with the fresh tasks.

The bloodiest period in the history of the Soviet Union now began.

Chapter Four

The Yezhovshchina

(1 9 3 6 – 1 9 3 8)

Nikolay Yezhov

INDISSOLUBLY linked with this name is the bloodiest chapter in pre-war Soviet history. Nikolay Yezhov was quite a different type from previous leaders of the Soviet security organs. Dzerzhinsky and Menzhinsky had come to power in the Communist movement. Yagoda's past had been obscure, but he too had made a career under Lenin. Yezhov, according to official information entered the Party as far back as 1917, but from the beginning he was a bureaucrat ('apparatchik') of the first water. He had taken no part in the vicissitudes of the civil war and the October Revolution. When he had risen to be head of the personnel department of the Central Committee, Stalin took the trouble to construct a 'revolutionary past' for his favourite. For instance, in the first edition of the *Short Manual on the History of the Communist Party of the Soviet Union*, it is stated that Yezhov was 'the originator of the military mutiny on the West Front and in Belorussia'. Nobody dared to point out how utterly untenable was such a statement, for Yezhov at that time was not yet sixteen. In the second edition of the manual the statement was omitted: Stalin had had it removed, certainly not from love of truth, but because Yezhov had in the meantime been unmasked and liquidated as an 'enemy of the State'.

Yezhov had no Cheka traditions, and that made him seem superior to all former chiefs of the security organs. For the task to which he was to devote himself Yezhov had already qualified under Yagoda. He well understood how to combine investigation of documents and the associated party purge with Stalin's terrorist plans against his own staff. He gave orders that each member of the Party and candidate for the Party had to fill up a questionnaire (the text of which was published by Trotsky abroad in the *Byulleteny Oppozitsii*) with particulars of his acquaintances and former friends. Yezhov was responsible for the fact that the new virtue of 'true Bolsheviks', i.e. denunciation, became an integral part of work for the Party. Moreover he was operating even before the Yezhovshchina with a favourite idea of Stalin's, 'double-dealing' (*dvurushnik*). It was an idea which was well calculated to destroy those who, although they had never had the slightest connection with any opposition group, had at some time or other spoken critically about the Party or Stalin himself. Yezhov thereby prepared the field for coming events. The party archives were now more important than the files of Yagoda's secret police. In the former were the dossiers from which Yagoda's sins of omission and commission, referred to in the above-mentioned telegram, were clearly indicated. Yezhov's star now shone brilliantly in the Party firmament. From 1934 to 1938 he was Secretary to the Central Committee, together with Kaganovich, Andreyev, and Zhdanov, and at the 17th Party Congress he was elected full member of the Central Committee. He was the embodiment of the new 'qualifications' which Stalin demanded from his colleagues: blind obedience, fanatical devotion, unconditional faith in the power of the State bureaucracy.

Scarcely was Yezhov appointed Chief of the NKVD than he started a murderous move against Chekists and the higher NKVD officers. All the People's Commissars of the NKVD in the Union republics, and usually their deputies as well, were summoned to a conference in Moscow and shot out of hand in the dungeons of the NKVD. Suicides of Chekists were of daily occurrence. Anyone who had had any connection whatsoever with Yagoda, even temporarily, began to tremble. Yezhov was particularly rigorous towards all Yagoda's investigation teams. Some of the investigating judges were shot without a hearing, their homes confiscated, and their families put out on the street without ceremony. Witnesses reported the tragic lot of the victims' children. Nobody dared to care for them or give them shelter. They became homeless beggars, and many of them committed suicide. Nine- and ten-year-old children, whose bodies were found in a wood outside Moscow, left a letter addressed to Stalin which contained the words: 'Our parents were honourable Communists. . . . The enemies of the people, the accursed Trotskyists, must have done this. . . .'[56]

While the annihilation of Chekists in the Soviet Union itself went on 'according to plan', Yezhov was causing great difficulties for the highly developed NKVD apparatus in foreign countries. All 'residents' (i.e. leaders of the illegal organs of the secret service abroad) and their agents were ordered to report to Moscow immediately. The elimination of those who obeyed was carried out without trouble. But as many Chekists refused to return, Yezhov formed 'flying groups' from 'apparatchiks' fanatically devoted to him who were placed under an 'Administration for Special Tasks' and took control of the whole foreign apparatus of the NKVD.

The subsequent hunting down of the remaining Chekists in the West was fully reported in the daily press. In the dark streets of Paris, Geneva, and other cities of Western Europe the police found many bodies of unknown persons perforated with bullet holes. The greatest excitement was aroused by the death of Ignats Reiss,[57] an NKVD agent in France, who shortly before had defected to Trotsky and whose letter to Stalin, published on the occasion, will be included in the documentation of the history of the NKVD. Slutsky, an old Chekist of Dzerzhinsky's time, was chief of the foreign department under Yagoda and had retained the post for a time under Yezhov; after his death, allegedly from a stroke, his body lay in state at the Moscow NKVD. The Chekist journal carried a notice of his death in which Slutsky was praised as a 'loyal follower of Stalin'. Many Chekists, however, had sufficient medical knowledge to be able to distinguish the face of a man dead from a stroke from that of a poisoned man with its characteristic stains.

A wave of mass arrests swept the country. The trials initiated by the security organs tore huge gaps in the Party lists. None of the Union republics was spared. In the Caucasian Soviet republics the chief organizer of the trials was Beria. In interrogations which lasted whole nights, often accompanied by torture, the most incredible confessions were extorted from such famous organizers of Soviet power in the Caucasus as the Georgian leaders B. Mdivani, M. Okudzhava, M. Toroshelidze, Z. Chikladze, and N. Kilnadze.

These served as a basis for proceedings brought in July 1936 against the so-called 'Georgian Centre', 'a paid agency of Fascism, the members of which have degenerated into an unprincipled band of spies, saboteurs, and murderers, into an unscrupulous gang of sworn enemies of the working classes'.[58]

The results of these proceedings, which took place in the Yagoda period, formed to a large extent the basis for the later Moscow trial of August 1936, against 'the Trotskyists and Zinoviev's terrorist centre'. The extorted Georgian confessions implicated a large number of Communists holding important positions. Did they suspect they were already on the list of 'Fascist agents'? Mostly they were Communists from the Caucasian republics, whom Stalin himself had brought to Moscow. In November 1936 Yezhov launched anti-Trotskyist proceedings in Novo-Sibirsk against a number of economic managers. Here too the well-tried methods of the security organs succeeded in making the defendants confess that economic failures, breakdowns, and accidents were entirely the fault of enemy agents. Thenceforward Soviet jargon included another favourite phrase of Stalin's—*vreditelstvo,* pernicious activity. This corresponded in the economic field with 'double-dealing' in party politics. In the Moscow trial the German engineer Stückling was sentenced to death as an alleged gestapo agent. The 'special department' (*spetschasti*) which already existed in the works now occupied the most important place in the industrial organization, with the duty of closely supervising directors and engineers as well as the workmen. The total control of the community by the security organs was an accomplished fact.

The second Moscow trial

The second Moscow trial against the 'Anti-Soviet Trotskyist Centre' was held from 23 to 30 January 1937, once again before the War Board of the Supreme Court of Justice of the USSR. Among the accused were two of Lenin's closest collaborators, G. L. Pyatakov and K. B. Radek, as well as seventeen other Bolsheviks of the older generation. In order to show that Trotsky was the chief enemy of the Revolution and responsible for all the conspiracies against Soviet power, Stalin had Pyatakov in the preliminary investigations kept under pressure until he declared himself ready to be a crown witness and testify to the correctness of the theory that Trotsky was the chief organizer of anti-Soviet conspiracies.

In court Pyatakov declared that at the end of 1935 he and Radek had decided to get in contact with Trotsky. As member of an official trade delegation he was sent to Berlin about that time. Radek, he said, had advised him to approach Bukhartsev, the Berlin correspondent of *Izvestiya,* who was in contact with Trotsky. At Vyshinsky's wish Pyatakov told the court his story in the following words: 'It was on 10 December, in the first half of the month. On that or the following day I met Bukhartsev, who, using a moment when we were alone, told me that he had heard of my arrival a few days previously and had informed Trotsky. He was now awaiting a reply from him. On the next day Trotsky's messenger arrived, and Bukhartsev took me to meet him, for just a few minutes, in one of the avenues in the Tiergarten. He showed me a short note from Trotsky on which was written: "Y.L., the bearer of this note, is completely trustworthy." The word "completely" was underlined, and from this I understood that the man coming from Trotsky was his confidant. I do not know his name. He introduced himself as Heinrich or as Gustav, I cannot remember exactly, but I think Gustav; it was probably a cover-name, or perhaps it was Heinrich after all. He said that he had a commission from Lev Davidovich [i.e. Trotsky] to arrange a meeting for me with Trotsky, as he expressly wanted a talk with me. As appeared later, this special emphasis derived from Radek's last letter to Trotsky. He asked me if I was prepared to travel by plane. I said I was, although I knew how risky such a step would be. But as I had already had a conversation with Radek on the subject, and as there were questions of extraordinary gravity and delicacy to discuss, I thought it better to risk the flight and meet Trotsky than to avoid the risk and remain in our existing state of uncertainty. In a word, I made up my mind, although, I repeat, there was a very great risk to me of being exposed and unmasked, and anything else you like, yet I resolved to make the journey. We arranged to meet next morning at the Tempelhof aerodrome. . . . He was waiting at the entrance and accompanied me. Previously he had shown me the passport which had been prepared for me. It was a German passport. All the customs formalities he saw to himself, so that I needed only to sign my name. We took our seats in the plane, started, and, with no intermediate landing, arrived about 3 p.m. at the aerodrome near Oslo. A car was waiting for us. We got in and drove off. We drove for about half an hour and came to a residential suburb. We got out and entered a small and not badly furnished house, where I met Trotsky, whom I had not seen since 1928. There my interview with Trotsky took place.'

Neither Trotsky nor neutral journalists knew what to make of this confession of Pyatakov's. The organ of the Norwegian Government party, *Arbeiderbladet,* published the following statement in January 1937, while the trial was still proceeding: 'A representative of this newspaper today made further inquiries at the Kjeller aerodrome: Director Gulleksen stated on the telephone that no foreign plane had landed there in December 1935.' The aerodrome director also assured the newspaper that according to their official records not a single foreign plane landed there in the whole period from September 1935 to 1 May 1936. Trotsky himself addressed several precise questions in the Press to Vyshinsky which revealed contradictions between the charges and the evidence of the witnesses. These corrections had not the slightest influence on the result of the proceedings. Pyatakov and most of the others were condemned to death. Four of the accused got off with long prison sentences.[59]

It is easy now to see the purpose of the trial. It was intended to 'convince' public opinion in the Soviet Union and throughout the world that the 'treason' even of such prominent Party leaders as Pyatakov and Radek and their espionage in the service of the Western powers were not at all 'exceptional'. The condemnation of G. L. Pyatakov fitted in with the cause of the Yezhovshchina proper, for Pyatakov was the deputy chairman of the Supreme Council of the People's Economy. The chairman of this institution, so important to the national well-being, was at the time Sergo Ordzhonikidze. In the course of the trial Pyatakov admitted that he had used his position in the Supreme Economic Council for espionage in the service of a hostile power. Moreover he had plotted Ordzhonikidze's assassination. But did Ordzhonikidze himself believe this fairy tale? When the Soviet security organs, consequent on Pyatakov's false confessions, began to arrest Ordzhonikidze's closest friends, Ordzhonikidze himself committed suicide on 18 February 1937. The Stalinists were wisely silent regarding this event. In all reference works treating of this period the popular

Sergo Ordzhonikidze is celebrated as a 'hero' and faithful vassal of Stalin. It was not until the 22nd Congress of the Communist Party of the Soviet Union in 1961 that a more detailed report on Ordzhonikidze's suicide was provided by Khrushchev: 'I was present at Ordzhonikidze's funeral. At the time I believed the published statement that his death was sudden, as we knew he had heart trouble. Much later, after the war, I learnt by chance that he had committed suicide. Sergo's brother was arrested and shot. Comrade Ordzhonikidze realized that he could no longer work with Stalin, although he had formerly been one of his best friends. Ordzonikidze had also held a high position in the Party. Lenin had known and valued him. The situation was so complicated that Ordzhonikidze could no longer work normally. In order not to collide with Stalin and in order not to carry the responsibility for his misuse of power, he resolved to put an end to his own life.'[60]

Kirov and Ordzhonikidze, ringleaders of the Stalinist malcontents, had now been disposed of. Ordzhonikidze had only been dead a few days when Stalin opened his campaign of bloody revenge against the delegates to the 17th Party Congress. The wave of arrests spread wider and wider. The atmosphere of those days is graphically described in memoirs published since 1960. A witness of these events, a certain Barvints, newspaper editor, writes: 'Suspicions grew. A wave of denunciations spread among the leading Party and trade officials and the scientists.'

Barvints continues: 'The editor received letters, some anonymous, others signed, in which Party officials of all grades were accused of sabotage and often deviationism. The Party Committee of the city of Kiev busied itself with the case of a certain woman called Nikolenko. She calumniated several Party officials and insinuated that in the Central Committee of the Ukraine Communist Party (Bolshevik) and in the Kiev city and area party committees there were protégés and protectors of enemies and that many Trotsky and Zinoviev supporters obtained their party cards through their connections.'[61]

The plenary session of February/March 1937

In this tense atmosphere a plenary session of the Central Committee of the Communist Party of the Soviet Union (Bolshevik) was summoned in February 1937 at Stalin's request. Stalin lectured

it on 'Faults in the Party's work and methods for the liquidation of Trotskyists and other double-dealers', in which he produced
his famous theory that with increasing progress in socialist development in the Soviet Union the class struggle would become more
intense. This justified his demand for terror to be given free play
in every sphere so that all enemy activity could be crushed. Stalin's
chief supporter at the meeting, Molotov, criticized the attitude of
the military leaders, who, he asserted, were refusing to embark on
the struggle against the 'people's enemies' in the army.[62]

At this session N. Yezhov gave a report about 'Lessons from the
sabotage, subversion, and espionage committed by Japanese, German, and Trotskyist agents'. This formed the basis for a resolution
which was accepted by the Committee and ran as follows:

'This plenary session of the Central Committee of the Communist Party of the Soviet Union (Bolshevik) is of the view that the
facts discovered during the investigations in the case of the Anti-
Soviet/Trotskyist Centre and its supporters in the provinces show
that the People's Commissariat of Internal Affairs is four years
behindhand in its task of unmasking these ruthless enemies of the
People.'[63]

The minutes of the plenary assembly of February/March 1937
have never to this day been published. That they exist in the Party
archives, however, is proved by many documents, especially those
published since the 22nd Congress of the Communist Party of the
Soviet Union (1961), which here and there refer to the minutes
and sometimes even quote verbatim from them. One may assume
that most of the Central Committee members who were elected by
the 17th Party Congress were reduced to silence either by fear or
from opportunism. It is certain, however, that there was a small
but dwindling group of officials who had the courage to oppose
Stalin and Yezhov openly.

Between February and May 1937 there were mass arrests
throughout the Soviet Union. The Terror was primarily directed
against the delegates to the 17th Party Congress and those chosen
by the Congress to be members of the Central Committee. In his
secret speech to the 20th Party Congress Khrushchev reported on
the extent of this action: 'It was established that of the 139 members of, and candidates for, the Central Committee elected by the
17th Party Congress 98, i.e. 70 per cent, were arrested and

liquidated in 1937 and 1938. . . . The same fate, however, befell
not only the committee members but also most of the delegates to
the Congress. Of 1,966 voting or advisory delegates 1,108, i.e.
over one half of all the delegates, were arrested under the charge
of counter-revolutionary crimes.'[64]

A St Bartholomew's Eve for the Party

The terrorist measures of Stalin and Yezhov were directed
against members of the most varied social groups. In the first place
Party, military, and economic cadres were affected. The disappear-
ance of almost the whole of the Army High Command was a particularly severe blow. In the West this macabre mass-slaughter of
Stalin's was known as the 'Tukhachevsky Case' from the main
figure in the process, Marshal Mikhail Nikolayevich Tukhachevsky.
He was one of the most striking and colourful personalities among
the Old Bolsheviks. Born in 1893, he began his military career in
Tsarist Russia. After passing through a Cadet Academy he joined
a Guards regiment as a lieutenant. He went to the front in 1914
and by February 1915 he had already won six decorations. In 1918
he joined the Bolshevik Party, and after that his military career
was meteoric. He held commands on various fronts in the civil war.
In April 1920 he was made Commander-in-Chief of the forces on
the Western front, and in May he was appointed to the General
Staff. In July and August 1920 he led the attack on Warsaw. This
adventurous undertaking, ordered by Lenin himself, ended in
fiasco. In this period the first rift between Tukhachevsky and Stalin
occurred. Lenin and Trotsky had ordered all the armies on the
Western front to be united into a single 'Western Army' under
Marshal Tukhachevsky, which was to start an offensive against
Warsaw. Stalin, who at that time was a member of the 'Revolutionary War Council' on the south front, disliked the plan intensely. He
sent Lenin a memorandum in the following terms: 'The Politbureau would do better not to bother itself with such stupidities.'[65]
Stalin issued a counter-order, the 1st Cavalry Army to capture
Lvov. This rash plan of Stalin's issued on his sole authority, was
one of the chief causes of the defeat at Warsaw. But Stalin pushed
the responsibility for the reverse on to Tukhachevsky. After the
Marshal's execution, the official reference books stated that the
advance of the 1st Cavalry Army on Lvov created the preliminary

conditions for the success of the Western offensive, which, however, 'the traitors Trotsky and Tukhachevsky frustrated.'[66] The
Stalinists suppressed the fact that Lenin himself was responsible
for all the operations. Later Lenin realized that in the Warsaw
offensive a series of mistakes had been made. In a recent publication
regarding Stalin's attitude in the Warsaw affair we read the following remark by Lenin: 'Childish thickheadedness! Who would
march to Warsaw via Lvov?'[67]

In spite of these tensions Tukhachevsky's upward progress after
the civil war and Lenin's death was at first unstoppable. He modernized the Red Army and was supported by Kirov, Ordzhonikidze,
and other Old Bolsheviks from the Stalinist camp. At the time of
the Weimar Republic, under his aegis, leading officers from the
German Army were trained in the Soviet Union. In June 1935 he
was appointed Deputy People's Commissar for the Defence of the
USSR and on 20 November of the same year he was promoted to
be Marshal of the Soviet Union.

In the liquidation of Tukhachevsky and other army leaders
Yezhov went to work with special care. One of the Marshal's closest
comrades from the time of the civil war was V. K. Putna, military
attaché at first in Germany and Great Britain and recalled from
England in the autumn of 1936. Yezhov had him tortured to obtain
the necessary confessions, which sealed Tukhachevsky's fate. In
May 1937 the latter was relieved of his post as Deputy People's
Commissar for the Defence of the USSR and made Commander-
in-Chief of the Volga Defence Area. He was arrested on 26 May,
sentenced to death after a secret hearing, and shortly afterwards,
on 11 June, executed. With him perished once-famous commanders in the civil war: Yakir, Uborevich, Eideman, Feldman,
Kork, Primakov, and Putna.

At a session of the Military Soviet called in June 1937 Stalin
declared that in the ranks of the Red Army 'a counter-revolutionary, Fascist military organization had been uncovered. It must be
radically destroyed in the shortest possible time.' At this session
Stalin blamed a long list of Army leaders and military and political
officials who were still at liberty. Gamarnik, the Deputy People's
Commissar for Defence and Chief of the Political Administration
of the Red Army, was stigmatized as one of the principals in this
'Fascist conspiracy'. He committed suicide before he could be

arrested. His successor as Chief of the Political Administration of
the Red Army was L. Z. Mekhlis. A few weeks later, in the middle
of 1937, Stalin delivered a crushing blow against the Red Army.
It was deprived of its best brains. Thousands of officers, almost
the whole of the General Staff, were arrested and liquidated.
Three-quarters of the Supreme Military Soviet, thirteen out of
nineteen Army Commanders, 110 out of 135 Divisional Commanders, were eliminated.

It was not known until the early sixties, long after Stalin's death,
with what consistent savagery the Party political apparatus in the
army had been treated. In August 1937 Stalin delivered an address
to an assembly of the political officers of the armed forces, in which
he praised to the skies the smellers-out of spies and denouncers,
and demanded from the political officers a complete extermination
of the 'people's enemies'. Mekhlis, the newly appointed Chief of
the Political Administration, was one of Stalin's most compliant
stooges in this affair. The Party apparatus in the army was shattered. The number of Party members in the armed forces in 1937
was halved between 1932 and 1937, when only 1,330 privates and
NCOs were left, i.e. less than 1 per cent of all Party members.
By the beginning of 1938 the Soviet armed forces were short of
over 10,500 Party political officers.[68]

Various explanations of Stalin's statement that a 'conspiracy'
had been discovered in the Soviet armed forces have been offered.
One of these seems very credible to us, although disputed by many
of the German political writers who deal with the subject. This
theory is that at the end of 1936 the White Guard General Nikolay
V. Skoblin, who was an active Soviet agent among the Russian
monarchists who had emigrated to France, sought out Reinhard
Heydrich, the head of the German SS, and informed him in confidence that Marshal Tukhachevsky for some time had been trying
to get in touch with the White *émigrés* and the German generals.
Skoblin gave Heydrich to understand that Tukhachevsky was at
the head of a conspiracy which was planning a coup to oust Stalin.
Heydrich passed on the information to the SS-Reichsführer Heinrich Himmler, who told Hitler. Hitler thereupon devised a scheme
to make use of the information so as to bring about a serious
weakening of the Soviet armed forces through Stalin himself. Heydrich was instructed to let the material regarding the alleged con-

spiracy get into Stalin's hands. He saw to it that the French minister of war, Daladier, and the Czechoslovak president, Beneš, were informed. As Hitler and his assistants had foreseen, they imparted their knowledge to the Soviets, Daladier to the Soviet ambassador in Paris, Potyomkin, and Beneš to the Soviet ambassador in Prague, Aleksandrovsky. Churchill mentions the story in *The Gathering Storm*, published in 1954, saying that it had been told to him verbally by Beneš, and in Volume V, *Closing the Ring*, he referred to it again, saying that Beneš's role in the affair probably started the Tukhachevsky prosecution. A statement in the French Chamber of Deputies in June 1947 also throws some light on the affair. Daladier said that his son, Robert, who was in Prague at the end of 1936, heard there of an alleged conspiracy of the Soviet generals with the German Reichswehr and Hitler. Beneš at the time was advising the French diplomats to be extremely careful in their contacts with Soviet officers.

In the West there appeared other more or less trustworthy documents regarding the intrigue between Hitler and Stalin. According to the memoirs of Walter Schellenberg, who was a major in the SS, a German agent was in contact with a confidant of Beneš's, who is said to have put him in touch with a member of the Soviet embassy in Berlin—probably Israelovich, at that time the representative of the NKVD in Berlin—from whom he demanded three million roubles for handing over the documents. The fee was promptly paid, within twenty-four hours. In this way the documents came into Stalin's hands by June 1937 and furnished him with the excuse for the massacre of the Soviet generals.

It is well known that Hitler's 'V' men were capable of such cunning. Without doubt the whole plot and its execution were concocted by Stalin. The denunciation of Tukhachevsky by Skoblin was the occasion, and then all went as Moscow planned.[69] The Russian publicist Lev Nikulin tells in his memoirs how admirably the murder of Tukhachevsky and his comrades suited the German generals' plans. According to him, Beck, the Chief of the German General Staff, said of the military situation in the summer of 1938: 'One need no longer look on the Red Army as an armed force, for the blood purge must have broken its spirit and turned it into a spineless tool.'[70]

The liquidated army leaders included the military theorists. The whole *élite* of the theorists was practically eliminated. Among them were world-famous experts like V. D. Grendal (1883–1940), Professor at the Frunze Military Academy, Y. M. Zhigur (1895–1937), deputy chief of the military-chemical establishment and also a professor at the Frunze Military Academy, Y. E. Slavin, a close collaborator of Tukhachevsky's and Kirov's, and Snesarev (1863–1937), known as a military theorist since the Tsar's time and author of *Questions of a Military Nature in the Light of Dialectic Materialism.* He was also a distinguished orientalist and founder of Soviet oriental studies. As an alleged member of a White Guard 'conspiratorial organization' he was arrested and sent to a concentration camp. Later, when he was stricken by a fatal illness, Stalin allowed his family to take him to Moscow.[71]

The Terror swept through the para-military organizations also. On 21 May 1937 *Pravda* asserted that the enemies of the people often succeeded in penetrating the leadership of the OSOAVIAKHIM (association for the encouragement of aviation, and air raid and anti-gas precautions). A few days later the President of the Osoaviakhim, Eideman, was removed from his post and replaced by Gorshenin, the secretary of the Central Committee of the Consomol. Shortly afterwards the whole of the Board were arrested, and Gorshenin himself was declared an enemy of the people and executed in November 1938. Even the underlings were not exempt from arrest. The Central Aero Club of the Osoaviakhim was worst hit of all.[72]

A group hit nearly as hard by the wave of destruction consisted of Party leaders. Only a few Old Bolsheviks survived. Kosarev, too, the leader of the Communist youth organization, was another victim of Stalin's executioners. The group of Party leaders from the Caucasus was very severely dealt with. Once the mountains of their homeland had resounded with their glory, now they were branded as traitors to the October Revolution. Among them were the former First Secretary of the Central Committee of the Communist Party of Armenia, Khandzhyan; the First Secretary of the Central Committee of the Communist Party of Georgia, Gogoberidze; the Georgian party official Mirzabekyan; Nazaretyan, who was once well known throughout the Caucasus; Narimanov of Azerbaidjan; Orakhelashvili the Georgian; and a hundred others.

The organizers of the Communist movement among the non-

Russian people, especially in Central Asia, were denounced as 'national diversionists' or 'bourgeois nationalists' and became victims of Stalin's 'reprisals'. One of them was F. Khodzhayev, who. like A. Ikramov (liquidated with him) was one of the founders of the Communist movement in present-day Uzbekistan. Perhaps the strongest and most important personality in this group was T. Ryskalov. For many years he was president of the Turkestan Executive Committee. He was one of the most-discussed Communist leaders and political strategists among the Muslim peoples.

Among the liquidated Ukrainians was Lenin's travelling companion Zatonsky, one of the founders of Soviet Ukraine. The purges had specially dire effects on the smaller groups of peoples such as the Yakuts and Buryats. There the October Revolution had laid the foundations for a national culture. Even in the twenties illiteracy had been vastly reduced. The teaching in the new schools was given in the national language and a young, native, intelligent generation was growing up. The Yezhovshchina purges cut short this promising development and caused these small races to fall back into the reactionary conditions of the Tsarist age.

In the West we often overlook the fact that the abolition of the 'captains of industry', i.e. that young and dynamic class of managers which developed in the early stages of the industrialization of the USSR, was one of the key points in the programme of the Yezhovshchina, or rather that the Yezhovshchina actually started with arrests among industrial personnel, for which Sergo Ordzhonikidze in his time was responsible. His suicide was as it were a protest against the mass-arrests of directors and engineers, especially in the armaments industry. Ordzhonikidze's successor, too, V. I. Mezhlauk, was arrested during the night of 1/2 December 1937, and with him the whole managerial class of the people's economy. Many of the managers of industry were liquidated in the same year. Among them, besides Mezhlauk, were 'captains of industry' M. L. Rukhimovich, Y. V. Kossior, S. S. Lobov, and A. P. Serebrovsky. The number of industrial managers goes into the hundreds. It was only later, after the 22nd Party Congress of 1961, that even their names were made known in various scattered publications, and by no means all of them. One of the best-known of these 'Red works directors' was the head of the Kharkov tractor factory, P. I. Svistun, a genius at organization and an outstanding expert. When in 1929 it was decided to build a tractor factory at Kharkov he was appointed constructional manager. Nineteen months after the beginning of the project the works were there, as though conjured up out of the ground. Similar services were rendered by another Red works manager under whose direction metallurgical works were built—G. V. Gvakhariya. Y. I. Vesnik was the organizer of the Soviet metal industry. He directed the building of the combine works at Magnitogorsk and Kuznetsk and finally built the 'Krivorozhstal'.

We have selected only a few names out of dozens, but they are enough to show what the Soviet Union owes to these 'Krupps' and 'Thyssens' of theirs, whom it then made victims of the Yezhovshchina and proceeded to devour. Without their devotion the industrialization plans could never have been realized, even to this day. Soviet periodicals, memoirs, etc., are silent about these men, and if one of them is perchance mentioned then only ashamedly and in an obscure corner. That would be a good theme for the famous Socialist realism! The Soviet historians so often boast of the rise to world power which backward Russia accomplished under Stalin. But did they mention the fact that the rise was paid for not only with the sweat of the Soviet workers and the privations of the whole nation, but also literally with the blood of the technical intelligentsia?

It is impossible for us to describe in all its details the long St Bartholomew's night of 1937. But there is one other group of Stalin terror victims which must be mentioned: the thousands of scientists, writers, and artists. Stalinism was essentially 'anti-intellectual'. It incorporated a type of society the outstanding characteristics of which were directives, force, and blind obedience. Even before Kirov's murder Stalin had started his terrorist measures against historians and economists. How many Stalinists (themselves later to be liquidated) supported Stalin's policy cannot now be ascertained. It is certain, however, that without their cooperation it would have been impossible. For instance a demagogic article of Stalin's, *Some Questions in the History of Bolshevism*, full of misrepresentations and falsehoods, was printed as early as 1931 in the form of a letter in the historical periodical *Proletarskaya Revolutsiya*. It could have been explained as the basis of the party line on historical research. Kirov, Ordzhonikidze, Tukhachevsky—

they were all still living at that date—applauded their future murderer and rejoiced when shortly after the appearance of the article the first purges among the historians took place. This article initiated the gross falsifications of history which reached their climax with the publication of the *History of the Communist Party of the Soviet Union: A Short Manual*. At the congress of the Union historians in December 1962, when a promising development seemed to be brewing, and a description and realization of the Stalinist epoch in all its barbarity seemed to be the future task of the Soviet community, several historians reported on the events of that period. I. I. Mints, one of the fathers of the study of Soviet history, declared that the publication of Stalin's letter in the *Prolatarskaya Revolutsiya* started a veritable battue among the older Marxist historians. Many historical experts were calumniated and subjected to persecution, others had to 'confess' their faults.[73] Among the liquidated were many who were leading lights in the study of Marxist history, such as N. M. Lukin. He had been a Party member since 1904 and was the founder of the Association of Marxist Historians. In the twenties he had represented the association at international congresses at Oslo, Warsaw, Cambridge, The Hague, and Paris. He was arrested in 1938 and died later in a concentration camp. It was many years after Stalin's death before he was rehabilitated. The savage persecution of the historian Piontkovsky is still remembered. M. N. Pokrovsky, well known for many articles in the periodical *Under the Banner of Marxism,* broke down under the fire of Stalinist critics. After his death in 1932 he was declared an 'enemy' of the new historical writings, and with him his whole school was outlawed. And yet he had been the true founder and organizer of the science of Soviet history. His articles on Russian history must be rated among the standard works of Marxism.

Uninformed persons might object, as some sort of justification, that history-writing, like economics and sociology, was an ideological science, and victimization was a necessary concomitant of the ideological conflict. Nothing could be falser. For Stalin the only question was the part science, art, and literature were to play in the shackled social order as planned by him. All these spheres had to be subordinated to one aim, the perfecting and consolidation of his own despotic power. Thus he sought from each sphere sufficient support to guarantee the fulfilment of his current scheme. The scientist must be an 'apparatchik', an obedient civil servant. Fear, which became a means of educating the whole community, was to fulfil that function in intellectual circles most of all. At the historians' congress of 1962, already mentioned, Madame M. V. Nechkina, who like Professor Mints was a member of the Academy of Sciences, described the effects of Stalin's method. 'Comrade', she declared, 'could not longer talk to comrade. One's thoughts and doubts could no longer be exchanged with friends, no matter how close, not only because a friend might next day be one's betrayer, but also out of consideration for the friend himself, from fear of putting him in a difficult situation by discussing this or that debatable question.'[74]

There naturally throve in this atmosphere the unscrupulous and not necessarily ungifted 'intelligence beast'. It was inevitable. Many a scientist was well aware that he could only keep his head and survive by denying his real convictions. This opened the door to the activities of charlatans of every sort, provided they pretended to be representatives of the Party. Not genuine talent, but conformism, became the chief virtue of a scientist. When under Stalin the university professor Trofim Lysenko, member of the Academy of Sciences, was promoted to be the sole right-minded exponent of the party line, all the adherents of other schools, particularly in genetics, were declared to be 'enemies' and persecuted. Among the biologists who were physically liquidated were capable scientists who anticipated future developments in biology. Only one example is quoted here. The Soviet Ukrainian biologist O. A. Yanata proposed to the Academy of Sciences in 1937 the use of chemicals for the destruction of weeds. The consequence was a political investigation and Yanata was accused of wanting to destroy by chemical means all the harvests in the Soviet Union. The man who had set up the first Chair of Botany in the Soviet Ukraine was arrested in 1937 and shot as an 'agent' on 8 June 1938.[75] At this time American scientists were already experimenting with his methods, which have since become an accepted part of agricultural science. In this sphere the Soviet Union is still backward, not least because no Soviet agriculturalist is willing to share Yanata's fate. After Stalin's death, under Khrushchev, Lysenko's star was still shining brightly, and it was not until Khrushchev's fall, at the end of 1964, that it became officially known that all his successes, especially the process of 'yarovizing'—hastening the growth of plants by the effects of temperature at the beginning of germination—had been nothing other than fraudulent eyewash.

Foreign Communists as purge victims

A special chapter of the Yezhovshchina is concerned with the liquidation of foreign Communists. Worst hit was the Communist Party in Poland. It began with the arrest of the well-known Polish writer Bruno Jasienski, author of the much-discussed novels *I am Burning Paris* and *Man Changes his Skin,* who was accused of being a Trotskyist and fellow-conspirator of Yagoda's. He died in a concentration camp in 1941. Another 'Trotskyist', Domski, was dragged out of a concentration camp in the mid-thirties and forced to accuse other Polish Communist leaders. Stalin and Yezhov then organized a St Bartholomew's Eve for the chief Polish Communists. They were invited to Moscow with leading Communists from Austria and Czechoslovakia for an 'important conference'. With the danger of an attack by Germany and a victory for Fascism before their eyes, the Polish Communists obeyed the treacherous summons to Moscow. They were arrested in most cases at the frontier and in some cases shot on the spot. Arvo Tuominen, former general secretary of the Finnish Communists, produced the most accurate reports about this crime of Stalin's.[76]

The presidium of the Comintern was summoned in the spring of 1937. After the experiences of Bela Kun (an account of whose fate comes later in this book) all present were convinced that it was again a question of unmasking 'traitors'. Strange that no Pole was present at the session, although the two most prominent Polish Communists, Lenski and Bronkowski, on the Central Committee, were members of the Executive Committee and the presidium of the Comintern, and two others, Walecki and Krajewski, were on the Control Commission of the Comintern; Krajewski was also the chief of the personnel department of the Comintern. The chairman at this session was Dimitrov. The main report was delivered by Manuilsky, who said: 'Comrades, I am compelled to reveal an affair which is so dark, dirty, and incredible that you have never heard anything like it. In July 1929, when our glorious Red Army was approaching the gates of Moscow, a Polish regiment with a strength of seven hundred men surrendered to us. We received them with open arms, because many were friends of the Soviets and even real Bolsheviks. Many Polish soldiers entered the Red Army as officers or political commissars, and some were given important posts in the Soviet Government. It is obvious that, because of the conditions in which this regiment gave itself up, we trusted these men. We have never investigated the past of these seven hundred men. So we fell into the trap set by our enemies.'

Manuilsky went on: 'Our enemies have often fought us with treacherous weapons, but never have they acted so cunningly as in the case of these seven hundred soldiers. Who could have thought that they were all selected spies, highly trained for their mission? It was quite an army of spies, who filled important positions among us and for seventeen long years practised their sinister machinations without being disturbed. Who organized this despicable conspiracy? Of course it was that Socialist traitor Pilsudski.'

Arvo Tuominen reports that all present were deeply moved by what they heard, especially when Manuilsky declared that even Lenski and Bronkowski were involved in the affair. This grand-scale use of *agents provocateurs* created grounds for a massacre of the Polish Communist leaders in the Soviet Union. Stalin was 'perfecting' the whole extermination procedure. While Bela Kun had been allowed to be present at the session of the presidium, the condemnation of the Poles took place without their being given a hearing. Dimitrov also stated that of those seven hundred Poles all who were still alive or could be found had already been arrested. They were shot in batches. Among those killed were the last general secretary of the Polish Communist Party and almost all the members of the Central Committee of the Party. The veteran of the Polish Communist movement, Wera Kostrzewa, died in a Moscow prison during the first hearing. All the Polish members of the Comintern apparatus were shot, with the exception of Felix Kon, the grey-haired widow Marchlewski, and Dzerzhinsky's widow. This was the cruellest blow for the Polish Communists, who were political prisoners exchanged between Warsaw and Moscow and thus were living in the Soviet Union. Many of them had already several years of imprisonment in Poland behind them. The exchange group included a number of non-Communist leftists of the Polish Socialist Party and the Peasant Movement. All of them without exception disappeared in 1937 into the dungeons of the NKVD.

Yugoslav Communists, too, suffered great losses. As reported by Josef Broz (Tito) on 19 April 1919, more than a hundred Yugoslav Communists perished in the Soviet Union during this period, including some of the founders of the movement: Filip Filipovič, Stjegan Cijvič-Stefek, Vladimir Copič. Voja Vujovič, K. Horvatin, and others. The Yugoslav journal *Vjesnik u Srijedu* published in April and May 1968 a series of reports about the Yugoslav Communists who were liquidated in the Soviet Union. These gave details about the following Communist leaders: Duka and Stjegan Cijvič, Mladen Conič, Vladimir Copič, Filip Filipovič, Kamilo Horvatin, Antun Mavrak, Kosta Novakovič, Rade, Grgur, and Voja Vujovič. The Soviet press immediately started a campaign against the author of the articles, Zvonko Staubringer, and accused him of 'anti-Soviet propaganda'. But that did not alter the fact that Staubringer's reports contained facts and nothing but the facts— facts on which no Soviet journal could throw any doubt.

Many German Communists fell victims to the Yezhovshchina. Some had been arrested in 1934, when Yagoda was still master of the NKVD. One of the best known of Stalin's victims was Hugo Eberlein, who had been a delegate of the Spartakus League to the congress which founded the Third International; he was highly esteemed by Lenin. Others were members of the Politbureau: Hermann Remmele, Heinz Neumann, Fritz Schulte, and Hermann Schubert. Then came Leo Flieg, the 'grey eminence' of the German Communist Party and organizing chief in the secretariat of the Central Committee; Hans Kippenberger, chief of the information service of the German Communist Party; Willy Leow, leader of the 'Red Front Fighters Association'; the long-time party officials and Central Committee members August Creutzburg, Paul Dietrich, Erich Birkenauer (Chairman of the Thälmann Committee in Paris), Alfred Rebe, and Theodor Beutling; the general secretary of the *Rote Hilfe*, Willy Koska; and the former editor of the *Roter Aufbau* in Berlin, Kurt Sauerland. Moreover Yezhov liquidated a group of German Communist journalists, including the chief editors of the *Rote Fahne* Heinrich Süsskind and Werner Hirsch, besides Heinrich Kurella, whose brother Alfred nevertheless still plays the part of an old Stalinist cultural dictator in the German Democratic

Republic. Finally, Felix Halle, a lawyer who defended German Communists in the courts, Johanna Ludwig, a member of the Landtag, and Max Hoelz, who was 'drowned' in the Volga in 1934. In all, between 1934 and 1939 several hundred German Communists disappeared in the prisons and concentration camps of Soviet Russia.

The murder of the Hungarian Communist leader Bela Kun may be regarded as a specially characteristic example of Stalin's mania for destruction. In 1956 Arvo Tuominen, former general secretary of the Finnish Communist Party, wrote in the periodical *Uusi Kuwalechti*: Kun was no oppositionist, no adherent of Trotskyism or any other such movement, but a loyal supporter of Stalin. Nevertheless in the spring of 1937 the 'Bela Kun case' suddenly appeared on the agenda of a session of the Comintern presidium. Stalin had directed Manuilsky to bring forward charges against him. These were concentrated on Kun's statement that the Communist Party of the Soviet Union was rather poorly represented in the Comintern and that its activity suffered thereby. Manuilsky questioned Kun, who was present, in an aggrieved tone of voice: 'Citizen Kun, do you know that the Soviet Communist Party is represented on the Comintern by Comrade Stalin?' The Presidium members present, who included the Finn Otto Kuusinen, the German Wilhelm Pieck, the Italian Communist leader Palmiro Togliatti, and the economist Eugen Varga, knew at once what was afoot. It was enough to hear Manuilsky addressing Bela Kun as 'Citizen' instead of 'Comrade'. Kun was furious: 'This is an abominable plot.' He knew that Stalin, Zhdanov, and Yezhov were on the presidium of the Comintern, but they were seldom present at the meetings. He attacked Manuilsky personally and said he did not believe that Stalin distrusted him, Bela Kun. Thereupon Manuilsky let loose: he produced documents forged by Yezhov to show that as far back as the time of the revolution in Hungary Kun was working with the Rumanian secret police and was thus a traitor. Kun tried to stem the flow of accusations by shouting *'Provocation, provocation!'* and demanding a personal interview with Stalin so that he could explain everything. The Comintern delegates who were present did not believe a word of the accusations, but were silent, knowing that Bela Kun's fate was already sealed. Yezhov's myrmidons were waiting outside the door. When the session ended, on the proposal of Dimitrov, the chairman, they arrested Kun and took him to a waiting van. He was shot soon afterwards. Bela Kun was rehabilitated in 1956, the first sign being an article in *Pravda* for 21 February, on the 70th anniversary of his birthday. The writer of the article was the Hungarian Communist Varga, the same Varga who had held his tongue at the Comintern tribunal in 1937. In the Kun affair Stalin had kept a semblance of legal procedure, but in the cases of thousands of other Communists leaders he saved himself the trouble of such a farce.

Spain was the scene of most brutal actions staged by Stalin and Yezhov. As already mentioned, Yagoda had seen to the preliminaries. The Terror involved Germans, Poles, and Spaniards. Even Soviet citizens who had fought Fascism in Spain in the volunteer brigades were not spared outrageous treatment by the NKVD. The victims included Antonov-Ovseyenko, the hero of the attack on the St Petersburg Winter Palace in 1917. Many fighters from Western Europe, Poland, and the Balkans were murdered in Spain, often shot in the back on the battlefield. Citizens of the Soviet Union were ordered home and, if they did not disappear into the Siberian concentration camps, mostly executed in Moscow. When the chief adviser of the Spanish general staff, the well-known Soviet General Berzin, intervened personally with Stalin against the blind fury of the NKVD's behaviour in Spain, he paid for his temerity with his head. Several responsible Communists in the international brigades were lured to Moscow for 'important discussions' and there disappeared for ever. Such was the fate, for example, of the old Polish Communist Gustaw Rwal, one of the leaders of the Polish volunteers in Spain, the 'Brigada Dombrowskiego'. Another tragic family history must be mentioned in this connection. Marina Tsvetayeva, a Russian writer of romantic novels, completely isolated and forgotten, committed suicide in the autumn of 1941 at Yelabuga on the Kama. Her husband, a former Tsarist officer, who had returned from abroad to his Soviet home, volunteered to go to Spain in 1936 to fight on the Republican side. In the memoirs of several who fought in the Spanish Civil War he is described as an outstandingly brave officer. On his return to the Soviet Union he was arrested and liquidated. His daughter Ariadna suffered the same fate.[77]

The hunt carried out by Stalin's and Yezhov's agents for

Trotskyists living abroad would need a chapter to itself. Trotsky had formed an international cover organization for his followers, the Fourth International. In many cases he succeeded in planting them in the ranks of international Communism. The NKVD answered the challenge with its usual measures, terrorism and murder. Even before Ignats Reiss, already mentioned, the Trotskyist Andreas Nin had been murdered in Spain. Trotsky was hard hit by the murder on 16 February 1938 of his son Lev Sedov, who was in charge of the whole organization of the Fourth International. Some months later, on 13 July 1938, the secretary of the Fourth International, Rudolf Klement, disappeared in Paris. Apart from assassination, Yezhov made frequent use of *agents provocateurs* in his efforts to split the Trotskyist international.

The last Moscow trial

The third Moscow trial of the 'Anti-Soviet Right Bloc and Trotskyists' took place from 2 to 13 March 1938, before the military board of the Supreme Court of Justice of the USSR. In its macabre theatricality the conscious intention was to mislead the general public. It was to be Stalin's day of reckoning with those satraps who still remained loyal to him. In the dock were prominent representatives of the right-wing opposition in the twenties: Nikolay Bukharin, A. I. Rykov, S. H. Rakovsky (representative of the first great school of Soviet diplomacy), N. N. Krestinsky, and others. And, quite incredibly, the twenty-two defendants, all charged with Trotskyist terrorism, included Yagoda. He was accused of having for fifteen years practised espionage in the service of a foreign power, of having been himself a secret accomplice of Zinoviev and Kamenev, of having acted in accordance with Trotsky's commission, and, on instructions received 'direct from Trotsky', of having had Kirov murdered in cold blood. Further, Yagoda was charged with having sprayed with poison the walls of Yezhov's office in order to get rid of a formidable competitor. Further, he had maintained a medical staff and his own laboratory in order to 'cure' to death such persons as he did not dare to murder openly. A 'faithful servant', even in the dock, Yagoda did not refuse a last service to his master. His statement began: 'The beginning of my activity hostile to the Soviet dates back to the year 1928, when

I joined the anti-Soviet organization of the Right. . . .' With seventeen others Yagoda was sentenced to death and shot. Only three, including Professor Pletnyev, escaped with their lives.[78]

Among the macabre stories that circulated during the trial and for long attracted the world's attention was the allegation that Yagoda had poisoned Maxim Gorki. The year 1914 saw the publication of the memoirs of a Madame B. Gerland, a former inmate of the Vorkuta concentration camp, who mentions her encounters with Pletnyev, grievously sick after the war. Pletnyev, who in his time had treated Gorki, told her that Gorki was in fact seriously ill with heart trouble. The disease, however, was due not to much to organic causes as to the tortures which he had suffered towards the end. Gorki wanted to get out of Russia at any price and live in Italy. Stalin forbade his departure because he believed that as soon as he went abroad Gorki would denounce him. Pletnyev declared that Stalin's agents had given Gorki poisoned sweets. When rumours about Gorki's poisoning began to circulate in Moscow, Stalin threw the blame for his death on to the doctors. Yagoda helped Stalin even during his trial by confirming this report. Pletnyev died in Vorkuta in 1953.

That Yagoda should have willingly obeyed Stalin's orders even during the third Moscow trial is to some degree understandable. What were the means used by Stalin, Yagoda, and Yezhov to extract confessions from revolutionaries such as Zinoviev, Kamenev, and Bukharin? Stalin's torturers suited their methods in each case to the physical and psychological nature of their victim. In many cases physical torture sufficed. If not, they had still more effective methods by working on the prisoner's morale. The cruellest of these was the threat of extending the punishment to the persons dearest to the prisoners: their wives, their children, their closest friends. On 7 April 1935 the Soviet Government passed one of the most barbaric laws known to twentieth-century justice. By this, on children from the age of twelve the same punishment as for adults, including death, could be inflicted. We know now that this law was one of Stalin's weapons in the fight against his opponents. Kamenev, for example, had to decide whether to confess to the imaginary crimes with which he was charged or to be confronted in court with his own son, who would admit that he knew his father was plotting to kill Stalin and Voroshilov. In that case not only his own fate would be sealed, but also that of his teenage son. For the fact that he had not denounced his father at the time was quite enough to win him a death sentence, in accordance with the new law. Zinoviev, on the other hand, who was noted for his loyalty, gave way in order to spare his friends. Stalin's secret police sought to convince nearly all their prisoners that they held the lives of their families and friends in their hands. Effective as this method doubtless was, it cannot in the last resort entirely explain the behaviour of all the Old Bolsheviks and revolutionaries.

The crimes of which Stalin accused his victims were monstrous. They extended from acting as paid agents and spies on behalf of German and Japanese intelligence, from sabotage and subversive activity with the object of harming the State's economic plans, to plotting the assassination of Stalin, Molotov, Kirov, Kuibyshev, and other Soviet leaders. Lenin's fellow-fighters were alleged to have favoured the restoration of capitalism in Russia and made preparations for overthrowing the Soviet regime! The Old Bolsheviks during the Moscow trials confessed to Stalin's myrmidons all these imaginary crimes. But terrorism and extortion are not in themselves sufficient explanation.

In the second trial Radek said with regard to his alleged connection with Trotsky: 'What proofs have you for any such connection? Apart from confessions by two persons: my own admission that I received letters and instructions from Trotsky, and Pyatakov's admission that he met Trotsky at Oslo. The evidence of all the other accused is based on our evidence. But, Citizen State Prosecutor, when you have to deal with admitted thugs and agents, what certainty have you that what we said was true?' And the intelligent Rakovsky said: 'Would it help to get at the root of the matter if I could prove that this is the first I have heard of many of the crimes, particularly the terrible crimes of the Right and the Trotskyists, and that I first met some of the alleged conspirators here in court? It does not make sense.'

The contempt of the defendants for Stalin and his creatures is clearly shown in these words. But why then did they confess to the crimes? And why, if they had confessed under the pressure of physical torture, did they not declare in court how their confessions had been obtained?

The defendants behaved in this curious fashion because they

wanted above all to serve the cause of the Communist Party of the Soviet Union. They knew that war was imminent and that the Soviet Union was in danger. They made their confessions because in the last resort they were convinced that Stalinism, even though it meant a deviation from the revolutionary ideal, offered the only chance of mobilizing the whole military strength of the Soviet Union against Fascism. It must not be forgotten that these opponents of Stalin were mostly theorists with a tendency towards intellectual speculation and not entirely sound philosophy. Stalin on the other hand represented a concrete programme in which everything seemed to serve a clear and unequivocal purpose. The confessions of Stalin's victims became credible because the accused, robbed of their association with the Soviet community by Stalinist terror, were forced to realize that their attitude, 'from an objective standpoint', was wrong. Consciousness of their political helplessness drove them to despair. Thus Stalin was able to obtain what he needed before the physical destruction of the Old Bolsheviks: their confessions, and their last services to the Party and the Soviet State. That is the only way to interpret Radek's words: 'We find ourselves in a period of the greatest tension, in a period preceding war. To all the anti-Party elements we say, before the Court and in full knowledge of our approaching punishment: If any of you has doubts of the Party, he must realize that tomorrow he may become a deviationist if he does not now fully and sincerely make a clean sweep of his doubts.'

Among the victims of the Moscow trial, Bukharin was clearly an exceptional case. He went so far as to start disputing with Vyshinsky, the public prosecutor, on various points in the charges. The American historian, R. V. Daniels, explains his attitude in the following terms. On many points Bukharin insisted obstinately on his personal integrity. On the other hand he felt it an inescapable necessity to condemn all opposition absolutely and to provide Stalin with the justification that he demanded. He searched his conscience to find reasons for compliance and accomplished something that one can only describe as a pure act of faith in the revolutionary Soviet regime. Bukharin said to the court: 'If one asks oneself: "If you must die, what are you dying for?", a black void opens before one's eyes, sudden and terrifying. There is nothing for which one can die if one wants to die without regret. On the contrary, all the positive good that radiates from the Soviet regime takes on a new dimension in the human spirit. That thought has completely disarmed me and forced me to bend the knee to my Party and my country. And if one asks oneself: "Good, supposing you do not die, supposing by a miracle you stay alive", what then have you to live for? Isolated from everybody, an enemy of the people, in a situation which has nothing human about it, completely cut off from everything that makes life worth living. . . . The result is the complete moral victory of the USSR over its kneeling opponents.'[79]

Stalin and his henchmen were not in the least interested in publishing these noble motives for the confessions of their victims; they were merely another means to their goal. But this chapter of Soviet history is not yet closed. The time will come when the historian will discuss it, not in hatred for Communism, not under the influence of the Cold War, but in search of the historical truth. In the shorthand reports of the Moscow trials even the Soviet historians will then find enough evidence to show that Stalin's victims were not enemies of the Soviet Union, and that their liquidation, impartially judged, was an inconceivable degradation of humanity.

The last Moscow trial was in many ways a 'success' for Stalin. Although the charges were as absurd as they were spurious, they were found credible in receptive Western circles, especially among bourgeois diplomats. In the summer of 1941 the American ambassador in Moscow. Joseph E. Davies, based his interpretation of the trials on the fact that in Russia there was no internal resistance cooperating with the Germans. He was alluding to the Trojan horses of the National Socialists, such as Henlein's organization in the Sudetenland, the crypto-Fascist elements around Tiso in Slovakia, or the Norwegian Quisling and his followers. The Moscow trials, according to Davies, can be thanked for this! After rereading the reports of the proceedings and his own notes . . . he found that the confessions and admissions wrung from the Russian quislings literally revealed all the methods of the German fifth column that we know of today. . . .[80]

How successful Stalin's stultifying action was after all! It was a psychological chess-move, and politically important that Stalin should arbitrarily correct Lenin's characterizations of the Bolshevik leaders. In Lenin's testament it was Zinoviev, Kamenev, Pyatakov, and Bukharin who were named as important personalities and worthy candidates for the succession. In 1938 Moscow trial was not the final emendation to Lenin's testament. Zinoviev, Kamenev, Pyatakov, and Bukharin had been executed as enemies and agents, but the most brilliant figure in the October Revolution, Leo Trotsky, did not die until 21 August 1940, when Stalin's agents murdered him at Coyacan in Mexico. Of the Bolshevik leaders envisaged in Lenin's testament for the succession not one was left in the Soviet Union after 1938. Only one man had survived, now without a rival: Stalin. . . .

Stalin's methods

After Stalin's death, the Soviet leadership published details of the Yezhovshchina technique, first at the time of the 20th Party Congress (1956) and then of the 22nd Party Congress (1961). Psychologists, sociologists, and writers asked themselves the intriguing question, how was it possible for men who had experienced the bitter fighting of civil war, and in some cases long years of imprisonment, to become Stalin's pawns? Something has already been said on this question in connection with the last Moscow trials. Stalin used two methods. On the one hand, his former comrades, who were vastly superior to him in moral fibre, were placed in a position where they were induced to put their care for the future of the Soviet State above their own well-being. On the other hand, he never shrank from using the most brutal methods of torture. As survivors reported, it started from the moment of arrest. Scarcely had the police car stopped before the house, scarcely had the NKVD men, mostly young thugs, begun their search, than came a hail of blows and kicks. Though the victim might have held a high position a few hours before, though he might be Marshal Tukhachevsky or Isaak Babel, he was maltreated. Woe to him who dared to say that he would make a complaint, he was merely treated with all the more cruelty! The victims knew what to expect. The secret police were not only told that they had enemies to deal with, they were instructed not to be squeamish in doing their duty; they could ignore all existing orders and instructions. In an address to the employees of the State Prosecutor's Office in March 1937 Vyshinsky declared, basing himself on instructions from Stalin: 'There are stages in the history of man, and in our lives, when the laws are seen to be obsolete, and one must push them aside.' This declaration of Vyshinsky's buttressed, both theoretically and juridically, the bandit methods of the Soviet security organs. According to Vyshinsky, the confession of the arrested man should be decisive in determining the sentence. And so the security organs did everything possible to extort a confession. The question of guilt as such was simply not a matter of debate.[81]

The basis for arrests were lists of persons checked by Yezhov, Stalin, and their closest associates. The lists were compiled by security organs at all levels. From certain recently published documents it may be inferred that Stalin insisted that anybody whose name was on the list should be liquidated without hearing his case. On one list submitted by Yezhov, Stalin wrote in his own hand 'Don't examine, just arrest!'[82] Stalin's most zealous assistants were Kaganovich, Molotov, and Malenkov. Kaganovich and Molotov not only took part in compiling the lists of persons to be liquidated, but often set a personal example in using the most brutal and arbitrary methods. At the 22nd Congress of the Communist Party of the Soviet Union (October 1961) Shelepin reported the following case. In June 1937 a high party official named Lomov (Oppokov) was denounced as a friend of Rykov and Bukharin. Stalin passed the letter to Molotov with the following remark: 'To Comrade Molotov. What should happen here?' Molotov replied: 'Immediate arrest. Lomov is a blackguard.' The man thus characterized was a member of the Commission of Soviet Control in the Council of the People's Commissars of the USSR and an Old Bolshevik, a Party member since 1903, a man who had been Lenin's closest associate in the first Soviet government.

At the same Party Congress several actions of a similar nature by Kaganovich were quoted. Especially sinister was his behaviour in the purges among the railway workers. Shvernik reports, for example, how Kaganovich as far back as December 1934 specialized in the uncovering of alleged conspiracies among the railway workers and even sought justification for punishing suspects in contravention of existing laws and regulations. In order to prove that on the railways 'anti-Soviet organizations' and organized 'deviationists' were active, Kaganovich had not shrunk from torture and the use of *agents provocateurs*. On 10 March 1937 he asserted

in an assembly of railway workers: 'I know no railway area headquarters, no railway network in which Trotskyist/Japanese
sabotage does not exist. . . . I would go further and say that there is
not one branch-line without saboteurs.' Shvernik further reported
that in the archives of the security organs there were thirty-two
personal letters from Kaganovich to the NKVD in which he demanded the arrest of eighty-five leading employees in the transport
service.

After Stalin's death documents were found indicating the
activities of Malenkov, who at the time of the Yezhovshchina was
one of the younger candidates for Party leadership but was no less
implicated in the mass-liquidations that his older colleagues in the
Party. At the 22nd Party Congress, mentioned several times
already, Mazurov, the Belorussian Party chief, threw some light
on events in the Yezhovshchina period in Belorussia. In 1935/6
the Party documents were examined, ostensibly for comparison.
Malenkov at the time was employed in the personnel department
of the Central Committee of the Communist Party of the USSR.
With Yezhov's support, he put forward a statement that in the
leading Party and State organs of the Belorussian Soviet Socialist
Republic a 'nationalistic organization' was active and on this he
based a demand for the expulsion of half the members of the Belorussian Communist Party. Goloded, the chairman of the Council of
People's Commissars of the Belorussian Soviet Socialist Republic,
dared to doubt the opinion of the Party leadership that there were
nationalistic elements in the Party. Thereupon Stalin and Yezhov
sent Malenkov himself to Belorussia to conduct in person a mass
annihilation of party officials and the representatives of a creative
intelligentsia. Shvernik enriched the history of Malenkov's heroic
deeds at the time of the Yezhovshchina with a description of the
purge led personally by him in America. Here, too, the existence
of a nationalist organization was alleged, and the allegation started
an action in which almost the whole leadership of the Central
Committee and the Council of People's Commissars of America
were arrested. The hearings were set on foot by Malenkov himself,
who used, in Shvernik's words, 'illicit methods' and did not scorn
the intimidation, beating up, and torture of victims with his own
hands. Serious charges were made against Voroshilov too at the
same congress. He had distinguished himself particularly in

liquidating his own comrades. Shelepin reported, for instance, that Voroshilov had annotated a letter written by Yakir, the commander of the Ukrainian military area (who was shot on the following day), with the words: 'I very much doubt the sincerity of this dishonourable man . . . Voroshilov. 9.6.1937.'

The real organizer of the mass-murders was, it is true, Stalin himself. There is much evidence that he personally ordered many arrests. He saw to it, for instance, that not only Marshal Blyukher (Blücher) but also his brother Pavel and his first wife were arrested. Stalin's thirst for revenge was apparently not satisfied by the shooting of Marshal Tukhachevsky; his wife Nina Yevgenyevna and his brother were arrested and executed. The Marshal's three sisters and his mother were sent to a concentration camp; his daughter, a minor, was arrested as soon as she came of age. She too was sent to a concentration camp. Example after example, name after name, of persons now known to have been executed, might be added to this list.

The attitude of the Soviet leadership

Which of the Soviet leaders supported the Yezhovshchina? It was impossible for the security organs alone to carry out the task imposed on them by Stalin, i.e. to exterminate the personnel of the political administration of the country, the armed forces, industry, and the cultural sphere. One group of political leaders must have not only accepted Stalin's plan but sedulously aided its execution. But who? The rift in the opinions of the Stalinist ranks began as long ago as the 17th Party Congress (1934). Whereas the majority of delegates wanted to depose Stalin from the general secretaryship and replace him by Kirov, there was also a group loyal to Stalin and blindly subservient to his intentions. This is best seen by a comparison of the list of Central Committee members chosen at the 17th Party Congress (1934) with those chosen at the 18th Party Congress (1939). At the latter only twenty-four members and candidates from the 1934 Committee were chosen, and the membership of the chief committees was completely altered. While of the 139 members and candidates of the Central Committee chosen at the 17th Congress, ninety-three had entered the Party before 1916, by the 18th Congress this Old Bolshevik group had shrunk to twenty-two, i.e. from roughly two-thirds of the strength of the Central Committee to a little more than a seventh. In the 1934 Central Committee there were only four members who had joined the Party after the Revolution and only two candidates who had joined the Party after Lenin's death, while the 1939 Committee showed seventy-four members and candidates (out of a total of 138) who had joined the Party after Lenin's death. Among the newcomers there were several leaders who had rendered valuable service but who now became agents of Stalin's Terror. To the first group belong those who took a direct part in the liquidations. The second group is composed of those who supported the Terror morally and by propaganda, but took no direct part in the murders.

The first group includes, besides Stalin, chiefly Kaganovich, Molotov (younger than the others), and Malenkov. Molotov's share in the atrocities has in part already been described. At the 22nd Party Congress his activities in this direction, supported by documents, were drastically illustrated, for his signature on many liquidation lists is indelible. The wicked deeds of Malenkov, Kaganovich, and Voroshilov have already been described, but those of Georgy Malenkov, Stalin's long-time associate, require elaboration. In the Yagoda period he was employed in the personnel department of the Central Committee. In 1934 he was appointed head of the office dealing with the leading Party departments of the Central Committee. His devotion to Yezhov is shown in the minutes of a conference of this office in the year 1935, in which Malenkov is reported as repeating time after time: 'Comrade Yezhov is quite right. . . . Comrade Yezhov has made illuminating comments on all points in the agenda.' In March 1936 Malenkov succeeded Yezhov as chief editor of the journal *Partynoye Stroitelstvo*. The two men certainly worked in close association. When in 1936 Yezhov devoted himself to work in the security organization, Malenkov inherited his post in the personnel department of the Central Committee. According to official records, Bulganin also was employed from 1918 to 1922 in the security service. Several other Party leaders of minor rank had the honour to have had something to do with the organization.

In the second group, so to speak, the fellow-travellers of the Yezhovshchina were people like Anastas Mikoyan and Nikita Khrushchev. These, in their speeches, thundered against the

Trotskyists and every conceivable other enemy. As an example we may quote from a speech Khrushchev made at Kiev in June 1938: 'Comrades! In two days, on 26 June, all voters in the Stalin constituency at Kiev will go to the polls and choose the first Ukrainian candidates for the Supreme Soviet of the Ukrainian Soviet Socialist Republic. You will give your vote to the Leader and Protector of the People, the great Stalin.' Khrushchev went on to describe the situation in the Ukraine after Yezhov's reign of terror. 'At the present time, now that we have uncovered the abominable machinations of the bourgeois nationalists, these Lyubchenkos, these Tsatonskys, these Khvylyas, and other *canaille*, who were plotting to sell the Ukraine, to sell the Ukrainians into slavery to the Polish magnates, the Polish capitalists, the German landowners, and the German capitalists, we know very well that you yourself, our Stalin, put forth your hand to clear the masks from the faces of this *canaille*. We thank you for it and greet the Bolshevik Party, we thank you and greet you, great Stalin, your best pupil, Nikolay Ivanovich Yezhov, and all of you who by your Bolshevist actions have destroyed these vermin.'[83] Such were the hymns he was singing at that time.

In conclusion it is worth mentioning that there was a group of important leaders who supported Stalin in the early stages of his terror and were obviously convinced that his measures served the interests of the Party. But as soon as they recognized the true nature of things they protested against the spread of terror to the Party personnel, and they paid for their courage with their blood. To this group of officials belonged Pavel Petrovich Postyshev, who contradicted Stalin at the February/March plenary session. He defended his colleague Karpov against those who denounced him for cooperation with the Trotskyists and accused him of treason. Postyshev is alleged to have said: 'I personally do not believe that a respectable Party member, who has gone the whole way with Socialism and has fought the pitiless fight against the opponents of the Party, can have gone over to the enemy camp in the year 1934. I don't believe it. . . . I can't imagine it possible for anyone to have joined the Trotskyists in 1954. It is a remarkable story. . . .'[84]

At the June 1937 plenary session of the Central Committee the Communist leader Kaminsky, very well known at the time, made a speech in which he openly condemned the Stalinist 'reprisals'. Shortly afterwards he was arrested and shot, with his best friend V. A. Kangelari. The case of Nikolay Kuibyshev is also deserving of mention. He was the brother of the party leader Valerian Kuibyshev, who died in January 1935 in mysterious circumstances. Nikolay Vladimirovich Kuibyshev was in 1937 the Commander-in-Chief of the Trans-Caucasian military area. At a session of the Military Soviet in November 1937 he protested strongly against the bloody persecution of so many meritorious officers of the Red Army. He was arrested shortly afterwards and shot.[85]

The above-mentioned cases lead one to think that the number of those who protested against the outrages was after all not so small. One of the most striking figures, a man who offered open resistance to Stalin's criminal policy, was Fedor Fedorovich Raskolnikov. As the 'Krasny Admiral' (Red Admiral) he was a popular hero of the civil war. In April 1918, when German troops occupied the Crimea, he received an order from Lenin to sink the Black Sea Fleet. He obeyed, then fought his way through to Tsaritsyn with a detachment of marines. In 1930 he entered the diplomatic service, and remained in it till 1938. He was in Sofia, the Bulgarian capital, when the Yezhovshchina broke out. Raskolnikov was one of the closest friends of Kirov and Sergo Ordzhonikidze. When he heard that his own name was on the list for liquidation he determined to defect. He escaped to France and thence issued a series of 'open letters' and protests. On 12 September 1939 he died in Nice of meningitis.

The importance of the role of individual Soviet leaders in the framework of the Yezhovshchina cannot be over-estimated. Stalin's despotism could not have arisen had not a minority of party officials who were hand-in-glove with the security organizations declared for Stalin and against a majority of active party members. This fact was not only decisive for the history of the second half of the thirties; it casts its shadow on present-day Soviet society.

The end of Yezhov

He who does not grasp the fact that Stalin, a sort of super-Machiavelli, was always intent on strengthening his despotic rule will never comprehend the dry data of the Yezhovshchina. While the terror carried out by his creatures still rage, and thousands of

Communists were handed over by the security organs to death and destruction, Stalin was planning a fresh move. On 5 March 1937 he delivered to the plenary session of the Central Committee of the Communist Party a lecture 'Concerning the deficiencies in Party work and measures for the liquidation of Trotskyists and other double-dealers', in which of all things he championed the thousands of innocent people who had been expelled from the Party. Stalin blamed the Party officials for 'indifference' towards everything that was happening in the Party. The Committee, he demanded, must condemn 'the practice of a formalistic, soullessly bureaucratic attitude' towards individual Party members. But it was not until January 1938 that the first signs of a change of front appeared. The plenary session of the Central Committee condemned downright the terrorist excesses of the secret police. The resolution was based on Stalin's speech of March 1937 and stressed that Trotskyists and other hostile elements had infiltrated the apparatus of the security organs and thence terrorized innocent and respectable Party members. Stalin was trying to stop the mass expulsions from the Party. After Stalin's death Party historians constantly refer to this session when they want to prove that the Party even at that time was full of life, and despite the Terror, despite Stalin's 'bad traits of character', was trying to correct his faults. But that is a gross distortion of the facts—the truth was quite different. In the despot's carefully worked-out plans this committee meeting was merely intended to conform with his scheme. At this session Postyshev, already snubbed, lost his position as candidate for the Politbureau, and two new assistants of Stalin's were promoted to the leadership class: Nikita Khrushchev, secretary of the Moscow region, who was appointed member of the Politbureau, and L. Z. Mekhlis, who joined the organization bureau of the Central Committee. From that time dated Khrushchev's participation in the intrigues against the high military command, as is proved beyond cavil from recent sources.[86]

Stalin's cynical assertion that the security organs were affected by hostile influences caused uncertainty and fear in Yezhov's staff. When Yezhov on 31 August 1938 was appointed to the post of People's Commissar of Inland Transport, it was common talk that he was on the way out. The terror machine, in conformity with natural law, continued at first to roll forwards, but visibly slackened in pace. By the beginning of 1938 things had gone so far that Lavrenti Beria, Stalin's fellow-countryman, organizer of the mass terror in Georgia, succeeded Yezhov as People's Commissar of Internal Affairs.

What happened to Yezhov? The circumstances of his death are still obscure. His end at any rate was very 'opportune' and not very exciting. He must have lost his senses, they said, when they heard he had fallen into disfavour; he had been removed to an asylum as a manic-depressive and had died there. Another version had it that he had been poisoned in his office as long ago as December 1938. Even the post-Stalinist historians can give no exact information about the 'reward' which Stalin in the end gave his loyal servant. In the *History of the Communist Party of the Soviet Union*, 1959 edition, it is stated: 'For their criminal activities Yezhov and Beria were appropriately punished.'[87] One thing is certain: there was no sentence or any other legal proceedings. The despot's will was Yezhov's fate.

Why had Stalin resolved to put an end to the Yezhovshchina? There were all sorts of reasons. Primarily the international situation. It was gradually becoming clear to him, as to his associates, that the war danger was ever more threatening. Moreover, as a result of the mass arrests, the civil service, military administration, and party organizations were no longer equal to their tasks. But probably the final reason was that this scheme for personal dictatorship had now been completely realized.

The historical function of the Yezhovshchina

It is not the real task of this book to trace the simple course of historical events. Even if dozens of factors, numberless names and happenings, have to be mentioned in order to give an idea of the situation, there is still one question to which the reply is all-important. The question is this.

What role did terror play in the history of the Soviet community, and what were its effects? The balance-sheet of the Yezhovshchina is two-sided. On the one hand it led to the mass destruction of the State's employees. Almost all the Old Bolsheviks who had survived the struggle for power and the civil war, and who filled key-positions in the community, were destroyed, as were those generations whose enthusiasm for the building up of the economy and culture of the Soviet Union had created the October Revolution. The flower of the Soviet community in every sphere of life was crushed. The Party was cut to pieces, as the following official statistics show.

Whereas the Communist Party of the Soviet Union had $3\frac{1}{2}$ million members in 1933, only 2 million were left in 1938. By the end of May 1937, in the Ukraine for instance, in the Kiev region, 54 per cent of all members of the Communist Party were arrested and for the most part liquidated; for the Chernigov region the figure was 48 per cent, for the Vinnitsa region 46 per cent, for the Odessa region 36 per cent. And here are two more cases that show the conditions at that time. During the Yezhovshchina, 207,500 members of the Ukraine Communist Party (Bolshevik), i.e. over half the membership, were expelled from the Party. In Turkmenia the Communist Party (Bolshevik) in January 1934 numbered 18,359 members and candidates, but in June 1938 (when the membership curve was slowly rising again) only 8,053.[88]

But the Yezhovshchina has another side. It created a new closed social order, which, it is true, retained some elements from the Lenin era, but was primarily a degenerate Leninism. In Lenin's time the Party was the strongest political power within the community, but now, under the influence of the Terror, it had become a mere bureaucratic apparatus. Although under Lenin democracy within the Party was completely distorted by the prohibition of fraction-parties, nevertheless Communist leaders and activists, even ordinary members, were looked upon as politically conscious persons, well informed regarding the current problems of their own society and the international situation, and capable of forming their own judgement. But a different type of politician was coming into the foreground. The *apparatchik* (civil servant), utterly subservient, whose qualities consisted only of a capacity to function without friction and to carry out directives from above exactly to the letter. There was a gulf between the Party apparatus and the mass of the membership. The *apparatchiks* were instructed not to engage in discussions with Party members, not even to inform them regarding the state of affairs, but only to publish orders and see that they were strictly carried out. While the whole internal life of the Party stiffened into formalism the political factor was reduced to a minimum. Stalin's account of the history of the Soviet

Union and his teaching of historical and dialectic materialism were revered like a religious catechism.

But this change in the role and life of the Party was only one feature of the new order, and not the most important. It was the despot's terror apparatus, i.e. the security organs, that formed the basis of the system. The NKVD was the most important instrument of public order within the community. Terror became institutionalized and the conclusive means for the 'development of Communism'. With the help of the Yezhovshchina the despot created a system which, efficiently disciplined, was above all a comprehensive and boundless reign of terror.

The generation of Old Bolsheviks, who had plumped for Stalin in the difficult time after Lenin's death, now proved a brake on the realization of the model of society as envisaged by Stalin. It must not be forgotten that Kirov, Ordzhonikidze, Tukhachevsky, and hundreds of others had been of the same mind as Stalin. The party line was not Stalin's work alone, but their common creation. In the early stage of Stalinism there was still a degree of comradeship among the Stalinists. But that could not last under a despotism. Criticisms, doubts, or efforts to make this or that 'better', were no longer tolerated and were ruled out by all possible means. They would only have spoilt the perfection of the line of command from above to below. What we today look upon as the cold-blooded murder of thousands of people was in Stalin's eyes nothing more than the elimination of foreign bodies from the normal path to 'progress'.

The year 1937 saw the birth of the order dominated by the tyrant Stalin, and its establishment was the 'historic function' of the Yezhovshchina.

Chapter Five

Lavrenti Beria, the great police reformer
(1937–1941)

Fellow-countryman of Stalin and Chekist

AMONG the henchmen of Stalin whose past is obscure the chief personage was undoubtedly Lavrenti Pavlovich Beria.[89] His fictitious biography was published on several occasions, first by Stalin and his chroniclers, then by Beria himself, and finally by Khrushchev, who after Beria's death produced a suitably garbled version.

One must agree with the historians of the Stalin era that Beria's role was quite out of the ordinary. As already mentioned, there were many causes for the termination of the Yezhovshchina. The security chiefs, from Dzerzhinsky to Yezhov, had always known how to create or refurbish a well-oiled apparatus of secret police. But the oft-changing functions of Terror as prescribed by Stalin, the dramatic turn of events, and repeated purges among the ranks of the Chekists themselves, weakened the apparatus. As a terror machine it functioned smoothly, but as a State apparatus in the real sense of the word it left much to be desired. Stalin's directive to Beria therefore was to transform the terror machine into a modern apparatus of State security.

According to his official biography—we rely on Volume V of the last edition of the *Great Soviet Encyclopaedia*, published in Stalin's lifetime—Beria was 'one of the prominent leaders of the Communist Party of the Soviet Union (Bolshevik), a loyal pupil and closest adviser of Y. V. Stalin's, born on 29 March 1899 in the village of Merkheali in the Georgian Soviet Socialist Republic, not far from Sukhum. His parents were said to be poor peasants. But as in 1915 he was able to complete a technical education in Baku, this statement seems doubtful. There are several other contradictory reports about Beria's social origins. A certain S. Danilov, who knew Beria from his student days, was sure that he always had plenty of money. Danilov also remembered that Beria's mother was twice married and had four children to bring up. The funds for Beria's education came, according to Danilov, from a rich textile merchant in Sukhum named Yerkomoshvili, in whose household Tamara, Beria's pretty half-sister, was a domestic servant.

In the official biography, Beria is said to have founded an illegal Bolshevik group while still at school in 1915. In March 1917 he joined the Russian Social Democratic Workers' Party (Bolshevik). In June of the same year he was called up and served as a pioneer on the Rumanian front, where he made Bolshevik propaganda among the troops. At the end of 1917 he returned to Baku, where he continued his studies and was active in various Communist organizations. In 1919 he obtained a diploma as technician and architect.

Many doubt the correctness of the statements about Beria's revolutionary activity between 1917 and 1919. There were dramatic happenings at Baku in 1918. In April the Bolsheviks seized power, but after a bitter defence were soon crushed, the students playing a prominent role, and it is strange that no official biographer of Stalin's time thought of attributing heroic deeds to Beria at Baku.

After the seizure of power by the Bolsheviks in Azerbaidjan Beria is said to have been sent to Georgia to carry on illegal work. He was arrested in Tiflis, but in August 1920, after a hunger strike by the political prisoners, he was released and expelled from Georgia. After his return to Baku he attended the local polytechnic.

Perhaps Beria wanted to be an engineer, but the Party decided otherwise and in April 1921 Beria joined the Cheka.

Between 1921 and 1931 Beria held responsible posts in various Soviet departments of espionage and anti-espionage. He was deputy chief of the Azerbaidjan Cheka, chief of the Georgian GPU, chief of the Trans-Caucasian GPU, and plenipotentiary of the OGPU of the Soviet Union. According to the official biography Beria rendered specially meritorious services about this time in breaking up the anti-Soviet Menshevik group, the nationalist groups of the Dashnaks and Musavatists, Trotskyists, and other anti-Soviet parties and 'capitalist agents'. He was rewarded with the Order of the Red Banner and the Order of the Red Workers' Banner of the Georgian, Azerbaidjan, and Armenian Soviet Socialist Republics. The scanty information about this part of Beria's career can now be supplemented. In the West and in the Soviet Union itself various more or less accurate reports of Beria's doings circulated, and these give a good deal of information about him. We know that the Bolsheviks succeeded in seizing power in Azerbaidjan, whereas in Georgia a Social Democratic regime prevailed at first. With the latter a peace treaty was concluded on Lenin's recommendation. But on 11 February 1921 Stalin ordered Ordzhonikidze to march into Georgia. The Georgian patriots put up a desperate resistance to the invaders. Reliable reports tell of a tough and bloody struggle. It was Beria's task to break the resistance mercilessly with the help of the Cheka. There is good cause to believe that Beria's association with Stalin dates from those dramatic days. Ordzhonikidze, who till 1925 was Stalin's trusted lieutenant for the whole of the Caucasus region, acted as intermediary for many years.

A former assistant of Beria's in the Cheka was E. Dumbadze, who escaped from Russia in 1930 and published memoirs containing informative details about Beria's doings in those years.[90] Beria's right hand at the time was a certain Mikhail Mudry, head of the 'agents' section', which was concerned not only in gathering information but also with arrests and executions. Dumbadze describes in his memoirs the special predilection of Beria and Mudry for the use of 'technical equipment' at interrogations. This, however, was not modern apparatus, but simply old-fashioned instruments of torture. About the torture chambers of the Georgian Cheka under Beria Dumbadze writes as follows: 'Most people imagine that the torture chambers of the Cheka were gloomy cellars fitted out with instruments of torture. I cannot say that they were the same all over Russia, but as far as concerns the Georgian Cheka which I am describing the reality was much simpler and much more horrifying than those fanciful descriptions. Simpler because they contained no modern apparatus; more horrifying because it is difficult to imagine anything more terrifying and revolting than the secret cellars of the Georgian Cheka'. Dumbadze attended the executions of 118 persons in a single night. The condemned were taken into the inner courtyard of the Cheka building, the Chekists tore off their clothes and tied their hands. They were then thrown on to trucks and at the place of execution compelled to jump down. Anyone who could not move was dragged down forcibly. The victims were drawn up on the edge of open mass-graves. Two of Beria's men, Shulman and Nagatyepov of the 'death squad', walked along the rows and shot each man in the head. Dumbadze describes the ghastly scene in detail; many naturally did not hold their head 'rightly', some tried to run away, others wept, screamed, or begged for mercy. Those who did not die at once were given a *coup de grâce* by the escort. Beria waited in his office for the report on the executions. Some accounts allege that he sometimes took a personal part in the massacres.

In order fully to understand Beria's personality one must first answer the question, who were his victims at the time in Georgia. The official Russian chroniclers mention several anti-Soviet persons whom Beria was told to liquidate, mostly Social Democrats and Mensheviks. Far and away the majority were students, workmen, or peasants' sons. Bloodshed was the mainspring of Beria's political career. His ruthlessness towards the Mensheviks in Georgia was a special recommendation in his candidacy for Stalin's favour.

In 1931 the Central Committee of the Communist Party of the Soviet Union (Bolshevik) transferred Beria's services to the Party. The background of this resolution, instigated by Stalin himself, is noteworthy. In all the Communist Party organizations in the Caucasus there was discontent, and the national departments were resisting Moscow's centralizing policy. Stalin believed that Beria was the one person in a position to restore order in the Caucasian party organizations, to get rid of Stalin's enemies, and put an end to internecine strife.

In November 1931 Beria was therefore promoted to be First Secretary of the Central Committee of the Georgian Communist Party and Secretary of the Trans-Caucasian Regional Committee of the Communist Party of the Soviet Union (Bolshevik). He proved his worth and in 1932 was promoted to be First Secretary of the Trans-Caucasian Committee, still remaining Secretary of the Central Committee of the Georgian Communist Party. The above-mentioned volume of the *Great Soviet Encyclopaedia* gives the following appreciation of Beria's services in these organizations: 'Under the direction of L. P. Beria the organizations of Trans-Caucasia and Georgia have accomplished a great work in the strengthening of the organization of their ranks and in the Bol-shevist education of their party members in a spirit of boundless devotion towards the Central Committee of the Communist Party of the Soviet Union (Bolshevik) and towards the great leader and teacher Y. V. Stalin.' As stated in a document of 31 October 1931 (a resolution of the Central Committee of the Communist Party of the Soviet Union), Beria restored order and discipline 'in a short time' to the whole Caucasus area. The resolution also emphasizes the value of his services in collectivizing the Caucasus region and carrying out of the Party directives in cultural and economic spheres.

In the documents of the time the future alliance between Stalin and Beria is foreshadowed. Some mention Beria's good services, others his prompt execution of Stalin's orders, especially in the agricultural sector. Not without importance for Beria's future career was the fact that the Georgian and Azerbaidjan Soviet Republic in the year 1935 was awarded the Order of Lenin for its successes in industry and agriculture. You can read about this in the *Great Soviet Encyclopaedia*: 'Under the leadership of L. P. Beria the Party organs of Trans-Caucasia have justified the con-fidence of the Central Committee of the Communist Party of the Soviet Union (Bolshevik) and its great leader Y. V. Stalin. They have achieved marked successes in the realm of Socialist develop-ment and secured the fulfilment of Stalin's first Five-Year Plan in Trans-Caucasia.' Beria, the former Chekist, was now the respon-sible Party leader for the whole of Trans-Caucasia, though that did not involve the abandonment of his control of the security organs. In the Caucasus there followed, one after another, the same reigns of terror as in the rest of the Soviet Union. It is wrong, however, to assume, as some publicists do, that Beria at the time was a mere representative of Yagoda or (later) Yezhov. Just like Yagoda or Yezhov, he received his orders direct from Stalin. Although he had to work closely with them, there is reason to believe that Stalin convinced Yagoda and Yezhov that in the extremely complicated problems of the Caucasus his fellow countryman Beria should alone be competent and entitled to make his own decisions.

When Kirov was murdered, the Caucasus was shaken by a wave of terror, which was characterized by one novelty: during the first monster action in Georgia and at the initiation of the practice of shooting without a legal sentence the statement was made that 'acts of terrorism' had been committed by the accused against the Secretary of the Georgian Communist Party, L. P. Beria.

In 1935 the official biography mentioned a unique event in Beria's life: he wrote a book. That is somewhat of an exaggeration, for it is merely a question of the publication in book form of a lecture which Beria gave to an assembly of active Party members on 21 and 22 July 1935. In this work Beria falsified all events in the Caucasus region so as to emphasize artificially the part played by Stalin in the history of the Communist Party in the Caucasus. The *Great Soviet Encyclopaedia* says on the subject: 'The importance of this book lies primarily in the fact that it deals in detail with the school of political strife which produced Y. V. Stalin, the closest collaborator and most loyal and consistent comrade-in-arms of the great Lenin, leader of the world's proletariat. This work contains extensive material showing the vast revolutionary labours of Y. V. Stalin at the time of the foundation and growth of the Bolshevik Party under the leadership of V. I. Lenin.'

The successful stalinization of the Caucasus and the 'scientific evidence' regarding Stalin's historical role in that region determined the future career of Beria. At the 17th Congress of the Communist Party of the Soviet Union (Bolshevik) he was made full member of the Central Committee. As the end of the Yezhovshchina approached, Stalin must have already had a clear plan for the employment of Beria in the security service. In some works on this period it is asserted that there was a rivalry between Stalin and Beria which was settled in favour of Beria, in that he warned Stalin that Yezhov was collecting compromising evidence and documents that incriminated all the Communist leaders, including Stalin. Such a statement might explain why the most important documents dealing with Stalin's role in the revolutionary workers' movement in Tsarist Russia were most easily obtainable in the Caucasus, as Trotsky later proved in his Stalin biography.

But even if this supposition were correct, it was of little

importance. The end of the Yezhovshchina had, as we have seen, deeper causes.

At the beginning of 1938 Beria was posted to Moscow. It is not known with what task he was first entrusted by Stalin. In the official biography it is simply said 'to work in Moscow', whence one may conclude that it was not only to work in the Party offices. In December 1938 Beria was appointed People's Commissar of Internal Affairs in the Soviet Union.

Relaxation of the Reign of Terror. Reform of the NKVD

The appointment brought about a certain thaw in the Soviet Union, the Terror abated, the security service was fundamentally remodelled. Of course it would be very naive to imagine that the thaw was Beria's work. The only person capable of enforcing such a decision was Stalin. Beria was only his puppet.

It is said that Beria's entire staff of espionage officials was recruited from the Caucasus. Eye-witnesses report that this had a disturbing effect on the Chekists: their new chiefs spoke broken Russian, and the Georgian language on the telephone sounded like conspirators' talk. The older Chekists and Communist leaders were the most upset. Even Khrushchev in his 'secret' speech to the 20th Party Congress complained that Stalin used to talk to Beria in the presence of other Communist leaders in a language incomprehensible to them. Like Yagoda and Yezhov, Beria, too, organized a drastic purge of the leading members of the Cheka. But this time the 'liquidation of the liquidators' proceeded in deadly silence. Yezhov's assistants were 'discreetly arrested' and secretly dispatched. The espionage apparatus in foreign countries was reorganized, and such affairs as occurred in the interregnum between Yagoda and Yezhov were not repeated.

During the shooting of Yezhov's assistants an episode occurred in the Soviet Ukraine which deserves mention, as it probably influenced the later relationship between Khrushchev and Beria. Even before Yezhov's fall Khrushchev was sent by Stalin to the Soviet Ukraine on a special mission. Yezhov's man in the Ukraine at the time, Leplevsky, was liquidated at Khrushchev's command. Khrushchev had brought with him O. I. Uspensky, who enjoyed his and Stalin's confidence. Certainly Khrushchev and Uspensky worked well together. When Beria was appointed chief of the

NKVD and automatically got rid of all the leading Chekists, Uspensky too was one of his victims. As his successor in the Soviet Ukraine I. A. Serov was nominated. Khrushchev kept on good terms with Serov, but he would hardly have forgotten the Uspensky episode.

Many believe that Serov, immediately after taking up his post in Kiev, started proceedings against some of Yezhov's men there. After a trial at which Khrushchev invited party officials from various parts of the Ukraine to be present, several were shot, others sentenced to long terms of imprisonment, because they had tortured innocent Communists, extorted false confessions, and carried out illegal executions.

Carrying out the new policy for the security organs, Stalin now sought to bring about a reconciliation with the party members who had been intimidated by the Yezhovshchina. He proclaimed a partial amnesty, whereby sentences of under five years were suspended. In Yezhov's time such sentences were awarded for trivial political offences, among which figured even making political jokes. This slight but clever concession was enough to foster hopes of a relaxation among the general public and party members.

Beria was the blind tool of Stalin in carrying out his orders, in the course of which he showed an original and remarkable talent for organization. He reformed the whole NKVD apparatus. The type of Chekist was changed. The expert came to the fore. The NKVD's policy under Beria was to restore the traditions prevailing in the final stage of Dzerzhinsky's Cheka and put an end to the treacherous assassinations and blind terror of the Yagoda and Yezhov period. Weight was laid on the expert permeation of all levels of the Soviet community. Anti-espionage and the development of secret apparatus for the collection of information were now to be principal tasks of the NKVD, replacing naked terrorism.

The NKVD already included the 'Chief Administration for State Security', GUGB, in which the problems of state security were handled. Beria made this institution into an elaborate machine functioning smoothly throughout the Soviet Union. A network of NKVD training schools was set up with a high school in Moscow and branches in the republics of the union with a unified curriculum of study. First of all Beria arranged for recruits to be trained in accelerated courses lasting up to three months, so as to be able to dispense quickly with the untrained Yezhov men. The curriculum comprised the following subjects: the history of the Communist Party of the Soviet Union, intelligence technique (including card-indexing, form-filling, collection and evaluation of information, interrogation, recruitment of agents, etc.), a course on criminal law, and full instructions regarding the enemies of Stalinism, i.e. Trotskyists, Bukharinists, Mensheviks, Zionists, bourgeois nationalists, religious organizations, *émigrés*.

The professional training of security sections was always Beria's chief anxiety. After the accelerated courses had facilitated an upheaval in the personnel of the security organs, Beria used all imaginable methods to make the training as thorough as possible. In the Moscow high school of the NKVD an *élite* of specially talented recruits was given a whole year's course to qualify them for leading positions in the security network. After the introduction in 1939 of a two-year training period those who qualified became lieutenants or captains in the NKVD. At the same time there were regular courses in the cities and smaller towns for officials and staff of the NKVD.

The central administration for State security gradually developed into a vast apparatus, numbering, according to experts, hundreds of thousands of persons by the beginning of the war. The most important part of the system was not so much the Chekists themselves as the army of spies and informers, who were commonly known as 'zekzots' (*zekretny zotrudnik*). On a lower level were the *zekretny osvyedomitel*, or secret news-collectors. The whole of Soviet life was permeated by these spies, whose business it was to get 'all elements hostile to the State' arrested and effectively nip in the bud any activity that might be dangerous to the State.

The NKVD apparatus under Beria consisted of the central administrations for state security, for the workers' and peasants' militia, for frontier and internal control, for fire protection, for punishment camps, for family registration, and for administration and economics. A central administration was established in 1935 for highways, roads, and motor transport, which in March 1936 was renamed 'Chief Administration for Highways and Roads' of the NKVD. In November 1935 a department was set up for the Survey and Map service, and another for Resettlement. In 1939

Beria founded the Chief Office of Archives, in September 1940 Chief Offices for Hydrotechnical Construction and for Railways.

The NKVD 'develops Socialism'

All these chief administrations of the NKVD were developed under the personal supervision of Beria. But a special service, in Stalin's eyes, was his reorganization of the chief administration for labour camps, or GULAG, with the purpose of using prison labour more rationally in the execution of the State's economic plans.

There is plenty of reliable information available as to GULAG activities under Beria. The GULAG, with its headquarters in Moscow, consisted of two sections: the Camp and Railway Administration and the Administration of Lines of Communication. The system of concentration camps was fully autonomous and the competence of the local authorities was abolished. It actually had its own armed force and police. Beria covered the whole Soviet Union with a network of labour camps geared to satisfy the demands of Stalin's five-year plans. For instance, in the Kuibyshev area lay the concentration camp system known as the *Bezimyenlag*, the inmates of which worked on a great munitions centre. It was divided into sections (*otdeleniya*), each of which in its turn comprised several 'camp points' (*lagpunkt*). The latter were not always permanent; roads and railways were built from mobile camps. Each 'camp point' held from several hundred to several thousand prisoners, and these again were divided into columns of from 600 to 1,800 men. The larger 'camp points' had smaller branch establishments or *podkomandirovki*. At the head of the next smaller units, each with only 25–40 persons, were 'brigadier' prisoners, under whom were *dezyatniki*, each in charge of ten prisoners. The prisoners while at work were guarded by an armed sentry, who was empowered to shoot to kill.

The degeneration of the bureaucracy in the life of the Soviet Union under Stalin naturally infected the labour camp system. A whole army of planners, accountants, book-keepers, norm-fixers, and other bureaucrats infested the head offices. Administration inside the camps was carried on by the prisoners themselves. The only free man was the camp leader; even his deputies might be prisoners. Men with criminal records were usually chosen for these posts and the camp administration was practically in their hands, which meant an additional burden for the political prisoners. In 1941 Beria issued an order that there must be another free man in each camp besides the camp leader, namely the political leader.

Distinct from the corrective labour camps (Russian abbreviation ITL) were the corrective labour colonies (ITK), which were under a special department of the NKVD, i.e. the administration of the detention institutes (OMS). The ITKs mostly housed minors and factory workers who had offended against the law of 6 June 1940 and were late for work or had left their place of work without permission.

In 1941 there were eighty groups of concentration camps, each group composed of from twenty to a hundred branches. After the Second World War precise information concerning all these camps was published in the West.

The preferential treatment and expansion given to the chief administration for State security, GUGB, gradually began to upset the whole of the NKVD. The aggregate staffs of all other departments of the People's Commissariat were many times less than that of the GUGB, and the constantly increasing budget for its expansion meant that there was less money available for other departments. However, this purely organizational problem was not the sole cause of the decision of the Soviet leadership in 1941 to carry out a drastic reformation of the NKVD. The international situation, the impending war, necessitated a further strengthening of the security service, and this could hardly be carried out within the framework of the NKVD.

The origin of the KGB

Thus it was that the law of 3 February 1941 took the Chief Office of State Security out of the NKVD and turned it into an independent ministry or People's Commissariat (*Narodny Kommissariat Gozudarstrennoi Bezopaznosti*—NKGB). Beria himself stayed at the head of the NKVD, and his former deputy, V. N. Merkulov, was appointed head of the newly formed NKGB. The importance of the security service in the Soviet Union was thereby still more emphasized on the eve of the war.

The question immediately arises, why Beria remained in the post of People's Commissar of Internal Affairs and did not become chief of the NKGB, and whether this meant a certain diminution of his power. The reply is simple: Merkulov was one of Beria's closest and most trusted collaborators, and the release of the Chief Office of State Security from the NKVD was only a bureaucratic separation. Merkulov was not thereby promoted to be Stalin's adviser on security. Beria continued to hold that position. Merkulov had to remain in close contact with Beria through the collaboration of the NKGB with the NKVD, but he was *de facto* placed under Beria, who was Stalin's adviser on all matters affecting security.

The NKGB continued to expand in rapidly recurring stages. Its competence now included supervision of the Red Army and Navy. The NKGB set-up comprised the following administrations or departments.

The Foreign Administration (*Inostrannoye Upravleniye*, INU) watched all foreigners in the Soviet Union, including the diplomatic missions. With the help of the intelligence department it collected information in foreign countries and kept its own resident officers in each western state, and it watched the *émigré* associations. The chief of the INU for that purpose kept contact through the NKGB with the People's Commissariat of Foreign Affairs. In general discreet attempts were made, especially just before the war, to include INU agents in the diplomatic missions of the Soviet Union abroad. Among the various departments of the Foreign Administration was one for the technical equipment of its members working abroad.

The Secret Political Administration (*Zekretno Politichechoye Ugravleniye*, SPU) supervised the whole of life within the Soviet Union. It comprised four large departments: for the suppression of illegal organizations, Trotskyists, Mensheviks, Bukharinists; for the supervision of nationalist movements among the non-Russian peoples; for the supervision of churches and religious sects; and finally for the supervision of all cultural life in the Soviet Union, including Press and broadcasting.

The Defence Department (*Kontrasvedyratelnoye Upravleniye*, KRU) protected the country against foreign spies, directed anti-espionage measures abroad, and supervised Soviet agents, including other intelligence organs. In view of the war menace this department was especially strongly manned. The KRU agents controlled, in accordance with a precise plan, all departments of Soviet life, especially industry, transport, and communications. With this object a special order was issued on 5 March 1941, whereby in all ministerial branches and in the larger industrial transport establishments, etc., cells of the KRU (designated 'O') were set up.

Other departments included one for roads and transport, a card index and files for suspicious persons and agents, and technical sections, e.g. for forging passes and the production of special weapons, and, of course, a very large interrogation department.

Operations in foreign countries

During the Yezhovshchina the purging of the officer corps deprived the military defence of its best brains. One of the most gifted organizers, Yan Karlovich Berzin, who from 1924 to 1935 had been Defence Chief of the Red Army and later Deputy Commander-in-Chief of the 'Red Banner Far-Eastern Special Army' and military adviser in Spain, was in June 1937 reappointed Defence Chief of the Red Army. During the Yezhovshchina he was arrested and in 1938 liquidated.[91] The operations of the military intelligence service were independent of those of the security organs. The so-called 4th Department of the General Staff was exclusively concerned with military information. Friction between military intelligence and the security service is usual in nearly every country. In the Soviet Union as elsewhere the security organs had long been discontented with the arrangement. Finally during the Yezhovshchina they attained their goal, which was the right to supervise all military formations. At first the experiment was made of putting leading Chekists on the staff of the Ministry of Defence. For example, Y. S. Unschlikht, member of the board of the NKVD, became also Deputy Chairman of the Revolutionary War Council of the USSR (1923-1930). This coordination was abandoned in practice after the Yezhovshchina, because (among other reasons) the 4th Department was drastically 'purged'. Together with Berzin, his closest colleague A. Korin was arrested and shot. All military intelligence officers resident abroad were recalled. The result was a series of scandals, which attracted worldwide attention. Many refused to return to the USSR, unwilling to fall into the hands of Stalin's executioners. Much dust was created by the case of V. G. Krivitzky, a representative of the 4th Department stationed in Western Europe, and author of *Ich war in Stalins*

Dienst! On the eve of the Russo-German war military intelligence specialists were trained in the General Staff Academy.

In 1939 a start was made in feverish haste to train new personnel for military intelligence, at first in accelerated courses, then in 'reconnaissance courses' (*kurzy razvedchikov*) of 3–6 months' duration. Later the 'Reconnaissance Centre' which Yezhov had abolished was reconstructed. Its task was to train highly qualified intelligence officers, and it was given the status of a military academy. Its courses lasted eighteen months, later extended to two years. The entrance examination was very strict, special weight being attached to general intelligence and physical fitness. Under the pressure of the events of 1940 the curriculum was reorganized and the training period reduced to six months. Other intelligence specialists were trained in the General Staff Academy.

Berzin had sent his cleverest and most experienced intelligence personnel to Germany, France, and especially Japan. The most important group was that centred around the later famous Dr Richard Sorge, who worked under the cover of correspondent of the *Frankfurter Zeitung*. Being in the confidence of the German ambassador in Tokyo, he was able to send much extremely valuable information to Moscow in many thousands of coded messages. The American intelligence chief, Major-General Charles Willoughby, who after the war had the opportunity to examine the Sorge file in Tokyo, reported that certainly the information which Sorge sent at that time was worth many millions of dollars to the Soviet Union.[92] Two messages were historically of vital significance: Sorge had warned Moscow, four months in advance, that Germany was planning to attack the Soviet Union. He also told Moscow that Japan would not in the foreseeable future attack the Soviet Union in the Far East. The Sorge case has two sides. On the one hand he will go down in the history of spying as the classic example of what a clever agent can accomplish. When Sorge had been arrested by the Japanese secret police and had been unequivocally convicted of activity as an agent, diplomatic and military representatives of Hitler's Germany in Tokyo were still convinced that the arrest of Sorge on 2 October 1941 was probably a political intrigue, because Sorge had received certain confidential information concerning the state of the Japanese-American negotiations, a State secret, as shown by an official report addressed to the State

Department and dated 14 November 1941.[93] The reverse side of his existence, which Sorge began to experience, consisted of the whims and distrust of the despot Stalin. Berzin, Sorge's chief, was executed by Stalin as a 'Japanese spy'. Consequently his closest colleagues would also be considered as traitors or at least be looked upon with grave suspicion. Towards the end of Khrushchev's period of office, when many themes could be discussed in the newspapers more freely, certain Russian journalists interested themselves in the Sorge affair. Their original motive was certainly not that of the young people who in 1966 wanted to make a German 'Hero of the Soviet Union' out of Sorge, although a few years earlier they did not yet know whether he was to remain the traitor denounced by the Stalinists. The journalists quite simply asked themselves how it was possible that Sorge had still not been rehabilitated by 1966. Why was the information radioed by Sorge to Moscow so mistrusted? In the eyes of Stalin and his intelligence specialists Sorge's reports were 'Japanese cock-and-bull stories', intended to lure Moscow on to false trails.

When on 5 November 1964 the Presidium of the Supreme Soviet of the USSR announced 'the award of the honourable title of Hero of the Soviet Union to Comrade Richard Sorge', the Soviet press drew attention to Stalin's attitude. On 7 November 1964 the organ of the Ministry of Defence, *Krasnaya Svyezda*, published a comment by Colonel A. Kalinin: 'The heroic deeds of Richard Sorge cannot be belittled by the fact that Stalin in his shortsightedness did not trust his information, even when confirmed from other Soviet sources. Reports of supreme importance were with unintelligent nonchalance marked "to be filed" or "to the archives".' The case of Sorge, despised by the despot Stalin even after 1953, is a classic example of the way in which the mentality which gave birth to the Yezhovshchina and inflicted such injury on the Soviet Union still persists in the heads of certain Soviet leaders. . . .

The attention of the Intelligence branch was directed primarily to Germany. The task was tackled with extreme caution, at the command of Stalin, who probably was already toying with the idea of a pact with Hitler. The Soviet agents went to work from other countries. They lived in France, Belgium, Denmark, Switzerland or Sweden, and thence directed their groups of agents in Germany. They were deeply mistrusted by the German Communist Party, which, as Stalin at least thought, was saturated with Gestapo spies. Only Ernst Wollweber enjoyed the full confidence of Stalin and Beria. He was almost the only Beria agent with the right to recruit and use spies from the ranks of the German Communist Party.

Another man who in the eyes of the Soviet security organs rendered invaluable service was Leopold Trepper, alias John Gilbert, who directed the ring of agents known as the 'Rote Kappelle' (Red Chapel). His team worked in Belgium and France, and only in an emergency did the Soviet Intelligence directly interfere.

Beria gave special attention to the training of his foreign agents. Time was short, everybody worked feverishly, and what was actually achieved in the circumstances was simply astounding. Russian intelligence officers, represented here by Viktor Sukolov, Mikhail Makarov, or Konstantin Yefremov, worked under West-European-sounding cover-names and spoke fluent French, Spanish, or German. They represented a new type of Soviet military agent— no longer a simple Trotskyist or a White-Guard-hater, but a trained conspirator with a deep knowledge of Western problems and imbued with the feeling that he must at all costs fulfil the task allotted by his country. They were no longer 'Revolutionaries', 'Champions of the World Revolution', or 'Fighters for the Victory of Stalin'. Their main job was to defend the Soviet Union against the menace of war.

On 23 August 1939 the Pact between Hitler and Stalin was signed. A transformation of the Soviet agents abroad into 'secret politicians' with a knowledge of foreign relations now became extremely urgent. Germany had become the most interesting object for all the Soviet intelligence services. Now was the time to intensify the work in Germany, but without annoying Hitler, for Stalin was anxious to avoid any unnecessary challenge to Germany.

In this new situation the appointment of Vladimir Dekanozov to the Soviet embassy in Berlin was significant. Born in 1898, he was a Georgian like Stalin and Beria. He had been a close friend of Beria's since his youth and had helped him to carry through the purges in Georgia. In 1938 he was deputy chairman of the Ministerial Council of the Georgian SSR and People's Commissar of Internal Affairs. When Beria became chief of the NKVD he took the talented Dekanozov with him to Moscow. Stalin regarded him as an extremely capable assistant and in 1939 made him Deputy People's Commissar of Foreign Affairs. Less well known was the fact that the same Dekanozov was the head of the information department of the NKVD and that he had been specially chosen by Stalin and Beria to reorganize the work of the information services abroad on the new lines. Dekanozov took Boglan Kobulov with him to Berlin, as counsellor at the embassy. Both men proved themselves during the Hitler-Stalin Pact negotiations as masters in Stalin's great game. They succeeded in providing the Soviet agents in Germany with the best possible opportunities and in reducing scandals to a minimum. Beria, Dekanozov, and Kobulov, through this commission of Stalin's, were welded into a sworn comradeship.

It is certain that Beria was also responsible for ferreting out the military secrets of other nations. The 4th Department of the General Staff, mentioned above, could no longer remain as disorganized as Beria would have wished, and it continued to strive for independence. The Yezhovshchina, too, had torn gaps in its structure, gaps which could not easily or speedily be filled. The most important fact was that Beria had not been able to abandon his obsolete ideas about the 'enemy'. Into his period of office fell the intensive preparations for the murder of Trotsky and others, chiefly *émigrés*—a task entrusted to the so-called 'Bureau No. 1'. Its head was P. A. Sudoplatov, a close associate of Beria's and a fanatical Stalinist who had been inherited from Yezhov. Sudoplatov possessed a special flair for the Western way of life and was admirably fitted to adapt Beria's plans to actual events in the West. His closest assistant was Leonid Eitingon, who in 1939 was ordered to draw up the plan for the assassination of Trotsky in Mexico. He chose as his tool a certain Ramon Mercader, who, calling himself a Trotskyist, managed to insinuate himself into the Trotskyist organization in the USA and thence to penetrate Trotsky's entourage at Coyacan in Mexico. On 21 August 1940 he reached his goal. He killed Trotsky by stabbing him in the back with an ice-pick.

Trotsky's murderer was no long-term agent; to carry out his commission he needed only the comparatively brief period of two years. The Trotsky affair showed clearly how precisely planned to the last detail the Soviet security service worked. They did not shrink from assassination, provided it was properly prepared. The murderer must never be a person who could be traced as a direct agent of the Soviet secret police, and wherever possible he should pose as an adherent or associate of his victim. In the Trotsky case he was a 'convinced Trotskyist', who was supposed to have made up his mind to assassinate Trotsky only when disappointed with his idol. Mercader told the court that he had been disillusioned by Trotsky when commissioned by him to go to Russia, murder Stalin, and make preparations for the assassination of other Communist leaders—an obvious, shameless lie.

This method was not invented by Beria, he merely perfected it and gave it legal status. To show this more clearly, we can refer to another case, which occurred before Beria's term of office. On 23 May 1938 the leader of the Ukrainian nationalists, E. Konowalets, was killed in Rotterdam by a bomb. The assassin, a certain Waluch, had made fairly lengthy preparations. Posing as a representative of the illegal Ukrainian nationalist groups in the Soviet Union, he got in touch with the organization of the Ukrainian nationalists abroad. He supplied the foreign Ukrainian press with information, reports, and articles, and took part in the quarrels among the leaders of the organization. One group, under Colonel Riko Jarry, was anxious to win him over to their side and supplied him with all kinds of information; another group, led by Konowalets, did the same. After the bomb attack in Rotterdam Waluch succeeded in escaping on a Soviet ship. If, like Mercader, he had been arrested and brought to trial, he would certainly have staged a similar farce and declared that he was a convinced Ukrainian nationalist and wanted to serve the cause out of pure idealism, but had been demoralized by the rifts and cliques in the Ukrainian organization.

It is clear that the Soviet security service was always 'a thing apart'. Apart from its purely intelligence work, apart from purely State Security duties, it was constantly entrusted with tasks that were not exactly typical work for a security organization. Thus from time to time its activities display various idiosyncrasies that are without parallel in history.

'Pure provocation', for instance, i.e. the use of *agents provocateurs*, was developed into a successful and elaborate police weapon.

It originated with Stalin, whose character it fitted admirably, and was warmly recommended by him during his struggles with the opposition. 'Provocation' soon became a valuable weapon in the arsenal of the security organs and its use constantly spread to new spheres, primarily to the campaign against the *émigrés'* associations. Many people still do not realize that the Soviet security organs were themselves often the instigators of an 'intensified struggle' against Communism abroad. *Provocateurs* sent by them stirred up a blind and uncritical anti-Communism among their opponents and did all they could to denigrate the Soviet Union. But their invariable object was thereby to get control over their opponents in order in the end to render the whole group harmless.

In the thirties there was a Russian anti-Communist organization consisting of representatives of the younger generation of *émigrés*, which was discontented with the activities of their monarchist and 'old-fashioned' elders. They wanted to adapt the anti-Communism of the Russian *émigrés* to the 'live' movements of Fascism and Nationalism; they called themselves the National Workers' Association and were later known under the Russian abbreviation of NTS. Even from the beginning of the thirties the GPU had quietly welcomed the new organization. A trained GPU agent, Baron L. N. Nolde, was sent at once to Belgrade, where the headquarters were situated. He was soon able to penetrate the leading circles of the organization and take up a responsible post in it. From him came a proposal to send several NTS groups to the Soviet Union. They were each to consist of three persons at most, and each group should continue its revolutionary agitation alone and independently of the others. Hundreds of young anti-Communists were in this way lured into the Soviet Union over the Polish and Rumanian frontiers—straight into the hands of the GPU. Some of them were converted by the Soviet Security organs and 'reversed', i.e. they were sent abroad again as 'representatives of the powerful anti-Communist Resistance'. In 1952 a Russian journal published in the United States, *Novoye Russkoye Slovo*, had some interesting information about this practice. The Soviet security organs had founded an 'illegal NTS organization' in Moscow, which advocated intensified anti-Communist action. Incidentally, Nolde was in touch with the anti-Communist organizations in existence. It is certain that he also had connections in the 2nd Department of the Polish security, which helped him to get his people into Russia. It is known that Polish security wanted to be sure that all this activity was really genuine. Polish agents were sent into the Soviet Union with some of the Russians, and the Chekists promptly staged a great performance in order to convince them of the genuine existence of a large-scale anti-Communist resistance movement. Thus a single success became a chain reaction.

After the Hitler-Stalin pact

On 17 September 1939 the Red Army crossed the Polish frontier and occupied Western Ukraine and Western Belorussia. The two Polish districts were incorporated into the Soviet Ukraine and Soviet Belorussia. When Germany invaded Denmark and Norway in April 1940, the Soviet Union speeded up their preparations to annex Lithuania, Latvia, and Estonia. By July they were able to consolidate their power in these states, which in August were absorbed into the USSR as new republics. In June 1940 Bessarabia and northern Bukovina were incorporated into the Soviet Union. The Soviet security organs, which were responsible for 'order' in the new regions, fell into a nervous state of feverish activity, especially when unusual and unexpected difficulties were caused by the Soviet-Finnish war.

The instructions to the security organs in the former Polish districts which now belonged to the Soviet Union were as follows: compilation of lists of hostile, suspicious, and unreliable elements, to be deported to Kazakhstan and other eastern republics of the Soviet Union; suppression of all nationalist and democratic organizations; creation of a network of secret agents and spies; and the preparation of measures to counter the growing war danger.

The great deportations from the former Polish districts began in 1939, from Lithuania and Latvia in 1941. When the German army occupied Lithuania in June 1941 the Soviet authorities were unable to remove or destroy their records. Lists left behind show that about 24 per cent of the whole population in the Lithuanian SSR were earmarked for deportation. After 1942 the Free Lithuanian embassy, resident in Switzerland, circulated photostat copies of these unique documents. They comprised not only the whole intellectual *élite* of Luthuania, but even philatelists and Esparantists, who Soviet security alleged belonged to 'international freemasonry'. Some Western observers remarked that the deportation lists for the parts of Poland occupied by the Soviets had been compiled on the same principle, although the political situation was quite different there. A considerable part of the Polish population displaced from this area, primarily higher civil servants, politicians, and 'colonists' (i.e. Polish peasants from West Poland who had recently been resettled in the eastern districts), and a large number of Ukrainians, Jews, and other elements. The deportations were usually to Soviet Asia, mostly to Kazakhstan. Some of the displaced persons were allowed to live as *volnonayomnye*, i.e. they could move about freely in their places of exile. The rest were sent to concentration camps, often in Northern Siberia, with forced labour in the forests of the taiga.[94]

In order to win Hitler's favour, Stalin shamelessly produced a convincing proof of his loyalty: in 1940 he handed over a group of German Communists to the Gestapo. One of these was Margarete Buber-Neumann, who had lived in the Soviet Union as a political refugee since 1935 and describes the affair in her memoirs.[95] Among those extradited were several German and Austrian Communists specially selected because of their Jewish origin. The handover took place at the railway bridge at Brest-Litovsk, and some of them had to be forcibly driven over the bridge by the NKVD guards when they refused to go voluntarily. Frau Buber-Neumann mentions a young workman from Dresden, who in 1933 had taken part in an armed clash with National Socialists in which one of the latter lost his life. He succeeded in escaping into Russia. In the trial of the arrested Communists all the blame was heaped upon him in his absence, so that he knew only too well the fate that awaited him. Most of the thirty extradited persons were sent straight to a concentration camp, where only a few survived.

The regions newly annexed by the Soviet Union, notably West Ukraine, Lithuania, and Latvia, became a field for experiments in which the effectiveness of the new security methods was tested. The whole area was covered with a network of *agents provocateurs* and spies. 'Provocation' became the common practice of the NKVD and the *provocateurs* played heroes' parts in the resultant political trials. To prepare for the liquidation of the head of the

Ukrainian Catholic Church, the Metropolitan Archbishop of Lvov, Cardinal Sheptytsky, the NKVD put a number of assistants at his disposal whose duties included a courier service between Lvov and the Vatican. One of them, a cleric, was instructed, besides taking messages to and from the Vatican, to deliver copies to the Gestapo on the way. The object was to provide 'proof' that the Metropolitan was collaborating with the Gestapo.

One of the most sinister events of the Second World War was the murder of Polish officers at Katyn. Although the Soviet Union is still trying to convince the world that this was one of Hitler's crimes, there is no doubt that it was the work of Stalin, Beria, and their henchmen. In September 1939 about 200,000 Polish soldiers fell into Soviet hands. The officers were carefully segregated from the men and treated not as prisoners-of-war but as prisoners of the NKVD. About 8,000, while being transported to Smolensk, were shot in a small wood about thirty miles west of that city.

The massacre was discovered by the Germans in the spring of 1943 and figured largely in Hitler's propaganda. But as in the meantime Hitler's mass murder of Jews, gypsies, and hostages had become known there were doubts as to whether the shooting of the Polish officers was really Stalin's work. Today, when an impartial judgement is possible, and when there are many witnesses in the West of the events at Katyn, it is certain that the Polish officers were shot in batches by a special NKVD squad with shots in the back of the neck, some of them with hands tied behind their backs.

One Russian *émigré*, M. Maksimov, reported in the July/August 1952 number of the Russian journal *Na Rubezhe*, published in Paris, what he saw with his own eyes. None of the papers found with the bodies (passes, family photographs, notes, diaries, Soviet newspapers, etc.) bore a date later than April 1940. The German occupation authorities, at the time, invited various international commissions to Katyn and made an exhibition of the articles found with the corpses. A professor of astronomy from Smolensk, Basilevsky, who had been present at the exhumation, gave a lecture on the subject to the Russian public at the former medical institute at Smolensk and, with tears in his eyes, accused Stalin of the crime. Maksimov, who heard the lecture, relates that the same Basilevsky, again in tears, gave evidence at the Nuremberg trials three years later. But this time, being a Soviet State witness, he alleged that the

Germans were guilty of the Katyn murders. The NKVD in the meantime had 'prepared' their witness.

What were the motives for the crime? The answer is only to be found in the primitive but widespread idea of the 'class struggle' innate in Stalinism. In the eyes of Stalin, Beria, and their followers the Polish officers represented the master class of Polish magnates (*pany*), who had to be exterminated. The thought that the officers could still be of use to Russia in its war with Hitler simply did not occur to them. Perhaps even the opposite thought passed through their minds: the Polish officers were potential or even actual agents of Hitler.

According to information originating in the Soviet Union there were several Katyn massacres. S. I. Karavansky, a prisoner in a work colony, made the following assertion in a petition addressed in 1966 to the Chairman of the Nationalities Soviet of the Supreme Soviet of the USSR. 'In 1940 the Latvian Republic is known to have joined the Soviet Union of its own free will, thereby obviating any form of reprisals against the Latvian Army. Nevertheless, strangely enough, officers of the Latvian Army, who had been invited to take part in tactical manoeuvres in 1941, were interned, and their fate is unknown. The fact remains that of these officers not one has returned home alive. Nor indeed did any of those thousands of innocent Letts who in 1940/41 were subjected to reprisals and deported.' Karavansky reports the wholesale deportation of the Latvian population from the frontier areas to Siberia. The inhabitants of whole towns as well as of villages were removed. If these mass deportations were really essential for military-strategic reasons, the same purpose could have been more humanely accomplished by moving them to areas in Estonia.[96]

That our assumption (that the Russians may have massacred the Polish officers at Katyn because they believed them to be potential Nazis) is by no means far-fetched is shown by numerous arrests ordered by Stalin about this time. Many Poles, Ukrainians, Belorussians, and other democrats or Socialists were arrested on suspicion of being Hitler's agents. They included Jews who had fled east through occupied Poland. A memorable instance is the case of two Jewish Socialists from Poland, Viktor Alter and Henryk Erlich, who after the fall of Moscow took refuge in the Soviet Union. One was taken to the NKVD prison in Moscow, the other to the prison at Lefortovo. Both were badly beaten up as 'Polish and Fascist agents'. We shall refer to their case again on a later occasion (page 157).

An unsuccessful duel with German security

Conditions in the Russian security service were wretched. Not only did the Stalinist leaders distrust those responsible for State security, but the work of the security organs was directed against their own folk. Khrushchev once compared Stalin very aptly to an artilleryman whose shells hit not the enemy, but his own ranks. Time pressed. There was no time to restore a shady profession to its previous level on a broader base, and it was difficult to convince the officials that the real enemies were not their fellow-countrymen.

It was not until the sixties that the Soviets opened their archives, but now the whole world knows what a weak opponent the Soviet security organization was at that time to German security. From October 1939 onwards German agents in large numbers were infiltrated into the Soviet Union. In 1937 and 1938 only single spies had been caught crossing the frontier, but in 1939 there were hundreds. The German intelligence used every opportunity to employ its newly formed special sections for subversive activity. It maintained contacts with nationalist circles among the Ukrainians, Belorussians, Letts, Lithuanians, and Estonians, and it even cooperated with certain offices of the Finnish Government. The Soviets were lucky in that the German intelligence services went to work on false assumptions and therefore made fundamental blunders. The spearhead of German security was on its side, too, strongly inspired by Nazist ideology. Most of their officers, even if they did not identify themselves with the racism of the National Socialists, were militant anti-Communists who, in many cases influenced by the *émigrés*, looked on the Soviet Union as 'a colossus with feet of clay'. Thereby they were misled into a completely false estimate, or rather underestimate, of the Soviets' military potential. On 5 December 1940 Hitler boasted at a secret conference that under the first blow from the German forces, the Soviet army would suffer a greater defeat than that of the French in 1940.[97] True, German intelligence was well informed regarding the Soviet military potential in the frontier area, but the actual strength of the Russian divisions as a whole was unknown. Both western and eastern sources confirm this.

In the East, and especially in the Soviet Union, there is silence even today regarding the fact that Nazi racialism, from the outset, was directed against the Russians, Poles, and Ukrainians as well as against the Jews. In their racial delusion the representatives of the 'master race' even rejected those who were ideologically akin, or in pure naivety believed that the Slav peoples in Hitler's 'New Europe' would have an easier time than under Stalin. In the eyes of Hitler gauleiters Poles and Ukrainians were destined to breed pigs for the 'master nation'. In the end many nationalists landed in German concentration camps, including, for example, Stefan Bandera, who was murdered in Munich after the war. Collaborators with the Germans on occasion received the SS shot in the neck meted out to Polish partisans and resistance fighters.

That the Soviet Union was so badly surprised by the German attack was not so much the fault of its intelligence service as of Stalin's chronic distrustfulness. On 25 December 1940 the Soviet military attaché in Germany received an anonymous letter. It contained precise information concerning Germany's military preparations for an attack on the Soviet Union. The war would break out during 1941. In February 1941 Soviet agents reported the transfer of German divisions from west to east. In March Soviet agents brought off a brilliant coup. They overheard a conversation between Antonescu, the head of the Rumanian government, and the German representative Bering, the subject of their talk being the coming campaign against the Soviet Union. Finally, on 10 April, the security service informed Stalin and Molotov of the substance of a conversation between Hitler and Prince Paul of Bulgaria, in which the exact date of the outbreak of war was mentioned. Richard Sorge confirmed the date from Japan. In May and June the NKVD repeatedly gave warnings of the impending offensive.[98]

Stalin was also officially informed from England about Hitler's intentions. But he remained deaf to all warnings. They disagreed with his own assessment of the situation. But characteristically Stalin's terror apparatus, even on the eve of the war, reacted in a particularly sensitive manner against alleged anti-Soviet conspiracies throughout the country. Everything that was happening at the time behind the German frontier simply did not exist for Stalin. In Soviet works of reference published after Stalin's death Beria as well as Molotov is blamed for Stalin's deafness to all these warnings.[99] The frontier guards came under Beria's authority, and he must have had precise knowledge of how many enemy agents were being infiltrated across the frontier. These numbered some five thousand between October 1939 and December 1940. In the same period German aircraft had crossed into Soviet air space over five hundred times. Beria, according to some works of reference, issued an order that they were not to be fired upon. Such was the situation in Soviet security on the eve of the German-Soviet war.

Chapter Six

In the Front Line of the 'Patriotic War'

Stalin orders a wave of blind terrorism

IMMEDIATELY after the outbreak of the war Stalin ordered the immediate liquidation of anyone anywhere in the Soviet Union who was suspected of espionage. The shootings mostly took place in the concentration camps and prisons, the most extensive massacres being in the Baltic Soviet republics, in Belorussia, and in the Western Ukraine.

A specially difficult problem was presented by the overcrowding of the prisons in these areas. In all the western regions of the Soviet Union the surprise attack of the German armies created chaos. There was no chance of evacuating the prisoners, for the Soviet authorities were not even able to evacuate their own services, records, and employees. So Moscow ordered all political prisoners to be shot. Criminals were released in large numbers on the very day when war broke out, and on the same day the shootings of political prisoners began. For example, on 22 June sections of the NKVD appeared at the Lvov prison and the warders began to drag the prisoners out of their cells. The executions were carried out at first against the chapel wall, and later in the prison courtyards. On 24 June the first women were shot. Many prisoners, in the hope of saving themselves, refused to obey the summons and barricaded themselves in their cells. They met their fate shortly before the arrival of the Germans, massacred in their cells with machine pistols and hand grenades. This ghastly slaughter lasted till 28 June. The German armies arrived at Lvov on the night of 29/30 June.

The murder of Viktor Alter and Henryk Erlich, leading Jewish Socialists in Poland, took place within the framework of this furious action of Soviet security 'against the spies'. For twenty years the two men, at the head of the Socialist organization of Polish Jews known as the 'Bund', had carried on a bitter struggle against any signs of Fascism, and in cooperation with other Polish Socialists had fought for the victory of Democratic Socialism. Not only in Poland, but also in the whole of the international workers' movement, they were well known as honourable and distinguished men. When war broke out in 1939 they took part in the defence of Warsaw against the approaching German troops, but fled eastwards later and were arrested by the Soviets. At the beginning of the German-Soviet conflict they were released, in accordance with the agreement between the Polish general Sikorski and the Soviet government, and evacuated to Kuibyshev. Eye-witnesses report that Alter and Erlich before being released had to be taken to sanatoria, imprisonment and torture having badly affected their health. They were allowed to resume correspondence with their relations in the USA. In December 1941 they were rearrested on Beria's personal instructions and immediately shot.

Why had the two Jewish Socialists to lose their lives at this juncture? The answer to this is very important, as showing the mentality of Stalin, Beria, and their myrmidons. From Beria's biography we know his way of reckoning with the Georgian Social Democrats and Mensheviks. Thence derived his conviction that every Menshevik, every Trotskyist, every Socialist, was an enemy who must be mercilessly destroyed. Had Stalin, Beria, and other Communist leaders been examined by a psychiatrist he would have concluded with certainty that their morbid conviction was quite genuine. These mental degenerates really believed that Mensheviks and Jews, like Erlich and Alter, would support Hitler if given an opportunity. When the American trades union leaders William Green and Philip Murray, together with Professor Albert Einstein, interceded for the imprisoned 'Bund' leaders with Molotov, who at that time was Foreign Minister of the USSR, they received a reply through Litrinov, the Soviet ambassador in the USA, that the two Jewish Socialists had been found to be 'anti-Soviet agents'. They had worked in the Soviet army for peace with Hitler and for this had been sentenced to death by a court martial.

Alter's and Erlich's fate was shared by hundreds of people with similar political views. Only a few are known to have survived this senseless massacre.

Apart from liquidating political prisoners and other enemies the security organs received another order: to leave behind a secret network in the territories occupied by the Germans. A similar instruction was given to the regional committees of the Communist Party of the Soviet Union. It was decided to set up such illegal committees everywhere, side by side with the party officials who normally were evacuated. The security organs had a part to play in staffing the secret party apparatus.

The nationalistic blindness of Hitler's policy suited the Soviet secret police very well. All German-speaking and reliable agents were labelled as 'Volksdeutsch' (i.e. Germans by race) and received instructions to report to Nazi party offices and infiltrate their staffs. This scheme, however, did not work out quite as desired, the advance of the German armies being too rapid. Nevertheless, by this method the Soviet security organs were able to achieve considerable results, especially in the Soviet Ukraine.

On the quest for optimal forms of organization

After the outbreak of the German-Soviet war, the National Defence Committee (Russian abbreviation GOKO) was founded on 30 June 1941. Its chairman was Stalin, with Molotov as his deputy and Voroshilov, Malenkov, and Beria as the other members. Later Mikoyan, Kaganovich, and Bulganin were co-opted. On 30 July 1941 the NKGB and NKVD were reunited into a joint People's Commission of Internal Affairs. This step was necessitated by the somewhat uncertain situation in the Soviet Union. The supervision of the whole civilian life of the country had to be tightened up, and for this purpose a strict centralization was chosen as the most suitable method. The stricter supervision of the Soviet army and fleet that was found to be necessary compelled Stalin and Beria to strengthen the special sections of the NKVD in military and naval staffs. At all social levels and in all Party and civil service departments a serious crisis developed, or more precisely a serious crisis of mood, which lasted until about 1945, when on all fronts the war was taking a favourable turn for Moscow. The

NKVD was unique in its display of toughness, iron discipline, and loyalty to the regime.

The NKVD troops rendered inestimable service in the defence of the Soviet Union. Their fanaticism contributed decisively to raising the morale of the fighting forces. Still more valuable were their services to the armaments industry. It was precisely in that sphere that Beria showed his great organizing ability during the war. True, on various occasions he was entrusted with combat duties—for example in August 1942, when the German armies were approaching the Caucasus and Beria with Kaganovich was organizing the defence in that region—but his chief task throughout the war was the equipping and provisioning of the troops. But the State security services, especially espionage, security, and intelligence, were still his responsibility.

During the bitter fighting with an enemy who was far superior to the Soviet Union in the first phase of the war it was obviously in the interest of the Soviet leadership to give priority to the practical and purely military factors in the army. Stalin probably realized this sooner than his chief assistants. He encouraged journalists and propagandists to soft-pedal their Communistic oratory and instead to appeal directly to pan-Russian chauvinism and the military traditions of Tsarist Russia. At this time relations between the Communist regime and the Russian Orthodox Church improved. The church was drawn into a whole series of patriotic campaigns and the Orthodox priests collected funds for the provision of tanks and planes, and organized gift parcels for the soldiers at the front and the wounded. But at the same time the Soviet security organs in no way slackened their unworthy activities among the troops. They spied on responsible generals and very often calumniated officers who had already lost their lives in the fight against Fascism. Among many cases of the kind one may quote as an example the fate of Lieutenant-General V. Kachalov.

In the fighting near Smolensk Kachalov's unit was given a specially difficult task. It failed, Kachalov's tank was shattered, and he himself was killed. The local peasants buried him in a common grave with fellow officers and other ranks. Although there are several witnesses of these tragic events and although even the Germans announced in their army bulletin that Kachalov, Commander-in-Chief of the 28th Army, had fallen in battle, in company with his staff, another version of the affair was circulated in the Soviet Union. Several years after Stalin's death a Soviet military journal reported that Stalin's specialists in security matters at the time had tried to make political capital out of Kachalov's death for the 'disciplining' of the officer corps of the Soviet army in their usual way.[100]

After the destruction of Kachalov's unit the responsible officers were summoned for an inquiry in Moscow. They rendered a true account of the battle, but Mekhlis, Stalin's henchman, had already formed a plan whereby Kachalov's heroic death could be twisted round and used for propaganda purposes. Mekhlis stigmatized the officers who had been summoned to the inquiry as 'political novices' and explained that Kachalov had certainly not been killed by the Germans. On the contrary, he had long been hatching a plan for going over to the Germans and had even invited some of his comrades to join him! Mekhlis alleged that Kachalov had seized the opportunity on this occasion—he was by no means dead, but was now fighting as a renegade with Hitler's armies against the Soviet Union. By such clumsy methods that violated human dignity the leaders of the security organs hoped to spur on army officers to be always on the watch. General Kachalov was not to be rehabilitated until 1955.

In 1943 there was again a series of changes in the organization of Soviet security.

First of all, in April the People's Commissariat of State Security (NKGB) regained its independence. Merkulov was once again at its head. The NKVD, under the leadership of Beria, was thereby relieved of the heavy problems of State security and became more and more an 'economic' organization. It was responsible for public order and particularly for the smooth functioning of the armaments industry, transport, and army reinforcements.

A second measure, of special importance for the war-time development of the security organs, concerned the special sectors of the NKVD in the army. Preparations for the great offensive of the Soviet armies compelled Stalin to strengthen the authority of the army commanders. With this object it had already been resolved, as far back as October 1942, to get rid of the 'war commissars' so hated by the troops and as a consequence to effect the principle of single command (*Yedinonachaliye*) by the army commanders. In April 1943 the special sections of the NKVD were removed from the army and converted into an independent security organization, directly responsible to the National Committee of Defence. This was the origin of the anti-espionage department of the People's Commissariat of Defence, with the title of 'Death to Spies', in Russian *Smerty Shpionam*, i.e. SMERSH. This gave Stalin all he needed. Firstly, it got rid of the previous two-way division in the supreme command of military security. Smersh became an integral part of the military apparatus and was placed, as a sole anti-espionage centre, under the orders of the National Committee of Defence by way of the People's Commissariat. Secondly, the establishment of Smersh strengthened the authority of the army commanders, who had previously been to a great extent dependent on the special sections of the NKVD.

At the head of Smersh was Viktor Semyonovich Abakumov, the new star of the Soviet security organization. He was a Caucasian (real name, Aba Kum) who in the thirties had become one of Stalin's trusted assistants.

In 1941, as Beria's deputy, he became the leader of the central army administration for anti-espionage. As the head of Smersh he proved himself a ruthless fanatic.

The anti-espionage duties of the security organization were transferred to Smersh. In its expansion Abakumov faced considerable difficulties. True, Stalin had abolished the supervisory organization of the NKVD in the army, but the actual supervision had of course to be maintained. Smersh thus had to function in such a way that the principle of 'sole command' of the army commanders and the soldiers' military pride was not damaged. Smersh was completely independent and did not even use the normal army means of communication. On each staff there was a Smersh office which *de facto* watched all officers. The methods, however, were radically changed. The size of the Smersh sections was not unduly inflated, as was the case with other similar organs, but kept as small as possible. In an army staff the whole Smersh personnel was not allowed to number more than a hundred, a mere fraction of the numbers employed in the former special sections of the NKVD. Supervision of the army was not, of course, the sole task of Smersh; it was more important to take effective measures against spies and traitors. One of their special tasks was to make use of selected German officer prisoners of war and captured agents for their own purposes.

Thus Smersh gradually became a weapon of offence. When the Soviet armies entered Poland, Rumania, and Hungary in 1944, Smersh was given more and more political tasks.

The NKGB attached great importance to the partisan movements in the German-occupied areas. Plans for them had already been worked out in 1941 by the staff of the NKVD. The first groups of any strength were formed in 1942. They were organized on military lines and received their orders from a central partisan staff under P. K. Ponomarenko, established in the Soviet General Staff on 30 May 1942. In August 1942 Voroshilov, Marshal of the Soviet Union, was appointed Commander-in-Chief on the staff of the partisan movement. Its expansion was the work of a conference of partisan commanders called at the Kremlin in September 1942. Stalin himself drafted its duties. By 1943 it formed an important element in Moscow's military plans. Its organization lay at first in the hands of the IVth Department of the NKGB. In the same year it was resolved to develop an intelligence service in the partisan groups, and a number of specialists were allotted to them. It was soon found that the partisans were not only militarily valuable, but that they could also exercise important intelligence functions. The NKGB was thus enabled to accomplish much that had had to be neglected before the war from lack of time. A number of terroristic acts, too, were carried out with the help of partisans, such as the attempt on the life of Wilhelm Kube in Minsk, and the murder of Otto Bauer, Vice-Governor of Galicia, who was shot in Lvov.

At the end of 1942 the NKGB succeeded in activating the network of its secret agents in the areas occupied by Germany. Their task was trenchantly formulated by Stalin himself—'to make life behind the enemy lines intolerable for them'. Their agents infiltrated all the activities of the Gestapo and other authorities.

In a journal published for Ukrainian *émigrés* a certain M. Selezy wrote about the Cheidze-Chapayev case.[101] Cheidze was the chief representative of the NKGB in German-occupied Ukraine. When it was certain that the Ukraine was about to be occupied by Soviet troops, he received instructions to insinuate himself into the Ukrainian nationalist movement. By chance, however, he was unmasked and later killed, but when he was caught he willingly divulged to the Ukrainian nationalists the methods used by the NKGB agents. Their principal task was to plant NKVD agents in the Gestapo and the staff of Koch, the Reichskommissar. Cheidze asserted that his agents were employed in all the larger towns of the Ukraine as interpreters and clerks. When it was found impossible to plant an agent in a Gestapo office at least a woman agent worked there as a cleaner.

The NKGB had two main aims in the German-occupied areas. In the first place they tried to obtain valuable military and political news. But it was still more important for them to render the shortsighted policy of the Germans in the occupied areas so unendurable that the population would look upon the return of Soviet power as a deliverance. Various means were adopted. In Rovno for example the Soviet agents shot a high German official and brought about blood reprisals on the Ukrainian nationalists. A further aim of the agents in this case was to encourage the destruction of the anti-Communist elements through the Gestapo.

Another classic example shows how the NKVD knew how to attain their objects with the help of the Gestapo.[102] In a town in the Donets basin a former White officer applied to the German security service for employment. He had papers to show that he had fought against the Reds in the civil war and had for this been persecuted under the Soviets. Colonel Kurochkin, as he called himself, was able to quote many respected citizens of the town as references. Now he was anxious to revenge himself on the accursed Bolsheviks. He knew all about the illegal Communist organization which had been left behind in the occupied area and he supplied a list of forty Party members. His story was foolproof. It was soon established that the persons on his list were in fact active Communists. One night they were arrested and shot by court martial. Colonel Kurochkin thereupon vanished without a trace. The solution of the puzzle was that all Party members had received strict instructions to accompany the retreating Red Army. Those who stayed behind were looked upon by the Soviets as traitors—and the Gestapo was made the instrument of their punishment. Kurochkin was able to carry out his instructions with ridiculous ease, and the Party members who had actually been sent to work illegally in the occupied areas were enabled thenceforth to carry on their activities unhampered.

The NKGB agents in the Ukraine succeeded in their efforts to stir up and inflame all quarrels in the occupied areas. During the German occupation, for instance, violent religious strife flared up between the 'Ukrainian Autocephalous Orthodox Church' and the 'Ukrainian Autonomous Church'. Cheidze declared that NKGB agents had stirred up the conflict most successfully. Even the leaders of the two opposing groups, Bishop Oleksy, head of the Ukrainian Autonomous Church in Kremyanetz, and Bishop Manuil, of the Orthodox Church, were both agents of the NKGB. Simple believers might think it was a church dispute about canonical questions, but the real object was to demoralize the faithful and undermine the authority of the Church. This was all the more important for the NKGB because Hitler was planning to use the church as a tool for training the people to be obedient.

Whole peoples deported

A new task for the Soviet security organs was in connection with the deportation of whole peoples into the eastern parts of the Union.[103] The first victims of this idea of Stalin's were the Volga Germans. On 28 August 1941 Stalin ordered that the 300,000 Germans of the 'Autonomous Volga Republic' should be resettled. One of Beria's chief assistants, I. A. Serov, was entrusted with the task. The Polish General Anders in exile, has written a graphic description of the event. He himself happened to be in the Volga Germans' territory and was an eyewitness of Stalin's crime. In the autumn of 1941 a battalion of parachutists, NKVD troops in German uniforms, descended on the territory. When the Volga Germans vociferously welcomed those whom they believed to be German soldiers, the NKVD had a good excuse for both a bloody massacre and the expulsion of the Volga Germans from their homeland.

With similar treacherous methods the Soviet security organs in 1943 and 1944 deported the Chechens, Ingushes, Karachayers, Kalmyks, and Krim Tartars. There are several accounts of these events. A student from Grozny told in the *Sotsialistichesky Vestnik* of September 1947 how the Checheno-Ingush Republic was liquidated. In February 1944 large NKVD units arrived in Studebakers at Grozny, capital of the North Caucasian republic of the Chechens and Ingushes. In the local press at the time there appeared articles such as 'Help our beloved Red Army in their mountain manoeuvres'. Soviet agents talked everywhere of manoeuvres, with the result that nobody found it at all strange that in all the towns and villages small garrisons should be posted. On 23 February 'Army Day' was to be celebrated everywhere in the republic. In the villages there were to be bonfires, dancing, and singing. But when the people assembled they were surrounded by soldiers: the men were arrested, the women and children with hand-luggage were ordered to take their places with their menfolk without delay. The houses of those who had not turned up for the festivities were searched and the occupants arrested. The action was so sudden and thorough that all the men in the whole Checheno-Ingush Republic were arrested in two or three hours. On 24 February they were taken with their families to Grozny and locked up in goods waggons. Students were mobilized to drive the people like cattle to the places of assembly and to transport the furniture left behind to repositories. Shortly afterwards Russian settlers, mostly from the Kursk and Orel districts, began to take over the houses of the Chechens and Ingushes. By the end of March life was once again running on 'normal' lines. It was merely that a republic had been deleted from the map of the Soviet Union, and a whole people transported to Central Asia and Siberia.

A sober balance sheet of the deportations gives some idea of how much suffering Stalin inflicted on the non-Russian peoples of the Soviet Union between 1941 and 1944.

August/September 1941: expulsion of the Volga Germans.
October/November 1943: deportation of the Karachayers.
December 1943: deportation of the Kalmyks.
February 1944: deportation of the Chechens and Ingushes.
March/April 1944: deportation of the Balkars.
June 1944: deportation of the Crimean Tatars.

According to Soviet sources, there were in 1939 some 407,690 Chechens, 92,074 Ingushes, 75,737 Karachayers, 42,666 Balkars, 134,271 Kalmyks, about 382,000 Volga Germans, and about 202,000 Crimean Tatars. It we deduct from the total of about 1,336,000 a bare third on account of war losses, mobilization, etc., we realize that more than a million people were affected by the deportations.

The concentration camp system during the war

The greatest Socialist economic organization, GULAG, was converted during the war years into a mighty armaments concern. Beria gave orders that the strictness of the discipline in the concentration camps should be somewhat slackened. 'Patriotic entertainments' were organized, newspapers were allowed, and hopes were encouraged that victory at the front would bring many benefits. But at the same time the prisoners' living conditions constantly deteriorated. Rations dwindled, the death rate rose.

Beria was responsible for the utilization of forced labour. Convicts built airfields and roads in the districts of Soroka, Onega, Kargopol, North Dvina, North Urals, and Pechora, and they excavated underground aerodromes in the Kuibyshev area. They built defences on the Manchurian frontier. American seamen report that convicts were also employed in unloading lend-lease goods in the White Sea harbours. Under the severest hardships they built strategic railways in the mountains of the Caspian Sea and in the North Caucasus.

Forced labour probably figured in Stalin's strategic plans as early as 1940. That is the only possible explanation of the fact that the number of forced labourers in the concentration camps in 1940 and 1941 grew from day to day. The labour reserves now consisted of Poles, Balts, and Bessarabians; later came German prisoners of war, Italians, Hungarians, and finally Japanese.

The fate of the Polish prisoners was exceptional. On the basis of an agreement between Stalin and the head of the Polish government in London, General Sikorski, hundreds of thousands of Poles were released from the camps in 1941 and many were even given permission to quit Soviet soil. In that way even during the war precise information about the Soviet concentration camps reached the West. Semi-official Polish organizations have calculated that from 1940 until the amnesty of 30 July 1941, about 270,000 of the 1,080,000 Poles in the Soviet camps perished. But even the Sikorski amnesty brought no lasting relief to the Poles in the Soviet Union. When two years later relations between Moscow and the Polish government in exile were broken off, the security organs started hunting out the Poles again, their activities being directed principally against the relatives of members of the 'Home Army', which was one of the strongest anti-German resistance organizations but acted in accordance with the instructions of the Polish government in exile.

One of the important but little-known 'services' performed by the GULAG during the war consisted of recruiting fighting groups from the concentration camps. A certain G. Kargaskov wrote on the subject in a periodical published in Paris under the title of *Na Rubezhe,* November 1951.[104] Its statements were confirmed by several ex-inmates of concentration camps. According to this article a special department was set up in the GULAG in October 1941 for the military mobilization of the prisoners. All prisoners who by 15 October 1942 had not been sentenced for breach of Paragraph 18 of the criminal code were in principle liable to military service. The GULAG army recruited from them was composed of 20 per cent criminals, 30 per cent *ukazniki* (those who had been late for work or produced goods of poor quality or committed petty thefts), 20 per cent persons who had committed offences (non-political) against the State, and 30 per cent collective-farm workers who had broken the collective-farm regulations. In the officers' opinion the GULAG thus had an army of a million and a half men at its disposal. That amounted to 10 per cent of all the men mobilized for the army during the war, but not more than 15 per cent of the total population of the concentration camps and prisons.

In April 1945 the Presidium of the Supreme Soviet of the USSR decreed new forms of punishment: death by hanging and imprisonment with hard labour. These sterner measures were intended to be more effective deterrents to spies, deserters, and saboteurs. But as at this time the Soviet armies were beginning to liberate more and more territories from German occupation, the measures at first affected principally the populations of those areas. Any form of contact with the Germans was adjudged by the NKGB and the war tribunals as collaboration with the enemy or as 'passive treason'. Thousands of people fell victims to this interpretation, which was later extended to the deported Russian workers and prisoners of war. Some estimate that the number of those condemned on such grounds ran into millions.

Tactics in Poland and other territories
occupied by the Red Armies

The Soviet security organs were faced with particularly difficult problems in Poland during the Second World war. Stalin was trying to create the pre-conditions necessary for a future pro-Communist development in Poland, for the pro-Communist resistance movement against the German occupation in Poland was much smaller that the well-developed 'Home Army' (AK) which acted under orders from the exiled Polish government in London.

As early as 1942 the 'IVth Department' of the NKGB worked out meticulously what were to be their future tactics in Poland. Josef Swiatlo,[105] a leading Polish security officer, who himself had taken part in many crimes committed by the Polish security organs in Stalin's time, fled to the West in 1954, and published sensational documents concerning the activities of the secret police in Poland. Among them were some illustrating the work of the Soviet security organs among the occupying Germans. As in the Soviet territories occupied by the Germans, *provocation* was adopted in Poland too as an effective method for attaining Soviet ends. The main objective was the Gestapo. All imaginable methods were used to gain as much influence as possible within it, and this served both to conceal the activities of one's own people and to bring about the liquidation of one's opponents through the Gestapo. Swiatlo reported that in the Poland of 1942 a special cell was set up with a Soviet Russian, Novotko, as its director, to supply the Gestapo with misleading information. The result was a fiasco. When Novotko came from the Soviet Union to Poland, he looked for a Communist whom he could plant in the Gestapo as a trustworthy agent. Finally he chose a Communist named Molojec, who had attended a Comintern school and had been in Spain during the civil war. Molojec, however, was an idealist and simply could not understand how genuine Communists could hatch such a scheme. Becoming convinced that Novotko was really a Gestapo agent, he shot him dead at one of their interviews. The Polish Communists later tried to twist the story round so as to make it appear that Molojec was a Gestapo agent. The head of the false information cell later appointed a second agent, Korab, who disappeared in the Soviet Union after the German retreat.

Encouraged by the success which they had enjoyed in the Ukraine, the Soviet security organs became obsessed by the idea of winning influence in the Gestapo at any price. They caused an organization to be set up, under two well-meaning and unsuspicious men, S. Grad and Slowikowski, which called itself 'Miecs i Plug' (Sword and Plough); they then planted in it a former Soviet agent, Hrinkiewicz, with the task of making the whole organization a tool of the Soviet security service. Grad and Slowikowski were betrayed to the Gestapo, and Hrinkiewicz took over the leadership of the cell. A certain Skonieczny became the intermediary between the 'Polish Freedom Organization' and the Gestapo, which he supplied with a constant flow of false information. By such methods the Soviets were able to direct the attention of the Gestapo to the anti-Communists in the Home Army.

As in other large cities, the Soviet security organizations succeeded in infiltrating their men direct into the Warsaw Gestapo. The representative of the NKGB in the Warsaw Gestapo was an old Communist from Lomtza named Ritter. For his services he was appointed after the war as the head of a department in the Polish Ministry of State Security, under the name of Jastrzemski. The German-sounding name, Ritter, had merely been used as a bait for the racial fanatics in the Gestapo.

Ritter was far from being the only Soviet agent in the Warsaw Gestapo, in which a goodly row of *provocateurs* had been planted. They were in regular communication with a special network which radioed their messages to Moscow daily. The same arrangements prevailed in other Polish cities, as indeed in all territories still occupied by German troops.

When the Red Army entered Rumanian, Czechoslovakian, or Polish territory, Smersh was always in the vanguard. Their original duty was counter-espionage, but they began to concern themselves more and more with political matters. There are fairly detailed reports concerning their methods. Shortly before the Red Army entered Poland, 'operations groups' were formed in Smersh, headed by Polish-speaking officers, who were also versed in local dialects. They looked primarily for German agents and collaborators—a term which, particularly in Poland, was of very wide significance. Apart from actual collaborators, hundreds of Polish non-Communists were liquidated who were actually anti-Nazi.

The arbitrary conduct of the operations groups was particularly marked in the Oder-Neisse region.

According to Swiatlo the operations groups in Poland were exclusively composed of specially trained Soviet security men, with only one or two Polish agents assigned to each group as interpreters. Swiatlo affirms that the Polish Communists, especially Gomulka, constantly complained to the authorities of the tyrannical behaviour of the Smersh groups. Their protests, however, achieved very little, but merely tended to discredit Gomulka. When he was arrested later on, they tried to use his protests against the arbitrariness of Smersh as proof of his disloyalty to the Soviet Union.

The activities of Smersh in other countries are reported by a certain N. Sinevirsky,[106] who was himself an interpreter in an operations group, later fled to the West, and published his memoirs in 1948. He was a Carpatho-Ukrainian, who, because of his linguistic talents—he spoke Russian, Ukrainian, Hungarian, Czech, and German—was assigned to the operations groups on the south-eastern front. Sinevirsky tells us that Smersh was divided into seven departments. The first supervised the front-line troops; the second or 'operations department' was always hunting down spies. In the chaotic circumstances of the war, when no regular criminal procedure was possible, the number of victims was enormous. The third or 'secret' department watched for 'suspicious developments' anywhere in the world. It was also responsible for compiling liquidation lists, even in non-Soviet countries, Germany for instance. The fourth department was concerned with interrogations; it extorted the necessary 'confessions', usually at night and with the use of Yezhovshchina methods. The judicial system of Smersh was the business of the fifth department. It basically resembled the so-called 'troikas' of the Yezhovshchina (page 37), with sentences delivered on a conveyor-belt. Apart from capital punishment, sentences of ten to fifteen years' hard labour were normal. Personnel and administration were dealt with by the sixth and seventh departments.

Sinevirsky illustrates his report from his own experiences. The Smersh officers were like a portrait gallery of fanatics and alcoholics in a chamber of horrors. At Košice, in Czechoslovakia, where Sinevirsky was employed, work went on day and night without a break. 'There were guards stationed in the corridors and interrogations going on in all the rooms. Sobs, screams, moans, pleas, combined to form a hellish symphony of terror. It was like a nightmarish torture-chamber, a monstrous mincing machine.' Košice was not the only place; wherever the Smersh groups appeared the story was the same.

Towards their western allies in the Hitler war the Soviet security organs adopted special tactics. According to David J. Dallin, in his book on Soviet espionage, there were various spy rings in the USA serving the Soviet General Staff and the NKVD or NKGB. The Soviet intelligence services planted a network of helpers and informants in various civil and military administrations, including American intelligence. In Washington there was a Soviet spy ring, which included among others, Harry Dexter White, father of the Morgenthau Plan, Major William Ullman, in military intelligence, and Maurice Halperin of the Secretary of State's office. President Roosevelt was greatly influenced by his numerous advisers, some of whom had had relations for years with the Soviet secret service. Soviet intelligence made unscrupulous use of the natural sympathies of the American people for the peoples of the Soviet Union who were their allies in the war against Hitler. Even while the Hitler war was at its height they made desperate efforts to infiltrate American intelligence. This was the period when the Soviet atom espionage began. Its success need not be gone into here.

The arrogance and unscrupulousness of the ambitious Soviet security service, combined with its primitive methods, were the cause of countless human tragedies. Among them was the fate of the Swedish diplomat Raul Wallenberg, who from pure idealism tried to save the Jews of Hungary from the murderous SS commandos. Officially a secretary at the Swedish mission in Hungary, he was in fact the leader of a department which, under the control of Ambassador Danielson, was organizing aid for the Jews in Budapest. On 15 January 1944 the Soviet forces occupied Pest, in which Wallenberg's office was situated. On the 16th Dekanozov, Beria's friend, acting at the time as Deputy Foreign Minister, informed the Swedish Ambassador in Moscow that Wallenberg was on the Soviet side of the front line and that measures had been taken for the security of his person and property. Wallenberg, however, disappeared into the dungeons of the Soviet secret police, who treated him as a good friend of the 'Zionist intriguers' and as a dangerous 'imperialist agent'. They believed they would have no difficulty in extracting from him statements to the detriment of Jewish organizations in the West. His eventual fate, in spite of energetic efforts by the Swedish government, remains obscure, even after Stalin's death.

For the sake of impartiality, it can here be noted that in many books and periodicals published after the Second World War—when the Cold War was already in full swing—it is stated that the American intelligence service paid back the Soviets in their own coin. In the American Bureau of Strategic Services there was a Russian department as early as 1941, which carried out systematic espionage in the Soviet Union during the war. It is stated several times that the Moscow military mission of the USA, with its branches in Odessa, Vladivostok, Murmansk, and Archangel, constantly indulged in such practices.

Final defeat of German intelligence

As the situation on the various fronts grew more favourable the Soviet security organs won a constantly growing superiority over the German intelligence. This was not primarily a result of the disintegration of German military power. Among other causes, lapse of time and conditions in the reoccupied or newly conquered territories fostered a new flowering in the art of espionage. The fact that Soviet security organs at the beginning of the war had fallen behind their German counterparts is attributed by present-day Soviet historians to a lack of trained personnel. Especially in the front-line areas the Soviets had to suffer many a defeat. The activities of German agents could not be speedily suppressed, and it was not until 1942 that the measures taken against them began to be more effective. More and more agents were detected and arrested. The year 1942 also saw an increase in the number of German agents who came over to Communism and declared their willingness to continue working—this time against the Germans. In 1943 a very important source of information for the Germans dried up. The wireless communications of the Soviet forces, between each other and between them and their headquarters, previously poorly disguised, were vastly improved by the use of freshly trained personnel.

As time went on, outstanding successes were achieved by the Soviet security organs in the German-occupied territories and even in the German intelligence service itself. 'Chekists' were scattered throughout the territories, some in the partisan detachments, others living openly in the cities or in the country. These managed to plant their own agents in the German security training schools. There were even Soviet agents in the German security section No. 103 who kept their headquarters informed as to German plans.[107] The Chairman of the Committee of State Security, V. Semichastny, stated in May 1963 that as early as 1942 the Chekists were in possession of important evidence about the military situation, obtained from the German army staffs. 'In the spring of 1943 information was collected regarding the transfer of German infantry and artillery divisions from Europe and Africa to the Kursk front and regarding an offensive of Fascist troops in that area.'[108] It seems that the work of the Soviet security service in Belorussia was particularly successful. Hundreds of diversion and espionage groups, numbering over 10,000 persons, were posted to that area, and they brought off several sensational coups. In August 1942, for example, a high officer in the German intelligence, Von Veith, was kidnapped and taken to Moscow by plane. A Comsomol girl played the chief part in the affair. She had been planted on Von Veith as a secretary and she lured him into a trap. Today she is working in a Minsk clinic. Another girl was planted in order to render harmless another high intelligence officer, Karl Kruck. A group of agents succeeded in kidnapping another security man, Kurt Schlegel.[109]

Recent publications throw further light on a number of political murders in Belorussia. From them it appears that Fabian Akinchits, an old Belorussian politician, who had once been a member of a famous democratic freedom organization, the 'Hromada', but in the thirties had gone over to the National Socialists, was shot dead on the instructions of the Soviet security service. The order was carried out by Akinchits's private secretary, Karpov. In December 1943 the mayor of Minsk, Vaclav Ivanovski, was murdered; in 1943 also, the editor of the *Belorusskaya Gazeta*, Kozlovski.[110] On the Soviet side one of the greatest coups of Soviet security, the attempt on the life of Wilhelm Kube, Gauleiter of Belorussia, is admitted only with great reluctance. The reason for his attitude is that the would-be assassin, N. Y. Khokhlov, fled to the West in 1954 and published memoirs which were painful for the Soviets.

Making a general survey of the activities of the Soviet security organs during the Second World War, we must conclude that behind the turbulent war scenes the most important and basic event was the amalgamation of the military intelligence service with the special departments of the NKGB and the formation of a unified anti-espionage central office, Smersh. Many Kremlinologists, among them Boris Meissner, rightly assert that the Soviet secret police emerged from the war not only stronger than ever, but also as the principal pillar of Stalin's autocracy. Later we will see that it was directly subordinated, not to the Central Committee, nor to the Politbureau or the Party Secretariat, but to Stalin himself. The Stalin personality cult reached its zenith during the Second World War; hand in hand with Stalin's rise the importance of the Party apparatus dwindled, especially that of the Central Committee.

Beria at the outbreak of the war played a paramount role in the security organization. He was Stalin's authoritative adviser on all security matters. But everything points to the conclusion that his direct influence on security gradually disappeared during the war. On the other hand, Beria's friends, like Abakumov and Kruglov, strengthened their positions, so that the balance of power gradually shifted. On many questions Stalin no longer needed Beria's mediation: Abakumov and Kruglov were sufficient. Beria's chief services lay in the armaments industry and transport. For this he was awarded the title of 'Hero of Socialist Labour' in 1943, and that of 'Marshal of the Soviet Union' in 1945.

In Volume IX of the *Bolshaya Sovietskaya Entsyklopediya*, which also contains the official biography of Beria, the task assigned to Beria is defined as 'raising the production of armaments and munitions in difficult wartime conditions'. We can also learn details of his war-time activities from other reliable sources, for instance that Beria was responsible for the civic defence committees, with the local NKVD apparatus as a backbone. He also had a share in the plan for the mobilization of man-power. On 30 June 1941, when a committee for the computation and distribution of man-power was set up by the Council of People's Commissars, Beria laid his plan before the first session. The speedy cure for a bottleneck in the munitions industry—the mass production of bomb-throwers —was his personal contribution.

Chapter Seven

Stalin's 'Second Yezhovshchina'

(1945–1953)

Changes in the organization of the security service

WITH the victory of the Soviets and their western allies over Germany came a new political development in the Soviet Union. Whereas before the war Stalin was a dictator who decided everything himself, the course of the war had forced upon him certain forms of collegiality. At first he frequently had to act in accordance with other people's opinions. Moreover during the first phase of the war he without doubt suffered from some sort of 'guilt complex'. From Khrushchev's 'secret' speech to the 20th Party Congress we know that in the first days of the war Stalin had no confidence in victory. 'All that Lenin created we have lost for ever', he said openly at a meeting of the Communist leaders.

Stalin at that time took a short step backwards from his autocratic attitude, he even tried to correct some of his former errors. Because he desperately needed capable officers, he released, for instance the survivors of the Tukhachevsky affair. Most of them, however, were human wrecks; only a few were still employable after all their tortures, but these included Marshal Rokosovsky, Marshal Kirill Meretskov, and Colonel-General (later Marshal) Gorbatov.

In time, however, Stalin gradually returned to his dictatorial ways. Once again he began to decide everything himself, he claimed to be a genius, infallible. It was Stalin who promoted himself to be *Vozhdy*, the Leader of the 'Great Patriotic War' and its winner.

The *Vozhdy's* rule was not based on the Central Committee of the Communist Party or on the rest of the party apparatus. During the war, as we have seen, there developed the nucleus of a new Stalin terror apparatus consisting of well-tried security officers of the NKGB—Smersh plus military intelligence. Out of them the post-war security service was constituted, and they also formed the group nearest Stalin, on whom he could fully rely.

The reorganized and restaffed security service occupied a new position in the Soviet system. True, it had previously become more and more Stalin's personal instrument, yet before the war there was always at least a loose connection between it and the Party apparatus. But after the war the security service was completely independent of the Party and under the direct orders of Stalin's private secretariat.

The head of Stalin's private office, or 'grey eminence', Aleksandr Poskrebyshev, was one of those creatures who had played an important part behind the scenes in the great purges and assassinations of the twenties. Poskrebyshev made his first appearance in 1922 as 'adviser for special tasks' in the Central Committee of the Communist Party. In 1928 he was appointed head of the 'special sector' in the secretariat of the Central Committee. In March 1939 he received the Order of Lenin for his 'exemplary and devoted activity'. He was responsible for the personal security of Stalin and submitted to him proposals for the composition of his innermost group of helpers. When the fighting on the fronts died down, he once again became the chief wire-puller in the Stalin circle. Those who knew the conditions at the summit of the Party after 1945 describe Poskrebyshev as an organizing genius with a phenomenal memory, and a master of intrigue. Few were able, as he was, to retain Stalin's trust and friendship until the dictator's death.

In foreign countries practically nobody was aware of Poskrebyshev's true role, until after Stalin's death semi-official indications showed that he was the link between Stalin the *Vozhdy* and his faithful guards the secret police.

NKGB and NKVD remained separate institutions from April 1943 until 1953. In 1946 all the People's Commissariats became Ministries, and the former NKVD from then on called itself the Ministry of Internal Affairs (MVD), while the NKGB became the Ministry of State Security (MGB).

In 1946 there were important changes in personnel in both ministries. Colonel-General Kruglov took Beria's place in January as Minister of Internal Affairs. Sergey Nikoforovich Kruglov was chosen in 1939 as a candidate for the Central Committee of the Communist Party of the Soviet Union and from 1943 to 1946 he was deputy director of Smersh. During the conferences of the 'Big Four' at Tehran, Yalta, and Potsdam he was prominent as the man responsible for security measures. His appointment as Minister of Internal Affairs was in no way a direct affront to Beria, for the most powerful political apparatus even after the war was still the MGB. Much more significant was the replacement of the Minister of State Security, Colonel-General V. N. Merkulov, by the Army General V. S. Abakumov on 18 October 1946.

Marshal Beria was now formally excluded from the direct leadership of the security organs. As deputy chairman of the Council of Ministers and Stalin's closest assistant he probably continued to coordinate the activities of the security apparatus at the highest level. Yet Western observers believe that Beria was entrusted with the 'super-espionage' task.[111] With the help of the information service of the former NKGB, military intelligence, and the economic espionage set-up, and with the use of all possible diplomatic connections, he created a special organization for atom espionage, which Stalin had declared to be a 'task of special importance to the State'. It is only this fact that makes the obscure role of Beria in the subsequent history of the Soviet secret police more comprehensible.

Abakumov led off with reforming the Ministry of State Security. In this he was able to make good use of the apparatus of the recently abolished Smersh.

It is significant that the Foreign Department was advanced to become the premier unit of the post-war MGB. Its duties were now much wider than before the war. As a consequence of the growing tension between East and West political espionage in foreign countries began to be of ever-increasing importance. New tasks, too, in the so-called 'People's Democratic States' automatically necessitated a vast increase of personnel in the Foreign Department. Originally there was only one department responsible for the supervision of all the 'People's Democratic States'. Very soon, however, each individual state in the eastern bloc was found to need its own department, which supervised its development along uniform lines. A completely new department was created to watch the *émigrés* from the Soviet Union and their activities. The Foreign Department of course continued to supervise the diplomatic service, the trade missions, and the Soviet representatives and agents abroad. Stresses and spheres of work, however, had changed since pre-war times.

The second great office of MGB was the 'Operations Department', the objectives of which were also now considerably altered. Whereas formerly it had busied itself with economic and technical tasks, preliminary investigations, the security of especially valuable objects, and the censorship of letters and the Press, it now became responsible for all internal security work. Its sphere extended from watching suspects to the organization of the large-scale use of units from MGB, MVD, and militia, from the arrest of individuals to the suppression of partisan groups and other illegal organizations.

The third great office of MGB was the Espionage and Anti-Espionage Department, fundamentally reformed. This took over most of the personnel of Smersh. It directed both military and political anti-espionage and supervised the whole Soviet army and fleet. Military intelligence, on the other hand, was still kept apart from the MGB apparatus; it had no anti-espionage duties but confined itself to the collection of purely military information.

The Secret Political Office, SPO, which had to supervise the whole civilian sector, was also reorganized to a great extent. Its departments specialized in certain sections of civilian life inside the Soviet Union. For instance, there were departments dealing with oppositional currents within the Party and with secret anti-Soviet organizations. The 5th Department supervised industrial establishments, the 6th university professors, school teachers, and instructors, and there was even a special department dealing with the religious life of the country.

Restoration of order in the Baltic states, Western Belorussia, and the Ukraine

Naturally, all these reforms were primarily dictated by post-war conditions. For the security organs the war was very far from being ended. Unrest was everywhere, especially in the Baltic republics, Belorussia, and the Ukraine, where there were still strong

anti-Soviet groups of partisans. Some of these groups were surrounded by MGB troops and destroyed in military operations.
But as a rule the partisans and other illegal organizations could
not be tackled by military action, as they were strongly backed
by the rest of the population. So the Operations Department of
the MGB adopted new methods, and these, incidentally, were
successfully used later against foreign spies.

In Moscow and two other cities of the Soviet Union volunteers
from 1945 onwards were taught in special courses how to deal
with rebel bands. They first learned the language of the area which
harboured the partisans. Picked teachers then acquainted them with
peculiarities of dialect and the history of the national group to
whose territory they were to be posted. They had to adopt the
nationalist attitude of the group in question and acquire a thorough
knowledge of its religious usages. Out of these volunteers partisan
squads were formed, with deceptively genuine equipment, and
sent into the forests. They lived a hard life for months—sometimes, e.g. in the Carpathians, for years—in the same conditions
as their opponents. Their object was to win the confidence of the
real partisans. In order to prove their genuineness and trust-
worthiness they sometimes fought side by side with the real
partisans against the Soviets. Only when they knew the whole
organization of a partisan unit and all their helpers did they show
their true colours and destroy them with the aid of the MGB
apparatus.

Although the MGB spared no pains to enable their people to
obtain entry into the ranks of the anti-Communist parties, their
agents were not always successful.

In the little Ukrainian-Galician town of Rogatyn a certain
M. Y. Dovhy, twenty-one years old, was working in 1947 as a
waiter in an inn. Of course nobody in the neighbourhood knew
that he was an MGB agent with the cover-name of Zoroka.
He spent much of his time with other young men who rendered
many services to the partisans, made himself out to be an ardent
anti-Communist, and offered to help them. The partisans wanted
butter, so he stole some from the inn where he worked. As the
amounts of stolen butter increased more and more, he for the
first time aroused the suspicions of the extremely wary partisans.
Their distrust was intensified when one day he applied to be

allowed to join the partisan group, alleging that the authorities were on the point of discovering his thefts. One of the leading partisans told him to his face that they did not trust him and required from him a better proof of reliability than stolen butter, i.e. they demanded that he kill the MGB chief of the Rogatyn district, Captain Anosov. Dovhy, who was in direct communication with the MGB headquarters at Stanislav, reported the facts and received permission to carry out the assassination. That evening he shot Anosov. Uselessly, because the security officer of the partisans had not been asleep. Dovhy was questioned and eventually had to admit his treachery. He was shot, and the well-organized partisans circulated a leaflet among the people of the Rogatyn district, entitled *How Captain Anosov died*.[112]

This example shows that it was far from easy for the MGB to restore order and security to all districts in which there were anti-Communist partisan movements. The partisan groups in Estonia, Latvia, Lithuania, Belorussia, and the Ukraine held out in some cases until 1952. Thousands of members of the security service fell on this front. The Soviet Ukraine party organ *Radyanska Ukraina* stated in its issue of 20 December 1957: 'In the post-war period the State security service, with the help of active party members and the Soviet, the Consomols, and the mass of the workers, have accomplished an important task in liquidating the armed bands of the nationalist resistance. During the German-Fascist occupation the bands of Ukrainian bourgeois nationalists amalgamated with *émigré* units. They armed themselves, and with the assistance of reactionary circles from the Western states hindered the rapid reconstruction of the economy destroyed in the war and normalization of the workers' lives. In the most difficult times of the struggle against the bandits, the Chekists of the Ukraine, the frontier guards, and the internal security forces displayed courage and bravery, some of them dying a hero's death.'

The Soviet supervision system in the People's Democratic States
   The Foreign Department of the MGB was engaged in a completely different area, i.e. the supervision of developments in the People's Democratic States, but in principle its methods were similar. In all these countries ministries of state security had been set up on the Soviet model. Stalin, who was extremely distrustful

of the Communist parties in People's Democratic countries, converted the ministries into instruments of Soviet policy. Nobody knew better than he what a deep rift existed between Moscow and the Communists of Poland and Yugoslavia. He himself and his creatures Yezhov and Yagoda had created the rift by shooting the old guard of Polish and Yugoslavian Communism.

Swiatlo, already mentioned as the security officer who fled to the West, gives a very precise account of how Soviet supervision in Poland functioned. A Bureau of the Soviet Adviser was set up in the Polish Ministry of State Security to serve as a link between the Polish State Security Service and the Soviet MGB. Formally the ministry was of course dependent on the Central Committee of the Polish United Workers' Party, but without doubt the Soviet Adviser General Lalin held the whip-hand. That, however, was not enough. The ministry was composed of seventeen departments, and there was a Soviet adviser in each department. The Soviets thus, without open interference from Moscow, controlled the whole political, economic, and cultural life of Poland. Besides the advisers in the Ministry of State Security there was also a representative of MGB resident in Poland with a separate staff. Moreover, when one takes into account the numerous Soviet advisers active in the Polish army and all economic staffs, one obtains a clear picture of the Soviet penetration of the People's Democratic states and their governments. This single example also shows the extent and powers of the Soviet security organs at this period.

Concentration camps and forced labour as permanent parts of the model Stalinist society

The hopes of millions of concentration camp inmates that they would be amnestied at the end of the war were not fulfilled. The number of prisoners did not decrease; on the contrary, it constantly grew. First came victims of the Smersh terror in the areas formerly occupied by the Germans. Thousands of people were sent to the camps as 'collaborators'. Ex-prisoners speak of a special group among them, women accused of having intercourse with Germans. In the camps they were branded as *s pod nyemtsa*, which means roughly that at one time they were 'under a German'. In all these cases a prominent element consisted of slanders, intrigues, denunciations, and personal enmities, often of the most primitive kind.

Later came the former Vlasov soldiers and men of every nationality who had fought on the German side. Many of the 'eastern workers' deported unwillingly to Germany also landed in the camps; it sufficed that during their period of forced labour they had 'collaborated' with Germans. An interesting though not very large group among the new arrivals was composed of former Russian *émigrés* who had been living in Poland, Yugoslavia, Bulgaria, and other East or Central European countries. Finally a large and important contingent consisted of German prisoners of war and, in the Far East, of Japanese war prisoners.

The new contingents were all treated by the State security organs as 'politicals'. Accordingly discipline in the camps, which had slackened somewhat during the war, was again tightened. In past years conditions in the camps had become stabilized; the generation of Old Bolsheviks, Trotskyists, and other deviants had been exterminated or reduced to insignificance. The camps had become to some extent normal economic institutions in the Soviet Union which were 'building Socialism'. The cruelly disappointed hopes of an amnesty, and the arrival of new 'politicals' with all its consequences produced in the old inmates a wave of disappointment and depression, further intensified by a recent worsening in living conditions. The equipment of the camps was not ready for the vast new intake, and food supplies were insufficient; the bureaucrats of GULAG needed time to reorientate themselves to the new conditions and gradually to set new plans in motion. It was not until 1948–50 that the situation improved. Then food supplies became ampler, and a start was made on paying wages to the prisoners: from 10 to (in exceptional cases) 40 roubles a month, which could be spent on margarine, jam, cigarettes, etc., at canteens inside the camps.

In 1948 a small reform was carried out in the concentration camps. All prisoners were re-registered and those who had been arrested for especially serious political crimes, for instance members of illegal anti-Soviet organizations, espionage suspects, etc., were transferred to *spetslagerya*, special camps with severer discipline, situated in the far north. Neither relatives' visits nor correspondence were permitted. Treatment was extremely harsh and no prisoner dared oppose the arbitrary orders of the guards. After release no ex-prisoner was allowed to return to his former home town, but had to settle in the vicinity of his camp. And as a rule he had to continue in the same occupation as in camp.[113]

For those left behind in the old camps conditions improved, not in any way for humanitarian reasons, but because it was necessary to husband labour reserves in view of the new tasks ahead. The new Five-Year Plan was started in 1946. A long series of projects in the plan were carried out by concentration camp labour, such as the reconstruction of the Stalin Canal, its extension from the White Sea to the Baltic, and the building of many new harbours and railways. There was actually a branch of industry which was monopolized by the concentration camps: the expansion of forestry in Siberia and other areas beyond the Urals was exclusively reserved for forced labour. In the first half of the plan, as a result of mental depression and insufficient food, a considerable fall in prisoners' productivity was noticeable. Then suddenly there was more to eat, medical treatment improved, and there was some relief for the sick. But the sole purpose of all these improvements was to raise production, without which the fulfilment of the economic plans would be impossible.

The 'perfection' of the Stalin system after the Second World War involved, among other things, a fresh differentiation in the 'Socialist society'. It is impossible to state exactly the total number of concentration camp inmates. Expert estimates vary between eight and twenty million. The latter figure is perhaps somewhat exaggerated, but if we say about twelve million in and around 1950, that would make about 16 per cent of the adult population of the Soviet Union. Apart from the large class of bureaucrats at various levels, the army and police, and the vast mass of workers eking out a bare existence in industry and collective farms, there arose a new and 'stable social factor', the slave class, or concentration camp inmates. It was only with their help that Stalin could carry out his plans. The prisoners' labour, measured in terms of modern technology, or even in comparison with free labour outside the camps, was certainly not used profitably. But that aspect of the matter had never much influence on Stalin, even in the case of regular labour. The concentration camps provided cheap labour, and the most important consideration was that it could be used in conditions, climatic and otherwise, that no ordinary labourer would stand.

The Zhdanovshchina

Especially difficult internal political problems in the ideological sphere faced the Soviet Communists after the war. Millions of Soviet citizens had come in contact with the Western way of life and culture during the war, and had returned home 'infected'. At the October Festival in 1946 Molotov assured the country that all of them had returned 'with still greater love for the Soviet Union and Soviet law and order'. But this was more of a wish than a fact. There were signs of disruption everywhere. To crush them, a fresh internal terror broke out, which will go down in Soviet history as the 'Zhdanovshchina'.

The most candid account of this spell of terrorism is to be found in the 1959 edition of the textbook *History of the Communist Party of the Soviet Union*. Here is an extract: [114] 'During the war many millions of men lived in territories which were temporarily occupied by the enemy. Millions of men were deported to Germany, many Soviet soldiers found themselves prisoners of war. All were given ideological treatment by the Hitlerites. During the anti-Fascist westward march of the liberating Soviet armies, some of our troops remained in the territories of capitalist states, and the reactionaries tried every conceivable means to influence them. In the western parts of Belorussia, the Ukraine, and the Baltic republics nationalist groups left behind by Hitler spread anti-Soviet propaganda among the population. By these and other channels many Soviet subjects came under an ideologically bad influence.' This revealing extract derives from Khrushchev's chroniclers, at a time when much of Stalin's teaching had already been contradicted. One can well imagine the feelings of Stalin and his close associates after 1945 towards millions of their Soviet fellow-citizens. All who had been in any sort of contact with the West were looked upon by Stalin as potential enemies, regardless of whether they came from German concentration camps or from prisoner of war camps or whether they had been forcibly deported to work in Germany. No wonder, then, that the security service became busier day after day.

Stalin found in Andrey Aleksandrovich Zhdanov the right man for stiffening the ideological backbone of the Party and the masses. Even before the Second World War Zhdanov had been one of the most prominent leaders of the Communist Party. The great trust that Stalin reposed in him is shown in his appointment as secretary of the Leningrad region of the Party in place of the murdered Kirov. All official documents of the Stalin period emphasize that Zhdanov belonged to 'the kernel of the Bolshevik party led by Stalin', which after Lenin's death had to bear the main burden of the struggle 'for Lenin's cause'. In war time, as a member of the war council for the Leningrad front, he was responsible for a sector of the front line, was promoted to Colonel-General in 1944, and thereafter was constantly employed in the party headquarters in Moscow. In September 1946, after he had been appointed Secretary of the Central Committee of the Communist Party, he began his large-scale ideological crusade with a speech to the active section of the Leningrad party organization about editorial faults in the literary journals *Svezda* and *Leningrad*.

'Guided by instructions from Stalin', he announced a great offensive against those Soviet writers who 'in the mire of a total lack of original ideas' kowtowed to Western culture and preached West European decadence. He demanded from writers that they should educate all the Soviet people, and especially the youth, in the spirit of Bolshevik pride and in faith in the invincibility of the Soviet system, and he pleaded in all his lectures for a return to the valued traditions of Russian culture. His campaign jumped from one subject to another. In June 1947 a struggle began for the restoration of Party principles in philosophy. Zhdanov demanded that 'professorial wisdom' should be made a bulwark against bourgeois ideas. In January 1948 he denounced formalism in music.

All this was by no means a merely educational measure. Zhdanov's concepts were an attempt to unite Russian nationalism and the acknowledgement of the Messianic role of Russian culture with the principles of revolutionary Communism. The existing repertoire of the categories of hostile persons who had to be liquidated, such as Trotskyists, spies, and enemies of the Party, was enlarged by Zhdanov to include 'cosmopolitans, Jewish and bourgeois nationalists, and Zionists'. Even in the early post-war years there were many arrests, mainly of intellectuals, based on the Zhdanovshchina. In practical terms the Zhdanovshchina was an attack on the non-Russian peoples of the Soviet Union and a tightening up of the situation in the ideological sector, including the Party. When, only a few months after Zhdanov's death in the

Kremlin, murderers commissioned by Stalin carried out their dastardly work, they were in any case ideologically and carefully trained beforehand by the Zhdanovshchina.

A speculation of the Western Kremlinologists: the struggle between 'Zhdanovists' and 'Malenkovists'

In the Soviet Union's concept of foreign politics and the correct attitude towards Communist parties in the Western countries there were difficulties, because Stalin had not yet taken a clear line. Many alleged that immediately after 1945 there had been two groups within the Soviet leadership, representing two different opinions on this subject. One group believed that the end of the war was not causing any worsening of the crisis in the capitalist world. A number of respected economists even dared to submit a scientific basis for this theory. Varga, a Soviet economic theorist of Hungarian origin, had published a book on *Changes in the Economy of Capitalism as a Result of the Second World War*, which put forward the followed theses. (1) 'Capitalist governments are in a position to make plans not only during the war but in peace time also.' (2) 'The USA will help in the reconstruction of Western Europe, and this reconstruction will be carried out on a capitalist basis.' (3) 'The relations between the colonies and their Western motherlands will be reformed.' Varga went furthest in this group of theorists and was consequently the object of the most violent criticism. The conception of the whole group, however, can be expressed in a single sentence: that the chief aim of Soviet foreign policy should be the strengthening of the Eastern bloc and the position of the Soviet Union itself. The prospect of a speedy revolution in the capitalist world must be looked upon with great scepticism.

Malenkov and his friends are believed to have shared this view.

The second group, to which Zhdanov and his followers adhered, counted on revolution in Western Europe and advocated the fostering of international Communism. They believed that internal difficulties in France and Italy would become so intense that seizure of power by the Stalinist parties would be a real possibility. In that case it was the task of the Soviet army to defend and consolidate what had been won. They were confirmed in their view when at that time France and Italy were swept by a wave of large-scale strikes and there were indisputable signs of political crises in the West.

The assumption that both groups, the Zhdanovists and the Malenkovists, were quarrelling with each other in the Central Committee misled a number of Western experts into all sorts of speculations regarding the true state of affairs in the Communist leadership after 1945. Zhdanov was alleged to have been supported by army circles and a number of economists like Voznesensky. The backbone of the Malenkovists was supposed to be a triumvirate consisting of Malenkov, Beria, and Khrushchev, whose connections with the security service counterbalanced Zhdanov's connections with the army. When in 1948 Stalin, after Zhdanov's death, ordered a bloody purge in the Party, the authors of this theory were triumphant, because they thought they had found the key to the understanding of events. The scarcity of news from the Kremlin led finally to such outspoken twisting of the facts as for example the assertion that Malenkov had been removed in 1946 from his post as Secretary to the Central Committee of the Communist Party and replaced by Zhdanov.

From the present-day viewpoint things look completely different. The theory that Zhdanovists were fighting Malenkovists, with Stalin a neutral observer of the contest, can no longer be upheld. Now it is clear that all the great changes between 1945 and 1953— the rise and fall of Communist leaders, the purges, intrigues, and assassinations—were entirely Stalin's work. It was not possible for either Zhdanov or Malenkov to take any step on his own initiative or to effectuate any personal ideas of his own, either in internal or in external policy. Nevertheless, when we spoke of two different conceptions of the international situation, and if there actually were at that time officials representing varying views, that was nothing more than a proof that Stalin himself had not yet made up his mind regarding the situation and the tactics he ought to pursue.

Events in the international sphere and the occurrence of economic difficulties in the Soviet Union in and around the year 1949 played into Stalin's hands by helping him to overcome the crisis. 'Revolutionary strikes' in France and unrest in Italy, both happening in 1948, did not bring the results for which Moscow yearned. The Berlin blockade was converted into a fiasco for Moscow by the prompt and energetic action of the USA. But worst of all was

Tito's 'heresy', a break between Belgrade and Moscow and the failure of the attempt to set up a command centre for all the Communist parties of the European East Bloc States—the Cominform. The attempt did not last long, for the Cominform—the information centre of the Communist and workers' parties—was not established until Spetember 1947, at the Schreiberhau conference of representatives from the Communist parties of Yugoslavia, Bulgaria, Rumania, Hungary, Poland, the Soviet Union, France, Czechoslovakia, and Italy. The Communist Party of the Soviet Union was represented at the conference by Zhdanov and Malenkov. The chief speech was delivered by Zhdanov, but those of Slansky, Djilas, Gomulka, and Anna Pauker were equally well received.

On 31 August 1948, at exactly the right moment, Zhdanov died. There simply had to be a change at this juncture. Stalin himself was to provide evidence that a medically contrived death was not out of the question. Shortly before Stalin's death a number of prominent doctors were arrested, and Stalin made them responsible for the death of Zhdanov among others. The spirit of Yagoda, the poisoner, lived on.

The question of whether there was a quarrel between the Malenkovists and the Zhdanovists is of little moment as an explanation of events subsequent to 1945. If we mention it here at all it is only as a concession to those Kremlinologists for whom literary disagreement with Communism and philosophical speculations are of more importance than facts, dates, and a sober analysis. From 1939 till Stalin's death there prevailed in the Soviet Union a social order which, in spite of certain shocks caused by war events, suffered no qualitative changes, but continued to develop according to a single law—the will of the despot, the perfecting at any price of the Stalin system. The scope allowed to Stalin's assistants for political initiatives of any kind was narrowed, and their functions were so completely restricted to the purely executive that any theorizing about a struggle for power behind Stalin's back must be described as pure fantasy. It forms part of that stage of Kremlinology in which our knowledge of the Soviet Union is necessarily of the scantiest.

What we call the 'Second Yezhovshchina', because of the methods employed, was no less macabre than the original Yezhovshchina of 1937. It consisted of a series of deliberate acts of malignant terrorism which at first affected only a few selected persons. On the basis of extorted confessions the 'guilty' men were tried in secret and condemned to death. Whereas the 1937 reign of terror struck blindly around and indiscriminately at persons of any social group, the second Yezhovshchina was better organized. The security organs were instructed to lay 'snares' (*dyelo*). In 1950 their number increased enormously, and the terror spread in ever widening circles. What Stalin was basically working for has still to be discussed.

The 'Leningrad Affair'

This is without doubt the darkest chapter in post-war Soviet history. The affair took the following course. In 1949 Stalin ordered the security organs 'to provide proofs of the treacherous roles played by certain prominent Communists'. He had several motives for this step. It is certain that some of the Party members disagreed with Stalin's attitude to Tito. Clearly there were among the Leningrad Communists an unusual number of malcontents, and Stalin informed the Leningrad party organization of the fact. His first blows were directed at the organization itself. Probably of equal importance was Stalin's intention to make a clean sweep of the Party leadership in Leningrad. The younger 'apparatchiks', who had gone through the hard school of war, were blindly devoted to him, and Stalin looked on them as more suitable collaborators than the old staff. Moreover he needed scapegoats for several failures in the first post-war Five-Year Plan. The victims of the 'Leningrad Affair' were a number of high Party officials, including some who had nothing whatever to do with the Leningrad party organization. The most important personage among the accused was Nikolay Alekseyevich Voznesensky, born in 1903 and a member of the party since 1919. From 1935 on he had worked in various planning offices in Leningrad; in 1938 he became Chairman of the GOS Plan for the Soviet Union, and in 1939 Deputy Chairman of the Council of People's Commissars of the USSR. He retained both these posts until his violent end. In the Second World War he was Stalin's closest assistant on the Defence Committee, and after 1945 he occupied a leading position on the State committee for the restoration of the economy in the areas liberated from the Germans. He became candidate for the Politbureau of the Central

Committee of the Communist Party (Bolshevik) in February 1941, and full member in 1947. At the end of 1947 Voznesensky published a work on *The War Economy of the Soviet Union during the Patriotic War* (Voyennaya Ekonomika SSSR v Period Otechestvennoy Voyny). It was the first attempt at a scientific treatment of the subject and was very well received. Nevertheless Stalin declared it to be anti-Marxist and 'unscientific'. M. Suslov, the Party theorist, was partly responsible for this verdict. On 24 December 1952, i.e. over two years after Voznesensky's death, *Pravda* published an unfavourable review of the book. At the beginning of 1949 Voznesensky was removed from all his posts. He was excluded from the Politbureau of the Central Committee and later from the Central Committee itself; he was forbidden to take up any employment whatsoever. Completely isolated, he stayed at home working on his book *The Political Economy of Communism*. All his letters to Stalin remained unanswered. Meanwhile his former associates on the GOS Plan had been arrested and the old game began again. Confessions were extorted from them, on the basis of which Voznesensky himself was taken into custody at the end of 1949. On 30 September 1950 he was shot. From evidence published after Stalin's death it is clear that Beria and Malenkov were not free from all part in the 'Leningrad Affair.'[115]

Another prominent victim of the Leningrad Affair was Aleksey Aleksandrovich Kuznetsov, born 1905, Party member since 1925. After 1932 he held various party posts in Leningrad, and in 1937/8 was second regional secretary there. For his services in the fighting around Leningrad he was promoted to Lieutenant-General and twice decorated with the Order of Lenin. In 1945/6 he was first regional and city secretary of Leningrad, and in 1946 he was promoted to be Secretary of the Central Committee of the Communist Party of the Soviet Union. He was arrested in February 1949. Together with Voznesensky and Kuznetsov other prominent leaders disappeared into the dungeons of the MGB. These included M. I. Rodionov, chairman of the ministerial council of the Russian SFSR, P. Z. Popkov, who succeeded Kuznetsov in Leningrad, G. M. Popov, secretary of the Central Committee and secretary of the Moscow Party organization, and Bolyakov, president of the Supreme Court of the USSR.

Soviet citizens first heard the details of the Leningrad Affair from the 'secret' speech of Khrushchev at the 20th Party Congress: 'The facts show that the Leningrad Affair likewise originated in the arbitrary and despotic attitude of Stalin towards Party members.[116] He blamed Beria and Abakumov for their share in the affair. But Khrushchev did not reveal all. In 1957, when he went on to attack Malenkov, several officials involved Malenkov in joint responsibility for the events in Leningrad. This attempt, however, to make Beria, Abakumov, and Malenkov alone responsible for the Leningrad Affair is unconvincing. The person really responsible for this campaign of extermination in the Communist leadership was Stalin himself.

While terror was still raging among the 'Leningraders', fresh difficulties, unforeseen by Stalin, cropped up. They were caused by miscalculations in the drafting of the second Five-Year Plan after the war. The first Five-Year Plan had ended in 1949 with a surplus. War damage to industry had been more quickly made good than was expected, much old machinery turned out to be still usable, and dismantled factories removed from Germany helped to get the Russian economy going again. The Soviet planners prided themselves on the achievement, but failed to realize that the productivity rate during the period of reconstruction of a ruined industry must necessarily be well above the average. To reckon on the same rate of increase in a second plan and to keep to it was impossible. Voznesensky and some of the others probably realized this and offered warnings. But Stalin and his ambitious Party planners were anxious to reach exaggerated targets. By 1950 it was already clear that the economy of the Soviet Union, as a consequence of miscalculations, was facing a crisis. The dismantled 'enemy factories' and machinery were by now in need of modernization or replacement. Reparations were out of the question. Bottlenecks began to appear in all the more important branches of industry.

It is known that some of the Communists murdered in the 'Leningrad Affair', notably Voznesensky, expressed views differing from Stalin's on questions of economic policy. However, they were not liquidated as responsible for the miscalculations in the planning field, but for a directly opposite reason. If the affair received any publicity whatsoever, they were shot precisely because

of their warnings. In the eyes of a success-drunk Stalin they were
defeatists, and Abakumov saw to it that defeatism could be proved
to be of a traitorous character.

The Yugoslav problem was also mixed up with the Leningrad
Affair. In January 1948, shortly before relations between Moscow
and Belgrade were broken off, a Yugoslav delegation headed by
Djilas arrived in the Soviet Union. They were coolly received in
Moscow, but very cordially in Leningrad. When relations between
Moscow and Belgrade continued to worsen, Stalin needed some
'proof' that the Yugoslav Communists were conspiring with certain Soviet Communists in order to split the Party. Moreover he
wanted to make an example of somebody in order to banish from
the minds of Soviet Communists any vestige of doubt that his line,
in opposition to that of the Yugoslavs, was the correct one.

It is difficult to say exactly how many people were liquidated in
the Leningrad Affair. At the 19th Party Congress in 1952 Kozlov
reported that in Leningrad city and region two thousand new
officials had recently been appointed. To make room for them, a
similar number at least must have been displaced. The figure is
much too modest, as Draconian measures were taken not only
against Party officials but also against various civil servants in
Leningrad and the region, against trades union officials, and even
against their kith and kin. A woman released from a Siberian concentration camp after Stalin's death said in a private conversation
that she and the wife of Y. F. Kapustin, second secretary of the
Party committee of Leningrad city, had been arrested. The latter
had stated that Party officials and other civil servants in a series
of trials had mostly been condemned to death by shooting, while
their nearest relatives had after brief court proceedings been
sentenced to imprisonment for periods of from five to fifteen years.
Wives of head officials had received sentences of as much as twenty-
five years.

Pogrom of the Jewish intellectual élite. The 'Crimean Affair'

When a totalitarian regime wants to divert public opinion from
its own insufficiences, it frequently—as we are taught by recent
history—resorts to the despicable expedient of making the Jews
responsible for all failures and miscalculations.

In the Soviet Union, too, this recipe has been followed since

7—TUOT * *

1948 in the case of Jews active in the political life of the country. The MGB prosecuted this campaign against the Zionists under the pretext that they formed 'the long arm of American imperialism'. About 1950 this criminal attitude was accentuated. The Zionists, they said, are not only hostile to us, they are saboteurs and noxious to our industry. The subsequent measures taken against the Jews have (as in the case of the Leningrad Affair) been given a collective name, the 'Crimean Affair'.

Stalin frequently used anti-semitic feelings in the Soviet Union for his own purpose.[117] In the liquidation lists of the Yezhovshchina there were always a number of Jewish intellectuals, politicians, and artists. In 1936, for example, Jewish writers such as Ittsig Kharik, Lev Süsskind, Duniets, and Bronstein disappeared into the dungeons of the Soviet security service; in 1937, Moshe Litvakov, Esther Frumkin, Moshe Kulbak, and Max Erlich. Jewish organizations in the West have published many documents to prove that even during the war, while Jews were being murdered by Hitler's special squads, Stalin did not cease from anti-semitic persecution.

In 1946 Marshal Chuykov, according to witnesses, began a purge of the Jewish officers in the Red Army. Nikolaus Nyaradi, the former Hungarian minister, gives a vivid picture in his memoirs of the anti-semitic feelings of the Communist leadership at this time. Although the Soviet Union laws forbid any sort of racial defamation, many Jewish Communists of Jewish extraction complained to him that everywhere they were greeted with the contemptuous name of *Zhid* (Yid). When Kaftanov, the Soviet Minister of Education, introduced Ilya Ehrenburg to Nyaradi, he said to him: 'You know he's a Jew, but in spite of that he's a prominent Communist and a good Soviet patriot.'

The part played by the Zhdanovshchina in this respect has already been described. It reached its apogee on 28 January 1948, with an article in *Pravda*: 'Cosmopolitans and anti-patriots are as dangerous to the Soviet Union as parasites on plants.' The theatre critics denounced in the article were without exception Jews. Even after Zhdanov's death the columns of the Soviet press were more and more filled with articles against cosmopolitans and Zionists.

In the autumn of 1948 there were happenings in Moscow, which, as witnesses report, filled Stalin with fury. During the New Year festival in and around the Moscow synagogues thousands and thousands of Jews assembled to welcome Mrs Golda Meir, Israel's foreign minister. Mrs Meir had come to Moscow to attend the festivities accompanying the opening of the Israelite embassy. There was a demonstration such as Moscow had not seen for years. It was renewed a week later, when the Jews celebrated their Day of Atonement. Thousands of Jews, filled with national pride, came to the Israelite embassy to see the offices, to ask for information regarding the possibility of emigration, and to inquire after relatives from whom they had been parted in the confusion of war.

It is easy to imagine how Stalin reacted, for in his eyes every nationality-conscious Jew was a follower of Zionism. He ordered fresh repressive measures, in Moscow above all. The MGB carried out a midnight raid on Jewish publishing offices and printing works, confiscating all the material found there and shutting down the businesses. The Jewish periodicals *Einheit* and *Emes*, published in Moscow, were closed down. The prosecution of the 'Jewish Anti-Fascist Committee' initiated a wild hunt for 'Zionists and saboteurs'. This committee had been founded in 1942 by Soviet Jews, 'to help the Soviet Union, Britain, and the USA overthrow Hitler and other Fascists', as *Izvestiya* wrote on 24 April 1942.

Most of the prominent Soviet Jews were on the committee. A deputation from it visited the USA in 1954 and collected from American Jews a sum of two million dollars, which it put at the disposal of the Soviet Government. The services of the Jewish Anti-Fascist Committee during the war were a valuable contribution to Allied victory.

Shortly after the demonstrations Stalin ordered the MGB to get rid of Shlomo Michoels, president of the Jewish Anti-Fascist Committee, who was a famous actor and producer at the Jewish theatre in Moscow and holder of the Order of Lenin. Like Kirov's bodyguard (page 81) he died in a car accident. On this occasion, too, he was the only casualty, and those who caused the accident were never found. Soon afterwards the devil broke loose. All the leading members of the committee, except Ehrenburg, were arrested, including such well-known personalities as S. A. Lozovsky, politician, trades union leader, publicist and diplomat; Shakhne Epstein, writer and secretary of the committee; Perets Markish, a famous Jewish poet, holder of the Order of Lenin; the writers

Ittsig Feffer, E. Gordon, and David Bergelson; and the literary critics I. Dobrushkin and I. Nusinov.

At the same time there were mass arrests of Jewish intellectuals throughout the Soviet Union. Among the Soviet writers of Jewish extraction arrested in the Ukraine was Leib Moiseyevich Kvitko, the poet.

Many of the arrested Jews were executed by the MGB after separate trials. Out of the bulk of them the secret police, in their customary way, manufactured a 'conspiracy', which was given the name of the 'Crimean Affair'.[118] In order to be able to understand the accusations hatched by the specialists of the MGB we must go into further details.

The Crimea was depopulated at the end of the war, mainly because of the forcible deportation of the Crimean Tatars ordered by Stalin. When the Crimea was recolonized by Russians and Ukrainians there was a great scarcity of wine-growers. Among the Soviet Jews a scheme was formed to resettle the Crimea with Jews. The tragedy was that the scheme originated from Jews who were Soviet patriots and definitely opposed to Zionism, and who were trying to stem the flow of Soviet Jews to Israel. They tried to convince the responsible persons in the Party and the Government that one could only counter the Jews' desire for emigration by offering them better opportunities in the homeland. The Crimea seemed the most suitable area. One must not forget that at that time thousands of Jews from the East were returning to their home towns and villages, where for various reasons they found life almost unbearable. Their former homes were occupied, their jobs filled; the Jewish families who had remained behind had perished in Hitler's camps.

The Soviet security organs twisted these efforts round, in a way that suited them. They extorted from Jewish writers and intellectuals the confessions that they needed to justify their accusations, e.g. that the Jewish Anti-Fascist Committee had become an agency of Zionism and American imperialism. They wanted to settle the Crimea with Jews so as later to be able to separate it from the Soviet Union and turn it into an anti-Soviet strongpoint.

All those arrested in the 'Crimean Affair' were shot in 1952. Only a few members of their families survived the rigours of the concentration camps and beatings up.

The Crimean and Leningrad Affairs are collective terms for a series of trials and executions. A study of the Soviet newspapers of the period shows that there were at least two series of liquidations in the Leningrad Affair. The Crimean Affair is characterized by trials for high treason and a series of individual liquidations, chiefly in Moscow, but in Kiev and Minsk also.

The destruction of the flower of the Jewish intelligentsia was accompanied in all the Soviet republics by ever-increasing pogroms. Worst of all was the fate of the Jews in the Ukraine, where there were constant trials of 'saboteurs and black marketeers'. The anti-semitic persecution worsened daily and approached its culmination shortly before Stalin's death.

The 'Mingrelian' and other affairs

Another wave of purges will go down in Stalinist history as the 'Mingrelian Affair'.[119] At the end of 1951 and the beginning of 1952 indications in the press showed that mass arrests were taking place in Georgia. Among those who disappeared at that time were First Secretary K. N. Cherkvani, Second Secretary M. Y. Baramiya, and Third Secretary Budzhiashvili, besides a large number of other civil servants from the various Party and government offices. It was not until after the 20th Party Congress that the background of the Georgian purges became known. Khrushchev said at the time: 'Forged documents were produced as proof that there existed in Georgia a nationalist organization which was planning the liquidation of Soviet power with the help of imperialist forces. The alleged plot was foiled by arresting a number of responsible party and state officials in Georgia. As was afterwards shown, the whole business was a slander directed at the Party organization in Georgia.'

After the Second World War there was a whole series of similar 'affairs', in which officers, factory managers, and scientific experts fell victim to Stalin's executioners. But we know much less about them than about the repressive measures of the thirties. It is only by a careful study of newspapers and periodicals that something can be learnt.

For instance, in 1950 Armenak Artemovich Khanferyants (Khadyakov) was sentenced to death at a secret trial, most

probably with a group of other officers. In 1942 he had been commander-in-chief of an air force army and had rendered great
services in the fighting for the reconquest of the Ukraine and
around Berlin, being promoted to Marshal of the Air Force in
1944. In 1945 he took part in the conference at Yalta. Another
well-known officer, Nikifor Zakharovich Kolyada, was awarded
the Order of Lenin in 1942 and later arrested. On his deathbed he
heard the news of his rehabilitation. Finally Lev Mikhailovich
Galler, who had distinguished himself in the civil war and escaped
the 1937 purge. His career was as follows: Deputy Commander-
in-Chief of the Navy, in 1938 Naval Chief of Staff, 1940–47
Deputy People's Commissar of the Navy. His official biography ends
in 1948, in which year he was most probably arrested. He died in
concentration camp in 1950.

*The monster trials of the NKGB in the People's Democratic
Republics*

Now let us turn our attention to the People's Democratic Republics, Russian satellites. It is not our intention to describe the
activities of the Soviet security organs and intelligence services
abroad, for we are concerned principally with the waves of terrorism in the history of the Soviet Union. But in the first place Stalin
looked on the People's Democratic Republics exclusively as his
personal domains, and secondly the goings-on there are well calculated to illustrate in a general fashion the methods of the Soviet
secret police.

The conflict between Moscow and Belgrade was historically
important not only for the stage which we in this book call the
'Second Yezhovshchina'. A definitive judgement of Yugoslav
Communism is not yet possible, but one thing is certain: we have
Tito and the Yugoslav Communists to thank for the unmasking,
while Stalin was still alive, of the criminal nature of Stalinism and
its methods of exploitation. Tito's resistance to Stalin led to the
dissolution of the Cominform, which, set up in 1947, was the information bureau of the Communist and Workers' parties. How
did it happen?

In a speech delivered at Stolice on 30 September 1949, Marshal
Tito accused the Soviet Union of having begun, immediately after

the war, to set the Balkan peoples against one another. This old imperialist policy—*divide et impera*—was used by Stalin in order more easily to further his own plans from a position of superior power. The Yugoslav Communists very quickly saw through the schemes of the Russian 'elder brother', and, although Yugoslavia after the war was in a state of extreme distress, its leaders did their utmost to cultivate friendly relations with their neighbours, especially with Hungary, Bulgaria, and Rumania. The government, for instance, declared itself ready to give financial assistance for reconstruction in Albania. Yugoslavia showed itself particularly tolerant in the so-called Macedonian question. Members of the Macedonian groups of people live in Bulgaria, Greece, and Albania, as well as in Yugoslavia. In the federal republic of Yugoslavia they were granted autonomy, and at the same time an enormous step forward in the history of national relations in the Balkans was taken in the 'Balkan Federation' project.

It is almost unknown in the West that Tito was not only the father of this project, but that in Georgy Dimitrov, the Bulgarian, he had a powerful ally. As long ago as 1947 the two men signed an agreement intended to solve the Macedonian problem. On easily understandable grounds Stalin condemned their efforts. Any movement towards emancipation among the Balkan peoples was a thorn in his flesh. Moreover, with his chauvinistic attitude, he had long ago subordinated Communist ideals to the imperialist interests of the Soviet State. For Moscow Bulgaria was important as a militarily strategic base, especially with reference to Greece and Turkey, of which Moscow wanted to have sole disposal. The idea of a Balkan Federation countered these plans. Dimitrov was an unlucky figure in the affair. On the one hand he probably recognized the true nature of Soviet Communism under Stalin, on the other the former favourite of Stalin lacked the courage to draw the necessary political consequences for his country. The Bled agreement was not kept, but Dimitrov, in spite of pressure from Moscow, had not given up his plans for a Balkan federation. He was merely looking for a form acceptable to Stalin. While the Yugoslav Communists strove for a complete federalization of the Balkans, Dimitrov proposed a form of federation between Bulgaria and Yugoslavia only. But Moscow was decisively opposed to any such

plans. Of no less significance than these political differences was
the resistance of the Yugoslavs to economic exploitation by
Moscow. When the situation was clearly deteriorating, Stalin put
in the Soviet security organs. After the Communist Party of
Yugoslavia had been expelled from the Cominform, the Stalinists
recognized the Communist leader Georgy Dimitrov as its greatest
enemy in the Balkans. In December 1948 Dimitrov risked arrang-
ing a secret meeting at Topčider in Serbia, at which Bulgaria was
represented by Traicho Kostov-Junev and Yugoslavia by
Milovan Djilas, Tito's closest associate at the time. There is no
official report of the meeting. Dimitrov tried to encourage the
Yugoslavs in their plan, and his final words to his Yugoslav allies
sound like the testament of an old warrior: 'Drzte czrsto', Hold
fast!

Meanwhile the Stalinist secret police machine was working at
full blast. In the Bulgarian leadership the Stalinists discovered a
devoted ally in the person of Chervenkov. When Vyshinsky, at
that time deputy chairman of the ministerial council of the USSR,
returned to Moscow from a conference of the United Nations in
Paris, he was accompanied by Dimitrov, who was alleged to have
been forced by illness to seek the medical help of the best Soviet
doctors. Three weeks later his corpse was despatched from Moscow
to Sofia. The Stalinists shed crocodile tears at the demise of a
trusted comrade. Numerous articles and obituaries honoured him
as a loyal son of the Cominform. But Stalin and his security organs
were by no means content with a single victim. In Bulgaria
Dimitrov's best friend, Traicho Kostov, was arrested under
suspicion of having, on Tito's orders, plotted Dimitrov's
death.[120]

The purges and liquidations in the Soviet Union were no out-
of-the-ordinary performances of the MGB. They took place even
in their own household. But what Stalin and the MGB were trying
to accomplish in nearly all the People's Democratic Republics was
in fact the proof of the perfection of their criminal methods and
also of the power of the Soviet security organs in the 'befriended'
states. A series of trials based on forged documents or extorted
confessions took place under the direct supervision of the Soviet
security specialists.

VICTIMS OF THE TRIAL OF BULGARIAN COMMUNISTS
(December 1949)

Condemned to death below: hanged
  Traicho Kostov-Junev
Condemned to penal servitude for life:
  Professor Ivan Stefanov Khadshi-Mateev
  Nikola Pavlov Kolev
  Nikola Nechev Petkov
  Ivan Slavov Gavronov
  Ivan Georgiev Tutev
Condemned to 15 years' penal servitude:
  Boris Antonov Christov
  Sonya Stefanova Tsoncheva
  Blagoi Ivanov Khadshi-Pantshov
Condemned to 12 years' penal servitude:
  Vasil Atanasov Ivansov
Condemned to 8 years' penal servitude:
  Iliya Ivanov Boyaltsaliev

In October 1948, in Albania, the deputy prime minister and minister of the interior, who was also secretary of the Albanian Communist Party, Lieutenant-General Kochi Dzodze, was arrested, and on 11 June 1949 he was shot. In January 1949 Gomulka, prime minister and general secretary of the Polish United Workers' Party was removed from his office, and in 1951 he was arrested. In June 1949 László Rajk with a group of Hungarian Communists was arrested and in October was sentenced to death by hanging on the basis of forged documents and extorted confessions. On 26 March 1949 Traicho Kostov, mentioned above, was expelled from the Politbureau and Central Committee of the Bulgarian Communist Party, arrested, and, in December of the same year, executed. One of the most impressive trials of the sort was that of Czechoslovak Communists and their leader Rudolf Slansky. The veterans of the Czechoslovak Communist movement were, through forged documents, branded as agents and without exception sentenced to be hanged.

In Poland the Soviet agents and their Polish minions were not so successful. They soon ran into difficulties. On 3 June 1950 the trial took place in Warsaw of General Tatar and his companions. Harsh sentences in this trial were to be a precedent for a trial of Gomulka. But they did not get so far. Gomulka and several of his imprisoned friends survived the Stalin terror and Stalin himself.

Preparations for a monster trial were in full swing in the DDR (East Germany), the principal figures in which were to be Paul Merker, Franz Dahlem, Kurt Müller, and Leo Bauer. Security specialists sought to extort confessions from the prisoners, e.g. that Franz Dahlem had been a 'French agent', and so on.

Stalin and the MGB succeeded by these purges in finally impressing the 'Soviet style' on the Communist parties of the states of the Eastern Bloc. They made use of intrigues, mutual accusations, torture. The arrests were in no single case founded on difference in political views. No, the accused must unquestionably be traitors, spies, 'paid agents of western intelligence services', etc. In these trials the Soviet advisers in the secret police forces of the Eastern Bloc states celebrated the greatest success in their history. Old experienced Communists like Rajk and Slansky, on non-Soviet soil, in Budapest with its Western culture and in golden Prague, 'voluntarily' admitted that they were in fact the criminals that they were charged with being.

The 'Soviet style' not only meant the public humiliation of Czechoslovak and Hungarian Communist leaders, but it poisoned the whole atmosphere. The Czechoslovak organ *Rude Pravo* of 24/25 November 1952 carried two letters which best illustrate the human depth which at that time was considered to be the greatest success of Russian security. Tomas Frejka, a teenager, wrote to the president of the state criminal court in Prague asking for the severest punishment to be inflicted on his own father, Ludvik Frejka, one of the defendants in the Slansky trial. This letter contained the following sentences: 'I demand for my father the severest punishment, the death sentence. I only now realize that this creature, whom one cannot call a man, because he has no trace of human feeling and dignity, was my greatest and bitterest enemy. As a devoted Communist I know that my hatred for all our enemies, especially for those who want to destroy our land, which is becoming ever richer and happier, and especially my hatred for my father, will always strengthen me in my struggle for the Communist future of our people. I request that this letter be shown to my father and that I may later be given the opportunity of saying the same to him personally.'

In the same number of *Rude Pravo* Lisa Londonova, wife of the accused Artur London, wrote as follows: 'After the arrest of my husband I believed, on the basis of what I knew of his life and activities, that he was the victim of traitors who were trying to hide their own vile conduct under the "London" case. Until the last moment, until 20 November, I hoped that the mistakes that he might have made could be made good, that he would answer for them to the Party and the People's court, and that after punishment for his faults he would have the opportunity of rejoining the Communist family.

'Unfortunately, since reading the charges, my hopes have been dashed. My husband was no victim, but a traitor to his Party, a traitor to the Fatherland. It is a hard blow for me. A traitor has lived with me and my family—we are all Communists. During the occupation my Father used to say: "I am proud that my children are in prison because of their loyalty to the Communist Party. I would rather see them dead than that they should become traitors." Now we see the father of my three children appearing before the People's Court as a traitor. I have the painful duty of telling my two elder children that their father is a traitor. They have promised me that all their lives they will behave as true Communists. As a Communist mother I rejoice, in the interests of the Czechoslovak people and world peace, that this band of traitors has been unmasked and rendered harmless, and I can only join all honourable people in demanding the punishment of the traitors.'

At the same time the purges were a step towards the realization of Stalin's new policy in the People's Democratic Republics after the failure of the Cominform experiment.

VICTIMS OF THE TRIALS OF THE CZECHOSLOVAK COMMUNIST LEADERS
(November 1952)

Condemned to death:
Dr Vladimir Clementis; Dr Otto Fischl; Josef Frank;

Ludvik Frejka (or Freund); Bedrich Geminder; Rudolf Margolius; Bedrich Reicin (or Reizinger); André Simone (or Katz); Rudolf Slansky; Otto Sling (or Schlesinger); Karel Svab.
Condemned to penal servitude for life:
Vavro Hajdu; Eugen Lobel; Artur London.

Stalin simplified the problem in a remarkable fashion. The Communist parties were robbed of their importance and influence on the government of the country by the liquidation of their older leaders, and in their stead a 'little Stalin' was installed: Bierut in Poland, Gottwald in Czechoslovakia, Rakosi in Hungary. These men were personally responsible to the Soviet Union for the functioning of the system. The only criterion of their rule was blind loyalty to the Soviet Union. Their backing was neither party nor army, but a security service led and directed from Moscow.

Stalin's preparations for the annihilation of the leaders' committees

About this time there were further important changes of personnel in the Soviet security service. At the beginning of 1952 Abakumov, Beria's intimate friend, was removed from his post and replaced by S. D. Ignatiev. Probably Abakumov was transferred to military intelligence. It is not possible to give details of the political reasons for this change. It was Stalin's first step towards the complete re-staffing of the secret police, towards the removal of Beria and his friends, and an attempt to make the security organs, with Poskrebyshev's assistance, into a still more subservient and trustworthy instrument for Stalin's crimes.

Ignatiev's appointment as Minister of the MGB shows certain parallels to Menzhinsky's. After Dzerzhinsky's death Stalin needed a man of straw in whose shadow he could do what he liked with the GPU. For the assumption that Ignatiev, too, was a man of straw there is plenty of evidence, especially the fact that he is still alive.

Semyov Denisovich Ignatiev, born 1903, was a typical Party *apparatchik*. Before the war he came to the fore as regional secretary of the Bashkir Autonomous Soviet Republic. After the war he was promoted to work in the Party's central headquarters, becoming in 1904 deputy chairman of the Committee for Party Control. Between 1947 and 1949 he worked in the secretariat of the Central Committee of the Belorussian Communist Party.

Ignatiev's appointment was favoured by the circumstance that he had never had anything to do with Beria and had no experience of the secret police. As for any connection with the supreme leadership, he was doubtless one of the protégés of Malenkov, who, for many years responsible for personnel, must have worked closely with Ignatiev. Perhaps what finally decided the appointment was Ignatiev's contacts with Poskrebyshev, with whom he supervised the Party as deputy chairman of the Committee for Party Control.

This change of leadership in the MGB was at the time the subject of violent disagreements among Western observers. Some of them almost guessed the truth. Today one can say with certainty what Stalin had in mind.

VICTIMS OF THE TRIALS OF THE HUNGARIAN COMMUNIST LEADERS
(September 1940)

Condemned to death:
    László Rajk; Dr Tibor Szonyj; Andras Szalai; Gyorgy Páleffy.

Condemned to penal servitude for life:
    Lasa Brankow; Pál Justus

Condemned to nine years' imprisonment:
    Milan Ognienovich.

For a better understanding of this step we must refer to another important event in the year 1952 which was closely connected with the changes in the MGB. After an eleven-year interval Stalin resolved to call the 19th Party Congress for October 1952. On 3 and 4 October, before the congress met, *Pravda* published Stalin's work, *The Economic Problems of Socialism in the Soviet Union*, which gave the personality cult a fresh impetus.

At the congress Stalin made a chess-move in the Party organization, a move incomprehensible to many and the meaning of which was for the first time revealed by Khrushchev at the 20th Party Congress. The Politbureau of the Central Committee, which according to the statutes is the highest body in the Party, had previously consisted of ten members. At Stalin's request its membership was enlarged to twenty-five.

What was the significance of that? It was Stalin's second blow against the Politbureau. The first had been in 1949, when he handed Voznesensky over to the MGB without a judicial sentence and without the knowledge of the Central Committee. Since then the Politbureau had no longer been a corporate body capable of making independent decisions and carrying them out according to the Party statutes. And now it was dealt a fresh blow. An example will make this clear: when a large business concern has three directors, the importance of each is recognized by everybody. But if the number is increased to fifteen, each is automatically devalued.

A Politbureau of ten persons would naturally comprise only the *élite* of the Communist Party. Formally it was of equal rank with Stalin. But now the authority of the previous members of the Politbureau was diminished; Malenkov, Beria, and Khrushchev were simply lost in the crowd. That was Stalin's object.

What did Stalin want in 1951, when he had the 'Leningrad Affair' behind him and the Party purges throughout the Soviet Union were once again in full swing? The answer is simple. The liquidation of Voznesensky and other leading Communists in 1949 and 1950 was only the beginning of the 'Second Yezhovshchina'. Its goal was the annihilation of Stalin's closest entourage, including Malenkov, Beria, and Khrushchev, and a sweeping change in the Party leadership.

Khrushchev said in his 'secret speech' that at that time nobody in the Party could be sure that he would be alive the morrow. Stalin began to accuse leading Communists, from one day to the next, of being foreign agents. Voroshilov, for instance, he described as an 'English agent' and ordered him to telephone before each session of the Politbureau to ask whether he might attend it. In Khrushchev's words: 'Sometimes Stalin gave him permission, but mostly he gave vent to his displeasure.' Not content with that, Stalin arranged for the MGB to 'bug' Voroshilov's apartment with a microphone. Khrushchev thus confirmed previous reports that Stalin with Poskrebyshev's help had installed a whole network of microphones to spy on Politbureau members, Party leaders, and higher civil servants.

During his first visit to Yugoslavia after Stalin's death,

Khrushchev, according to a Yugoslav journalist, remarked: 'We trembled before Stalin. We did not know whether we should ever come back when we were called to see him. New sinister figures, previously unknown to us, constantly loomed up in Stalin's immediate proximity. . . .'

It is precisely these sinister figures swarming around Stalin and Poskrebyshev that were no good omen for Stalin's former guards. At the 20th Party Congress Khrushchev declared quite openly: 'Apparently Stalin intended to get rid of the old members of the Politbureau. He had often said that the Politbureau members ought to be replaced by new. When after the 19th Congress he proposed to elect twenty-five new members to the Central Committee presidium, he was aiming at the dismissal of all the existing Politbureau members and their replacement by less experienced people who would then publicize his glory. It is to be assumed that he was simultaneously working for the eventual annihilation of all the old members of the Politbureau, so as to conceal the shameful deeds he had committed, those deeds with which we are today concerned.'

We do not want at this juncture to examine in detail which of his old comrades Stalin at that time wanted to keep and which he wanted to get rid of. Some experts, like Nikolayevsky, assert that Kaganovich lost no whit of Stalin's favour as long as the latter was alive. Opinions regarding Malenkov are divided; it is only certain that his position was badly shaken in 1952. For the events in the security service the question of Beria's position is of special importance. There is now sufficient concrete evidence to establish it in some detail.

Since the end of the war Beria had no longer been lord of the secret police. The recent changes in its organization presaged badly for himself. Much for which Beria could have been blamed had now been achieved by Stalin with the help of Abakumov, Beria's friend. On the basis of the 'Crimean Affair' Stalin could easily stigmatize Beria as an 'agent of Israelite Zionists'. Lucian Blit, an assistant of Erlich, the liquidated leader of the 'Bund', and Alter, an eye-witness of the events, reported that Beria had been a friend of leading members of the 'Jewish Anti-Fascist Committee', and especially of Michoels. Still more, when Michoels and Feffer went to the USA in 1944, they did so on the recommendation of Beria, who, through the delegation, wanted to obtain funds from

JEWISH SOVIET INTELLECTUALS LIQUIDATED
BY STALIN
1936–42

I. E. Babel; Yasha Bronstein; Ittsig Kharik; Aleksandr Khazhin; M. P. Khavkin; Khemerinsky; Chaim Duniets; Max Erlich; Tsvi Friedland; Esther Frumkin ; Chaim Gildin; Gorokhov; Koblentz; Yankl Levine; M. Levithan; I. Lieberberg; Moshe Litvakov; M. Lraffes; V. E. Meyerhold; Merezhin; P. Zhprach; Lev Süsskind; Rakhmil Weinstein; Zinberg.

1943–53

David Bergelson; I. Dobrushkin; Shakhne Epstein; Ittsig Feffer; Elie Gordon; David Hoffstein; Moshe Kulbak; Leib Moiseyerich Kvitko; A. Lozovsky; Perets Markish; Shlomo Michoels; I. Nusinov.

the American Jews and at the same time elicit their sympathy for Moscow. In the 'Crimean Affair', however, it was 'proved' through the MGB that Michoels and Feffer had only gone to America in order to make connections with American imperialists and the Zionist headquarters. Now it needed only a little step, and Beria could be shown up as the chief conspirator against Stalin.

Still worse for Beria were the happenings in Georgia and the already mentioned 'Mingrelian Affair'. As Beria's authority in Moscow began to fade, he sought support from his fellow-countrymen in Georgia. This was a clever move, as many Georgians had influence with Stalin. Beria did his utmost to fill the staff of the Georgian Communist Party with his own nominees. The crowning point of his efforts was the 14th Congress of the Georgian Communist Party in January 1949. When glancing through the report on the Congress, one discovers a remarkable thing. The glorification of Stalin followed the usual impressive line: he was vaunted as the leader of genius. But Beria, Stalin's 'nearest comrade', was exalted at much greater length. Beria's marionettes in Georgia took pride in reminding everybody of all the details of Beria's services to the Caucasus. At the end of the congress two separate greeting messages were sent: one to Stalin and one to Beria.

Beria's success in the Caucasus, however, was of short duration. Somebody (read Poskrebyshev) spun a spider's web of intrigue within the leadership of the Georgian Communist Party, which finally culminated in the 'Mingrelian Affair'. Beria fought desperately to save his protégés. There are indications that the staging of the Mingrelian Affair entailed enormous difficulties for the MGB. There is every probability that Abakumov sabotaged Stalin's instructions. At any rate, the secret trial of the 'Georgian nationalists' did not take place until 1952, after Abakumov had already been removed from the MGB. In the course of the Mingrelian Affair it was 'proved' that the chief conspirators in the Georgian Central Committee were in the service of Turkish imperialists and working for the secession of Georgia and the Caucasus from the Soviet Union and their incorporation in Turkey. All of them were Beria's protégés, so it was quite a small step to brand Beria as the chief conspirator and agent of 'Turkish imperialism'.

Dark clouds began to gather over Beria's head. But there arose another difficulty, which, however, it is difficult to verify documentarily. All the experts believe that Beria was responsible for Soviet atom espionage. Some even say that the institute directed by him was 'State Trust No. 1' and that the most secret channels of Soviet intelligence cooperated there in the struggle for nuclear and atomic weapons. There is now much to indicate that Stalin was not satisfied with the work of the institute, for his plans for the production of atomic weapons could not be realized to the degree he envisaged in his ambitious dreams.

That Beria lost his power over the Soviet security service after the Second World War, quite certainly by 1950, was stated by Khrushchev in his secret speech. He mentioned that Stalin had entrusted Kuznetsov (liquidated in the 'Leningrad Affair') with the supervision of State security. As a matter of fact, that is one of the most important pieces of evidence of Beria's tottering position. The theory that he too was destined to liquidation must be near the truth.

Arrest of the 'Murderous Doctors'

Meanwhile security services throughout the Soviet Union were working at high pressure. The prisons were crammed with Zionists, bourgeois nationalists, and cosmopolitans. Persecution grew daily more intense.

In the winter of 1952/3 Stalin instructed Ignatiev and his deputy Ryumin to organize a 'doctors' conspiracy'. The proceedings began with a woman doctor, L. F. Timashchuk, sending Stalin a letter with general accusations against the leading consultants at the Kremlin hospital, who were entrusted with the care of the health of Stalin and other prominent personages. As Khrushchev told the 20th Congress, Ignatiev was told to 'prove' the charges. Five prominent doctors, Professors Vovsi, B. B. Kogan, Feldman, Grinstein, and Etinger were accused of being Zionist agents, and three others, Vinogradov, M. B. Kogan, and Yegorov, of having for years been agents of the British secret service. Stalin's orders to Ignatiev were short and sharp. 'If you cannot force a confession out of the doctors, you will lose your head.' When Khrushchev made these revelations at the 20th Party Congress, there was an uproar among the delegates. He went on: 'Stalin sent for the investigating judge, gave him his orders, and instructed him what investigation methods to use. In fact, however, they were quite simple: "Beat, beat, and again beat".'

Two of the arrested doctors, Professor M. B. Kogan and Professor Y. G. Etinger, died under maltreatment, but the others yielded the desired confessions. Stalin then summoned the members of the Politbureau and distributed among them the confessions of guilt. The appropriate passage from Khrushchev's speech reads as follows. 'After the confessions had been distributed, Stalin told us: "You are as blind as kittens. What would you do without me? Our country will be ruined because you don't know how to recognize its enemies".'

The general public was informed of the doctors' affair in a very brief report which appeared on 13 January 1953 in *Pravda* and *Izvestiya* as a communiqué from the Tass press agency. 'It is announced that the MGB had succeeded in unmasking a conspiracy among nine Kremlin doctors' (actually fifteen, as afterwards officially stated). 'The defendants were charged with the murder by poison of Zhdanov and the former Chief of the Political Administration of the Red Army, Colonel-General Aleksandr Shcherbakov. Further they had tried to poison Marshals Konev, Vazilevsky, and Govorov, Army General Shtemenko, and Admiral

Levchenko. Moreover they had by their treatment damaged the health of the Supreme Soviet Leader.'

The official communiqué continued: 'It was established that all these murderous doctors—human monsters who trampled on the sacred flag of science and befouled the dignity of science—were paid agents of foreign intelligence services. The majority of the members of the terrorist group (Vovsi M. S., Kogan B. B., Feldman A. I., Grinstein A. N., Etinger Y. G., and others) were in communication with the international Jewish bourgeois-nationalist organization JOINT, which was founded by the American information service allegedly for the provision of material aid to Jews in other countries. In reality this organization, under the direction of the American information service, carried on large-scale espionage, terrorism, and revisionist activities in a number of countries, including the Soviet Union. The defendant Vovsi admitted under interrogation that he had received a directive from the USA "regarding the annihilation of leaders of the USSR" sent by the JOINT organization in the USA via the Moscow doctor Shimeliovich and the well-known Jewish bourgeois-nationalist Michoels. Other members of the terrorist group (Vinogradov V. N., Kogan M. B., Yegorov P. I.) were proved to have been agents of the British intelligence service.'

The whole affair was accompanied by violent attacks on the Soviet security services. The MGB was blamed for lack of vigilance and for inefficiency in the contest with enemy agents. But what was Stalin's object in making these reproaches? Who if not the security organizations had discovered the conspiracy of the 'murderous doctors', and who by the arrests had foiled the plans of the British, American, and other espionage services?

The answer to this question betrays one of the many objects at which the suspicious Stalin at that time was aiming. At the head of the MGB was his man of straw, Ignatiev, the apparatus itself was not yet entirely free of all the people who owed their careers to Beria and Abakumov. Behind Ignatiev's back Stalin was already creating his own security service, which would carry out his instructions blindly. We shall return to this subject, because it was only known later, after Stalin's death, who was to be his 'new Yagoda'. Stalin was trying to carry out the 'renewal' of the MGB as quickly as possible with his 'dialectic' method, so he criticized the MGB for its blindness and slackness. But it was only the older officials that he blamed. With his new staff he showed by the unmasking of the 'murderous doctors' what 'correct work' should be like.

Death of the despot

What actually happened behind the Kremlin walls between January and 5 March 1953 confers probability on even the wildest fantasies—even the maddest speculation might hit the mark. Quite certainly people defended themselves against the butchery of the 'Second Yezhovshchina'. Perhaps they even tried to put a straitjacket on the maniacal Stalin and bring him under their control. At any rate, on 15 February 1953, shortly before Stalin's death, the commander of the Kremlin guard, Major-General Pyotr Kosynkin, who was responsible for Stalin's personal safety, died. Did somebody perhaps use Stalin's old method and remove a bodyguard in order to facilitate access to the dictator?

Great excitement was caused at the time by the opinion of Franz Borkenau, who at the moment when the 'Doctors' Affair' became known prophesied Stalin's early death.[121] His reasons were logical: the doctors in charge of Stalin could decide on his life or death. So somebody 'provoked' the 'Doctors' Affair' in order to get control of the supervision of Stalin's health and give him a fatal injection.

There are many versions of Stalin's death. It is possible that a doctor's comment is correct: the fact that a 74-year-old man was resolving to get rid of his closest assistants and was about to carry out a bloody purge in order to change the basic development of the Soviet Union was sufficient to cause a coronary.

When the Kremlin had turned itself into a nest of intrigues, when murders increased every day and a reign of terror was raging throughout the country outside the Kremlin walls, Yosef Vissarionovich Stalin died, on 5 March 1953, at 9.50 p.m. Stalin combined in one person Bonaparte and Robespierre. But his death interrupted the greatest scheme of his life: the 'Second Yezhovshchina' remained incomplete.

Chapter Eight

The security service under the 'Imperialist Agent' Beria

(March–July 1953)

Destruction of Stalin's terror system

No sooner was Stalin dead than a *coup d'état* took place that was of infinite importance in the development of the Soviet Union and its history. Stalin's principle of leadership and therewith the basis of the whole Stalinist system were fundamentally altered.

There are several more-or-less well-founded speculations about the part played by Malenkov after Stalin's death. Many are of the opinion that he was chosen by Stalin as his successor. Such speculation, however, is now of no importance. The essential point is that immediately after Stalin's death a new theory for the leadership of the Soviet Union carried the day, a theory that had nothing in common with Stalin's. Instead of one-man dictatorship, 'collective leadership' was proclaimed, and Malenkov, who was appointed to the chairmanship of the Council of Ministers, was promptly shorn of some of his authority: he lost the important post of Secretary to the Central Committee of the Communist Party.

Without the immediate switching-off of Stalin's terrorist machine all this would have been impossible. Even while the long line of Muscovites was filing past the dictator's bier to pay their last respects, his successors were taking the first steps to do away with his terror apparatus.

They began by dissolving his private secretariat. Poskrebyshev was not seen among those invited to attend Stalin's funeral. A rumour was going around that immediately after the announcement of Stalin's death Poskrebyshev had been arrested by a posse of secret police under Abakumov's command. At the same time, so it was said, all the records found in Stalin's office and in seventeen other rooms were impounded. Other measures were directed against the MGB.

On 7 March 1953, two days after Stalin's death, the Soviet Press published a joint resolution of the Central Committee of the Communist Party, the Council of Ministers, and the Presidium of the Supreme Soviet of the USSR regarding the reshaping of the government and the party leadership. Beria was appointed Minister of Internal Affairs. On 15 March the Supreme Soviet resolved to amalgamate the Ministry of State Security with the Ministry of Internal Affairs. That does not mean that until then the MGB had been working on its own. Only one day after Stalin's death the 'collective leadership' had decided to liquidate the MGB.

On 6 April the public learnt of the measures taken by Beria against the MGB in the name of 'collective leadership'. On 10 April an article appeared in *Pravda* under the heading 'Soviet Socialist legality is inviolable'. It began with a question that went to the heart of the matter: 'How could it come about that in the Ministry of State Security, whose duty it was to protect the interests of the Soviet Union, a frame-up was fabricated whose victims were honourable Soviet citizens, distinguished in Soviet science?' The answer given in *Pravda* was very precise: 'The former Minister of State Security, S. Ignatiev, displayed political blindness and carelessness. It has turned out that he was taken in tow by criminal adventurers such as the former Deputy Minister and Director of the Investigation Department, Ryumin, who was in direct charge of the investigations and is now under arrest.' The documents which had led to the arrest of the Kremlin doctors had been forged, the confessions had been extorted. 'The organs of the MGB', continued the article, 'have damaged Soviet legality in the crudest fashion and have been guilty of arbitrary acts and abuse of power.' Finally Soviet citizens were assured that the government of the Soviet Union was determined to punish the criminal behaviour of the security service and to bring about a state of affairs in which such arbitrary actions could never be repeated.

Beria had a number of members of the MGB in Moscow and also in the Union republics arrested. The number of arrests in the provinces in general was remarkably small. The old tradition, according to which with every change of policy in the security service the heads of ex-Chekists had to roll, was maintained on this occasion too, but to a lesser extent. This is shown in the further fortunes of Ignatiev. With the break-up of the MGB he was automatically deposed as Minister of State Security. A second blow was struck him on 7 April, when he lost his post as Secretary to the Central Committee. Nevertheless he was not put under lock and key, as had previously been the normal practice. There were divergent opinions as to the reason for this, but actually the whole business seems to have been quite simple. Ignatiev was only a figure-head. For Stalin the feeble *apparatchik* was only a 'front man' behind whom the MGB was reorganized to suit his purpose. So just as the new inquisitor Yagoda had grown in stature in the shadow cast by the feeble Menzhinsky, Ryumin, one of the most dangerous of the creatures chosen by Stalin and Poskrebyshev for the removal of the whole of the old Stalin guard, began his handi-work behind Ignatiev's back. Ignatiev described in detail to the collective leadership the circumstances in which he had been forced to work. In consequence he was simply downgraded and used for other jobs for which he was better suited. He went back to Bash-kiria, where some months after Stalin's death he was re-elected to the First Party Secretaryship of that territory. In October 1960 he was relieved of this post too, ostensibly on account of his poor state of health. But this was no longer serious politics: Ignatiev was quite simply pensioned off.

Events in Georgia

What happened after Stalin's death, on Beria's initiative, is informative for several reasons. Firstly, the view that Beria's authority dwindled more and more after the Second World War was confirmed. We learn something about the method of working that Stalin had forced upon his closest collaborators on the eve of the 'Second Yezhovshchina' and—what is even more important—some light is thrown on the chaos among the top leaders, rightly called the schizophrenia of the leadership apparatus, caused by Stalin's death.

In the course of the 'Mingrelian Affair', already mentioned, even some of Beria's friends had fallen victims to the purge. The then Minister of State Security, Rukhadze, arrested leading members of the Georgian Party and State bureaucracy indiscriminately. This put Beria in an embarrassing position. Officially he was obliged to approve the wave of arrests that was going on entirely in accordance with Stalin's wishes, but by circuitous means he tried to check it a little. At about this time A. Y. Mgeladze was appointed First Secretary of the Georgian Communist Party in place of K. Charkviani, and in April 1952 Beria put in a personal appearance at the change of appointments. It was characteristic of the situation then prevailing that on 15 April 1953, when the 'Father of the People's' corpse had hardly grown cold, Beria exploded his Georgian bombshell. Mgeladze, who had barely been a year in office, was deposed, and Rukhadze, Minister of State Security, who on Stalin's instructions had contrived the 'Mingrelian Affair', was arrested. The importance attributed by Beria to the Caucasus situation may be gauged by the appointment of Dekanozov, one of his most intelligent and reliable colleagues, to be Minister of Internal Affairs in the Georgian Republic. The Caucasian journals poured out songs of praise for Beria, extolling him as the restorer of justice, the man they had to thank for the return to a genuine national policy. The survivors of the 'Second Yezhovshchina' in Georgia were released from prison and some of them were reinstated in their official jobs.

The Soviet works of reference which appeared in the sixties are either completely silent about these matters or twist them to suit their own ends. Although it has been established that Rukhadze was arrested on Beria's instructions, they state that 'in April 1953 the Presidium of the Central Committee of the Communist Party of the Soviet Union' investigated the 'Mingrelian Affair' and ordered the arrest of Rukhadze, one of Beria's protégés.[122] Any comment on the credibility of this explanation would be superfluous. Naturally Beria tried to win friends for himself among the Party executives in the national republics, a move that afterwards earned him the official accusation that he had maliciously stirred up mutual animosity among the peoples of the Soviet Union.

Stalin's representatives were also chased out of the Baltic republics, the Ukraine, and Belorussia. The events in the Ukraine caused the greatest stir. The Party leader L. G. Melnikov was relieved of his post as First Secretary of the Central Committee as responsible for the Russification policy in the Ukraine.[123] Presumably Beria encouraged the Party cadres to take this step. Khrushchev was not yet in a position to voice his opinions very strongly, and the other prominent Party leaders were out-and-out adherents of the hard-line, centralizing course. It may well be supposed that in the period that followed Stalin's death, when no one knew which way the wind would blow, Khrushchev and Beria poached on each other's preserves in looking for supporters in the struggle for power. Both must have aimed at winning the favour of the non-Russian Party leaders. This supposition is supported by several memoirists. The film director A. Dovzhenko, for instance, tells of an astonishing *volte-face* on Beria's part. In 1944 Dovzhenko was summoned to Stalin's presence and made to listen to a violent criticism of his latest film. Beria, who was present at the interview, said in a rage, 'We'll show you how to see things in the right light!' After Stalin's death a colleague of Beria's turned up one day and suggested to Dovzhenko that he should get in touch with Beria again. 'He would do anything for you.'[124]

In Stalin's day Dovzhenko was subjected to all kinds of vexations. But his films found favour with the intelligentsia and he was personally very popular. He died in 1965. In Germany, too, his film *Earth* made a big impression in the early thirties.

Reform of the security service

Stalin's terrorist apparatus having ceased to exist, Beria found himself faced with the extremely difficult task of finding suitable recruits for the security service and of employing them in the most effective manner. In Georgia his friend Dekanozov, whom we have already mentioned, had become Minister of Internal Affairs. In the Ukraine, Mieshik held a similar position. In other republics Beria made use of 'material to hand'. Either the Ministers of Internal Affairs retained their positions or—as happened more frequently—they were replaced by ex-MGB ministers.

Beria's chief concern was the reform of the headquarters office of the MVD in Moscow. The functions of the former KGB were now taken over by the newly erected 'Chief Administration of State Security', Kobulov being selected as its head. He had been a colleague of Beria's in Georgia. After 1945 he was in charge of the espionage organizations in the part of Germany occupied by the

Red Army. Beria brought him straight back from there to Moscow. Gogolidze, another old pal of Beria's, was appointed his deputy and director of the operations office. Abakumov was allotted a particularly 'delightful sphere of operations', the directorship of the investigation department. But only a few of Beria's old friends had had MVD experience. Some of the security experts he obtained from prisons and concentration camps. Among these, for instance, was General Leonid Eitingon. This old Chekist, being a Jew, had been arrested by Stalin in the course of his anti-semitic campaign. There are various accounts of his arrest, the most credible being that of his former colleague Khokhlov,[125] who fled to the West. According to him, Eitingon, who was responsible for the organization of terrorist activities, frequently travelled abroad. On returning from a journey in January 1951 he was arrested on the charge of having concealed in his house a large quantity of American dollars. The real reason for his arrest, however, was presumably that he had arranged Trotsky's murder and had trained the murderer Jackson, *alias* Mercader. Probably Stalin thought that the time had come to erase this trace of the past along with the others. Eitington came out of his concentration camp a sick man. After he had recuperated to some extent in the Kremlin hospital, Beria re-employed him in his old craft. He was appointed deputy director of the department of terrorism and deviation.

The 'collective leadership' had decided to have a thorough clean-up of the State Security headquarters and commissioned Beria to seek volunteers from the Comsomol and Party to fill the positions of responsibility. Strangely enough, experienced diplomats and politicians with no practical knowledge of security were suddenly found in many of the key positions. For instance, the deputy director of the First Chief Administration for Counter-Espionage was Colonel M. G. Gribanov, who was a trained diplomat and had worked in the European Department of the Foreign Ministry. Still more interesting was the appearance of Aleksandr Semyonovich Panyushkin, an even more distinguished diplomat than Gribanov, now occupying the post of Director of the Second Chief Administration, i.e. the Foreign Department. In 1944 he had been Soviet ambassador in China, later a principal in the Foreign Office, Soviet ambassador in the USA in 1947–52, and shortly afterwards Soviet ambassador in Peking for a year. These appointments were very significant. They show what efforts were being made to find suitable personnel for the security service and that the persons preferred were not too deeply involved in its past history.

On the other hand, Beria had no intention of completely abolishing any of the departments of the security service. There is probably no security authority in the whole world which would willingly relinquish any of its spheres of duty. Departments of the Soviet State Security service that dealt with the organization of terrorist activities in the West, those entrusted with the production of special weapons, and those engaged in faking documents, or in 'bugging' foreign diplomatic missions in the Soviet Union, continued their activities almost undisturbed.

Beria's term of office saw the beginning of various developments which indicated a certain slackening in internal policy. For example, quite a number of matters were withdrawn from the competence of the State Security service, and the frontier guards were again subordinated to the military power.[126] What is quite certain is that Beria began to work on plans for the abolition of the concentration camps. This has been confirmed by released prisoners. The disengagement of the GULAG from the authority of the MGB and its absorption by the Ministry of Justice were certainly begun in Beria's time.

Moreover, the first plans for the reform of the criminal code and the juristic underpinning of the 'restoration of legality' began to mature. On 18 June 1953 the Soviet Press carried an article by the Public Prosecutor of the USSR, G. Safanov, stating that 'in the performance of their honourable and responsible duties' the security organizations, law courts, and public prosecutor's offices 'must punish most severely any violation of the rights of private Soviet citizens and relentlessly expose the machinations of criminal elements that endanger the reputation or the property of Soviet citizens'. But the most important feature of the article was its denunciation of anonymous informers and the snooping methods that had hitherto prevailed.

That was published one day after the rising in East Berlin on 17 June—at a time when Beria's career was nearing its end.

End of Beria

On 10 July 1953 *Pravda* carried a report on the plenary session of the Central Committee of the Communist Party, which read: 'The plenary session of the Central Committee of the Communist Party has accepted a report of Comrade Malenkov of the Presidium of the Central Committee on the criminal anti-State and anti-Party activity of L. P. Beria, which aimed at undermining the Soviet State in the interests of foreign capital, and on his treasonable attempts to put the Ministry of Internal Affairs above the Communist Party and Government of the Soviet Union. It has been resolved to eject L. P. Beria from the Central Committee of the Communist Party and to remove him from the body of the Communist Party as an enemy of the Communist Party and the Soviet people.' Simultaneously the Presidium of the Supreme Soviet of the USSR announced that Beria had been deposed as First Deputy President of the Council of Ministers of the USSR and as Minister of Internal Affairs of the USSR, and that it had been resolved to refer Beria's case to the Supreme Court of Justice. In a leading article which appeared in the same issue of *Pravda*, under the heading 'The unshakable unity of the Party and the Soviet People', Beria was violently abused, the principal charge against him being that he had put a brake on those directives of the Party and the Soviet Government which were intended to strengthen Soviet justice, and on the measures proposed for the promotion of agriculture. He had tried 'to break up the friendship between the peoples of the Soviet Union', he had been guilty of 'bourgeois-nationalist deviations', and finally he had tried 'to put the Ministry of Internal Affairs above Party and Government and to misuse the organizations of the Ministry of Internal Affairs both at headquarters and in the country, in opposition to the Party and the Government of the Soviet Union.'[127]

When we examine the causes of Beria's downfall the first question that arises is whether there was a special political 'Beria line' and whether he followed any programme that diverged from that of the 'collective leadership'. The Kremlinologists and observers of these events in the Soviet Union differ vastly in their opinions. A thorough investigation shows, however, that on the whole Beria kept to the line worked out at the time by the 'collective leadership'. It is very doubtful whether he was pursuing any particular aims in the international sector or within the internal political programme that were in conflict with the general policy of the Soviet leaders then in power. There were deeper causes of Beria's downfall than mere differences of opinion on this or that problem.

The discovery of the power of bureaucracy was one of the foundations of Stalinism. With the help of bureaucrats, blindly obedient recipients and executors of orders, together with complete disregard of any democratic agitation or initiative 'from below', Stalin managed to realize his daring projects in an economically backward country. As we have seen in our outline of the history of the Soviet Union's security service, the Yezhovshchina was no accident or result of one of 'Stalin's outbursts of rage', as some of Khrushchev's biographers would have us believe. Without the destruction of the Old Guard of the Bolsheviks Stalin could not have turned the Communist Party into a blindly obedient apparatus. For Stalin the Party was superfluous as 'a political factor in society'. The Yezhovshchina transformed the Party into an apparatus that was completely estranged from the bulk of the people.

This statement does not ignore the fact that the role of the Party in the bureaucratic system under Stalin was still more important than that of the economic apparatus, the army, or even the police. The security service naturally formed the chief support of Stalin's personal dictatorship, but it stood above the Party only to the extent that Stalin put himself above the Central Committee, the Politbureau, and other Party institutions. We should not forget that no post other than that of General Secretary of the Central Committee was the starting and finishing point of Stalin's position of power, and that everything that he did, including what he arbitrarily ordered to be done, paying no attention to his innermost circle of advisers, was done 'in the name of the Communist Party'. That the Soviet system continued to function under Stalin was due to his ingenuity in 'playing' the various 'apparatuses' which Wolfgang Leonhard in his book *Kreml ohne Stalin* calls the 'bureaucratic pillars of Stalinism'. The integrating and dominant power in the community was not the Communist Party, the Central Committee, or the Politbureau, nor was it any other bureaucratic apparatus—it was Stalin himself.

But let us return to the situation in the Soviet Union after Stalin's death.

The integrating power was no longer in existence. In its place, a 'collective leadership' had seized the rudder of state—a completely new social phenomenon in the Soviet Union. What still existed as a solid fact was the bureaucratic apparatus that had been nurtured to maturity in the bosom of Stalinism.

Today we have numerous indications that in the main Stalin's successors had two varying conceptions of the function of collective leadership or—expressed in sociological terms—the formation of a new integrating social force or institution. One group's conception upheld to a certain extent the *status quo* and the autonomy of the bureaucratic apparatus represented by themselves. Needless to say, they acknowledged the leading role of the Central Committee and the Communist Party, but they thought that a *modus vivendi* would have to be worked out between the Party and the existing apparatus, a formula which would ensure the control of the apparatus by the Party but also the possibility of independent action by the apparatus. Others were applying a 'Leninist conception' to the problem, which was not a *modus vivendi* with the apparatus but its total subordination to the Party. The first conception was advocated not only by Beria, who had to pay for his opinion with his life, but later also by Malenkov, who stood up for the independence of the economic apparatus. Later still, the economic bureaucracy was championed by Saburov, Pervukhin, and others, and finally by Zhukov, the 'little Bonaparte', who fought for the independence of the military apparatus within the framework of the Soviet system. The second conception was favoured by Khrushchev and a number of senior party officials. It would be quite wrong to imagine that the Stalinists were solidly in favour of one conception or the other. All Stalin's successors were 'Stalinists', and the most prominent of Stalin's 'yes men' were on one side or the other. This controversy was the product of a completely new historical situation.

Such was the general background behind Beria's downfall. To advocate the independence of the security service must have been of evil omen to all those who still had vivid memories of Stalin's terrorism. Consequently the subordination of the police to the Party leadership was taken for granted even by those who, for example, supported the self-sufficiency of the military or the economic apparatus.

There were interesting and authentic reports of the suspicion with which all the members of the collective leadership viewed what was going on in the security service. As early as April, for instance, Beria is said to have flown in a special plane to visit almost all the capitals of the Union republics, where he had lengthy talks with security officials. The other Communist leaders became suspicious, and there are several persons who maintain that Malenkov of all people, who had so much on his own conscience, was the most distrustful of them all. The Polish Communist Seweryn Bialer, who fled to the West in 1956, tells of an incident which, if it really happened, must have shaken the whole Party leadership to the core. When one of the members of the Presidium of the Central Committee went on duty to Lvov, Beria instructed the chief of the MVD there to shadow him. But, instead, the security officer promptly reported the matter to Party headquarters. Suspicions of Beria were now confirmed. When finally he had the Kremlin guard made up of his own people the other Communist leaders felt themselves to be utterly unsafe. There were also stories going around that Beria had adopted the practice of having the telephone conversations of prominent Communist leaders tapped. It was clear that he had broken the pact to decide everything 'collectively'. From this point onwards it was only a short step to his liquidation.

Beria's overthrow therefore was an act of self-defence on the part of the collective leadership against the possible resumption of terrorism against the Party bureaucracy and its leaders. This is confirmed by official documents which stated that Beria was trying to put the MVD above the Party.

The way in which Beria was overthrown is fairly accurately known. As the police units were under Beria's command, Zhukov and the army were drawn into the conspiracy against him. At a session of the Presidium of the Central Committee of the Communist Party Malenkov spoke in justification of the proposal to depose Beria as Minister of Internal Affairs and expel him from the Presidium of the Communist Party. The Presidium adopted the proposal, and when Beria refused to accept the resolution he was arrested by a group of generals in the presence of all the Presidium members. Observers reported from Moscow that on 27 June motorized units of the army were seen driving through the streets of Moscow in the direction of the Kremlin and that shortly afterwards they came back at high speed. That evening Beria was no longer among the Party leaders attending the opera.

On the same day rather more than a hundred senior security officers, Beria's adherents, were arrested. As everything went off without any serious disturbance, a plenary session of the Central Committee of the Communist Party was held on 7 and 8 July, when the 'Beria case' was dealt with.

It was not until December 1953 that the names of the security officers who had been arrested along with Beria were officially disclosed. This was done by way of a report from the Public Prosecutor's office published in *Pravda*. From this it transpired that along with Beria the following colleagues were found guilty: the former Minister of State Security and latterly Minister of State Control, V. N. Merkulov; the former People's Commissar of Internal Affairs of the Georgian Republic, afterwards Deputy Minister of State Security, and finally Deputy Minister of Internal Affairs of the USSR, B. C. Kobulov; the former director of a department in the NKVD and finally Minister of Internal Affairs in the Georgian Republic, V. G. Dekanozov; the former People's Commissar of Internal Affairs in the Georgian Republic and finally director of a department in the Ministry of Internal Affairs of the USSR, S. G. Gogolidze; the former director of a department of the NKVD of the USSR and former Minister of Internal Affairs of the Soviet Ukraine, D. Y. Mieshik; and the former director of the investigation department in particularly important affairs in the Ministry of Internal Affairs of the USSR, L. V. Vlodzimirsky. It was stated in the Public Prosecutor's report that during the civil war Beria had been an 'agent of nationalist organizations in the Caucasus, that at the time he was already working for the British intelligence service and simultaneously supporting the Mensheviks. He was a traitor to the Fatherland and a spy who had sold himself to foreign intelligence services.'

At the end of December 1953, following a resolution of the Military Council, all the persons cited were condemned to death for high treason and shot.

Let us now consider the significance of Beria's downfall in so

far as it affected the Soviet system. It occurred at a time when one
of the most important constitutional alterations was being undertaken in post-despotic Soviet society. The destruction of the Stalinist terror apparatus, the proclamation of the return to 'Socialist
legality', the beginning of the rehabilitations and the release of the
victims of the Stalin terror hitherto held in custody—all that was
of less significance than the new status in the Soviet system with
which the security service now had to rest content. From now on
it was to be only an auxiliary organization of the Party and was not
to pursue any 'independent policy'. It could only move within
exactly defined limits, and various tasks, fundamentally alien to it,
which had been entrusted to it under Stalin were to be transferred
to other State offices. It was at this juncture that Nikita Khrushchev came to the fore; he it was who showed the most energy in
promoting this social change which was to be of such far-reaching
importance, and in this he was supported by most of the leading
Party bureaucrats. But very few of them really understood whither
it was actually leading them, that from now on terrorism was no
longer to be accepted as the foundation of the Soviet system. Most
of them followed Khrushchev simply for the sake of self-preserva-
tion, rejoicing that the security police had been stripped of its
powers and their own skins saved.

Chapter Nine

On the way to 'Socialist Legality'

(1953–1958)

After Beria's downfall

BERIA'S overthrow brought about a crisis in the leadership of the Soviet security service that was not finally disposed of until 1956. Proceedings were taken against several security officers and in some of them cases originating in the 'Yezhovshchina' were to be cleared up. A commission was appointed to deal specifically with the rehabilitation of victims of the Stalinist terror. In other cases the connections between certain security officers and Beria were investigated. This resulted in Chekists being arrested, tried, and even shot.

On 14–19 December 1954 a show trial was held in Leningrad by the Military Council of the Supreme Court of Justice of the USSR. The accused were the former Minister of Security of the USSR, V. S. Abakumov, and five of his colleagues: A. G. Leonov, former director of the investigation department for State Security of the USSR; V. I. Komarov and M. T. Likhachov, former deputy directors of this department: and I. A. Chernov and Y. M. Broverman. Abakumov, Leonov, Komarov, and Likhachov were sentenced to be shot, Broverman was sentenced to twenty-five years in a labour camp, Chernov to fifteen years.

There was much that was spurious in this trial. At the time Malenkov, Bulganin, and Molotov were still in very strong positions. Later, when the trio came into conflict with Khrushchev, it became known that they too had been responsible for the 'Leningrad Affair'. In the course of Abakumov's trial Turko, former secretary of the Leningrad District Party Committee, who had survived the 'affair', appeared in the witness box. Only shortly before he had been released from a concentration camp and was still showing the marks of his experiences there. He told in detail how he had been maltreated and what he knew about the fate of his friends. But he did not tell all. It was not until 8 July 1957 that he recounted in the *Leningradskaya Pravda* how he had been summoned by Malenkov to the secretariat of the Central Committee of the Communist Party and had been forced to give false evidence against the Communist leaders in Leningrad. He had kept quiet about that when Abakumov was being tried. By shooting Abakumov and his friends the regime wanted to show that it was determined to put an end for good and all to the falsifications, the fabrications of cases, and the arbitrary conduct of the security organizations.

Accordingly, in July 1955, the former senior State Security official Ryumin was executed. In the following November a group of Georgian security officers were liquidated, including the former State Security Minister of the Georgian Republic, Rukhadze, and his deputy Tseretelli. The last reports of the shooting of security officers date from April 1959, when, according to them, the ex-Premier and Minister of Internal Affairs of Azerbaidjan, M. D. A. Bagirov, was shot, along with three senior police officers. Bagirov was accused of collaborating with Beria and of participating in the physical destruction of leading Party members.[128]

Not all the security officers shot at this period were Beria's collaborators. Some of them in fact were his opponents. Beria's downfall did not have such an adverse effect on the further development of the security service as has been commonly supposed. It was only at the top that a crisis developed; apart from that, the collective leadership endeavoured to continue on the new course assigned to the security service, which, incidentally, was initiated in Beria's term of office. The events of this period are still viewed in a somewhat nebulous light. Let us try to make some of them a little more distinct.

Take, for instance, the case of Ryumin. A communiqué on this appeared in the Soviet press on 23 July 1955. In fact, Ryumin had been arrested as far back as April 1953, as the chief organizer of the 'doctors' plot'. The grounds on which sentence was pronounced were vague. It is quite clear, however, from various documents and the evidence of witnesses in the trials of the time that it was not only because he had cooked up the 'doctors' plot' that Ryumin was shot. In the course of the proceedings, in which only prominent Party functionaries took part, it transpired that Ryumin was the chief of those commissioned by Stalin and Poskrebyshev to prepare false documents for the intended proceedings against the whole of Stalin's old guard. Hearsay has it that it was a question of preparations for the liquidation of Malenkov, Khrushchev, Molotov, and even Beria himself. Ryumin's execution may be regarded as the epilogue to all those measures of self-defence taken by the Communist leaders against the Stalinist terror which most probably began in Stalin's lifetime. The case against Ryumin therefore had nothing to do with Beria's downfall. In a way it was quite a fair trial inasmuch as Ryumin was not a scapegoat for the sins of others, but was in fact 'a criminal of the first class' whose importance during the whole of the 'second Yezhovshchina' was exceeded only by Poskrebyshev's.[129]

The case against Bagirov also calls for careful scrutiny. A detailed examination of the interrelations of the Soviet leaders from the Caucasus is always fraught with peculiar difficulties. In this area the intrigues, murky cross-connections, and personal conflicts seem to defy elucidation. It is almost certain, however, that towards the end of his life Bagirov was no adherent of Beria's. If he had been, so prominent a personality would have had to share the fate of Beria's close collaborators in December 1953. Psychologically this would have been of advantage to the collective leadership, since Bagirov was hated as Stalin's representative in Azerbaidjan. Between 1921 and 1930 he had been the leading Chekist in Azerbaidjan and Beria's closest collaborator. Since 1953 he had been President of the Council of the People's Commissars of the Soviet Socialist Republic of Azerbaidjan and First Secretary of the Central Committee of the Communist Party of Azerbaidjan; in 1939 he was promoted to membership of the Central Committee and in 1952 to the candidacy for the Presidium of the Central Committee of the Communist Party of the Soviet Union. He had received the Order of Lenin five times and had been decorated with various medals, including that of 'Distinguished Chekist'. In the hands of this favourite an inordinate amount of power had accumulated; Stalin found in him a representative who would carry out his instructions from Baku. Under Bagirov's supervision the purges, especially in Georgia, became a permanent phenomenon after 1950.

Few proceedings were taken against those responsible for the terror. Possibly there were some held in secret in which particularly flagrant cases were dealt with, without the public's knowledge. But these were certainly exceptions. Proceedings such as those taken in Western Germany where immediate participants in mass murders were brought to account in public trials were unknown in the post-despotic Soviet Union. All that could happen to anyone there was that he might lose his job or be demoted; many were just pensioned off. And doubtless not a few took refuge behind other officials—which is also said to have happened elsewhere.

Serov as the new security chief

After Beria's arrest S. N. Kruglov was appointed Minister of Internal Affairs. He was an old Chekist who after completing his studies at the Industrial Academy in Moscow transferred to the economic department of the OGPU. His training stood him in good stead in the Cheka: he was one of the directors responsible for the administration of the concentration camps—GULAG—and became its head after the Yezhovshchina. During the war he was on the staff of Smersh, where he was in charge of the 'operations section'. He was responsible for the security measures at Tehran, Yalta, and Potsdam and won his way into the good graces of the 'Big Three'. He made a favourable impression on President Truman and was on good terms with men at the highest level, being dubbed a Knight of the British Empire and enrolled in the American Legion. From 1946 to 1953 he was Minister of Internal Affairs of the Soviet Union. As we already know, he succeeded Beria in this post. After Stalin's death he is said to have re-entered the organization of the MVD under Beria; according to another, seemingly convincing, version, he was transferred to the armed forces when this change of offices was taking place. After Beria's arrest he obtained his post for the second time. Colonel-General of State Security Kruglov was assuredly never a devoted henchman of Beria's. His re-appointment was due to his organizing ability.

For the history of the Soviet security service, however, what happened at the headquarters of the Administration of State Security is of importance. The crisis in this apparatus that followed the destruction of Beria's set-up seemed to hang on for rather a long time. It was not until March 1954 that important decisions were announced: on 3 March the Chief Administration of State Security was again—apparently definitively—separated from the Ministry of Internal Affairs. It was now called the Committee of State Security (*Komitet Gozudarstvennoy Bezopaznosti*, KGB). Its Chairman was General I. A. Serov.

The establishment of the KGB did not mean merely—as in the past—a purely formal separation of the State Security apparatus from the Ministry of Internal Affairs. In the Council of Ministers of the Soviet Union there are various State commissions whose importance depends on their sphere of activity. They are usually set up because certain tasks cannot be dealt with by one ministry alone but need a broader basis. To take one example, the State Planning Commission. The problems of planning cannot be solved within the framework of a Ministry of Planning; they overlap into the territories of all the other ministries. The State Planning Commission is thus a 'super-ministry', an institution with far wider competence than a single ministry.

The KGB is a similar case. It is an organization that cannot work only within the limits of its own apparatus; it is a super-ministry responsible for all questions of security in the Soviet State.

Serov, born in 1905, is no longer an unknown figure to us.[130] In 1938 he completed his military education in Leningrad and entered the army as an artillery officer. In 1939 he passed out of the Red Banner Frunze Military Academy and was then appointed to the People's Commissariat of Internal Affairs. So his new field of activity was with the armed forces of the NKVD. This was probably the reason why the liquidation of Yezhov had no detrimental consequence for him, apart from the fact that he was only just beginning his career. In 1939, when Beria was filling his new staff appointments for the Union republics, Serov was appointed Minister of Internal Affairs in the Ukraine. This brought him into close touch with Khrushchev, who also was then officiating in the Ukraine. Under his patronage Serov became a member of the Politbureau of the Central Committee of the Ukrainian Communist Party. At that time the security organizations were faced with a difficult task, the incorporation into the Soviet Union of a former Polish territory, Western Ukraine. In February 1941 Serov rose still higher. He was transferred to Moscow, elected candidate for the Central Committee of the Communist Party of the Soviet Union, and became the First Deputy Minister for State Security under Merkulov. Documents which fell into the hands of the German army during the war disclosed that Serov had also been entrusted with the incorporation into the Soviet Union of Lithuania, Latvia, and Estonia. He signed the notorious 'Order No. 001223', which contained instructions for the deportation of those peoples. Tom Whitney, foreign observer for the Associated Press, afterwards wrote that as a result of this order thousands of Baltic citizens were carried off to Siberia.

When in July 1941 Beria amalgamated the NKVD with the NKGB Serov was appointed First Deputy People's Commissar of Internal Affairs in the USSR. During the war he was frequently in command of armed forces of the NKVD at key points on the front, and he took part in the defence of Moscow and in the Caucasus fighting. He also directed the removal of industrial equipment from Stalingrad in 1942 and 1943. But Serov did not confuse his services to the purely military sphere. He was also entrusted with 'operational' tasks, such as the deportation in 1944 of the Chechens, Ingushes, Kalmyks, and Crimean Tatars. We already know the way in whch he liquidated the republic of the Volga Germans. In 1944 he was a deputy commander at the front, but this was only a preparation for fresh 'operational' duties which he was to undertake in the Soviet-occupied part of Germany. After Germany's capitulation he was Deputy Commander-in-Chief under Marshal Zhukov of the Soviet forces in Germany, where he was entrusted with state security questions. In 1945 Serov was promoted Colonel-General and later full General. He bears the title 'Hero of the Soviet Union', he is a sextuple recipient of the Order of Lenin, and he has been decorated with several other orders and medals. When the MVD and the MGB were separated again in 1946, he was given the post of First Deputy Minister of Internal Affairs in the Soviet Union under Colonel-General Kruglov. For the successful execution of the building works on the Volga-Don Canal by the employment of concentration camp prisoners he was rewarded with still another Order of Lenin in 1952.

After the second amalgamation of the MVD and MGB Serov was very probably once again one of Beria's deputies. He retained this post until March 1954, when the Supreme Administration of State Security was separated again from the MVD and this time was converted, under his direction, into the Committee of State Security, the KGB.

It seems rather curious that the 'collective leadership' placed such confidence in a man who year after year under Stalin and Beria had been forging ahead unchecked. But it is easy to see from Serov's biography that his special qualities favoured his advancement. He had always been entrusted with 'operational' duties. He had little to do with the political intrigues of Stalin, Poskrebyshev, and Ryumin, nor with Beria's machinations. A Chekist with an exclusively military education, he had simply carried out the measures decided on by the NKVD. He was an experienced organizer on the grand scale and was devoid of any 'taints' dating from the time of Yagoda and Yezhov. His organizing ability made him a security officer of an unusual type which fitted him admirably for a career under the collective leadership. Stalin's successors needed someone who could organize the transformation of the security service, who was in a position to cope with the personal conflicts that were going on at the top of the service, and who could keep the security apparatus working as if on oiled wheels. By fulfilling this task Serov seems to have justified the trust put in him. At the 20th Party Congress of the Communist Party he was promoted to membership of the Central Committee. Abroad, however, he met with some slight setbacks. In March 1957 he appeared in London to arrange security measures with his British opposite numbers on the occasion of the visit of Bulganin and Khrushchev. The leading English newspapers attacked him violently on account of his past. Serov defended himself in *The Times* of 2 April 1956 on the ground that the British correspondents had been misinformed. 'Look at me', he said to an interviewer, 'do I look like Ivan the Terrible?' Nevertheless, on account of this reception he was recalled to Moscow. His commission in England was taken over by Major-General N. S. Sakharov.

When Serov had successfully performed the organizational tasks that had been set him, he was sent packing. But this was at the end of 1958, when, instead of an organizer, a new man with a feeling for the political finesses of the Khrushchevist line was to come to the top of the security organization.

Uprising in a concentration camp

The setting up of the KGB and the transformation of the security service took place against a background of a series of measures taken by the Soviet leadership which became known as the 'return to Socialist legality'. Some Soviet authors appear to see a connection between this development and Beria's liquidation, but the facts point to a series of events that began while Beria was still alive.

By September 1953 the Central Committee and the Government of the Soviet Union had done away with the infamous 'special sections of the NKVD'.[131] The abolition of these bloody tools of terrorist justice allowed the Soviet people to breathe a little more easily for the first time. Incidentally, the text of the resolution has never been published, but that the step had been taken was obvious from other documents. Moreover, some Western correspondents reported at the time that the special armed force of the security service, including the frontier guards, had been put under army command. There are no official documents about this either. It is certain that not later than Beria's brief term of office the frontier guards were once more under KGB authority. At various times the special units of the security service numbered between 500,000 and 800,000 men. They were equipped with the latest weapons and even with fighter aircraft.

The critical situation of the security service following Stalin's death, and the tendency towards a general relaxation, had a marked effect on the concentration camps. As we already know, the first improvements in camp conditions were made during Beria's term of office. The news of the rehabilitation and release of some of the prisoners raised the spirits of those who were still detained and created a new atmosphere. From 1953 onwards there were incidents in various camps, the most serious being the insurrection at Vorkuta.[132]

In July 1953 fifty goods trucks arrived at Vorkuta with prisoners from the Karaganda camp. When the newcomers learnt about the severe conditions prevalent at Vorkuta, which were even worse than at Karaganda, they refused to work. The strike soon spread, and very soon the rebels were in control of all the compounds. As it happened, one of the richest coal measures in the Soviet Union was situated at Vorkuta and the complete stoppage of production there was bound to have swift and serious economic effects. The camp staff were uncertain what to do, and owing to the changing atmosphere in Moscow dared not take drastic measures against the rebels. So they began parleying with them and offered a six-point programme to alleviate their living conditions. Incidentally the programme throws some light on the conditions then prevailing. Freedom of movement inside the huts would no longer be restricted; the hut doors would not be locked; the occupants of the different huts could visit each other; the bars outside the hut windows would be removed; the numbers on the left sleeve would be taken off; every prisoner might write to his family once a month; every prisoner who performed his duties satisfactorily might meet his family once a year; and, finally, every prisoner might apply to have his case reviewed by a special commission.

But the proposals made by the camp staff were not accepted by the mutineers. They elected their own camp leaders and demanded to speak directly to the Government of the Soviet Union or to representatives of the Central Committee of the Communist Party. Derevyanko, the MVD general immediately responsible for the security of the camp, made two attempts to call a meeting of the rebels, so as to bring the strike to an end, but all his efforts were in vain, and, as the situation was worsening, the insurrection had to be forcibly suppressed by units of the MVD and the army. Some sixty-four prisoners were killed and many others were wounded.

The uprising at Vorkuta had a considerable effect on the other concentration camps in the Soviet Union. A wave of unrest ran through nearly all the camps in the RSFSR and Kazakhstan. In the West there were detailed accounts of the Vorkuta mutiny, but very little was written about what was happening in the other camps, with the exception of the special regime camp at Kingir, a settlement about 300 miles from the town of Karaganda. The rising there broke out in May 1954 and was crushed at the end of June by means of tanks; 500 prisoners, including 200 women, lost their lives in the unequal combat. The prisoners at this camp made demands of the NKVD officers and camp administrators that covered sixteen points. These included an amnesty for minors and the disabled and the revision of sentences. Other demands were for more humane treatment, the removal of the numbers, the removal of the bars from the hut windows, and the introduction of an eight-hour working day. The prisoners were also unanimous in asking for the repatriation of foreigners. An interesting feature of this revolt was that it was led by a certain Kuznetsov, who was one of the conquerors of Berlin.[133]

The astonishing feature of this wave of mutinies was that it affected, almost simultaneously, hundreds and thousands of prisoners in every type of camp though they were completely isolated from one another, even reaching the camps where maximum secrecy was in force. The Soviet at last realized that a modification of the camp system could no longer be postponed and that this heritage of Stalin's could not be preserved even with terrorist methods. While Beria was still in command the first of several commissions was set up to examine the situation and introduce revisional procedures for those who had been unjustly condemned. It is an historical fact, however, that the impetus towards camp reform came from the inmates themselves and cost the lives of hundreds of human beings.

The lip service paid by Stalin's successors to legality and humanity came later. The concentration camp system inherited from Stalin was, if not abandoned, at least greatly modified. In 1957 the Chief Prosecutor of the Soviet Union, P. I. Kudryavzev, stated that 70 per cent of the camps had been given up and that only 2 per cent of the inmates remaining in the other camps were political prisoners. Life in the remaining camps became appreciably more bearable. Since then, released prisoners on arriving in Western countries have confirmed the truth of these official statements.

Life in the Soviet Union was also greatly alleviated by the amnesty decrees of the Presidium of the Supreme Soviet of the USSR. By the first amnesty of 27 March 1953 the penalties for certain breaches of duty and economic offences, and a whole series of other minor offences, were revised. On 10 January 1955 the law regulating the penalties for petty thefts was re-worded, and on 17 September of that year those who had been found guilty of collaborating with the German occupying forces were amnestied. All these amnesties were enshrined in a broadly formulated ordinance of rehabilitation for the victims of the Stalinist terror, beginning with Yagoda's term of office. The survivors were set free and recompensed, and reprisals against their families were abandoned.

The decree of 24 May 1955, on the Public Prosecutor's superintendence of the security organizations, is of particular importance. As far back as 1922 Lenin had instructed a special commission to work out a system by which every Soviet official functioned under the supervision of the Public Prosecutor. Later, the Prosecutor's obligation to supervise officials was embodied in the Constitution. During the 'personality cult' period every effort was made to whittle away this decree. We have already seen the methods used by Stalin to free the security service from control. Now the Central Committee issued fresh regulations to enforce the Prosecutor's supervision, and these were ratified by the Supreme Soviet. Article II of the new statutes made the Prosecutor responsible for the maintenance of 'Socialist legality'. Since 7 April 1956 the Public Prosecutor's office of the USSR has included a special department for the superintendence of the security organizations. This department sees to it that the current laws are strictly observed by the secret police in every branch of their activities. Another department controls the prisons and the training and corrective camps.

The value of having Serov, a gifted organizer, at the head of the security service is shown by the fact that at the very time when the security organizations were being shaken to their foundations by radical changes there was no pause in the activity of the armed forces.

Thanks to the constant perfecting of their methods and their greater experience, the work of the security organizations was not nearly so badly impaired at this turning-point of their history as it had been during the transition from Menzhinsky to Yagoda or from Yagoda to Yezhov. This was true especially of the Soviet security apparatus working abroad. Regardless of whether the departmental head in Moscow was removed from office or was beginning to make a name for himself, all the permanent officials in the security service were left undisturbed to continue working with their secret organizations abroad. This was one of the reasons for their successes after Stalin's death.

Another reason for their efficiency lies in the use of *agents provocateurs* planted by the Soviet security men inside the *émigré* organizations. We know that they had no fear of anti-Communism. On the contrary, they fanned it into a white-hot frenzy, calculating that in this atmosphere they were more likely to secure the top jobs inside the anti-Communist organizations. Even before Stalin's death, when the Western intelligence services—generously financed as part of the Cold War—contemplated extending their area of operations in the Soviet Union with the help of *émigrés*, *Pravda* reported on 19 December 1951 that a military tribunal of the Supreme Court of Justice of the USSR had condemned to death two 'American diversionists', A. I. Ozmanov and F. K. Sarantsev, parachutists who had been picked up by security men. Afterwards it became known that they had formerly served in the Vlasov army and had fallen into the hands of the Soviet security police in the territory of the Moldavian SSR.

On 27 May 1953 *Pravda* reported the execution of four other Russian *émigrés* coming from Munich. This time too the report of the Ministry of Internal Affairs contained the statement: 'The diversionists' parachutes were found at the places where they landed.' Rumours that there were traitors in the organizations that were supposed to carry out these commissions with the aid of one of the Western intelligence services were confirmed when in 1953 a certain Georg Müller, alias Khorunzhy, a collaborator in the NTS organization of Russian exiles, was arrested in Frankfurt and afterwards sentenced. According to Press reports, he had been working as an instructor in a secret school of the NTS at Bad Homburg, where persons were trained as anti-Soviet agents. According to one account he had had no difficulty in joining this school and in then sending regular reports to Soviet intelligence. Another version was mentioned in three brochures circulated by *Nabat*, the Russian exile publishing concern in Munich. This said that the real agents had remained in the aforesaid group of Russian exiles and that Müller had merely been used as a cover, so that they themselves could continue their treacherous work.[134]

There were other important events at this period, this time in the Ukraine. There the security forces had to fight hard for their successes. In the Carpathian Mountains of south-west Ukraine, a very favourable terrain for the partisans, the UPA or the Ukrainian army of resistance had settled down to a domestic existence after the war. In 1948 and 1949 they still possessed a secret network of dug-outs where, guarded by armed partisans, there was a regular printing works for the production of anti-Soviet broadsheets, periodicals, and pamphlets. Today Soviet sources admit that the struggle with the UPA caused them severe losses. One can well understand this when one considers that the UPA had experienced leaders and was obviously supported by a section of the Ukrainian population. It was not until 1950 that the last dug-outs fell into the hands of the Soviet agents, but even then resistance was not completely quelled. On 5 March 1950 the commander of the UPA, Roman Shukhevych, cover-name Chuprynka, was killed at his secret headquarters near Lvov.

Only time will show what happened to the resistance movement in the years that followed, but it looks as if the security organizations cleverly exploited the situation of the Ukrainian exiles for their own ends. The Soviet agents found that an excellent opportunity to fish in troubled waters was provided by the conflict between the radical wing of the Ukrainian nationalists, headed by Stefan Bandera, and the wing that adapted itself to the new conditions in the Western world and gathered around the chief representatives outside Russia of the Supreme Council of Ukrainian Liberation, the UHVR. Even better opportunities for countering the partisan movement were offered by the collaboration between a Western intelligence service and a wing of the Ukrainian nationalists in exile.

The epilogue to these connections so fatal to the Ukrainian national movement was enacted in May 1954. On the 19th, the eve of the great celebrations commemorating the tercentenary of the union of the Ukraine with Russia, Radio Kiev announced the execution of a certain Okhrymovych, who had been sent from Munich to work illegally in the Soviet Union. The communiqué alleged that he had confessed his guilt and had given a full account of the treasonable activities of the OUN abroad and of his fellow spies in the Ukraine. There can be no doubt that the Soviet security service dealt a mortal blow to the Ukrainian anti-Communist resistance round about the year 1953, at a time when various anti-Communist organizations thought that better opportunities for illegal activity in the Soviet Union had been created by Stalin's death.

The destruction of an extensive spy network in Belorussia was described in Soviet literature under the heading 'Square B-52'.[135] As in the case of the Ukraine, the connections between a Western intelligence service and a Belorussian national liberation centre on foreign soil played an important part in the affair. Circumstantial Soviet accounts, supported by numerous photographs, tell how Belorussian political exiles had formed a group of *émigré* agents, who were trained at several places, one of them being a secret school at Kaufbeuren in the Bavarian Allgäu, run by American intelligence. Later, four of these agents, whose real names and photographs were published by the Soviets but who went under the pseudonyms of Joe, Ben, Fin, and Karl, were flown from Frankfurt via the Baltic to Belorussia. They were dropped by parachute in the dense forests around Naliboki. The security men were waiting for them on the very same night. If we are to believe Soviet sources, this is what happened. During the night, headquarters in Moscow received two messages. One came from the Soviet air defence stations, which kept a perpetual watch along the whole length of the Soviet frontier, equipped with the latest radar apparatus. They reported that a plane without distinguishing marks had crossed the Soviet frontier during the night and had recrossed it an hour later. The second message came from the Soviet radio monitoring stations. These had long since learned the best way to keep a watch on the activities of the spy headquarters in Frankfurt. On the night in question an American transmitter tried for a long time without success to make contact with a spy in Belorussia by means of the code signal 'dvi de maye'. Finally they picked up three radio messages in cipher sent from somewhere in Belorussia to Frankfurt.

This incident illustrates the methods used by present-day Soviet security organizations. All the information they receive is carefully sifted by experts, and in this case it provided them with valuable clues to the place where the parachutists had taken off. And how did they proceed from this point?

The matter was handed over to the 'operations section'. Experienced security specialists immediately went to the areas in which the agents were calculated to have been dropped. The method used

at this juncture is very significant. The parachutists would naturally be looking out for anti-Communist elements, so 'anti-Communists' were set on their track. The agent Fin fell into the trap at
Baranovichi, when he confided to a certain Semenenko: 'A short
time ago I was in West Germany, where I met some people who
were struggling to bring about a decent existence for the Belorussians.' Later, with growing confidence, he told his 'friend' that
three more comrades of his were living in the forest. Semenenko
sent up-to-date progress reports on the matter to the operations
section, and after a time he made the acquaintance of the other
three agents. The intelligence centre in Frankfurt received the
optimistic message, 'Contacts made with local population. Have
enlisted Semenenko for the job.' So as to learn as much as possible
about the group leaders in the West, the security specialists decided
not to arrest the four agents immediately but to let them go on
working for a while. They settled on a method that had already
been tried out in the campaign against the Ukrainian partisans. A
body of security officers went into the forest, giving themselves out
to be 'illegal anti-Communists'. Rumours about the 'foresters'
spread through the neighbourhood. Soviet sources described sar-
donically the way in which they were armed. A security officer had
visited the local museum and found there some old carbines that
the partisans had used in the civil war against the Red Army.
Rusty old German machine-guns and water-bottles from the First
World War were also taken into the forest, and a headquarters was
set up in a dug-out also dating from the First World War.
The play was staged to the last detail. One day Semenenko
imparted to the parachutists his 'lifelong secret'—he knew there
were partisans living in the forest who had been fighting the
Soviets for years. The spies and the 'foresters' were soon put in
touch with one another. 'Those are the sort of chaps we need', said
the spies. The Soviet writers must have chuckled when recounting
the first meeting, at which the following conversation is said to
have taken place.

'Well, boys, shall we fight the Soviets together?'

'Certainly, mate. We have heard all about you from Semenenko.
We've been in the field a long time now. What about you? We
can't leave the woods, you know. Soon we shall have no strength
left, and no money. We live like animals, and no one gives us any

help. With only four of us, we can't do a thing. We shall just be wiped out.'

'If you help us, we'll help you. There are powerful people in the West who look after us, and when we have finished the job we won't go back without you.'

The parachutists radioed their headquarters that they were in touch with a group of bandits who had evaded the law by taking to the woods. As the days went by the two groups became more and more friendly, and when the secret police had learnt enough, incident 'Square B-52' was brought to an end by the arrest of the agents.

It would be inappropriate here to mention all the details of this affair, nor is its dramatic side important. What is illuminating is the host of minor jobs that had to be done by the operations group of the security service in order to obtain a success.

A good example of how enemies of the State are discovered is provided by the liquidation of a group of agents—American and Swedish, according to the Soviet version—working in Estonia.[136] Under the headline 'Spies arrested and unmasked' a report appeared in *Pravda* of 7 March 1957 containing the following lines: 'In December 1956 the Soviet security service apprehended the Swedish spy Endel Mumm in the very act of communicating by means of a pocket radio with his espionage headquarters in Stockholm. Already in the past the security service have arrested several groups of spies who had been smuggled into the Estonian Union Republic by Swedish intelligence. Thirteen other agents were arrested along with Endel Mumm; among them were Harry Wimm, Johan Maltis, Evalds Hallisk, Ustel Lembit, and Aksel Pors.'

Here again the essential feature of the incident was the connection between Western intelligence services and the exile organizations, in this case Estonian. Soviet sources maintain that the 'Estonian National Council' had a hand in the affair by recruiting collaborators. The selected agents were trained in Stockholm and were provided with accommodation addresses and a genuine address in Helsinki. When this group was rounded up it was found to be in possession of twelve transmitters, cipher codes, invisible ink, automatic weapons, pistols, and ammunition, camera, field glasses, maps, forged Soviet passports and military identification cards, over 200,000 roubles, 600 watches, and 60 pieces of jewellery.

Towards the end of 1960 a documentary film about the discovery of these spies was being shown in the Soviet Union. The story as thus depicted had all the makings of a thriller. The three spies were taken to Estonia in a motorboat. Each had been allotted a different task. They separated on landing, having arranged to meet again in specified places.

One of them, Jonas, had been told to contact a man called Saaliste, the head of a network of agents. Two weeks previously, however, Saaliste had been liquidated. There could be no better illustration of the methods employed by the Soviet security service than the way in which it dealt with Saaliste. He was living in a dugout in a forest, and special observation measures were taken in the area in which he was thought to be hiding. It became known that a keeper by the name of Jansen was regularly buying more provisions than he himself could have needed. The explanation he gave to the shopkeeper was that he wanted them for his woodmen. This aroused suspicion and it was found that he was not employing any workers. Suspicion grew when one day he wanted an accumulator repaired. The local postwoman, who worked for the security service, called on Jansen to tell him that she had dropped the accumulator on the way to him and it was ruined. On hearing this Jansen turned pale with anger. At the same time the radio monitoring service reported that after the accumulator had been taken to be repaired a secret transmitter had gone silent. A variant of the methods already known to us was now employed. One day when Jansen, laden with provisions, was leaving the village he was set upon by bandits. He himself was left unharmed but they relieved him of his foodstuffs. The whole district now buzzed with rumours about a band of deserters or robbers living in the forest. Naturally no one knew that it was a group of Chekists who had been sent there, had built a dug-out, and were living there like bandits. Jansen tried day after day to meet up with them and was finally successful. They showed the utmost caution, apparently fearing that he would betray them to the police. Jansen, however, finally convinced them that he himself was an enemy of the regime and they engaged him as a purveyor of provisions. Naturally he informed Saaliste and his three companions about

his working for the bandits and suggested that Saaliste contact
their chief. Finally a meeting took place, both sides taking extreme
precautions. Saaliste was for a union of the two groups and it was
agreed to construct a common winter quarters. To celebrate the
opening of the new and more capacious dug-out Jansen procured
an appropriate quantity of spirits. While they were drinking each
other's healths the bandits proposed, to show how great was their
mutual trust, an exchange of weapons—a proposal that met with
willing acceptance. Suddenly the chief bandit began to embrace
Saaliste and adroitly crushed the phial of poison sewn into his
collar. Saaliste, finding himself in danger of being poisoned, cut
away a piece of his collar. At that moment the game was up. The
bandits levelled their weapons at Saaliste and his three men, who
attempted to defend themselves, but the weapons for which they
had exchanged their own were unloaded. A shot into the roof of
the dug-out was a signal for Chekists waiting outside. They rushed
in and took the bewildered Saaliste and his men into custody.

When Jonas went to look for Saaliste, he fell into the hands of
the police. Of course he was not immediately arrested, but from
that time on not a step he took went unobserved. When the time
was ripe he was arrested in Tallinn.

Willi, the second agent, tried to poison himself when his
identity was exposed during a visit to an acquaintance. The
secret police managed to keep him alive and his admissions played
a useful part in the liquidation of the whole group.

Susi, the leader of another group of spies, was rendered harmless in an unusual way. This case was a classic example of the
Soviet methods of counter-espionage. Susi used to visit in Tallinn
an old college girl-friend of his, Hilde Jarwin. His friend Herbert,
who had been killed in the war, had been engaged to Hilde, and
Susi was sure that Hilde's apartment would make ideal quarters
for himself. He had an unpleasant shock on his first visit, however,
to find that Hilde had acquired another fiancé, in the person of
one Ernst Borstel. Susi explained to Hilde that after the war he had
taken refuge in the Caucasus, where he had lived in a village with
deported Estonians. But he had no desire to go back there; he
intended to stay in Tallinn. Meanwhile he was becoming better
acquainted with Hilde's new fiancé. Borstel's father was a well-
known architect, but his son lived all alone in his own apartment,

and owing to his passion for motor-cycling was always short of cash. Susi turned this weakness of Borstel's to good use. When anything was needed for the motor-cycle, Susi lent him the money, asking nothing more than a receipt. They became good friends, and Susi moved into Borstel's apartment. When he was completely sure of Borstel, he engaged him to work for the Swedish intelligence. They went by motor-cycle to various places, where they picked up radio messages from the Stockholm headquarters. When funds ran out and life became more difficult, they decided to make their way back to Sweden through Finland. At Tallinn they bought tickets for Leningrad. While Borstel was taking leave of his fiancée, Susi waited for him in the street. Suddenly he was surrounded by civilians and before he knew what was happening they bundled him into a car. He was taken to security headquarters in Tallinn and interrogated by an officer. Susi protested against the arrest, since his papers were in order and he could call on Hilde and Borstel as references. At that juncture a door opened and the interrogating officer said to a man in the uniform of a captain in the security force, 'Tell Susi the whole story, and then he will see that the game is up'. When Susi looked at the newcomer he saw that it was Borstel.

This case illustrates other methods adopted by the Soviet security service. Susi and his assistants were being shadowed by Soviet agents when they were still in Stockholm. Once when he was in his cups Susi told 'someone' that he had a close friend in Tallinn called Hilde, who had been an assistant in a confectioner's shop during the war. He did not mention her surname, but what he said was more than sufficient for the Soviet officials. They checked on all the Hildes in Tallinn who had worked in confectioners' shops during the war. There were only four of them and the right one was soon found. Long before Susi arrived in Tallinn, Hilde was working for the secret police. So Susi was under observation from the start. He was not liquidated straight away but unwittingly helped the secret police to discover the identity of his employers, thus adding to the knowledge of its opponents which the Soviet security service already possessed.

From 1956 onwards the Soviet press published any number of reports of such affairs as this—brief items, or eye-witness accounts, or longer, detailed stories. A careful study reveals in all of them a sense of superiority on the part of the Soviet security services. They are always the heroes, never putting a foot wrong. Genuine names and addresses, telephone numbers, and other particulars are frequently given in these reports. Addresses in Western Germany are also noticeably frequent, and sometimes particulars of the American training establishments for intelligence agents are given.

In 1962 a slim volume of 152 pages reporting cases such as those we have described appeared in the Soviet Union.[137] Naturally these stories must be read with caution—a piece of advice which does not apply exclusively to the products of Soviet 'journalism'. But it would be equally wrong to dismiss them as pure fantasy. The booklet in question, for instance, contains photographs of spies under arrest, their equipment, and so forth. And many of the addresses in Munich and Frankfurt are genuine enough. If, after Stalin's death, the Western intelligence services really did imagine that their opportunity had come, they were soon disillusioned. Shortly after the 20th Party Congress the Soviet security service was once again full of confidence. It had warded off external threats to the Soviet Union and at the same time had seen to it that the social transformation inside the USSR was proceeding undisturbed. Its status within the system was retained, thanks to Nikita Khrushchev and his right-hand man in matters of security, Serov.

The 20th Party Congress

The 20th Congress of the Communist Party of the Soviet Union, held in 1956, was in some respects a turning-point in the history of the Union. So far as the security service was concerned, the Party reaffirmed its approval of the policy of 'the establishment of Socialist legality'. In his speech Khrushchev said emphatically that 'the Beria gang sought to withdraw the State security service from the control of the Party and the power of the Soviet, and to put themselves above Party and Government, also to create an atmosphere of lawlessness and arbitrariness within the service'. On the other hand, he warned the Communists against 'a certain distrust of the personnel of the security service'. 'The personnel of our State Security Service', he said, 'are for the most part honourable men devoted to our common cause.' He also drew attention to the further extension of the Western intelligence network. 'We know that reactionary circles in various capitalist countries are openly supporting agitation against our country and even boast of it. Suffice it to say that since 1951 the USA has been spending 100 million dollars a year on this work of propaganda against Socialist countries. Consequently we must use every means of intensifying revolutionary watchfulness among the Soviet people and strengthening our security services.'

The chief feature of the 20th Party Congress was the emphasis laid on what Mikoyan called the 'enforcement of Leninist-Socialist legality to its fullest extent'. The new function of the security service was clearly defined on three main principles: the further consolidation of 'Socialist legality'; the rehabilitation of Stalin's victims and the related revaluation of the various stages in the development of the security service; and finally a certain narrowing of the security service's area of activity, with the surrender of some of its previous duties to 'social institutions'.

After the 20th Congress new measures were taken to strengthen 'Socialist legality'. On 19 April 1956 the Presidium of the Supreme Soviet of the USSR annulled the decree issued on 1 December 1944 by the Presidium of the Central Executive Committee of the USSR 'on the procedure to be followed in legal proceedings in cases involving the planning and execution of acts of terrorism'. Similarly it annulled the decrees of 1 December 1934 and 14 September 1937 'on the insertion of amendments in the standard penal codes and the procedures to be followed in legal proceedings in the Union Republics'. A few days before these annulments the new 'Decree regarding the State Prosecutor's Office of the USSR' had been passed and a department had been established to superintend the investigations conducted by the State Security Service. This was the first time that juristic publications contained strong criticism of A. Y. Vyshinsky, who had not only acted as State Prosecutor in the 'Moscow trials' but had also provided theoretical support of Stalin's terrorist justice.

A current of healthy fresh air followed in the wake of the 20th Party Congress. Soviet man, drilled by Stalin into blind obedience, plucked up courage again. As though the flood-gates had been opened, a torrent of debate poured out over the country, and not only was the past discussed at public meetings but private opinions were voiced at home and among friends. The younger generation was astonished to hear its elders' stammering explanations of why they had taken a hand in such doings. For the younger generation at least a new era opened with the 20th Party Congress, and though in the political world the cold wind familiar to their grandfathers soon began to blow again, in the world of technology, economics, and culture, and indeed in everyday life, the voice of youth could now be clearly heard.

The 'Anti-Party Group'

Shortly after the Party Congress a bitter dispute arose among the Soviet leaders, who had been anything but unanimous since Stalin's death. In June 1957 the climax was reached. At the time, even men who had taken a direct part in the reprisals and mass murders were still holding leading posts. Kaganovich, Molotov, and Malenkov tried to use their positions to put a brake on the new trend. The current rehabilitations especially could certainly not have been to their liking, seeing that their own misdeeds might be brought into the light of day. And there were other reasons for their attitude. Khrushchev and a section of the Party bureaucrats were well aware that the whole of Soviet society needed radical reform if it were to make any progress. The conservative wing of the Party, however, was opposed to any such aspirations. These functionaries, many of whom, even in 1957, were more acceptable than Khrushchev to the Party bureaucracy, organized what developed into a regular conspiracy. It was joined by Shepilov and even by another Chairman of the Presidium of the Supreme Soviet of the USSR, Marshal Voroshilov. At a session of the Presidium of the Central Committee of the Communist Party they decided to depose Khrushchev from the First Secretaryship of the Central Committee. In June 1957, in dramatic circumstances, a plenary session of the Central Committee of the Communist Party was convened; the Party leaders who had engineered the affair and thenceforth went down in the history of the Communist Party of the Soviet Union as the 'Anti-Party Group' were themselves relieved of their offices. Later on, when the conflict between Moscow and Peking came to a head, Molotov and his adherents made another attempt to divert the general trend, but failed. They were ousted for good and all, and now lead lonely lives as pensioners in retirement—mere relics of a bygone epoch.

The events of June 1957 are extremely important for our theme. One of the causes of the victory gained by Khrushchev and his group over the 'Anti-Party Group' was that popular opinion was on their side. They spread it abroad that the Anti-Party men wanted to return to the old state of things and were opposing the elimination of the consequences of the personality cult. Popular opinion also favoured the new masters inasmuch as those dispensed with were not, as in Stalin's time, given a shot in the back of the neck but were re-employed in other, presumably uninfluential, positions. And it was an indication, obvious to everybody, of what was meant by 'Socialist legality'.

The penal laws of 1958

At the meeting of the Supreme Soviet of the USSR on 22–25 December 1958 certain penal laws were passed. The distinctive feature of this session was that it was largely a turning away from the 'materialist' definition of crime that was the norm in Stalin's time. Under Stalin not only was crime universally defined as 'a deed endangering society', but, in addition, the 'principle of analogy' was introduced into the penal laws. In accordance with this principle, deeds which were similar to those to which a penalty was attached in the penal code could also be punished. One need not be a jurist to see how such elastic paragraphs facilitated arbitrary interpretation of the laws. At the aforesaid session the Soviet administration of justice adopted the 'formal definition' as universally recognized by modern legislators, according to which the term 'crime' is applicable only to what is expressly prohibited by the penal laws. This means that from that time onward only those actions forbidden by law rendered the doer liable to criminal prosecution.

This change of policy entailed the annulment of various arbitrary enactments of the Stalin era. In addition, reprisals against persons alleged to have been in contact with 'criminal circles', the 'enemy of the people' stigma, and numerous terrorist measures, such as those taken against a defector's family, were abolished.

By the new legislation, 'no evidence to be submitted to a court of law, the State Prosecutor, or an investigating judge shall have

a predetermined significance'. The judgement of the court, therefore, is to be based solely on the evidence given in the course of the
trial. Suppositions and suspicions must be excluded from the proceedings, and the guilt of the defendant must be proved to the
court.

We shall not enumerate all the effects of this reform but confine ourselves to the measures which have reformed and—in comparison with the Stalinist era—transformed the operations of the
security service. In former days anyone could suffer the heaviest
penalties, including death, at the hands of the special units of the
NKVD, without judicial proceedings. The courts were arbitrary
too; the judges had to follow Stalin's instructions, and especially
his henchman Vyshinsky's recommendations and interpretations.
They were obliged to base their verdicts on the 'Socialist sense
of justice', the Russian counterpart to the 'healthy national sentiment' of the Hitlerian regime, in which the decisive part was played
by secret reports, 'expert' opinions, unsubstantiated suspicions, and
the rest. In those days the grounds for a judgement, especially in
political trials, were rarely given. The present-day Soviet laws, on
the other hand, go back to the old principle *nullum crimen sine
lege* (no crime without its corresponding law). This is self-evident
in Western countries, but was not so regarded by the Soviet
bureaucracy corrupted by Stalin.

This change of policy in the Soviet administration of justice
should not be overlooked. Western jurists see in it a new trend, of
an importance not to be underestimated. It is thanks to Khrushchev
that, as Klaus Westen says, we can feel assured of a genuine progress in the administration of justice, as exemplified by an improvement and normalization of conditions and a movement towards
the restoration of legal security.[138]

But do not let us put too much trust in the Soviet administration
of justice. One of its most vital problems remains unsolved: who
or what guarantees the security of the law? Without going into
theoretical discussions one may say that there can be no question
of any such guarantee so long as the 'Party spirit', normal throughout Soviet society, dominates every sphere of activity, including
the administration of justice. This Party spirit makes almost a
farce of any legal and effective control over civil servants, and the
effect on judicial impartiality is easily imagined. Consequently

the danger of arbitrary interpretation of the law is still very great and very real. This is not a digression; it has a great deal to do with our main theme—terrorism in Soviet society. The laws of 1958 delimit the new position of the security service within the system. Naturally the service will continue to do its utmost to interpret in its own fashion certain criminal actions and the relevant paragraphs. But a relapse into sheer arbitrariness—the essence of terrorism—to the extent prevalent under Stalin, is now unthinkable, because the security service can no longer act on its own account.

Every jurist who has studied the subject is aware of the danger of trial and sentence being manipulated when so-called 'political crimes' are involved. The penal law divides them into crimes which are a special danger to the State, and other crimes. The former include treason, espionage, terrorist acts against the State and State organizations, terrorist acts against representatives of foreign States, acts of 'deviation' and sabotage, anti-soviet agitation and propaganda, war propaganda, the organization of highly dangerous crimes against the State with a simultaneous adherence to an anti-Soviet organization, and highly dangerous crimes against another 'Socialist State'.[139] 'Highly dangerous crimes against the State' are punishable with a maximum of 15 years' imprisonment and confiscation of property, or with the death penalty and confiscation of property. Other, not so highly dangerous, crimes against the State are punishable with lengthy terms of imprisonment; in addition, according to the decree of the Supreme Soviet of the USSR of 18 May 1961, they are punishable with deportation for up to five years. The catalogue of punishment is very extensive and differs substantially from that of other countries, including the 'people's democracies'. It comprises penalties unknown in the rest of Europe: deportation (*sylta*) as well as loss of liberty; banishment (*vyzylka*); 'corrective labour' with loss of liberty, which means hard, mostly manual, labour; loss of the civil right to fill certain posts and engage in certain activities; money fines; public reprimand; and the death penalty. Loss of liberty may mean either a term of imprisonment or confinement in a 'corrective labour colony'. Deportation means that a citizen may be condemned by the court to move from his place of residence to some other specified place; banishment means that, in addition, he is prohibited from residing in specified localities.

At this point we shall skip the development of legal norms and the whole administration of justice under Khrushchev and go straight to later events. The propitious start that was made in 1958 soon came to a standstill. In 1958 the Soviet authorities were still stressing the educational qualities of punishment. After 1960 they achieved an almost complete about-turn, and the catalogue of crimes to which the death penalty was attached grew longer and longer. In May 1961, for instance, death became the penalty for the embezzlement 'to a specially large extent' of state or communal property, also for coin forgery. In July 1961 the applicability of the death penalty was again extended, this time to speculation in currency and foreign exchange. According to ordinances set out in Articles 22 and 25 of the 'Principles of Penal Law', the long list of offences punishable by death include the following: high treason, espionage, sabotage, acts of terrorism, gangsterism, the professional manufacture of false coins or paper money for the purpose of passing them on, the putting into circulation, either professionally or in large quantities, or counterfeit coins or paper money, speculation in foreign bills and paper money, the infringement of currency regulations by a person previously convicted of infringing currency regulations or of speculating in foreign bills or paper money, wilful murder in aggravated circumstances according to the articles of the penal laws of the USSR and the Union Republics relating to wilful murder, the plundering of state or public property to a specially great extent, and particularly serious crimes in time of war or in theatres of war in circumstances specially laid down in the laws of the USSR. For the time being capital punishment may be carried out by shooting.

Execution by shooting can also be meted out to specially dangerous habitual criminals, and to persons convicted of serious offences who terrorize other prisoners or repeatedly assault the prison staff, or join with others for the same purpose and take an active part in these criminal activities.

This catalogue was enlarged in February 1962 by the extension of the death penalty to attempts on the life of a member of the militia or people's militia when performing his duty, also to cases of corruption of officials.

Capital punishment in the Soviet Union
The course of legislation from 1917 to 1962 is as follows:

23 March 1917: abolition of capital punishment.
21 January 1918: restoration.
17 January 1920: abolition.
May 1920: restoration.
26 May 1947: abolition.

The 1947 decree of the Presidium of the Supreme Soviet of the USSR included the following sentence: 'In accordance with the wishes of the trades unions of the workers and employees and of other representative organizations which express the views of the broad masses of the people, the Presidium of the Supreme Soviet judges it unnecessary to have recourse to the death penalty in time of peace.'

12 January 1950: restoration.

By this decree of the Presidium of the Supreme Soviet of the USSR, capital punishment was restored in the case of 'traitors, spies, and persons trying to undermine the State'. The justification for this measure was that '... in consideration of the statements made by the Union Republics, the trades unions, the peasants, and the cultural workers, the decree abolishing capital punishment must be rescinded'.

30 April 1954: extension of the death penalty to the offence of murder in aggravated circumstances.
25 December 1958. The law concerning the responsibility of the criminal law for dealing with crimes against the State provided for the death penalty for the following offences: high treason, espionage, sabotage ('deviation'), acts of terrorism, banditry, and murder. The death penalty was also permissible in the case of other specially serious offences committed in war time or in battle conditions.
27 October 1960. The penal code of the RSFSR provided the death penalty for banditry, acts of terrorism, high treason, espionage, and murder.
5 May 1961. By a decree of the Supreme Soviet of the USSR the death penalty was extended to the 'embezzlement of state or public property to a specially great extent' and professional coin-forgery.

1 July 1961. Further extension of the death penalty, on this occasion to currency and foreign exchange speculation.

15 February 1962. Extension of the death penalty to attempts made in aggravated circumstances on the life of a member of the militia or people's militia performing his duty or when engaged in social activity; also to the use of force in aggravated circumstances.

20 February 1962. Extension of the death penalty to cover the 'passive' corruption of officials.

No statistics of the administration of justice being issued in the Soviet Union, specific computations can only be based on Press reports. Professor Maurach, an expert on the administration of justice in Eastern Europe, reports that in 1962 181 persons were sentenced to death and executed. Most of these convictions were not for political offences but for murder, robbery with violence, embezzlement, currency speculation, and, in more recent times and more and more frequently, bribery and corruption. Between May 1961 and May 1963, according to the same authority, 160 death sentences were passed on economic offenders.[140]

These figures clearly show a shift of emphasis from the educational function of punishment to the primitive object of deterrence. Under pressure from the Party leadership the highly controversial theory that capital punishment can play a positive role in society has prevailed in the Soviet administration of justice. This attitude is controverted by the declaration on universal human rights adopted by the General Assembly of the United Nations in December 1948, which solemnly affirmed the right to life of every human being. Throughout the centuries the arguments for and against capital punishment have been debated time after time in every country in the world, but the latest results of research made in those countries which have abolished the death penalty indicate that opinion is inevitably moving in that direction. The French Union for the Abolition of Capital Punishment, for instance, held a meeting on 8 December 1960 at which famous criminologists for the first time thrashed out the problem. It was further debated in June 1961 at the Royaumont conferences, which came to the conclusion that both historical evolution and factual observation showed that capital punishment was an anachronism. The primitive arguments brought forward in its favour were no longer in conformity with modern ethics and were no longer in line with modern treatment of criminals. It was also declared that the purpose of punishment could no longer consist in the deterrence of the individual or of society at large by means of excessive severity. History has shown, it was stated, that, regarded solely from the standpoint of deterrence, punishment was of no effect. Excessive harshness did not produce a lessening of criminality or recidivism. Consequently other methods must be found of keeping criminality within bounds. The essence of the new attitude adopted by those who took part in the Royaumont conferences is that respect for human life must be absolute, both on ethical grounds and also because of the duties which the modern world acknowledges are owed by society to fundamental human rights.[141]

The extension of the death penalty in the Soviet Union which took place after the 22nd Party Congress must be regarded as a menace for several reasons. Here too it has been demonstrated that increased severity of sentence and additions made to the list of offences liable to capital punishment have in no way diminished serious crime. This is confirmed even by the Soviet press itself. Since the first report of any length on the death sentences carried out in 1941, crimes of this nature have increased every month. This in itself is enough to make one doubt the efficiency of the extended death penalty. And there are two other important considerations that question the rightness of this policy. In every modern state crimes such as murder, robbery with violence, and the like are committed, but many of the offences punishable with death in the Soviet Union are extremely rare in other countries. The cause of the discrepancy is easily discovered. It is first and foremost the Soviet system that favours the commission of these offences; secondly, the Soviet Union could put a stop to all currency offences in twenty-four hours if it came into line with Germany, France, and many other countries, and adopted regulations current there.

Finally, the whole matter is important when viewed from still another standpoint. When in May 1947 the death penalty was abolished in the Soviet Union for a short time, with a great deal of propagandist palaver, the relevant decree stressed that the Soviet Union was thereby setting the rest of the world 'an example of real Socialist humanity'.[142] The idea, therefore, that capital punishment is an assault on human dignity is not alien to Soviet politicians and jurists. But after the 22nd Party Congress had announced the new Communist programme and proclaimed the attainment of a higher social standard as the chief goal of Party activity, the death penalty became an essential component of every measure serving to achieve this purpose. However, no one with any belief in progress can regard the Soviet's hypertrophy of capital punishment as a promotion of Socialist legality.

Reform of the concentration camp system

Another retrogressive tendency is shown in the continual extension of the so-called corrective labour colonies, which are—to call things by their right names—simply forced labour camps. According to the new Soviet penal law passed in December 1958, a stay in a corrective labour colony was a mild form of punishment. In the course of time, this institution, which was meant to replace the concentration camp, became extremely complex. According to Soviet sources, it takes the following forms: (1) General corrective labour colonies (*ispravitelno-trudovye kolonii obshchego rezhima*); (2) Strict corrective labour colonies (*strogogo rezhima*), primarily intended for recidivists and habitual criminals; (3) Severe corrective labour colonies (*osobogo rezhima*), most of whose inmates are criminals dangerous to the public or persons whose sentences have been commuted from execution to a long term of imprisonment. The corrective labour camps for young persons are dealt with in a chapter to themselves. According to Soviet penal law, offences committed by persons over fourteen years of age are punishable by the law applicable to adults. Soviet law makes no special provision for the correction of young persons such as is customary in progressive states in the West. In practice, however, since 1958, they have been sent to serve their sentences in special corrective labour camps for youth. So far as is known, there are two classes of these camps, training methods varying with the gravity of the offence.

It became known in 1964 that in some of the republics, such as the Russian Soviet Federated Social Republics of Kazakhstan, Uzbekistan, and Moldavia, certain so-called corrective-labour settlement colonies (*kolonii-pozelenya*) have been established, where living conditions are supposed to be easier than in those we have mentioned above. Persons who have served part of their sentence in corrective labour colonies and have received a certificate of good conduct are transferred to a corrective-labour-settlement colony.

Failure of 'social justice'

Under Khrushchev the administration of justice proceeded by fits and starts: important trials that were positive and progressive in character went hand-in-hand with ultra-reactionary ones. The reasons, of course, were not entirely of a personal nature. While Khrushchev was in office, the Soviet leaders often showed their desire to eradicate the negative features of the system, but there is a big difference between wanting something and putting it into practice. Once more it was shown that Soviet society had not yet rid itself of its heritage of depotism. Without wishing to excuse certain proceedings that took place within the Soviet system, one must, to be impartial, admit that here as everywhere else intrinsically good ideas come to nothing when they are faced with reality and prove to be utopian. One example of this is the attempt made by Khrushchev and his collaborators at the time to insert the 'social element' into the preservation of justice, the combating of crime, and the maintenance of public order. The attempt failed, but because of the results that ensued it calls for a detailed treatment.

One of the measures taken to include the 'social element', i.e. principally the workers in the factories and the 'white collar' employees in the large concerns, was the establishment of a 'People's Militia'. Together with the regular militia these groups of volunteers were to help maintain public order in both town and country. The Comsomol and the trades unions were exhorted to join them. By the middle of 1960 there were more than 80,000 detachments of 'People's Militia'. They comprised a fantastic number of 'social guardians of public order', two and a half million of them. The experiment got off to quite a promising start. Party bureaucrats and the general public talked only of defects in organization, which would disappear as soon as the 'People's Militia' had settled down. Actually, as it turned out, the experiment proved to be still-born. The people just took no interest in it. In addition, there was friction between the 'People's Militia' and the regular militia, which was not removed by lengthy speeches made at numerous conferences and meetings by representatives of the bench, the public prosecutor, and even the security service, about the duties and problems of the 'People's Militia'. At first, in 1959 and 1960, the newspapers were falling over themselves in praise of the way in which the 'People's Militia' had brought about a diminution in petty swindles, vagabondage, hooliganism (to use a favourite Soviet expression), and offences committed when under the influence of drink. But this did not last long. It soon became apparent that in actual fact the 'People's Militia' was quite incapable of checking the growth of juvenile delinquency and the ever-spreading hooliganism. As we shall see, it was not until Khrushchev's downfall, namely in 1966, that firm conclusions were drawn.

Even more serious consequences ensued from the fiasco of 'social justice', by which was meant a stronger infusion of the 'lay element' into the administration of the law. This idea, too, was progressive and positive in its outlook. What was envisaged was a people's court in its true sense, not the perverted Nazi sense. These 'social arbitrators' were to be given the competence to pass judgement on minor transgressions of the law. A similarly positive tendency had shown itself in 1957, when a law against 'anti-social elements' and 'parasites' was drafted and submitted for discussion, at a time when the whole of Soviet society was in a state of flux following Stalin's death. The days when society could be totally manipulated were gone; even under Stalin it had never been completely possible. In these days leaders proposing any legal project had immediately to reckon with the opposition of public opinion or certain social groups. Such indeed was the fate of the law against 'anti-social elements' and 'parasites', which did not go unopposed. Some jurists went so far as to warn the country that the 'judgements of the general public' could easily lead to abuses and the revival of arbitrariness. Preparations were made for these judgements to be given at the citizens' assemblies in the appropriate neighbourhood, collective farm, or settlement. These lay courts were empowered to sentence a delinquent to a term of penal servitude ranging from two to five years or to a correspondingly longer period of deportation. 'Through these social judgements', observed the Tadzhik jurist Bolshakov in a discussion on the significance of this form of social justice, 'persons could be robbed of their freedom without any proper legal procedure. The question of guilt can never be satisfactorily decided in a public assembly. Only a court of law is in a position to establish whether a man is guilty or not. And I am not alone in that opinion.' But Khrushchev and his colleagues were deaf to all such warnings. They were fascinated by this 'modern' idea that would not only ensure the punishment of 'anti-social elements' but would also arouse the citizen's sense of justice. That in fact the idea was a snare and delusion had to be admitted by Khrushchev even before his abdication.

What had happened? Today, when we look at the question from a certain distance of time, we are struck first by the bureaucratic corruption of this kind of 'social justice'. Instead of a case being properly dealt with, a bureaucratic ritual was performed. Suppose that in a certain factory a worker had stolen something. Instead of being passed to the militia, the case is heard by the 'Comrades' Court'. Naturally a trial of this kind can be held only after working hours. On the judges' bench sit the accused's fellow workers. A 'social' prosecutor presents the case; the accused is defended by a 'social' counsel. Everybody is tired and wants to go home. What is particularly important is that everyone present is aware that he may be the next to stand trial. The speeches keep to a prescribed pattern, and the conclusion is always the same: they all hope that the accused will mend his ways. Finally they sentence him to some prescribed punishment. The court rises. Judges and audience crowd to the door, eager to get home as quickly as possible. How a satisfactory result is to be obtained in this way is a mystery.

To give another illustration of the contradictory tendencies in Soviet society in general, and not only in the administration of justice: to arouse greater interest in the administration of justice among the lay judges and the personnel in the factories it was decided to allow every collective to apply on behalf of the defendant in a regular court of law for suspension of sentence and a period of probation. In such cases the collective went security for the accused, that is to say it undertook to 'improve' the delinquent. This procedure (called *na poruki*) was certainly permissible only in less serious cases. But as many of the laws consist of elastic paragraphs and as it is often left to the judge's discretion to draw the line between serious and petty offences, the experiment did nothing to strengthen a sense of justice or concern for the maintenance of public order—as the legislators had hoped—but had precisely the opposite effect. The number of applications for suspension of sentence rose by leaps and bounds, and there were cases of respected citizens putting in *na poruki* applications on behalf of habitual and recidivist criminals. There were loud protests from the Press. A feebly inculcated feeling for justice on the one hand—a heritage from Stalin's time—and the absence of firm guarantees of legal security on the other resulted in 'ineradicable daily habits' gaining the upper hand. For any number of reasons (sympathy with the accused's family, the factory's need of his skill, or just because, after all, he was quite a decent chap) a group would frequently decide in favour of the accused and make light of his offence.

The only way, then, in which the Soviets could profit from 'social justice' was to misuse it for the purpose of political revenge—a very dubious 'success'. To mention briefly a typical case: in February–March 1964, just before Khrushchev's departure, a Leningrad court dealt with the case of the Russian writer Yosif Brodsky, who was arraigned on the charge of being an 'anti-social and parasitic element'. He was sentenced to five years' hard labour. The disgraceful means employed to achieve this end were revealed in shorthand notes of the proceedings which found their way to the West and were published in various newspapers, including some in Germany.[143] Brodsky was accused of having gained his livelihood by casual labour in order to indulge himself to the full in literature. The twenty-four-year-old writer and translator tried to explain to the judges that writing and translating was as honourable a kind of work as any other. The linguist and *littérateur* Admoni, a professor at the Herzen Institute, gave the accused an excellent character, praised the high standard of his translations, and affirmed that he devoted much time to his literary activity. 'So it is nonsense', he said, 'to accuse Brodsky of being work-shy. It's impossible to bring a charge of laziness against a man who works like Brodsky—so hard and for such long hours—who is not always thinking of money but is prepared to exist on the barest necessities so as to perfect himself in his art and produce literary, high-quality translations.' The shorthand note of these proceedings against Brodsky is a terrifying document of Soviet reality. The puppet witnesses whose strings were pulled by people behind the scenes and who were made to strut into the box as 'representatives of the people' slandered Brodsky and very often described his work as 'horrible and anti-Soviet compositions', without any real knowledge of the works or even knowing whether Brodsky wrote them. Most shocking of all was the attitude of the female 'Comrade Judge', who did not bother to examine the case objectively but continually attempted in uncouth, demagogic fashion to play down anything that told in favour of the accused.

Rehabilitation of the deported peoples

To deal with a positive aspect of the administration of justice under Khrushchev we shall hark back to one of his most important steps: the rehabilitation of the peoples deported by Stalin during the Second World War. Khrushchev had already denounced this barbaric measure of Stalin's in his secret speech at the 20th Party Congress. On 9 January 1957 the Presidium of the Supreme Soviet of the USSR decreed the restoration of the autonomous territories of the Balkars, Chechens, Ingushes, Kalmyks, and Karachai. On 11 January 1957 the same body decreed the detachment of the Chechen territory from the Georgian SSR and its incorporation into the Russian Soviet Federated Socialist Republic. At the February meeting of the Supreme Soviet of the USSR in 1957 these measures were hailed as a return to the nationality policy of Lenin and were confirmed by law. Then on 29 July 1958 the autonomous Kalmyk territory was transformed into the Kalmyk Autonomous Socialist Soviet Republic. This was the beginning of the gradual return of the deported national groups.

Even if Khrushchev and his adherents had wanted to make amends for Stalin's criminal treatment of these nationalities, it was now hardly possible to do so completely. Some of the victims had taken root in their new settlements and were no longer interested in returning to their homeland. For the Crimean Tatars the reparation came too late; their numbers had been seriously depleted by their compulsory evacuation from sunny Crimea to lands subject to a harsh climate. And since in the meantime the Crimea had been 'presented' to the Soviet Ukraine, political demographic conditions had undergone so great a change that a restoration of Tatar autonomy in the Crimea was out of the question.

An even more protracted business was the rehabilitation of the Volga Germans. It was not until Khrushchev had fallen that it was learnt that when his term of office was nearing its end, namely on 29 August 1964, the Presidium of the Supreme Soviet of the USSR had adopted a decree in respect of them. In this it was stated that in the Second World War the greater part of the people of German origin in the Soviet Union had sided with Russia. Meanwhile they had settled down in their new homeland. The decree guaranteed them cultural autonomy and other benefits there, but not a word was said about restoring the Autonomous Republic of the Volga Germans. So the map of the Soviet Union is no longer the same as it was. Nevertheless, what has happened must be accepted as evidence of the willingness of Stalin's successors to mitigate the consequences of his misdeeds.

Espionage—a fine art . . . and a base handicraft

Every intelligence service aims at making itself proof against crises; one way of doing this is to provide the Government with exclusive information of such importance that not only the service's right to exist but, if possible, its indispensability is beyond question. Naturally it is not everywhere that the taxpayer can test for himself the actual usefulness of this institution. In post-despotic societies, the situation seems to be rather different from that in the USA, for instance. There the public has become so critical of the various forms of intelligence service that their boasts no longer have much effect. It is otherwise in the Soviet Union. The services there—and by this we mean the KGB (Committee for State Security) and the armed forces—do their best to show that they are unassailable. And in fact, under Khrushchev, they could point to some successes.

At Karlsruhe in July 1963 three members of the Federal German intelligence service were up for trial, in the course of which it transpired that a Soviet agent by the name of Heinz Felfe had held a leading position in the Gehlen organization from 1950 on; in other words, he had been watching the organization—he had even been working at its headquarters at Pullach—and had provided the Soviet Union with information. The three accused men admitted that they had delivered to the Soviet intelligence service 15,000 photo-copies of documents in the possession of the Gehlen organization of the Federal Republic, besides twenty tape-recordings. General Gehlen, a member of the German General

Staff under Hitler, had recruited for his organization a number of well-tried associates, including the aforesaid Felfe, a former member of the SS and a Nazi agent in Switzerland during the war.[144] This was only a partial success on the part of the Soviet intelligence. It was true that its agents were able to spy on Gehlen's espionage organization from the inside and supply Moscow with valuable material, but the exposure of the group signified, after all, one of Moscow's failures. The same can be said about the notorious case of the Swedish colonel-general of the Air Force, Stif Erik Constans Wennerström, who was exposed after years of service for the Soviet intelligence and was sentenced to lifelong imprisonment. In him the Soviets had a first-class purveyor of top-secret material from USA and NATO headquarters. But here too the final exposure injured Moscow's morale; it revealed defects in the Soviet spy system and was not exactly an advertisement for its faultless working. Another question arises: how many Soviet masters of their craft are still sitting pretty in the Western intelligence services?

Of course even these cases of exposure will take their place in the history of espionage as *chefs-d'oeuvre* of the higher flights of the profession, but in the recent history of the Soviet secret service there was one case that shocked the Soviet public and enhanced the prestige of the Western services. On 19 May 1963, following his trial, a colonel in military intelligence (GUR), Oleg V. Penkovsky, was executed in Moscow. From April until the time of his arrest he had succeeded at various times in passing information to the West, using for the purpose photocopies, microfilms, and tape-recordings. His reports, touched up with obvious clumsiness by the Western intelligence services, appeared in several languages and became best-sellers everywhere.[145] Penkovsky produced far less than his Western counterparts, Felfe and Wennerström, but it was enough to raise considerable dust. It was a long time since anything like this had happened in the Soviet Union. To think: a functionary in a key position in military intelligence who deliberately put himself at the service of the West! Whatever its importance, Penkovsky's treachery certainly shook the Kremlin, according to German observers, who were probably right.[146]

Once again it has been established that the Soviet intelligence service is at its best in its traditional sphere of activity, among the *émigrés*, especially the groups of extremists, and that it is most successful there. But who, in either the East or the West, is interested in, or has any knowledge of, the human tragedies involved in these activities? There was an epilogue to the battle between the Soviet security service and the so-called Ukrainian rebel army, the UPA, whose deeds have already been recounted. Shukhevych-Chuprynka, the commander-in-chief of this organization, which for years had given the Soviet authorities a great deal of trouble, was killed in 1950. He was succeeded by V. Kuk. Three years later there were clear signs of dissolution in this resistance group. What actually happened, the secret archives of the Soviet authorities have not yet revealed, but some light was thrown on the affair round about 1960 by the Soviet security service itself. The Ukrainian *émigrés* could hardly believe their eyes when in the autumn of 1960 they read in a journal published in East Berlin in the Ukrainian language an open letter from V. Kuk to his 'comrades and friends' abroad. It appeared that he had been arrested by the Soviets and had afterwards been pardoned together with his wife. According to his account he was now living as a free citizen in the Soviet Union. He appealed to the *émigrés* to give up the struggle against the Union, to offer no assistance to the Western intelligence services, and to help promote progress at home. *Inter alia*, the appeal stated that many of the errors inherited from the Stalin era had been corrected and that those that still remained would soon be cleared away.

Whether or not this ploy had any political significance, the story of Myron Matviyeyko, the former head of the security section of the radically nationalist Ukrainian group that went by the name of OUN-Bandera, is still more macabre. His name has been linked with numerous political murders committed after 1945 in the Western-occupied zones of Germany. It is no longer possible to fix the number of persons murdered by these Radical Ukrainian fanatics of the Right, since no one was interested in bringing them to light, but one thing is certain: Bandera instructed Matviyeyko to enter the Ukraine illegally for the purpose of bringing back into line with his organization the illegal groups that had fallen away from Bandera's Right Radicalism. On 24 November 1960 Matviyeyko made a speech on Radio Kiev from which it appeared that as soon as he had crossed the frontier he had put himself at the disposal of the Soviet security service. He is suspected, not without cause, of having played no small part in the final extermination of the resistance groups. Moderate nationalist circles are in no doubt that his activities in Western Germany had been agreed upon beforehand with the Soviet intelligence, and that the illegal groups had been warned that he was an *agent provocateur*. Some journals in fact claimed that there was proof of this.[147]

For the Russian *émigrés*, too, the Soviet security service had a surprise in store. We have already referred to the Shulgin affair. At the end of 1960 a Russian news-sheet published in East Berlin carried an open letter from Shulgin to the Russian *émigrés*.[148] This made out that in the thirties, after the affair already related, he had led a humble existence in a small Yugoslavian town, where in October 1940 he had been arrested and taken to Moscow. In his open letter he wrote that after a searching interrogation he had been sentenced to a long term of imprisonment on account of his counter-revolutionary activity, but had been pardoned in 1956 and along with several others had been released from the prison camp. The letter seemed to be genuine. He was writing, he said, not as a Communist but quite the opposite. 'I am a mystic. Mysticism combines badly with materialism. I appeal to the *émigrés* to help the Communists, to fight against the spectre of war, not because I believe the Communist doctrine to be infallible but because the Communists have the right way of thinking about this matter, namely the fight against war. Their feelings are humane and their actions are for the good of mankind.' But one would search in vain for a word of honest reasoning about his own past. Shulgin was a reactionary monarchist and a notorious Jew-baiter. The letter was merely about his wrong tactics. As time went on Shulgin became still more a publicist, and there are some who say that he became a friend of Khrushchev's. He died in 1965.

The affair of the Algerian politician Ben Barka, and the murder of the Congolese politician Patrice Lumumba, merely go to show that the Western intelligence services also do not shrink from murder. It is plain from the history of the Soviet security service that murder is just a method like any other. Even in Khrushchev's term of office it treated itself to one of those 'heroic deeds'.

On 8–19 October 1962 the Federal Court of Justice at Karls-ruhe tried a case against Bogdan Stashynsky, a thirty-one-year-old

Soviet citizen. He described himself as an employee of the Soviet Committee for State Security and admitted that at the behest of the KGB he had murdered two Ukrainian exiles living in Munich —in 1957 Dr Lev Rebet and in 1959 Stefan Bandera, leader of the Right Radical 'Organization of Ukrainian Nationalists' (OUN). If all that Stashynsky said was true it shows without a doubt that the Soviet security service still had the same mentality as under Stalin and that it still indulged in the same criminal practices. Marxism has never considered terrorism against individuals to be a fitting way of fighting its opponents, and Lenin too spoke out against it. It was not until the Stalin era that this weapon was taken into the Communist arsenal. After Stalin's death the Soviet leadership must have realized how short-lived were the effects to be gained by this means, that it brought no real success but merely betrayed the true character of the men who employed it. As a typical Right Radical, Stefan Bandera had no scruples in using individual terrorism against his 'enemies' (there were many Ukrainians among the victims of his organization), but Dr Lev Rebet was a representative of those Ukrainian intellectuals who were clearly on their way towards democracy. Only a barbaric and criminal brain could conceive the idea of justifying the murder of two Soviet Ukrainian *émigrés* on the ground that they constituted a danger to one of the greatest powers in the world. An aggravating circumstance of the malicious liquidation of the two exiled Ukrainians is that it took place in a foreign country. So it was not only a shocking repudiation of human rights but also a violation of the sovereignty of another country. Clearly the Soviet politicians are not aware of the harm they do themselves by this kind of action.

At his trial at Karlsruhe Stashynsky described in detail how he had killed the two Ukrainian exiles with an air pistol. There were several articles in the West European Press and also some pamphlets giving a full account of the murders. According to them it had been a shortsighed undertaking of the Soviet secret police from the very beginning. The scandal was only increased by a number of statements made by the East European intelligence services which could hardly be taken seriously. They tried to show that Bandera's murder had been committed by Professor Oberländer, a formerly active Nazi and ex-Minister; or if not by him then by one of the mutually contending groups of the OUN, or even by the West German 'spy organization', the Federal intelligence service.[149]

Changes in the KGB

These diversions have no direct bearing on our theme, but they serve to complete the picture. Turning again to the changes that took place in the Russian security service, let us study the changed face of terrorism under Khrushchev.

After the Beria débacle the security officers tried to give the history of the service a fresh coat of paint. 'Back to Dzerzhinsky!' was the watchword. This, in the opinion of the functionaries of the security service, had been the only stage in its history that had accorded with 'Leninist principles'. A whole staff of historians were recruited who busily refreshed the memories of their contemporaries with the 'heroic traditions' of the Chekists in Dzerzhinsky's time. There were no obstacles to this enterprise, since all the witnesses of the time when the Cheka had been founded had fallen victims to Stalin's terror. Now they have been rehabilitated, and the bookshops are piled high with the stories of their heroic deeds.

The Yagoda, Yezhov, and Beria stages are either passed over in silence or attempts are made, often very clumsily, to show that even then there were Chekists who kept faith with Leninist principles, and in the worst times of the Stalinist terror, during the Yezhovshchina, set their face against arbitrary actions, tried to help their fellow-citizens, and paid for it with their lives. The daily papers also carried accounts of the lives of these 'famous Chekists'. There were not many of them. There are accounts, for example, of how the Kazakhs Dzhakupov (Dungane) and M. Mazanchin, the Georgian A. N. Mikeladze, and a few others had refused to obey orders to kill their friends. The search for 'suitable subjects' seems not to have been too successful, but in the early sixties films were shown in which the good Lenin-loyal Chekists were doing their best to preserve decent human standards in the security service, even during the Stalinist terror. The feelings of those who saw these films were not reported.

Another sign of change was the effort made to develop prophylactic measures. Responsible security officers gave lectures everywhere on the dangers that threatened a citizen immediately he got caught up in the network of the Western anti-Soviet organizations.

Minor offences such as accepting a gift from a foreigner were still rated as political crimes but were no longer burdened with the leaden weight of treason. The sinner was now graded as 'politically immature' or as 'led astray by the enemy'. In fine, an attempt was made to look for extenuating circumstances, to dispel the spy mania and the oversensitiveness to slight transgressions that were rampant in Stalin's days, and no longer to regard every political joke coming from the 'Yerevan transmitter' as high treason. In No. 8/1959 of the legal journal *Sovietskoye Gozudarstvo i Pravo* an article by V. S. Tikunov explained the new attitude of the KGB. An interesting point about this article is that its writer had recently been a leading functionary in the Comsomol and consequently was doubtless one of the new Chekists called to fill responsible posts in the KGB. From this source we learn that the process of renovating the cadres of the KGB had been completed about 1959 and that all unreliable members or those with tainted pasts had had to retire from the organization. Several were exposed as 'impostors' and punished. The new cadres, wrote Tikunov, were recruited 'from Party and Soviet functionaries, Communists of experience and attainments, highly cultivated and educated'. These functionaries took over all the top positions in the KGB. With their assistance the new policy has definitely won through. The prime importance of this statement is that in every case the KGB now respects the law.

The most trenchant changes were those made in the investigation department of the KGB. This is now composed of experienced lawyers. Recently a large number of capable judges and advocates have been transferred to this department. It has been laid down that an investigating official of the KGB must have completed a course of legal studies and must have practised in the courts for a prescribed period.

Changes in personnel

Today, if the head of the security service had to be replaced, the Soviet leadership would be actuated by other motives and would be aiming at other objectives than those of Stalin's day. Then the security service was an instrument of force in the hands of a despot. The slightest alteration in his plans was followed by a change of personnel in the security service. Now State security has a permanent, established position within the system, and the motives for replacing the head of the security service are primarily of a professional nature: the leadership would have come to the conclusion that under its new controller the apparatus would work better within the limitations and competence marked out by the Party. On 9 December 1958 Serov was replaced by a representative of the younger generation, A. N. Shelepin. No one in the Soviet Union would question the value of the services rendered by Serov in the difficult transitional period following the downfall of Beria; nevertheless there were several good reasons for his removal. In the first place, he represented the older generation, and by the mid-fifties the generation problem had become an urgent one in the security service and had resulted in an appreciable rejuvenation in the apparatus. Secondly, there were certain things in Serov's past that told against him. There was no doubt that he had been involved in various terrorist activities under Stalin. Thirdly—and this seems to have turned the scales—by training and mentality he was unfitted to deal with the new situation. The security service had to be directed by someone with a flair for politics. Khrushchev made a wise choice in appointing Shelepin as its chairman. Aleksandr Nikolayevich Shelepin, born in 1918, was a student at the Moscow Institute of Philosophy, Literature, and History, and in the war with Finland served as a political officer at the front. Joining the Party in 1940, he was Secretary of the Central Committee of the Comsomol of the USSR from 1943 to 1958. Simultaneously he had been since 1945 a member of the Council of the World Federation of Democratic Youth and was elected its Vice-Chairman in 1957. In 1954 he was a member of the Foreign Affairs Committee of the Soviet of Nationalities in the Supreme Soviet of the USSR. It was already clear at the 20th Party Congress that he would climb still higher up the ladder of success. He was, for instance, a member of the committee appointed to work out a new Party programme. In April 1958 he joined the Party headquarters as director of the department for the Party organizations of the Union Republics in the Central Committee of the Communist Party.

From these brief biographical details it can be seen that Shelepin was free from encumbrances acquired in the Stalinist era. Although, according to various sources, he must, willy-nilly, as a leading functionary in the pro-Soviet World Federation of Democratic Youth, have had to deal with all kinds of 'security questions' (such as the protection of the organization from 'undermining'), he was not directly concerned with the work of the secret police. A step nearer to 'security' was his appointment as director of the department for the Party organizations. This department at Party headquarters is concerned with the personal particulars of those actively engaged in the Party apparatus. He could hardly have filled this office without close collaboration with the security service.

But Shelepin grew up in quite a different stable. He was the typical young *apparatchik* devoted to the Party, with a sharp eye for the ever-changing niceties of Party policy and a highly developed adaptability. In one respect he was reminiscent of the source of his inspiration, Khrushchev, namely in his untiring industry and inexhaustible energy. He owed his success to Khrushchev, though not directly, according to hearsay. The part of go-between, so it is said, was played by Khrushchev's son-in-law, A. I. Adzhubei, once chief editor of the principal organ of the Comsomol, the *Komsomolskaya Pravda*, then chief editor of the Government journal *Izvestia*, which set the tone for the whole of the Soviet press under the rule of his father-in-law. On Khrushchev's fall from power Adzhubei was fobbed off with the editorship of the international edition of the periodical *Soviet Union*.

At the 21st Congress of the Communist Party (27 January to 5 February 1959) Shelepin delivered his maiden speech before the august assembly, explaining in simple but spirited terms the new platform of the KGB: it was to be an organization completely subordinate to and directed by the Party. 'In the last few years, under the immediate direction of the Central Committee of the Communist Party of the Soviet Union, its Presidium, and Comrade Khrushchev in person, revolutionary legality has been fully restored, and those guilty of its violation punished.' Every Soviet citizen could now sleep peacefully in his bed, knowing that arbitrary acts of the security service were no longer possible. Furthermore, a 'fundamental restriction of the competence of the KGB organizations' had been decreed, the 'moral and political unity' of the Soviet citizens and a lively contact between the KGB and the general public made it possible to carry out the measures proposed by the Central Committee of the Communist Party for the reformation of the KGB. 'Punitive functions have in fact been greatly restricted throughout the country and will remain restricted in the future.' The sword of the security service was pointed primarily at enemies of the Soviet Union and spies. 'The imperialistic, aggressive powers set their highest hopes on the work of undermining, spying, diversion. . . . At the present moment, for instance, more than 20,000 persons are employed in the Central Intelligence Agency of the USA. The annual expenditure of this organization exceeds $1,500,000,000. . . . In West Germany alone the USA has more than forty spy centres, and in West Berlin there are more than sixty espionage organizations maintained by capitalist countries. . . . The American intelligence service is engaged in terrorist assaults and political intrigues, and it hatches conspiracies in various countries, especially in the Near and Middle East. . . . The enemy is up and doing, and is looking for any split in our ranks.'

Shelepin's term of office was relatively brief. The situation, especially on the economic front, was becoming increasingly difficult, and in 1961 there was another change in the government. Shelepin was entrusted with a different field of work, which Khrushchev considered to be of great importance, namely the management of the apparatus whose function was to control 'on a social basis' the maintenance of order in the factories, collective farms, and other institutions. That, in Khrushchev's judgement, it was the half-baked Chekist Shelepin who appeared to be the most suitable person for the control of every sphere of Soviet society by the Party and the State gives one furiously to think.

The next head of the security service, Vladimir Yefimovich Semichastny, a Ukrainian by nationality, was born in 1924 and has belonged to the Party since 1945. He was thus six years younger than Shelepin and had not attained his predecessor's level of education; whereas Shelepin went to an academy, Semichastny proceeded no further than an intermediate school. Both were for several years active members and officials in the Comsomol. In 1954 Semichastny was moved from the Ukraine to the Comsomol headquarters in Moscow, where he acted as Secretary, and in 1958 he was appointed First Secretary of the Central Committee of the Comsomol in succession to Shelepin, who took over the direction of the Department for the Party organizations in the Central Committee of the Communist Party in the Union

Republics. Later, too, he followed in Shelepin's footsteps. Shortly after the latter had been appointed Chairman of the Committee for State Security in December 1958, Semichastny succeeded Shelepin again, as director of the Department for the Party organizations. In August 1959 he was switched to work in the Central Committee of the Communist Party of Azerbaidjan and was selected as Second Secretary and member of the bureau of this committee. When the party leadership in Azerbaidjan declined to fall in with Khrushchev's proposal to abolish the privileged position of national languages, in the interest of educational reform, and Khrushchev as a result initiated a sort of purge in Azerbaidjan, Semichastny had to act as Moscow's special representative at Baku. His recall to Moscow followed rather suddenly, shortly after the 21st Congress of the Communist Party of Azerbaidjan in September 1961, when he was elected to the Central Committee of this Party and was confirmed in his appointment as Second Secretary and member of the bureau of the Party. Only two months later he had risen to the position of Chairman of the Committee for State Security of the Council of Ministers of the USSR.

The reason for Semichastny's appointment as head of the KGB was the same as in Shelepin's case. Semichastny had no experience as a Chekist but he had certainly done well as an *apparatchik* of the Party, though with certain limitations. He had had no regular career in the Party apparatus because he was too young, and it was from the Comsomol apparatus that he had been promoted to Party headquarters. The Comsomol, of course, is as much bureau-cratized as the Party, but there are certain differences. There is still a certain 'enthusiasm' about the work in the Comsomol and it is nothing like so monotonous as in the Party apparatus. Semi-chastny was assuredly a fanatic, for certain incidents in his past life showed that he was inclined to go to extremes. When the campaign of persecution against Pasternak (who died in its course) was at its height, Semichastny, then Secretary of the Comsomol, demanded his banishment abroad.

In spite of his appointment as head of the KGB, Semichastny was only a party functionary who had no say in the political direction to be taken by the security service and was responsible only for the 'quality' of its work.

The 22nd Party Congress

The 22nd Congress of the Communist Party of the Soviet Union was held in Moscow on 17–31 October 1961. It took a long step forward on the road to 'Socialist legality'. We shall deal here only with its more important features.

This Congress laid down the Party's new programme, in which it pledged itself to the 'strict observance of Socialist legality, the eradication of every kind of infringement of the law, and the elimination of criminality and its causes'. These were to be its prime tasks. Further, 'the administration of justice in the USSR would be carried out in complete accordance with the law'.[150]

The programme laid great stress on the education of the citizens, an emphasis closely related to the Congress's promise to replace the dictatorship of the proletariat by the 'Soviet democracy of the classless society of the whole people'. This new theory of the character of the Soviet state was the starting-point of every attempt to introduce persuasive methods instead of compulsion for the maintenance of public order and to educate the people. Unfortunately it needed only a few years to show that the way to hell was still paved with good intentions. But the fundamental importance of the 22nd Party Congress so far as progress towards 'Socialist legality' was concerned lay in a different direction. To the great surprise of many of those present, Khrushchev and his supporters persisted in exposing Stalin's crimes to a wholly unexpected extent. One speaker after another produced overwhelming evidence to prove that Kaganovich, Malenkov, Molotov, and Voroshilov had been implicated in the crimes of the thirties. The public was even more astonished to learn, much later, of the enormous extent of the crimes committed by Stalin and of the vast numbers of his victims. Stalin's role as the driving force behind all these outrages was described in detail. This settling of accounts with Stalinism culminated in the Congress's decision to shift Stalin's corpse. The wording of this decision ran: 'To continue to keep the coffin with the mortal remains of Y. V. Stalin in the Lenin Mausoleum is intolerable. His grievous contraventions of Lenin's testament, his abuse of power, his mass reprisals against honourable Soviet people, and other misdeeds in the days of the personality cult make it impossible for the coffin with his mortal remains to remain any longer in the Lenin Mausoleum.' The

Khrushchevists had several aims in passing this measure, and the worsening relations with the Chinese Communists also had to be considered. Not the least of their motives, however, was to pacify public opinion and to satisfy the demand for guarantees of legal security which society was beginning to express in ever more clamorous tones. And in the event the de-Stalinization measures did produce positive effects on the whole administration of justice.

Another outcome of the Congress was the definite condemnation of the theories propounded by Stalin's personal lawyer Vyshinsky. Khrushchev also proposed the erection of a monument in Moscow to Stalin's victims, with the obvious hope of ingratiating himself with the people. 'The comrades propose', he announced to the Congress, 'to remember for ever the distinguished functionaries of Party and State who were the victims of unjust persecution in the period of the personality cult. We concur with this proposal.'

Even incurable pessimists began to believe that the Congress would rapidly be followed by the creation of the normal rule of law and that the practices current in the Stalin era were finished with for good and all. It looked as if the forces that wanted to reintroduce compulsion were in retreat. Possibly the more enlightened members of the Party bureaucracy really had at this moment the same desires as almost the whole of the population, especially the young. But to some degree these sanguine hopes proved illusory. It was not so much the personal attitude of Khrushchev or other party leaders that caused the disappointment; it was largely the intrinsic difficulties of the general situation, principally in the economic and social domain. Moreover, the bureaucracy, which had hardly changed at all since Stalin's time, and a Party involved in the toils of the old autocratic techniques were incapable of even comprehending the new objectives.

Relapse into reaction

After the 22nd Party Congress a wave of storm and stress swept over the Soviet community. It had two main features. First came a spontaneous movement with the slogan 'Give us the truth about the past!' Even some of the Party functionaries sympathized and headquarters went so far as to issue an instruction to give the people fuller information about the terrorism and tyranny of the Stalin epoch. At the Party meetings which began in November 1961 in all the republics further shattering details about the events of 1937 and the time of the 'second Yezhovshchina' were revealed. But the people wanted to know still more, and a serious conflict between the general public and the Party bureaucracy ensued. The latter was prepared to be comparatively generous in extending the limits within which this way of settling accounts with Stalinism could be carried out, but it had no intention of allowing these limits to be overrun, leaving it with no control of public opinion.

The 22nd Congress started another movement of even more far-reaching importance: the young intelligentsia went over to the offensive. They mistrusted their elders and would not contain themselves in silence. They accused the older generation of having been aware of what was going on and demanded to know who would guarantee that the past would never be repeated. In this dispute the young writers were especially prominent and were soon leading public opinion. Although supported by several of the older writers, it was not long before they were at loggerheads with those writers who favoured a dogmatic, neo-Stalinist line. Poems and stories about the reign of terror appeared more and more frequently until finally it came to an open conflict between the young intelligentsia and the Party bureaucrats. This caused Khrushchev and his adherents, who only shortly before had been promoting de-Stalinization, to beat a shameful retreat. In December 1962 and March 1963 Party leaders and cultural experts met to exchange views. Cornered in argument by the younger set, Khrushchev suddenly began to defend Stalin. At the meeting on 8 March he exclaimed with emotional solemnity: 'We believed him and supported him. Nothing else was possible. . . . At that time Stalin was leading the Party in its fight against the enemies of the Revolution and in Socialist reconstruction. Besides, everybody knew of Stalin's share in the revolutionary struggle before the October Revolution, during the Revolution, and in the years that followed.' Although he had only just been speaking of Stalin's crimes with the relish of a connoisseur, Khrushchev had suddenly changed his tune. Certainly, he declared, the Party had condemned Stalin's abuse of power and still condemned it, but, he added immediately by way of qualification, 'In spite of all that, the Party appreciates Stalin's services to the Party and the Communist movement. Even today our view is that Stalin was truly devoted to Communism, that he was a true Marxist. That cannot and must not be denied. When Stalin was taken to his tomb, there were many, including myself, with tears in their eyes. They were real tears. We knew that Stalin had some personal failings but we believed in him.'[151]

To pacify his hearers, Khrushchev went so far as to say that he and his friends had only known of Stalin's despotism 'after his death and the exposure of Beria, that arch-enemy of the Party and the people, that spy, that vile *agent provocateur.*'[152] Khrushchev's *volte-face* slowed up the promising change of policy. Moreover, Khrushchev thwarted the efforts of the younger writers to have done with certain traditional phenomena harmful to the Soviet Union, such as anti-Semitism. 'We no longer have any anti-Semitism' was his reply to the questions on this subject put to him by the younger writers, prominent among whom was Yevtushenko. Finally, Khrushchev saw to it personally that not so many reports of experiences in concentration camps appeared in books and periodicals.

The strained relations between the Party and the intellectual *élite* was only one of the many negative results of the 22nd Party Congress, which had started out so promisingly. In the second half of the Seven-Year Plan (1959–65) it became increasingly clear that the targets, especially in so far as the modernization of the economy was concerned, would not be reached. The development in agriculture which up to about 1959 had been steadily improving was now in a state of collapse, largely as a result of Khrushchev's experiments, particularly his narrow-minded policy for the 'virgin lands' of Kazakhstan. This failure naturally aggravated the irritability of the leading politicians, Khrushchev in particular. The difficult economic situation, added to the social unrest already described, presented a serious threat to the Party leadership. History began to repeat itself. As difficulties grew, so did the tendency to settle every question that cropped up with orders from above and finally a resort to compulsion. This reactionary movement was helped along by the failure of the 'social measures' already noted. Only a few months after the 22nd Party Congress a new trend could be discerned: the widening of the sphere of competence of the security service.

In November 1962, when the Soviet Union was celebrating the

85th birthday of the co-founder of the secret police, Feliks Dzerzhinsky, an interview with the General of the security service, N. F. Chistyakov, appeared in the Press, in the course of which the journalists asked Chistyakov what was at present engaging the attention of the investigating officials of the KGB.[153] The General replied that besides having to deal with the agents of the Western intelligence services, they were waging a campaign against persons committing such dangerous crimes against the State as high treason, diversion, sabotage, smuggling, the betrayal of State secrets, and infringements of the currency regulations. Chistyakov acknowledged that no further cases of sabotage had been reported in recent times, but it is easy to see from his list of offences that the extension of the death penalty automatically entailed the extension of the KGB's sphere of influence. This raises the question why currency offences and embezzlement should come within the domain of the KGB. They are simply crimes which in a system free from political hysteria would not be dealt with at all by the political police. In a state based on law they would be the concern of the financial authorities, the criminal police, and the public prosecutor. The fact that this is not the case in the Soviet Union is fraught with incalculable dangers. The delimitation of spheres of competence is certainly an extremely knotty problem in any society, but in the Soviet Union it is a socio-political question of cardinal importance. Under Khrushchev the Communist Party has succeeded in removing many of the abuses deriving from the Stalinist era, but the problem of determining the position of the security service in the structure of Soviet society will remain insoluble so long as the Party leaders allow its activity to extend into unspecified fields.

That is how matters stood at the end of Khrushchev's term of office, i.e. in October 1964. The presumed desire to take a leap forward from the arbitrary methods of Stalin's time into conditions befitting a constitutional state was not realized. Nevertheless historians must credit Khrushchev with the fact that under him many barriers were removed and the use of many despotic techniques was abandoned.

Chapter Ten

Brezhnev and Kosygin
proceed with caution

T H E RE were many reasons for Khrushchev's fall. Probably the most important was the chaotic state of things resulting from his dilettanish experiments in all directions, especially in agriculture and law. His bequests to the corresponding departments of Soviet life were as might have been expected. The complete failure of his 'social justice' experiment was shown in the fact that the general public, contrary to all his hopes, lost interest in the suppression of crime and maintenance of public order; on the contrary, the public's apathy towards such matters was revealed. The only result of the experiment was a fresh bureaucratic apparatus scattered throughout the country. Khrushchev was deaf to the opinions expressed by many Soviet jurists warning him of the abuse and fatal consequences of the 'comrades' tribunals'. The expected democratization of society did not fit into the existing bureaucratic structure.

The most absurd consequences followed. In the last weeks of the Khrushchev era the newspapers and periodicals carried alarming reports. In one collective farm in the Ryazan district, for instance, the 'leaders' committees', i.e. the chairman of the collective farm, the chief agronomist, and the Party representative, had formulated a plan whereby the judgements which the comrades' tribunals were to deliver in the coming years were settled in advance. They simply determined that 'in accordance with the ordinance of the Presidium of the Supreme Soviet of the RSFSR dated 4 May 1961, at least four to eight persons were to be expelled from the collective farm'. Whether suitable cases would actually present themselves in the course of the year was quite immaterial. The law against 'parasites' was not looked upon as an instrument for punishing the guilty, but as a device for carrying out a 'systematic social duty'.[154] The bureaucratic feeling for justice was in a pretty miserable condition. If there was no 'parasites' available they simply sentenced to expulsion a few honest peasants who for some reason or another had not fulfilled their allotted quotas of work.

Such abuses inflamed the conflict between jurists and bureaucrats. Many jurists used the opportunity to divert the course of justice into other channels and to adapt 'Socialist legality' to the demands of modern society. And in fact, even under Khrushchev, they could boast of certain successes. The reform of the scientific institutes of jurisprudence had already begun in 1960, when the 'Institute of State and Justice' in the Academy of Sciences of the Soviet Union was reorganized, in connection with which the whole network of juristic research institutes was modernized. The 'Union Research Institute of Criminality' was converted into a 'Union Institute for Research into the Causes of Criminality and for the Study of Prophylactic Measures against the Criminal Class'. Further, the 'Union Institute of Juristic Sciences' became the 'Union Scientific Research Institute of Soviet Legislation'. This development is still proceeding, and it is to be hoped that the new generation of jurists will help new ideas to surface. In the study of Soviet conditions one must always bear in mind such developing processes and not overlook their complicated stratification, as so-called Kremlinologists frequently do. Of course, such processes can only become effective in everyday life when the Party on its side is willing to make certain concessions. There are enough progressive forces available, and it will only depend on circumstances if and when their hour will strike. Khrushchev's fall was obviously not a propitious moment. Another area in which Khrushchev's successes felt the effects of his heritage was in the control of society by State and Party. Such control is of extraordinary importance in the Soviet system. We must here distinguish between technical control, exercised in Russia as in every other country by tax and health departments, etc., and a 'socio-political control', a typical Soviet institution, which the Party exercises through its own apparatus or by an apparatus specifically created for the purpose. The duty of this 'socio-political control' was to determine whether the policies of the Party and Government were being carried out in practice, and for this purpose it sought to gain an insight into individual concerns and factories, collective farms, and other social institutions. But in the fifty years of its existence the Soviet system has never been able to discover any effective method of exercising this form of control. Again and again new means are tried, and in 1962 Khrushchev had the idea of creating a new organ for unified control, viz. the 'Committeee of Party and State Control of the Communist Party and Ministerial Council of the Soviet Union' (*Komitet Partyno-gozudarstvennogo Kontrolya ZK KPSS i Sovieta Ministrov SSSR*). Shelepin was entrusted with the chairmanship of this committee. But it was soon evident that Shelepin's enormously expanded apparatus, which, according to the statistics of mid-1955, comprised 3,390 Committees of Party and State Control in the republics, with 164,000 honorary functionaries, and was based on no fewer than 710,000 'groups' and 'posts' for the control of factories, concerns, construction works, collective farms, and other works, was of little use and could play no really positive role. More and more often there were disputes between the 'People's Controllers' and works directors who rejected any interference in their competence. The result was the same as in the case of the People's Militia: the People's Controllers were despised and ostracized by the general public.

Moreover, a completely unforeseen phenomenon presented itself: the controlling organs of Party and State not only collected information regarding actual conditions in the country, but began to develop an existence of their own and became a power instrument that was constantly increasing its strength. The consequences for their chief Shelepin were disastrous. In December 1965 the Committee of Party and State Control, an unlucky relic of the Khrushchev era, was once again reorganized. The new organization was renamed 'People's Control' and constitutionally lost to a large extent the strong position within the system that Shelepin's apparatus had enjoyed. Shelepin lost his job and had to go back to his work in Party headquarters. The whole upset brought at least one advantage: the Party no longer looks upon and used 'socio-political control' as a kind of police control. Nowadays it instructs the 'People's Controllers' not so much to spy on the works directors and collective farm chairmen in order to collect 'conspiratorial material', as Shelepin was wont to do, but rather to provide technical criticism on actual abuses and grievances.

A test of justice: the Party and the intellectual élite

A third area in which tensions had formed under Khrushchev was between the Party and creative writers and artists, and especially the younger intelligentsia. Western observers, like Giuseppe Boffa, the Italian, stress that this problem is decisive for the future of the Soviet community. The younger generation is better educated. It has grown up in a different atmosphere from that of their fathers and grandfathers who handled the levers of power. Its mentality was created not on the blood-drenched battlefields of the civil war but by the fall of the idolized Stalin and the conquest of space.

When the framework decreed by the official party line of 'Socialist realism' proved too cramped and outdated for the realm of literature and art, and young writers found fewer and fewer opportunities for publishing poems, tales, and treatises that had little regard for the party line, a kind of 'unofficial' literature was born. The young writers were no longer dependent on fees provided by the Press and publishing houses, but were supported directly by the general public. Writers and poets, as well as composers, singers, and musicians, were (and still are) invited to give paid lectures, readings, and performances to the clubs of the technical intelligentsia who could earn good money in the factories and collective farms. The works performances are often strongly critical of the Establishment. There artists can experiment on new forms of poetry and literature, new songs, a new language of music, and their mostly youthful audiences support them with enthusiasm. Many young scientists, the direction of whose researches do not suit the concepts of 'scientific bureaucracy', find themselves in a similar situation. Even before the end of Khrushchev's rule a series of such 'unofficial' works were smuggled abroad and reproduced there in several languages. The natural result was tension between Party and creative artists. The political leadership is still influenced by Stalinist ideas of governmental technique and is consequently incapable of solving this problem in a contemporary fashion and in the interest of a progressive development of the Soviet community. The end result is a reaction into the methods of terrorism and barbarity.

In the second half of 1965 two Russian writers, Andrey Sinyavsky and Yuri Daniel, were arrested in Moscow. The general public only learnt of it in January 1966 from an article by D. Yeremin, the secretary of the Moscow section of the Association of Soviet Writers. In a jargon worthy of a Stalin prizeman he wrote: 'Enemies of Communism have found what they were looking for—two renegades, for whom double talk and shamelessness have become a religion. Hidden behind the pseudonyms of Abram Terz and Nikolay Arzhak, the two men have for several years sent abroad to foreign publishers and had published abroad the dirtiest slanders against their country, against the Party, and against the Soviet system. . . . In the end they sank so low as to commit crimes against the Soviet State. Thereby they have excluded themselves from the community of the Soviet people. From petty fault-finding they have ended up in high treason. These mudlarks have not only raised their hand against the Soviet community, but they have sprayed their poison over all progressive people, over their ideals, and over the holy fight for social progress, democracy, and peace.'[155]

The trial of the two writers was held in February 1966. They were charged with having since 1956 smuggled out of the country a long series of writings, using a French woman scientist, Hélenè Pelletier-Samojska, as a go-between. These articles, under the pseudonyms of Abram Terz and Nikolay Arshak, first appeared in the Polish periodical *Kultura*, published in Paris, and afterwards in nearly all the Western countries.

It is true that the investigation methods of the Committee of State Seecurity, KGB, cannot be compared with those used in the Stalin period. This became evident during the trial. In the old days Bukharin, Zinoviev, Pyatokov, and other leaders of the October Revolution were subjected to such physical and moral pressures that they said exactly what the security service wanted them to say. That things are different today is to be clearly seen from Sinyavsky's final speech. 'The prosecution's arguments have failed to convince me. I maintain my previous attitude. The prosecution's arguments give one the feeling of standing in front of a brick wall against which one runs one's head without being able to penetrate it and reach the truth. Certainly I am "different", but I do not consider myself an enemy. I am a Soviet man, and my writings are not anti-Soviet. In this fantastic, electrically charged atmosphere anybody who is "different" can be considered an enemy. But that is not an objective way to the truth. Above all I cannot see why enemies have to be invented, why an interpretation of literary works which relies on criticizing each individual letter of the alphabet has to set up one Aunt Sally after another'.[156] The Moscow press published only extracts from his speech, and the 'producers' of the proceedings saw to it that the declarations of the two young writers were greeted with laughter and ridicule.

The trial was nothing for the Soviet Union to be proud of. For the first time the Communists of the West dissociated themselves from such an example of 'cultural politics'. In *L'Humanité*, the organ of the French Communist Party, Louis Aragon condemned the attempts of the Soviet leadership to use terror as a means of controlling cultural politics.[157] Similar views appeared in the Communist organ *Unità* and in the Swedish and British party papers. *Pravda* of 22 February 1966 reported that the trial of Daniel and Sinyavsky had started a fresh anti-Soviet campaign, but wisely refrained from mentioning that the bitterest comments on the trial were made by Communists. Even in the Soviet Union the affair did not meet with such a smooth reception as usual. And when the claque in the court mocked the two defendants, the militia outside had some difficulty in dispersing the protesting literature students and other young people. It is to be hoped that the inspirers and organizers of that monstrous trial will reflect on all this and find some means of complying with the demands of their own youth and those of their French and Italian friends.

There is another point of interest to us: for the first time since Stalin's death, so far as is officially known, the Committee of State Security officiated as investigators in literature proceedings, in order to control them in favour of the bureaucratic clique and the Stalinist minority among the writers themselves. With this purpose in mind, certain vaguely worded paragraphs in the criminal code were given a suitable interpretation. In their overpowering desire to create a precedent on 'educational' grounds, the Committee went so far as to pervert justice for immediate political ends. An expert jurist of the West rightly condemned the verdict with these words: 'The Supreme Court of Justice of the RSFSR has clearly shown that—in contravention of the Soviet Constitution, by which the courts are subject to the laws alone—it has been subordinated to political considerations and cannot exercise its duties, which are to decide according to the spirit and the letter of legality.'[158]

Almost simultaneously the security organs in other parts of the Soviet Union took harsh action against young writers. The persecution in the Soviet Ukraine started in 1963. Two writers were arrested because they had taken out of the country manuscripts of the deceased writer Vasyl Symonenko, which were issued in book form in 1965 by a Ukrainian publishing house in New York.[159] The two writers were released, but the State security service prepared a fresh blow against the Ukrainian intelligentsia. In July 1966 they arrested more than seventy persons, who after harsh and lengthy hearings were sentenced to imprisonment. They were mostly young scientists and students who were accused of having circulated forbidden literature. Only in a few cases were lawyers or representatives from the writers' association allowed to be present. In the Ukraine, as in Moscow, the action of the authorities met with resistance from the intelligentsia, and the Central Committee of the Communist Party was overwhelmed with protests.

Details of other practices on the part of the KGB leaked out. The Russian writer Tarsis (the name is a pseudonym), who received an official exit permit at the beginning of February 1966 and was shortly afterwards deprived of his citizenship, reported that other writers besides himself had been shut up in mental hospitals. Naturally much that Tarsis says seems exaggerated, and one is obliged to take it with a grain of salt. But Chinese Communists, too, have repeatedly said that practices like shutting up people of divergent views in asylums is not uncommon in the Soviet Union. The same allegation is made by Chinese students who have been expelled from Russia.

This hardening attitude in the sphere of 'cultural politics', and its effects on the administration of justice, are indeed unpleasant phenomena, but one must not dramatize them, for social conditions have altered since then, and a totalitarian manipulation of the courts of justice is no longer possible. But the dwindling of the use of terrorism as a basis for social development into a simple directive cannot disguise the fact that those in power are making use of this directive more and more frequently, and in new areas, e.g. in art and literature. In any case the happenings quoted serve to test the sincerity of the phrase 'Socialist legality'. We have seen one interpretation at least.

Forcible measures for the maintenance of public order

The history of the security service clearly shows the close involvement of the political police with the Ministry of the Interior. The first phase of the return to 'Socialist legality' saw a separation of the security service from the Ministry of the Interior that is the first requisite for every constitutional state. The separation took place in March 1954, shortly after Beria's execution. The Ministry of the Interior, the MVD, was separated from the Committee of State Security, the KGB. In January 1960 the Ministry of the Interior was abolished as a federal ministry, and from then on there was a ministry of the interior in each component republic of the Union.

When the federal ministry was abolished, Russian jurists, Party theoreticians, and journalists wrote proudly that the Soviet Union was setting a good example to the whole world in the sphere of jurisprudence. It was dispensing with the centralization of internal affairs, which were now to be transferred *in toto* to the competence of each republic of the Union. This was indeed an important event, but the happy state of things did not last long. The ministry of the interior in each republic was very soon changed into a ministry for the maintenance of public order, and stress was thereby laid on certain factors. Its primary duty became the suppression of youthful delinquency. Experience showed that such social organizations as the 'People's Militia' and the 'Comrades' Courts' were ineffective. This drove the Soviet leaders into a complete reversal of policy and to a renewed use of drastic administrative measures to cope with the problem. At a meeting of the Supreme Soviet of the USSR in August 1966 a federal Ministry for the Maintenance of Public Order was established. That meant that the existing fifteen republican ministries were returned to the competence of the Ministerial Council of the USSR, with its own headquarters in the Government. This reorganization meant a relapse into centralization. It was thought that an expansion of the powers of the central government would facilitate a stricter and more effective use of measures for the maintenance of public order. The old idea that orders, edicts, and compulsion were still the methods that promised the most success was optimistically resurrected.

The Ministry for the Maintenance of Public Order took under its charge all the places of banishment, penal institutions, reformatory colonies, colonies of forced labour (i.e. concentration camps), etc. The competent administration (*Upravleniye Mest Zaklyncheniya*) publishes a monthly journal for the prisoners entitled *K Novoy Zhizni* (Towards a New Life), the very title of which shows that its chief aim is to contribute to the re-education of the prisoners.

The August 1966 resolution of the Supreme Soviet was preceded by an ordinance announcing stronger measures against youthful delinquency. 'No hooligan act is to be left unpunished' was the watchword. Offences committed under the influence of drink were to be only the more severely punished. Drunkenness was no longer to be an extenuating circumstance but was to incur an increase of sentence. Stricter measures were to be taken to curb misbehaviour by teenagers. The year 1966, no less than Stalinism, showed what a visionary Lenin was when in 1919 he declared pontifically: 'There are no youthful criminals'.[160]

Of course the whole problem must be viewed against the general social background. The part played by demographic conditions must not be underestimated. By 1966 the great wave of children born just after the war were ready to go out into the world and the regime was not in a position to provide enough jobs for them. As early as 1965 there were signs of increasing unemployment among them, especially in medium-sized and small towns. Schools were unable to accept all those who wanted further education. Such a state of things was a fertile seed-bed for anti-social conduct among young people and, worst of all, was inevitable under the Soviet system. It is particularly in regard to youthful delinquency that the remedy of administrative ordinances used to the extreme by Stalin's party bureaucrats now proved to be sensationally inadequate, disregarding all up-to-date methods of coping with the problem. It is a sad enough fact that the Soviet bureaucrats had no eyes for anything beyond forceful measures, using terrorism as a remedy, as in the case of the young writers and artists. Worst of all, they put the blame, not on the Soviet system but on 'imperialist propaganda' and 'the disruptive influence of the West'. This attitude encouraged those forces which, when there is a question of an immediate political advantage, always decide in favour of the latter. It is easy to see that 'Socialist legality' is still in its birth-pangs. . . .

The tendency to enlarge the list of political crimes not only harbours potential danger to the administration of justice but in many cases involves immediate drawbacks. Thus it became known that in September 1966 the criminal code of the RSFSR, i.e. the republic which sets the tone for the other fourteen, was 'enriched' by many new crimes: for wilfully spreading insulting statements about the Soviet system (and we all know what that can include), imprisonment for up to three years; for insulting State emblems and flags, up to two years; for forming groups which commit a breach of public order, up to three years. It reminds one of Heine's advice: 'When three men stand together, they should separate' (Wo dreie beienander stehn, da soll man auseinander gehn!). After Stalin's death the tendency was to tone down ambiguous laws which might be interpreted to suit the Government's convenience, or those which punished merely for the sake of prestige, but the tendency was again reversed. And that at a time when the Soviet Union was preparing to celebrate its fiftieth anniversary. Must not the real Russian *élite* be a trifle thoughtful when it remembers such a retrograde policy?

The 23rd Party Congress of the USSR

The Party Congresses are highly important milestones in the history of the Soviet Union. The 20th, in 1956, had marked a real break. It signified a change in the post-despotic phase of the Soviet community. The leaders at the time realized that the excesses of the Stalin era must be removed. The security service had been given a new position within the system, and there was a slackening of tension in various departments. The 21st Congress, in 1959, proclaimed a Seven-Year Plan and the determination of the Soviet leadership to achieve a qualitatively superior stage of development and with it the preconditions for a flourishing 'Communist society'. The 22nd Congress, in 1961, was pervaded by the Utopian ideas of Khrushchev and his supporters, who believed that the highest form of social development could be realized quite soon, i.e. in about twenty years, when the Soviet State would become a People's State. Violence and administrative measures would be replaced by ideologically educational methods, and the people would take an ever larger share in all the multifarious details of community life.

The 23rd Party Congress, held in March/April 1966, was largely devoted to a cool and factual stocktaking of Soviet life in all its aspects. It showed that the leaders had renounced the fantastic ideas, the irresponsible aspirations towards a 'rosy future', and all the other relics of Khrushchev's time. The present-day Soviet rulers profess reform. They are moving much faster than Khrushchev in that direction, as is shown by the economic reforms that they decided upon in 1965. Their efforts are concentrated on the minimizing of risks and difficulties. They are convinced that it is the strengthening of the executive in both Party and State, and not the democratization of the people, that is the most 'sensible' policy for what is likely to be a complicated future, success in which cannot be guaranteed.

None of the present leaders imagines that a relapse into terrorism as a basis for comprehensive development would be valuable, or even possible. Only blindly or maliciously 'anti-Communist' demagogues refuse to admit the fundamental difference between the despotic tyranny of Stalin and the present system. The Soviet leaders are not thinking of dispensing with terror entirely as a regulative factor, but terror no longer takes the form of arbitrary action against the people; it has been 'tamed by law'. Whereas terror disguised as law diminished under Khrushchev, another development became apparent from the 23rd Congress onwards. It became clear that conservative elements, pro-Stalinist or neo-Stalinist, were trying to take advantage of the situation by a tendency to emphasize Stalin's positive achievements, to put a brake on the rehabilitation of Stalin's victims. Many voices clamoured for a harder line in 'culture politics' and in other undesirable directions.

That these reactionary elements met and meet with resistance, and that if they had prevailed the worst consequences would have ensued, is shown by certain happenings on the eve of the Congress. A group of the intelligentsia submitted to the Central Committee of the Communist Party a memorandum with a warning against any form of re-Stalinization. It was signed by twenty-seven scientists and writers, some of worldwide repute. They included Tvardovsky, the chief editor of *Novy Mir*, and the writers Ilya Ehrenburg, Konstantin Paustovsky, Konstantin Simonov, and even Aleksey Surkov, formerly well known for his Stalinist sympathies. Among the other signatories were eminent film producers like Room and Chukhray and the prima ballerina of the Bolshoi Theatre, Plisetskaya. Under such pressure the Soviet leaders instructed N. G. Yegorychev, first secretary of the Moscow City Committee of the Communist Party, to prepare a tranquillizing address to the Congress. 'Personality cult, infractions of the Lenin norms and principles of Party life and Socialist legality,' he said, 'everything that hindered our forward progress, were decisively rejected by our Party, and there will never be any return to the past. A reliable guarantee for this is the line taken by the 20th Party Congress and the October plenary session of the Central Committee of the Communist Party of the Soviet Union'.[161] The assembly received the address with applause. But what gives one cause to think is that the Congress carefully avoided any criticism of Stalin's despotic rule and any form of tribute to the victims of Stalin's terror.

The real problems of 'Socialist legality' were not really tackled at the Congress. The only speaker who mentioned the subject was the Chairman of the Presidium of the Supreme Soviet, N. V. Podgorny. 'One must strengthen the responsibility of the ministries and government offices for the maintenance of legality in the works and industrial concerns under their orders, one must expand the supervisory powers of the State Prosecutor over the correct administration of the laws, one must not tolerate any injury to the rights and interests of the workers. We must be ever on our guard against an inattentive and indifferent attitude towards workers' proposals and complaints. The attention of all Soviets must be drawn to the need to solve these problems.'[162]

If we extract from the speech of the party chief Brezhnev one passage, which must be regarded as a rhetorical flourish rather than a statement of principle, it is the only reference to 'Socialist legality' out of the vast documentation of the 23rd Party Congress. This is it: 'The Soviet laws, which incorporate the norms of Socialist order as tested by experience, are the expression of the will of the workers. . . . In the campaign for a further strengthening of Socialist legality much will be done by the organs of the militia, the State Prosecutor, and justice.'[163]

Does all this not signify that in the Soviet Union many hopes have had to be abandoned, because a democratic apparatus, in every detail historically obsolete, has shown itself incapable of meeting the demands of a society which is constantly modernizing itself? Or is it an attempt to stabilize certain despotic practices? Any effort to answer such questions would burst the covers of this book.

In May 1967 there were further personnel changes in the Committee of State Security. Its chairman, V. Semichastny, was replaced by Yuri Vladimirovich Andropov. Andropov is a Party expert on the 'Socialist countries. He is a Russian, born in 1914 and a Party member since 1939. His political career began in 1936 as a not unimportant Comsomol functionary. He is thus one of the politicians who started successful careers under Stalin and whose mentality is thoroughly imbued with Stalin's despotic methods of government. After Stalin's death he was appointed ambassador in Hungary, and in 1956 he was one of the organizers who set on foot the Soviet intervention which crushed the Hungarian revolution. After 1957 he directed the 'Department for the Socialist Countries' in the Central Committee of the Communist Party of the Soviet Union. He had no direct experience of State Security work, but from his success in the Party apparatus it is obvious that he had a certain aptitude for collecting information—among other qualifications. The shake-up in staffing showed that the Soviet leaders were beginning to realize the increasingly dangerous situation in the Eastern bloc. Stalin constantly spoke of 'capitalist encirclement' as the Soviet Union's greatest peril. Since 1945 he had been almost entirely surrounded by Socialist countries, yet the danger, far from dwindling, was apparently worsening as the years passed. The conflict with the People's Republic of China seemed at first to be merely an ideological dispute, but it soon assumed a form threatening the security of the USSR. Chinese Communists sought to spread their propaganda in the Soviet Union itself, legally at first, then by subversive methods, claiming that their 'Marxist-Leninist Revolutionary Movement' was working for the fall of a 'clique of revisionist renegades'. Exacerbated by a petty ideological quarrel, the Chinese suddenly raised claims to Soviet territory. Chinese leaders openly declared that the revisionist clique in Moscow must be pruned and punished. Their policy was to influence Communist movements all over the world and in particular to assist pro-Chinese groups in any Socialist country. So much for the Eastern wing of the 'encirclement'.

In the West prospects were not much brighter. Firstly, Rumania had for some time been a source of anxiety, for it avoided all Moscow's attempts at tutelage and interference, apart from flatly turning down the Brezhnev doctrine. There followed a series of remonstrances regarding failure to collaborate in COMECON and the Warsaw Pact.

The development in Czechoslovakia that began at the end of 1967 came as a complete surprise to the Soviet Union. The great majority of Communists in Czechoslovakia, backed by the intelligentsia and the trades unions, had realized that a Soviet type of government was bound to be definitely harmful for a country with a democratic tradition and flourishing industries. In 1968 the distaste took a dramatic form.

Chapter Eleven

In the Shadow of the Brezhnev Doctrine

I N 1967/8 it became clearer than ever that the Soviet leadership with Brezhnev and Kosygin at the helm neither would nor could solve by political means the conflicts within Soviet society or within the world movement towards Communism. The ideological dispute with the Chinese Communists developed into a quarrel in which hard words eventually gave way to tanks and rockets. Events in Czechoslovakia took a similar course. The Czechoslovak Communists under Dubček had no desire to desert the Warsaw Pact or the Soviet community, still less were they thinking of restoring capitalism or joining NATO—as the Brezhnevists asserted. Backed by the majority of the Czechoslovak people, they wanted to create a new type of society, differing in many points from the Soviet model, but they still intended it to be basically Socialist. The Soviet leaders, however, could not allow the Czechoslovaks to go their own way in such matters, so here, too, the Soviet tanks had the last word.

In such an atmosphere the Soviet security service, backed by the Party, was able to strengthen its position in the Soviet hierarchy. Brezhnev and his followers began to discover more and more new 'enemies'—revisionists, Maoists, and the rest. Even left-wing students in the West were promoted by these imaginative thinkers into 'enemies' and 'the long arm of imperialism'. The older Chekists, especially in the provinces, had not yet abandoned methods that dated from Stalin's time. They had maintained an immense network of spies, suspecting on principle everything that lay beyond their restricted horizon, and now their attitude was encouraged

by the Soviet leadership. Repression was justified by a belief
that in face of the new tensions in the Soviet Union itself and in
the Communist republics the use of such a weapon as the security
service was quite indispensable. It is characteristic of the Soviet
system that when faced with internal difficulties and social pressures the Party bureaucracy should feel obliged to strengthen its
security service, which is the nearest tool to hand. In cases when
conflict cannot be avoided by discussion, or when the Party thinks
it cannot afford any latitude, the political police are brought in as a
last resource.

Fresh trials of writers and the young intelligentsia

We have already reported in some detail on the first proceedings
against writers in Moscow. The Soviet leaders' aim was to establish examples and precedents in order to intimidate the younger
intelligentsia. But they achieved the directly opposite result. From
all parts of the country came declarations of solidarity with the
arrested and convicted writers, and in many towns there were protests against the sentences. Larissa Daniel, the wife of the writer
Yuri Daniel, was joined by Pavel Litvinov, grandson of the diplomat, in issuing an appeal to world opinion. They protested against
the trials and the sentences passed on Ginsburg, Galanskov, Dob-
rovolsky, and Lashkova. They stigmatized the proceedings as a
KGB intrigue, and the judges and public prosecutors as KGB
tools. 'We appeal to the general public throughout the world, but
in the first instance to the Russian public. We appeal to all who
still have a conscience and courage. Demand the public quashing
of these shameful proceedings and the punishment of those who
instituted them! Demand that the victims be freed!' Madame
Daniel and Litvinov admitted that they had sent copies of the
appeal to progressive Western newspapers with a request for
maximum publicity in the press and on the radio.

Among those who openly protested were people of all social
classes, simple peasants as well as respected university professors,
Party members and others, young and old. In Moscow a leading
part was played by General P. G. Grigorenko, who offered himself
as a witness in the case against Ginsburg, Galanskov, and the
others, but had been refused as 'unreliable'. Pyotr Grigoryevich
Grigorenko, born 1907 at Borisovka in the Ukraine, had joined

the Party as long ago as 1927. In 1937 he passed the Academy of the General Staff. He took part in the fighting against the Japanese in the Far East, and after 1943 he fought on the German front and was twice wounded. After the war he was a professor at the Frunze Military Academy until the end of 1961. Khrushchev had ordered drastic measures to be taken against him, merely because at Party metings he had demanded an end to Stalinism and control over the activities of the security service. In the autumn of 1963 he founded a group which called itself the 'Society for the Rebirth of Leninism'. On 1 February 1964 he was arrested, with his sons and friends. The authorities ordered him to be taken to the Zerbski Institute in Moscow to have his mental state examined. Later he was transferred to a prison hospital in Leningrad, and in August 1964 he was expelled from the Party. He was discharged from hospital in April 1965 and, although he had rendered valuable military service at the front, he was deprived of his general's rank and his title as 'Candidate for the Academy of Sciences', and his pension was cancelled. The security organs were particularly vindictive towards Grigorenko because he bravely took the side of the Crimean Tatars in the campaign for the restoration of their national autonomy. But more about this later.

The wave of arrests, trials, and intimidating sentences swelled visibly in 1968, after the Soviet intervention in Czechoslovakia. On 25 August a small crowd in the Red Square in Moscow tried to voice its protest, and in consequence five more persons were tried on 9 October: Pavel Litvinov, Larissa Daniel, Vadim Delone, Konstantin Babitsky, and Vladimir Dremyuga. All the accused stood their ground fearlessly. Outside the court a street demonstration took place, at which, according to Western observers, between a hundred and three hundred people took part. Among them was Grigorenko, who collected signatures for a petition of protest. KGB men hustled the crowd and tried to provoke a riot. The demonstrators denounced them as 'Nazis' and 'pigs', and in other endearing terms.

A complete account of the arrests and trials in Moscow and Leningrad alone would occupy more space than can be spared here, but documents concerning them were smuggled into the West and there is no reason to doubt the authenticity of these. When analysed, they show that the resistance included, as well as scientists and students, technicians, engineers, collective farm leaders, and simple workers. The attitudes of the various groups differed considerably: from indignant condemnation of the march into Czechoslovakia and solidarity with Dubček to such radical rebelliousness as that of the Kolokol group from Leningrad, whose slogans were 'Down with the dictatorship of the bureaucrats!' and 'Long live the dictatorship of the people!'.

Conflicts and clashes in the Ukraine

Events in the Soviet Ukraine deserve special treatment. We have already related how in 1965 and 1966 two waves of arrests swept through the youthful intelligentsia there. Vyacheslav Chornovil, a journalist, collected all the papers dealing with the arrests, including letters from the corrective labour colonies, manifestos, protests, etc. Some copies from this collection reached the West, where they were published in Ukrainian, Polish, and English. Chornovil's work includes portraits of twenty 'criminals', the most notable of whom perhaps was F. Y. Karavansky. Before his arrest he had tried to present a memorandum to the Polish and Czechoslovak consul in Kiev, drawing the attention of Communists in the outside world to the discrimination practised against the Jews in the Soviet Union.

How fundamentally the situation had changed, and what a new climate had been created by the arrests and Party terrorism meant to bring the public to heel, is apparent in the documents dealing with the Moscow, Leningrad, and Kiev trials. 'Fear has been overcome'—thus the Polish writer and critic Josef Lobodowski described the situation in his foreword to *Ukraina 1956–1968*, published in Paris in 1969. 'Instead of show trials, the courts sat behind closed doors. Instead of humiliating self-criticism and confessions there were written protests addressed to the highest authorities and smuggled through the barbed wire of the concentration camps. There were demonstrations in the streets and squares outside the courts. In Kiev and Lvov youths and girls threw flowers in front of the "black Marias" in which the prisoners were being carried off.'

In all the Ukrainian protests the struggle against the suppression of nationality and Russification figured largely, but was met by the favourite KGB trick of denouncing every protest against injustice as 'bourgeois nationalism'. In the Ukraine as in other non-Russian republics the KGB assumed the right of deciding the point at which legitimate national aspirations degenerate into 'bourgeois nationalism'.

Fight of the Crimean Tatars for their homeland

The nationalities problem also played a leading role in the struggle of the Crimean Tatars for their rights. The racial groups deported by Stalin and robbed of their autonomy were being registered and rehabilitated one after another. Last on the list came the Crimean Tatars, in virtue of a decree passed by the Supreme Soviet on 5 September 1967. It was no genuine rehabilitation, however, as the Autonomous Republic of the Crimea was no*. restored. As in the case of the Volga Germans, the decree merely meant that all discriminatory measures in force until 1967 were abolished, and that the Crimean Tatars were no longer to be second-class citizens in their own Socialist homeland. Disappointed at these half-measures, the Tatars resumed the struggle for the recovery of their autonomy. Those living in Moscow, supported by Russians and Ukrainians, collected signatures for petitions to Party and State. General Grigorenko figured prominently in the movement.

In the areas where they had been forcibly resettled the Crimean Tatars set up a strong organization, with committees in every locality and the young intelligentsia as a spearhead. In an appeal to the public opinion of the Soviet Union and the West they claimed that the official rehabilitation, though it cancelled the charge of treason that had been levelled at them, confirmed 'our expulsion from our homeland and our liquidation as a nation'. Although the Tatars had legality on their side, and although in the first place they tried to persuade the Central Committee of the Communist Party of the justice of their demands, the KGB was called in, from 1968 onwards, to crush the movement by the use of *agents provocateurs* and wholesale arrests. On 21 April 1968 thousands of Tatars assembled in the town of Chirchik near Tashkent in the Uzbekistan SSR, to celebrate the anniversary of Lenin's birthday. Military and KGB units dispersed the gathering by force and arrested several persons. In May a Tatar deputation went to Moscow to present a petition to the Central Committee. They were arrested and sent back to Tashkent. In 1969 proceedings were taken in Tashkent against ten of the Tatar leaders, who included persons of various ages and professions. Among them were a twenty-three-year-old nurse, a fifty-four-year-old electrician, and a teacher, Izmail Yetsydzhiyev, who for his services in defence of Sebastopol had been awarded the title of Hero of the Soviet Union. Two young physicists in the group represented the new generation of Soviet intellectuals: Rollan Kadiyev, aged twenty-nine, whose work on the Einstein theory of relativity had won high praise, and Isset Khairov, aged thirty-one and a Party member.

General Grigorenko asked to be called as witness for the Tatars at the Tashkent trial, but was arrested by the KGB and for the second time sent to a mental hospital.

A new category of political offenders—the mentally sick

In a letter addressed to the Attorney General Grigorenko described the Russian psychiatric institutes as 'the most terrible of all prisons'. In the Soviet Union, as in other countries, there are legal powers to send certain people, e.g. alcoholics, sexual offenders, and a certain category of the mentally sick to suitable institutions for medical treatment. In the Soviet Union there are two types of psychiatric establishments, general and special, the latter with extremely strict control. The KGB has adopted the practice of sending political undesirables to these institutions, where they disappear for good. *Zumasshedshiye prestupniki,* mentally sick criminals, is the term for persons whose political activity displeases the authorities and is 'dangerous to the public', and from whom society must be protected. According to the current law, all mentally sick persons who are a danger to the public can only be declared to be so by a competent court. On admission to a psychiatric institution the patient has to be examined by a committee of three specialists within twenty-four hours, so as (in theory) to avoid any possibility of error. At a later date, too, an expert committee decides whether the treatment shall be continued or stopped.

Western newspapers reported many such cases of 'mentally sick political offenders'. Here are a few cases out of dozens. Ivan Yakhimovich, former head of a collective farm, attracted attention by denouncing certain illegalities and by protesting against the occupation of Czechoslovakia. He was detained for many months in the psychiatric department of Riga prison hospital. Nikolay Danilov, for many years an investigating judge, resigned his position on conscientious grounds; he thereby incurred the hatred of the security service and is now in the psychiatric department of the prison hospital in Leningrad. Viktor Kuznetsov, a Moscow artist, was arrested on account of his contribution to a debate at Moscow University and was taken to a psychiatric clinic. After his discharge it was found that the shock therapy used on him had been without effect, so he was sent back for further treatment. Another political offender in a psychiatric clinic is a student, Ilya Rips, who on 13 April 1969 set light to himself in front of the Freedom Monument in Riga as a protest against the prohibition of Jewish emigration to Israel.

The methods commonly used in the treatment of political 'undesirables' are further illustrated by the following cases. In February 1968 a candidate in physical-mathematical science, Aleksandr Volpin, and a translator, Nataliya Gorbanevskaya, were forcibly removed to a psychiatric clinic. On the 14th militia called at Volpin's home and he was taken to a hospital fifty miles from Moscow, without notification to his family. After ninety-nine scientists, who included well-known professors and holders of Lenin prizes, had protested to the Minister of Health, the conditions in which he was detained were somewhat ameliorated.

Another case is that of Vladimir Borisov of Leningrad, who wrote an open letter to the United Nations in defence of Grigorenko. He was arrested and taken straight to a psychiatric clinic, actually to the department for dangerous lunatics. When he tried to escape, he was removed to the psychiatric department of a prison reserved for convicts.

General (retd) P. G. Grigorenko was declared 'not responsible for his actions' at Tashkent in February 1970 and sent back to a mental hospital. His wife T. M. Grigorenko addressed an open letter to world opinion on 3 March, showing that the reason for this treatment was simple—he thereby lost the right of defending himself before a court and explaining his actions. In Madame Grigorenko's own words:

'My husband was thus condemned to the most dreadful punishment that can befall a sane man. From today's date he is declared insane and deprived of all civic rights. He would have revealed all the offences against the law that occurred during the investigation of his case (e.g. that he was beaten up and forcibly fed) and the groundless nature of the charges against him would have been exposed. My husband has never told a lie and he has slandered no one. . . . He has never been an agitator against the Soviet system: he has only protested openly and fearlessly against the consequences of Stalinism in our country. For that he has been given a punishment beyond compare for its inhumanity and its cynicism.'

At the same time Grigorenko's memoirs detailing his treatment in mental hospitals appeared in various Western journals. There is no doubt that, just as in Stalin's time, the KGB has recruited a group of physicians for its own ends, who, grievously offending against the basic laws of medicine, act as blind tools of the KGB by incarcerating political undesirables. There are very many of this new category of criminals, and their number is daily being augmented. On 30 May 1970 all the Western press agencies carried a report that a few days earlier the well-known Soviet biologist Yaures Medvedev had been arrested at his home in Obninsk, ninety miles from Moscow, and taken to a mental hospital. Medvedev had criticized the Party's interference in natural science, which he considered to be one of the chief reasons for the backward state of Soviet biology. His detention unloosed a wave of protest from Soviet scientists, a number of whom, world-famous and including Kapitsa, sent a protest to the Ministry of Health, the State Attorney's office, and other government departments.

Grigorenko's memoirs reveal that the therapeutic treatments used in these clinics are rough and ready in the extreme, liable to cause serious damage to sane people. Violent shock therapy with injections can cause insanity in normal persons. The patients are constantly reminded that their release depends on the success of the treatment: to be 'cured' means complete subservience and silence.

LIST OF TRIALS AND ARRESTS 1967-1970

Date and place of trial or arrest	Arrested person	Charge	Sentence
Nov. 1967, Leningrad	Trial of Igor OGURTSOV, translator from Japanese, Mikhail SADO, Orientalist, Evgeniya VAGINA, writer, and AVEROCHKINA, lawyer	Leaders of the All Russian Christian Socialist Union for the Liberation of the People	OGURTSOV 15, SADO 13, VAGINA 10, AVEROCHKINA 8 years in a strict corrective labour colony
8-12 Jan. 1968, Moscow	Trial of the writers Yury GALANSKOV, Aleksandr GINSBURG, Aleksey DOBROVOLSKY, and Vera LASHKOVA	Anti-Soviet propaganda and agitation. Galanskov for offences against the currency laws	GALANSKOV 7 years strict camp; GINSBURG 5 years camp, DOBROVOLSKY 2, LASHKOVA 1
14 Feb. 1968, Moscow	Arrest of Aleksandr VOLPIN, candidate in physical mathematics, and Nataliya GORBANEVSKAYA, interpreter	Participation in the demonstration against the arrest of Galanskov, Ginsburg, Dobrovolsky, and Lashkova	Removal to a psychiatric clinic
4 March to 5 April 1968, Leningrad	Trial of Vyacheslav PLATONOV, Orientalist, Nikolay IVANOV, art historian, Leonid BORODIN, headmaster, Vladimir IVOYLOV, agriculturist, Mikhail KONOSOV, locksmith and evening student at the Gorki Institute of Literature, Sergey USTINOVICH, graduate of Leningrad University, Yury BUTSIN, Valery NAGORNY, Aleksandr MIKLASHEVICH, and Yury BARONOV, engineers, Georgy BOCHEVAROV, graduate of Leningrad University, Anatoly SUDAREV, translator,	Members of the All Russian Christian Socialist Union for the Liberation of the People	PLATONOV 7 years camp, IVANOV and BORODIN 6, IVOYLOV 3, KONOSOV 4, USTINOVICH 3½, BUTSIN, NAGORNY, and BARONOV 3, BOCHEVAROV 2½, SUDAREV,

Date and place of trial or arrest	Arrested person	Charge	Sentence
4 March to 5 April 1968, Leningrad	Anatoly IEVLEV and Vladimir VERETENOV, chemists, Olgred SOBAK, mechanic, Oleg SHUVALOV, and Stanislav KONSTANTINOV		IEVLEV, and VERETENOV 2, SOBAK, SHUVALOV, and KONSTANTINOV 14 months
March/April 1968, Moscow	Arrest of A. FETISOV, agriculturist, M. ANTONOV, M. BYKOV, and O. SMIRNOV, architects	Criticism of the Soviet system	Removal to psychiatric clinics in Kazan and Leningrad
20 Aug. 1968, Simferopol	Arrest of Mamedi CHOBANOV, a Crimean Tatar	Resistance to State authority	3 years in prison
21 Aug. 1968, Leningrad	Arrest of BOGUSLAVSKY	Protest against the intervention in Czechoslovakia	5 years in strict camp, reduced on appeal in Oct. 1968 to 3 years camp
27 Aug. 1968, Simferopol	Arrest of Mubein YUSUPOV and Fakhul ISMAILOV, Crimean Tatars	Resistance to State authority	YUSUPOV 1 year in prison, ISMAILOV 6 months
4 Sept. 1968, Simferopol	Arrest of Tsekeriya ASANOV, a Crimean Tartar	Resistance to State authority	1 year in prison
9-11 Oct. 1968, Moscow	Trial of Konstantin BABITSKY, Larissa BOGORAZ-BRUKHMAN, Vadim DELONE, Vladimir DREMLYUGA, and Pavel LITVINOV	Demonstration in the Red Square in Moscow against the intervention in Czechoslovakia	BABITSKY 3 years camp, BOGORAZ-BRUKHMAN 4 years, DELONE 2 years 10 months, DREMLYUGA 3 years, LITVINOV 5 years
18 Oct. 1968, Lvov	Arrest of Pyotr GORODETSKY, priest	Slander of the Soviet State and social order, offence against the law for the separation of Church and State	Unknown

Date and place of trial or arrest	Arrested person	Charge	Sentence
22-28 Oct. 1968, Tashkent	Trial of Lyuman UMEROV, Idris KASYMOV, Shelket SEITABLEYEV, Lennar GUSEYNOV, and Yusuf RASINOV	Publishing a news bulletin on the events in Chirchik on 21 March 1968 and an appeal to writers and artists	UMEROV, RASYMOV, and SEITABLEYEV 1 year in prison, GUSEYNOV and RASINOV 1 year probation
17-26 Dec. 1968, Leningrad	Trial of Yury GENDLER, lawyer, Lev KVACHEVSKY, chemist, Evgeny SHASHENKOV, engineer, Nikolay DANILOV, lawyer, Anatoly STUDENKOV	Distributing leaflets on the intervention in Czechoslovakia	GENDLER 3, KVACHEVSKY 4, STUDENKOV 1 year strict camp, DANILOV and SHASHENKOV removal to a prison mental hospital
24 Dec. 1968, Moscow	Trail of Viktor FEINBERG	Demonstration in the Red Square in Moscow against the intervention in Czechoslovakia	Removal to a psychiatric clinic
End of 1968, Moscow	Arrest of BOGANOV, a workman from Elektrotal	Treason (conversations with foreigners)	Unknown
End of 1968, Kolomna	Arrest of Bishop Vasily VELICHOVSKY	Unknown	Unknown
1968, Lithuania	Trial of Verute KODENE, a woman member of a collective farm	Resistance to the Soviet State 20 years previously	10 years
22 Jan. 1969, Moscow	Arrest of ILIN	Attempt on the lives of the cosmonauts Beregovoi, Nikolayeva-Tereshkova, Nikolayev, and Leonov	Removal to a psychiatric clinic
26-29 Jan. 1969, Kiev	Trial of A. NAZARENKO, V. KONDRYUKOV, and V. KARPENKO, workmen in the Kiev waterworks and evening students at Kiev University	Anti-Soviet propaganda, distributing leaflets condemning the Russification of the Ukraine and the Shevchenko celebrations in Kiev	1 year camp
19 Feb. 1969, Moscow	Trial of Irina BELGORODSKAYA	Circulating a letter describing the cause of the arrest of Anatoly Marchenko	1 year camp

Date and place of trial or arrest	Arrested person	Charge	Sentence
23/24 April 1969, Simferopol	Trial of Gomer BAYEV, engineer, Crimean Tatar	Slander of the Soviet State and social order	2 years camp
May 1969, Tallinn	Arrest of Gennady GAVRILOV, KOZIREV, and PARAMONOV, officers of the Baltic Fleet	Forming the Union for the Struggle for Political Rights	GAVRILOV 6 years strict camp, KOZIREV 2 years; PARAMONOV removal to a psychiatric clinic at Charnychousk
May 1969, Leningrad	Arrest of BERGER, BRAUN, VODOPYANOV, and MANCHESKY	Distributing 'Samisdat' literature and books published abroad	Unknown
13–16 May 1969, Kiev	Trial of Boris KOCHUBIYEVSKY, radio engineer	Anti-Soviet views and attempt to emigrate to Israel	3 years camp
21 May 1969, Moscow	Trial of Ilya BURMISTROVICH, mathematician	Distributing the works of Daniel and Sinyavsky	3 years camp
28 May 1969, Kiev	Trial of Nikolay BERISLAVSKY	Attempted suicide by fire	2½ years strict camp
June 1969, Leningrad	Arrest of Yury LEVIN, technician at the Scientific Institute for the Mechanical Processing of Minerals	Writing letters to persons abroad which criticized Soviet policy towards Czechoslovakia	Unknown
June 1969, Leningrad	Trial of Svetlana AMETOVA, Rashat BAYRAMOV, Ayder BARIYEV, Itstset KHAIROV, Munira KHAKIKOVA, Ruslan EMINOV, Ridvin GAFAROV, Izmail YETSYDZHIYEV, Rollan KADYEV, and Ritsa UMEROV	Distributing literature protesting against the fate of the Crimean Tatars	AMETOVA, KHALILOVA, GAFAROV, YAZYDZHIYEV, and UMAROV 1 year camp, BAYRAMOV and KADYEV 3 years, BARIYEV and KHAIROV 18 months, EMINOV 6 months
20 June 1969, Moscow	Trial of Sergey SARYCHEV, scientific assistant in the Institute of Oriental Studies	Anti-Soviet utterances	2½ years strict camp

Date and place of trial or arrest	Arrested person	Charge	Sentence
End of June 1969, Moscow	Arrest of Major (retd) Ivan GRISH-CHUK	Organizing a demonstration against housing conditions in Beretsky near Kiev	Unknown
June 1969, Latvia	Arrest of a daughter of the writer Birute GEYLANE	Flying a Latvian flag	18 months camp
16 July 1969, Moscow	Trial of Viktor KUZNETSOV	Distributing the works of Daniel, Sinyavsky, Tarsis, etc.	Removal to a psychiatric clinic at Kazan
18 Aug. 1969, Leningrad	Arrest of Boris SHILDKROT, student	Distributing an appeal to students to fight against Stalinism and for the democratic reorganization of Soviet society	Referred for examination in a neurological clinic
28 Aug. 1969, Nyrob, prov. Perm	Trial of Anatoly MARCHENKO, author of *Moi Pokazaniya*	Anti-Soviet statements	2 years strict camp
Sept. 1969, Ternopol	Trial of ten persons	Distributing 'Samitsdat' literature about the nationalities question and intervention in Czechoslovakia	Unknown
2 Sept. 1969, Kiev	Trial of Boris TALANTOV, teacher of mathematics	Writing articles on religious themes	2 years camp
12 Sept. 1969, Moscow	Arrest of A. E. LEVITIN (KRASNOV), author of religious books	Unknown	Unknown
2 Oct. 1969, Riga	Trial of Ilya RIPS, student	Attempted suicide by fire	Removal to a mental hospital
13 Oct. 1969, Noginsk	Trial of Mikhail RYZHIK	Refusal of military service	18 months in a corrective labour colony
5 Nov. 1969, Leningrad	Arrest of B. O. MITYASHIN	Sending letters to the editors of Soviet journals protesting against the arrest of the demonstrators at the Ginsburg trial	Unknown
7 Nov. 1969, Riga	Arrest of A. MISULOVIN and E. KIEPINA	Tearing down a Soviet flag	MISULOVIN 18 months imprisonment, KIEPINA 1 year

Date and place of trial or arrest	*Arrested person*	*Charge*	*Sentence*
19 Nov. 1969, Leningrad	Trial of Vladimir BORISOV	Signing a letter to the United Nations	19 May 1970 suicide in the sick ward of the Butyrka prison
20 Nov. 1969, Moscow	Arrest of Vyacheslav VAKHMIN, student	Unknown	Unknown
26 Nov. 1969, Kharkov	Trial of Genrikh ALTUNYAN, radio technician	Anti-Soviet propaganda, circulation of leaflets slandering the Soviet State and social order	3 years camp
1 Dec. 1969, Moscow	Arrest of Irina KAPLUN and Olga IOFFE, students	Distributing 'Samitsdat' material and preparing a protest against the celebration of the 90th anniversary of Stalin's birthday	IOFFE removed to a psychiatric clinic
23 Dec. 1969, Moscow	Trial of Viktor KRASIN, agriculturist	Parasitic way of life	Deportation to the Krasnoyarsk district for 5 years
1969, Leningrad	Arrest of two history students of the Herzen Institute of Pedagogy	Circulating material from the libraries which was reserved for selected students	Unknown
1969, Lvov	Arrest of Vasily RYBAK	Sending an article to *Pravda* protesting against the suppression of the Ukrainian language and the forced assimilation of the Ukrainians	Unknown
1969, Rostov	Arrest of Dr SHER, biologist	Unknown	Unknown
1969	Arrest of A. A. PETROV-AGATOV	Unknown	Unknown
1969, Moscow	Trial of Erich DANNE of Riga, an employee on an air line	Importing anti-Soviet literature	Unknown

Date and place of trial or arrest	Arrested person	Charge	Sentence
End of 1969, Krasnodar	Arrest of PETRENKO, an engine-driver	Sending a letter to A. A. Grechno, Minister of Defence, criticizing the policies of the Soviet Government, the intervention in Czechoslovakia, disorder in the Krasnodar industries, and Brezhnev personally	1 year imprisonment
1969, Riga	Arrest of Fritz MENDERS, aged 24, one of the founders of the Social Democratic Party in Latvia	Unknown	5 years strict camp
1969, Leningrad	Arrest of SLAVINSKY	Unknown	Unknown
1969, Kiev	Arrest of I. GRISHUK	Unknown	Unknown
1969, Roshal	Arrest of V. LUKANIN	Unknown	Removal to a prison mental hospital
1969, Chernovtsy	Arrest of GAY	Communicating with Ukrainian nationalists	Unknown
1969, Estonia	Arrest of 31 officers of the Baltic Fleet	Re Alekseyev's letter protesting against the intervention in Czechoslovakia	Unknown
1969, Gorki	Arrest of two professors and two students at Gorki University	Unknown	Unknown
1969, Vladimir	Arrest of Vladimir BORISOV, former chairman of the Soyuts Netsavizimoy Molodeshi	(The legally founded Soyuts was then disbanded)	Removal to a mental hospital
1969, Krasnoyarsk	Arrest of Elena ROGALEVA, PETRASHKO, and POTEMCHENKO	Anti-Soviet propaganda, distributing fly-sheets, setting fire to militia buildings, public prosecutor's office, and law court	5 years each in a corrective labour colony
1969	Arrest of Galina SELIVONCHIK	Attempt to hijack an aircraft	13 years camp
Jan. 1970, Tallinn	Trial of Teet KALLAS	Unknown	Unknown

Date and place of trial or arrest	Arrested person	Charge	Sentence
5-13 Jan. 1970, Saratov	Trial of SENIN, ROMANOV, KULIKOV (gymnastics trainer), KIRIKIN, BOBROV, and FOKEYEV, students	Setting up an anti-Soviet organization; anti-Soviet propaganda	SENIN 7, ROMANOV, KULIKOV, and KIRIKIN 6, BOBROV 4 years strict camp, FOKEYEV 3 years camp
8 Jan. 1970, Yangyul, Uzbekistan	Arrest of Nuri ABDURAIMOV	Unknown	3 years camp
12-19 Jan. 1970, Tashkent	Trial of Ilya GABAY and Mustafa DZHEMILEV	Preparation and circulation of various documents, including the letter of the twelve to the Budapest council of the Communist and Workers' parties; the appeal to scientists and artists, signed by I. Gabay, Y. Kim, and P. Yakir; appeal to Moscow citizens for aid to the Crimean Tatars	GABAY 3 years camp, DZHEMILEV 3 years strict camp
19-27 Jan. 1970, Dnyepropetrovsk	Trial of I. G. SOKULSKY, N. G. KULCHINSKY, and V. V. SAVCHENKO	Preparation and circulation of an appeal to the youth of Dnyepropetrovsk; circulating so-called 'report from Beria', etc.	SOKULSKY 4½ years strict camp, KULCHINSKY 2½ years camp, SAVCHENKO 2 years (reduced to 3 years probation)
22 Jan. 1970, Leningrad	Arrest of Gennady TRIFONOV, labourer in the Kalinin works at Leningrad	Attempt at suicide by fire	Unknown
Jan. 1970, Leningrad	Trial of Eruand LALAYANTS, translator and orientalist	Sending anonymous letters to various institutions, signed 'Central Office of the Russian Socialist Party'	Several years in a corrective labour colony

Date and place of trial or arrest	Arrested person	Charge	Sentence
29 Feb. 1970, Sverdlovsk	Arrest of Lev UBOZHKO, engineer physicist	Possessing fly-sheets distributed by foreigners in Moscow, defending Grigorenko, Litvinov, and Gulanskov	Unknown
Feb. 1970, Ryazan	Trial of Yury VUDKA, Shimons GRILYUS, FROLOV, Valery VUDKA, MARTIMONOV, and ZASLAVSKY, students at the Radio Technical Institute at Ryazan	Founding an illegal group, 'The New-Type Marxist Party'	Y. VUDKA 7, GRILYUS and FROLOV 5, V. VUDKA 3 years strict camp; MARTIMONOV and ZASLAVSKY probation
3 Feb. 1970, Lvov	Trial of BEDRILO, agriculturist	Preparation of the appeal of seven convicted Ukrainian writers and of a fly-sheet concerning Makhukha's suicide	2 years camp
26/27 Feb. 1970, Moscow	Trial of P. G. GRIGORENKO	Anti-Soviet activities	Removal to a psychiatric clinic at Kazan
20 March 1970, Kiev	Trial of BAKHTIYAROV, student	Anti-Soviet propaganda	3 years camp
March 1970, Begovat, Uzbekistan	Trial of Maurem MARTYNOV, Crimean Tatar writer	Speech at the grave of A. E. Kosterin; signing various documents regarding the Crimean Tatars	2 years probation
March 1970, Angron, Uzbekistan	Trial of Seydomet KHALIZAYEV	Anti-Soviet propaganda	1 year camp
March 1970, Uzhgorod	Arrest of Raiza BEKDUALIEVA, teacher	Writing letters to foreign statesmen	3 years camp
10/11 March 1970, Kharkov	Trial of Vladimir PONOMAREV and Vladislav NEDOBORA, engineers	Slandering the Soviet State and social order	3 years camp
13 March, 1970, Moscow	Trial of Vladimir GERSHUNI, mason	Slandering the Soviet State and social order	Removal to psychiatric clinic
16 March 1970, Moscow	Valeriya NOVODVORSKAYA, student	Distributing fly-sheets against the intervention in Czechoslovakia	Removal to psychiatric clinic in Kazan

Date and place of trial or arrest	Arrested person	Charge	Sentence
22 March 1970, Rostov	Arrest of Pyotr EGIDES, candidate in philosophy	Letters to Soviet authorities protesting against conditions in the Soviet Union	Unknown
25 March to 24 April 1970, Gorki	Trial of Mikhail KAPRANOV, former student, expelled for anti-Soviet utterances, Sergey PONOMAREV and Vladimir ZHILTSOV, students, and Vladen PAVLENKOV, history teacher	Anti-Soviet propaganda	PAVLENKOV and KAPRANOV 7 years strict camp, PONOMAREV 5 and ZHILTSOV 4 years camp
April 1970, Obninsk	Arrest of Valentina ZINOVYEVA	Anti-Soviet agitation	Unknown
13-18 April 1970, Riga	Second trial of Ivan YAKHIMOVICH, philologist, graduate of the Latvian University, chairman of the 'Yauna Gvarde' kolkhoz	Letter of protest to the Communist Party	Removal to a psychiatric clinic in Riga
24 April 1970, Kharkov	Trial of Arkady LEVIN, engineer	Signing and distributing letters to the United Nations Committee of Human Rights, à propos the arrest of Grigorenko	3 years camp
30 May 1970, Obninsk	Arrest of Yaures MEDVEDEV, biologist	Criticizing the Soviet Government for introducing politics into science	Removal to a psychiatric clinic
1970, Petrosavodsk	Trial of a student	Distributing a pamphlet, 'Sakat Kapitala', by Y. Vudka	4 years camp
1970, Kishinev	Arrest of SUSLONSKY, teacher	Circulating Samitsdat literature	Unknown
April 1970, Leningrad	Trial of A. N. ZEMTSOV, student	Damaging a portrait of Stalin in the Kirov Prospekt, Leningrad	1 year strict camp (on probation)
April 1970, Leningrad	Trial of YEZHOV, engineer	Tearing down a portrait of Stalin near the public library in the Nevsky Prospekt, Leningrad	1½ years corrective labour at his former place of employment, with a 10% deduction from his wages

Date and place of trial or arrest	Arrested person	Charge	Sentence
10 April 1970, Leningrad	Trial of VOLKOV, technician	Tearing down a portrait of Stalin at the Elektrosila underground station, Leningrad	1 year strict camp
May 1970, Tashkent	Arrest of Nurfet MARAKHAZ	Collecting information about the Crimean Tatars	Unknown
21 May 1970, Akulovo, in the Ryazan district	Arrest of Andrey AMALRIK	Distributing anti-Soviet literature in the Urals	Unknown
June 1970, Kemerovo	Trial of Vladimir VEKSHIN	Anti-Soviet propaganda	Unknown
1 June 1970, Ivano-Franlovsk	Arrest of Valentin MOROS	Possessing books published in the W. Ukraine before 1939; also because of his MSS 'Moisey i Datan', 'Chronika Soprotivleniya', and 'Sredi Snegov'	Unknown
9-15 June 1970, Estonia	Trial of Rayvo LAPP, laboratory assistant at Tartu University, Andres VYSU, taxi-driver, Enn PAULYUS, locksmith, and Sven TAMM	Possessing firearms and founding an organization 'to fight against Soviet power in the case of a conflict between the Soviet Union and Estonia'	LAPP 5, VYSU 3½, PAULYUS 2½ years camp, TAMM 3 years probation
15 June 1970, Leningrad	Arrest of Eduard KUZNETSOV (Riga), Aleksandr MURZHENKO (Losovaya, Ukraine), Yury FEDOROV (Moscow), Silva SALMANSON (Kuznetsov's wife), Anatoly ALTMAN (Riga), Mendel BODIYA (Riga), Vulf SALMANSON, reserve officer, and his brother Izaak (Riga), CHNOCH and his wife (Riga),	Attempting to hijack a plane at Leningrad	Unknown

Date and place of trial or arrest	Arrested person	Charge	Sentence
15 June 1970, Leningrad	PENSON, a painter (Riga), Mark DYMSHITS and his wife and daughter (Leningrad), Georgy BUTMAN, GOLDENFELD, Solomon DREYSNER, Lassal KAMINSKY, L. KORNBLIT, Vladimir MOGILEVER, David CHERNOGLAZ, and, on the way to Odessa, Lev YAGMAN	Attempting to hijack a plane at Leningrad	Unknown
July 1970, Leningrad	G. VERTLIB, lawyer, G. SHUR, engineer, and V. BOGUSLAVSKY, engineer	Attempting to hijack a plane at Leningrad	Unknown
July 1970, Leningrad	Arrest of Dr Revolt PIMENOV, scientific assistant at the Mathematical Institute	Anti-Soviet propaganda	Unknown
7 July 1970, Moscow	Arrest of Yulia VISHNEVSKAYA and Vladimir TELNIKOV	Resistance to the State power during the trial of Nataliya Gorbanevskaya	Unknown
9 July 1970, Tiflis	Venyamin DZHANASHVILI and Abram DZHANDZHIKHANASHVILI, Georgian Jews	Applying for permission to emigrate to Israel	Unknown
5 Aug. 1970, Riga	Arrest of Boris SHAFNER and Aaron SPIELBERG	Taking part in an attempt to hijack a plane at Leningrad	Unknown

Back to the Ministry of Internal Affairs (MVD)

In the course of this study of the Reign of Terror in the Soviet Union there have been many references to the connection between the political police and the organs responsible for the maintenance of public order. At certain periods the two departments were united, usually when it was considered necessary to thrust the element of force and fear still more deeply into the private life of the Soviet citizen. From time to time the two departments were separated from each other, the aim being to facilitate both the activities of the political police and the concentration of the People's Commissariat (i.e. ministry) on its own specific purposes, as occurred particularly during the Second World War. After Stalin's death, or rather after Beria's execution, an appropriate separation was carried out between the KGB (Committee of State Security) and the MVD (Ministry of the Interior). The MVD ceased to exist *qua* Union ministry in 1960, and in 1966 a Ministry for the Maintenance of Public Order was created in each republic of the Union. The Soviet leaders used the occasion to announce in triumph that a Socialist country was able to carry out a decentralization of the offices responsible for public order, proclaiming the step as a progressive and democratic achievement. But that happy state of affairs was not destined to last for long.

The Socialism of the Soviet Union is no magic charm against the problems that beset every modern industrial country: youthful delinquency, vandalism and hooliganism, alcoholism, drug-taking, and the rest. Few people in the West are aware of what a headache the drug habit is to the Soviet authorities. There are frequent newspaper reports of Comsomol members smoking drugged cigarettes and even injecting themselves in public, quite regardless of the stares of passers-by. An open letter addressed to the Soviet leaders in March 1970 by three professors, A. D. Sakharov, V. F. Turchin, and R. A. Medvedev, and published in all the leading Western newspapers, drew attention to the problem: 'Alcoholism is gaining ground in the most tragic fashion, and now we are faced with the dangers of drug-taking. Crime flourishes in many parts of the country, and in more than one city corruption is rife.'

On 29 November 1968 the newspapers published the decree of the Presidium of the Supreme Soviet whereby the Ministry for the Maintenance of Public Order was renamed the Ministry of Internal Affairs. So—back to the MVD. The press commentaries gave several reasons for the change of name. The militia must be better trained and their effectiveness improved. Traffic offences, alcoholism, and particularly the illegal possession of firearms by young people needed stricter control and severer measures. It was believed that a greater efficiency was obtainable by centralizing and tightening up the whole system of maintaining public order. The need to protect both State and private property was becoming more and more pressing. The failure of the prophylactic measures hitherto employed was openly admitted, and fresh hopes were put in the resuscitated MVD.

The need to enlarge the scope of the KGB was another motive for the decision of the Soviet leaders. The MVD is not a political organ, and cooperation with the State Attorney's department and the courts of justice is obviously essential. There were many signs of the growing discontent within the Party bureaucracy that on the one hand the activities of the KGB had been better organized and made more effective, with a more powerful influence on the general public, while on the other hand the failure of the organs responsible for public order was becoming more and more evident. The balance between the two departments was to be restored by better organization and greater financial expenditure. It is significant that the system of corrective labour colonies, which lies within the competency of the department responsible for public order, was to be further expanded.

That there is no possibility of perfect cooperation between the KGB and the MVD is acknowledged in an article by Colonel-General N. Shchelokov in the *Kommunist Moldavi* No. 2, 1970. Even collaboration with the State Attorney's department needs to be improved. In the authoritarian system of the Soviet Union such phenomena are quite normal: overlapping competencies, departmental disputes, parallel duties and activities, are everyday occurrencies. Intrigue and jealousy are becoming traditional in the relations between MVD and KGB. But all this is of minor importance compared with the question of what the reconstitution of the MVD means to the man in the street, even if it does not take over the duties of the political police. As against a firmer attitude in questions of the public well-being it brings him manifold threats of reprimands, punishments, and fines. He is faced with a long catalogue of punishable faults and offences which had previously been considered ridiculously trivial. But as it is generally admitted that the training of the militia leaves much to be desired, the tendency now is to judge a case on purely formal and bureaucratic lines, rather than treat it with a sense of proportion and equity. The Soviet citizen is certainly as much interested as other nationals in the preservation of public order. It is ominous that the militia is being specially trained in the suppression of mass demonstrations and other forms of disorder, and the results of the training are already visible in the handling of trifling disturbances in Moscow and in the crushing of the Crimean Tatar demonstrations.

Chapter Twelve

With Terror into the Seventies?

IN 1967 fifty years of Soviet rule in Russia were celebrated. All that had happened since 1917, and the way it happened, is unthinkable without the security organs. In a period of a mere fifty years the role of force and terror has frequently changed, but at no time have the leaders dispensed with this tool entirely. Our analysis of the performance and the varying guises of the Soviet security service was primarily meant as a contribution to the understanding of the past and future of a country which has become a great world power, second only to the United States. Even though the reader is occasionally offered sensational material, the main object of the book is an account of the historic function of the security service and of the use of force and terror in the successive stages of development of the Soviet system. The security problem still plagues the Soviet community at the present time, when through the development of science and technology all industrial countries are facing new and enormously difficult problems —political, economic, social. Can a society in which the use of compulsion far exceeds what is necessary to maintain order and security, and even invades the thoughts and private lives of the Soviet citizens, can such a society which watches and muzzles the individual to such an extent compete successfully with the rest of the world?

Readers of the Samitsdat provided by a Soviet underground publishing system are supplied with a list of arrests and political trials which is certainly incomplete and possibly omits dozens of cases. It is a striking fact, however, that the wave of political prosecutions, which ebbed after Stalin's death and notably after the 20th Party Congress of 1956, rose to a flood again in the last years of Khrushchev's rule, and especially since 1967. Why should this be so? The answer must not be a mere observation that Terror is again triumphant in the Soviet Union, for such a recrudescence primarily reflects a serious crisis in the whole system and failure in a leadership which is incapable of dealing with modern problems and possibilities while Brezhnev remains at its head. Despite their condemnation of the personality cult, the Soviet leaders still rely on terror as a rein for guiding social progress. They utterly fail to realize that traditional violence and terror can no longer cope with the ever-rising flood of 'diversionist' thinking, open letters, appeals to world opinion, and groups which form oases of free thought and discussion, culminating in demonstrations and direct action. This movement must not be over-estimated, but it may well figure as the significant problem of the next few years.

We must now attempt an historical retrospect in outline.

Lenin and his companions certainly considered terrorism as a necessary evil. Even in the earliest days of Bolshevism they worried about the possible dangers that might arise from a misuse of political police power. But in Dzerzhinsky's personality Lenin seemed to have a guarantee that such misuse would be restricted to an absolute minimum. The security service was to be 'the servant of the Revolution': it would destroy the enemies of Communism in Russia, it would tear down the barriers that stood in the way towards a new society. Situations like those which arose on the ruins of Tsarist Russia during the October Revolution, when lawlessness was rampant, law and order dissolved, and the helpless people was delivered over to an unknown fate, have occurred more than once in the history of mankind, and that fact must never be forgotten. Still nothing can justify the barbarity and murders of that period. According to their lights the Bolsheviks were waging a bitter struggle against the superior forces of their adversaries, in order to carry out the demands of history. The use of terrorist measures and restrictions on liberty were Lenin's way of reaching his political goals more quickly. These goals retained their rosy Utopian hue at least until the beginning of the twenties. Lenin was fascinated by 'the first proletarian state', i.e. the Paris Commune of 1871, and he believed that the Soviet State should incorporate the best elements of that famous political experiment; popular election of officials, strictest control of the State machine by the people, replacement of police by a people's militia, abolition of the army in favour of new ways of arming the people. In his celebrated thesis for the Bolshevik party programme of 1917 Lenin wrote: 'The substitution of a people's militia for the police is a change that is the logical outcome of the whole course of the Revolution and is being carried out in most parts of Russia. . . . There is only one way to prevent the return of the police, namely the establishment of a people's militia, to be incorporated into the army: the standing army must be replaced by a general arming of the people.'

When Lenin, after the victory of the Revolution, developed from a rebel and a prophet into a statesman, he sobered down in many ways. He became a spectator of the process which had begun under his immediate direction. Dzerzhinsky's security service adopted policies which had nothing to do with defending the achievements of the Revolution. Even Lenin's lifetime saw the start of a lunatic development which mocked all Socialist ideas. The secret police became the main support of the Party, and the Party itself found itself more and more represented by a single man—Stalin. Lenin did nothing to put a brake on this process, and nothing in the world can absolve him from the responsibility. It was Lenin himself who proposed Stalin as the General Secretary of the Party. His constant use of the phrases 'Counter-Revolution', 'betrayal of Marxism', etc., created a favourable seed-bed for arbitrary interpretations. Such phrases implied condemnation not only of the White Guards but of the resistance of the starving peasants, the longings for freedom of peoples long oppressed by the Tsarist yoke, and the limit of intolerance was reached when all tendencies in the working classes which did not happen to conform to Bolshevist theory were similarly anathematized.

And yet all this is of minor importance compared with Lenin's blindness and deafness to the dangers innate in such a concentration of power. Theo Pirker, the sociologist, is right when he writes: 'Lenin's testament—including the first sentence, in which he speaks of the "enormous power" that is concentrated in the hands of the General Secretary—contains no fundamental criticism of the power system. Perhaps Lenin had his eye on a different person as the Party leader. But he made no judgement on Stalin as a statesman, nor did he propose any reform of the constitution. That would have been very difficult for him, for Stalin was his own creation—from the "nationalities question" on which Stalin published a paper before 1914, with an introduction by Lenin, to Stalin's election as General Secretary in 1922. The "enormous power" in Stalin's hands was the concentration of power which Lenin had handed on to him.'[164]

After the deaths of Lenin and (especially) Dzerzhinsky the security service became the principal tool of the General Secretary of the Communist Party of the Soviet Union. At Stalin's instigation, Yagoda and Yezhov separated the political police from the Party, causing the departments of State and Party to lose all control of the secret police. The 'Sword of the Revolution' became the 'Scourge of the Revolution'. Without the destruction of Lenin's companions, without the liquidation of the whole generation of Old Bolsheviks, the setting up of Stalin's despotic and bureaucratic system would not have been possible. But that was not the end. Terrorism became for the Stalinists the most important tool of all. It would be quite wrong to think that Stalin merely wanted to create a system of intimidation. Terror, which in Lenin's view was a useful tool only to be used in the last resort, became institutionalized under Stalin. Still worse, Stalin's 'genius' showed itself in the equating of terror with 'Socialist legality'. The dividing line which Lenin had drawn between the two now disappeared. In this way there arose a new social order with the security service as its basis. This is the only possible explanation why many of Stalin's victims did not simply rot away in the dungeons of the secret police but could be brought before the courts to be sentenced with all the formalities or normal justice.

By his terrorism Stalin made fear and uncertainty into 'organizational methods', into instruments for educating people in Communism. Terror became a stimulant for increasing economic productivity. This precisely is the essence of the 'historical function' of terrorism under Stalin. After the Yezhovshchina, after the bloody purges, it was not abolished, but expanded to fresh depths. With the help of the security service a million-strong army of convicts was created so as to form part of the plan for 'building Socialism'. Nor were terrorizing methods confined to forced labourers. By Draconian laws Stalin sought to squeeze the last drops of effort out of the 'free' workers. He had no other policy than to expand his despotic system to the limit when he could finally profess himself satisfied. This is the conclusion which we have tried to prove by our description of events in the thirties, during the war, and in the 'second Yezhovshchina'. Until his dying day Stalin remained true to his principles, and the 'doctors' conspiracy' was his swan-song.

After Stalin's death there were many changes, but one can hardly speak of any steady progress. The security service was deprived of its unique powers and given a new position in the Soviet system. Its activities were put under the control of the Party, it must observe the law meticulously, and any relapse into arbitrary conduct was to be sharply censured. The abolition of terrorism became necessary through the general improvement in the economy. In the first phase the Soviet leaders cut down the arrogated powers of the security service primarily in order to assure the personal safety of themselves and their bureaucrats. Later they realized that in a society that was anxious to modernize itself almost nothing can be gained through terrorizing methods. The worker or technician, using modern machinery and responsible for a complete process, can only do his best when allowed a considerable degree of independent decision. A scientist cannot make any progress in his research work if he is conscious that any failure in his experiments can be ascribed by an ignorant 'security expert' to 'sabotage'. The 'historical role' of terrorism is played out, even in such an undemocratic type of society as the Soviet Union.

Of course the Party leaders' anxiety to keep full control of the community persists even now, for that is one of their innate characteristics. That is why they so often cast around for fresh administrative measures of compulsion whenever difficulties accumulate and social tensions threaten to become explosive. And they lack the courage to restrict the activities of their security service to the minimum.

The Soviet leadership professes to want a constitutional state based on law and justice. In this connection the year 1958 is of special significance. A reform of the judicature was resolved upon, and definite guarantees for civil rights were given. But everything stuck half-way. For the social future of the Soviet Union the decisive question is how such desirable principles as a constitutional state work out in the practical administration of justice and find an echo in the everyday life of Soviet citizens. After fifty years' existence the Soviet community, like the American, is still a classic example of the 'unfinished society'.

One must also bear in mind that the *élite* political groups in the Soviet Union have inherited from Tsarist Russia a fatal lack of feeling for justice. Before 1917 the population of the Russian Empire were helpless subjects of the autocratic Tsars, whose arbitrary rule often took the most barbaric forms, especially in Central Asia. The Revolution brought little change in this respect, for the Tsarist despotism was merely replaced by the 'dictatorship of the proletariat.' The increase of Soviet power in the Stalin era was a rare example in world history of how a consolidation of power and a political system can go hand in hand with unbridled tyranny and lawlessness. Khrushchev and his supporters in the post-despotic phase of Soviet society relinquished the inquisitorial methods of Stalinism, but they never freed themselves from a naively subjective attitude, and this is confirmed by a study of recent history. Certain 'genuinely Russian' ways of thinking are hard to eradicate. They consider social institutions, with guarantees and norms sanctioned by law, as unimportant, and their manipulation for political reasons, or indeed just to suit one's convenience, quite permissible, since 'everything depends solely on the leader, on him who stands at the head of the Party and represents the people'. Khrushchev never actually said this, but we are bold enough to put the following words in his mouth: 'When I, and other men as good as I am, when we are in power, then everything is all right; when the leaders are bad men, no institution can prevent evil consequences.'

The reformation of the Soviet judicial system and the consolidation of 'legality' is an extremely difficult problem, and tradition, inherited mental attitudes, and other factors come into play. The present Soviet community is burdened, it is true, with the heritage from Stalin, but that is not the only source of evil. Today's basic problem is clearly defined in a publication of the International Committee of Jurists: 'So long as the administration of justice is an instrument of state policy, and so long as the judges administer the law according to the directions of the Party or the Government, the people of the Soviet Union will be as helpless in face of their courts as they are in face of their Party's monopoly of power: it must endure without protest the consequences of the errors and failures that are inevitable over and over again in every totalitarian state. Time alone will show how far the efforts of which we have spoken will approach their goal, a fresh conception of "Socialist legality" or, what would be better still, true legality.'[165]

The hopes expressed in 1962 have in the meantime been bitterly disappointed. It is clear that the political leaders, contrary to all logic and against their own interests, have failed to shake off the chains of the past. The explanation of this phenomenon must be a sociological one. What is known in the Soviet Union as the 'real model' (i.e. practical or power politics) has prevailed, i.e. the Party and social *élite* were too weak to throw off the past and they capitulated to traditional forces and institutions. Persistence in terrorism is due less to the KGB's ambition than to the Party leaders' deliberate use of them as a means to an end. What is known in the West as the Brezhnev Doctrine not only concerns the fraternal Communist countries, but is based on internal political strategy. Of the frequently quoted inevitability of the doctrine there can be no question, for it derives solely from the carefully planned tactics of the Party leadership.

Let us return to the original question—can the Soviet Union with an obsolete set of administrative tools meet the requirements of the seventies? In addition to the interpretations of Western Kremlinologists, we are now in a position to benefit from first-hand information supplied by the Soviet intelligentsia. Their demands can be formulated as follows: democratization of the Soviet system; no interference by the Party in science and art, and particularly in literature; the abolition of social injustices; a fair nationalities policy; and the abandonment of Russification, chauvinism, and anti-Semitism.

In the economic sphere their proposals extend from recognition of the autonomy of industrial concerns and a general restriction of centralization to recognition of the economic laws that govern the Socialist markets. As for the KGB, the liberal 'programmes of the democratic movement in the Soviet Union', signed by 'the democrats of Russia, the Ukraine, and the Baltic', demand 'the abolition of the political penal apparatus and the State security system as being an unconstitutional organization, the maintenance of public order to be left exclusively in the hands of the militia'.

Other liberals demand that the internal duties of the KGB be confined to counter-espionage. Complete amnesty for all political groups is the minimum demand of all. Even today one can speak of an anti-KGB movement in the Soviet Union. Open letters, protests, and manifestos relentlessly reveal the malpractices of the security service. Valentin Moros, a Ukrainian detained in a corrective labour camp, has written a comprehensive study of the KGB under the title of *A Report from Beria*.

Again and again the question is raised—how far can the resistance influence social development and alter conditions in Russia? Certainly it consists at present of only a few small groups, opposing an overwhelmingly powerful governmental system and the indifference of the vast majority of the population. Nevertheless a certain degree of optimism is permissible when one remembers that the dissident groups are composed of students, writers, and, more recently (one is surprised to learn) of mathematicians, physicists, and biologists. These are precisely the people who are stamping their personalities on Soviet society in an age of technological progress and automation.

There is yet another ground for qualified optimism. Perhaps the Party bureaucracy, with Brezhnev at the helm, will one day remember the great theme of the teaching of Marx and Engels—that it is not the ideas and orders of a ruling class but the permanence of social contradictions that form the real mainspring of human history.

TABLE SHOWING THE DEVELOPMENT OF THE SOVIET SECURITY SERVICE

VECHEKA
7 (20) December 1917: F. E. DZERZHINSKY

GPU
6 February 1922: F. E. DZERZHINSKY

OGPU
January 1923: F. E. DZERZHINSKY
from July 1926: V. R. MENZHINSKY

NKVD
10 July 1934: H. YAGODA
from September 1936: N. Y. YEZHOV
from December 1938: L. P. BERIA

NKVD
3 February 1941: L. P. BERIA

NKGB
3 February 1941: V. N. MERKULOV

NKVD
30 July 1941: L. P. BERIA

NKVD
April 1943:
L.P. BERIA

NKGB
April 1943:
V. N. MERKULOV

SMERSH
April 1943:
V. S. ABAKUMOV

MVD
January 1946:
S. N. KRUGLOV

MGB
18 October 1946: V. S. ABAKUMOV
from the beginning of 1952: S. D. IGNATIEV

MVD
15 March 1953: L. P. BERIA
from July 1953: S. N. KRUGLOV

MVD
S. N. KRUGLOV
from 1 February 1956:
N. P. DUDOROV

KGB
13 March 1954: I. A. SEROV
from 9 December 1958: A. N. SHELEPIN
from 13 November 1961:
V. Y. SEMICHASTNY

MVD
13 January 1960:
Dissolution of the Ministry of
the Interior as a federal ministry

KGB
from 18 May 1967:
Y. V. ANDROPOV

Establishment of the Federal Republican Ministry
for the Maintenance of Public Order 18 July 1966
from 18 September 1966: N. A. SHCHELOKOV

Renamed Ministry of the Interior on 28 November 1968
from 28 November 1968: N. A. SHCHELOKOV

Notes and Sources

1. Russia used the Julian Calendar until 1918, but gave it up after the Revolution. 1 February 1918 in the Julian Calendar became 14 February in the Gregorian Calendar. Dates in our text before February 1918 include the Julian Calendar date, in brackets.

2. A detailed and well-documented biography of Lenin is that by D. Shub: *Lenin*, published by the Limes Verlag, Wiesbaden 1952.

3. D. Popov, the well-known Soviet historian, states in his *Grundriss der Geschichte des Bolschewismus* (published by the Association of Foreign Workers in the USSR, Moscow/Leningrad 1934) that there were 210,000 industrial workers in Russia in 1825, 560,000 in 1860, and 870,000 only two years later, in 1862. After that, of course, the numbers grew enormously. But in training, traditions, and organization they were in no way comparable to the Western working classes.

4. According to N. Zubov, *F. E. Dzierzhinski, A Biography*, published by the State Publishing House for Political Literature, Moscow 1965, p. 154 ff.

5. According to D. Shub, op. cit., p. 334.

6. Official biography of Dzerzhinsky in the *Bolshaya Sovetskaya Entsiklopediya*, Vol. 14, Moscow 1952, p. 250 ff. In 1951 the Marx-Engels-Lenin Institute of the Communist Party of the Central Committee published an album entitled *Feliks Edmundovich Dzerzhinsky (1877–1926)*. Every Soviet work of reference contains a biography of Dzerzhinsky. In our account of Dzerzhinsky's personality several statements by his contemporaries were used. The most detailed of the biographies of Dzerzhinzky published in the Soviet Union is Zubov's (see Note 4). Its documentation has been used on various occasions in this book in our accounts of the activities of the security organs under Dzerzhinsky.

7. Lenin's attitude to the question of terrorism is discussed by F. M. Burlatsky in *Voprosy Istorii KPSS*, No. 462, p. 162 ff: *Lenin o Demokraticheskom Kharaktere Diktatury Proletariata* (Lenin on the democratic character of the dictatorship of the proletariat).

8. According to *Istoriya SSSR*, No. 4/1965, p. N121.

9. N. Zubov, op. cit., p. 196.

10. For Lenin's changing attitude to terrorism see D. Shub (op. cit.), and E. J. Scott, 'The Czeka, Soviet Affairs', in *St Anthony's Papers*, No. 1/1956, published by Chatto & Windus, London.

11. P. G. Sofinov, *Ocherki Istorii VECHEKA* (outline of the history of the

Vecheka), published by the State Publishing House for Political Literature Moscow 1960, p. 18.

12. Also known as 'revtribunals'. For their organization and development see D. S. Karev, *Organizatziya Suda i Prokuratury v SSR*, published by the Lenin State University, Minsk 1960, p. 87.

13. Quoted from George F. Kennan, *Amerika und die Sowjetmacht*, Vol. II, *Die Entscheidung zur Intervention*, published by Steingruben Verlag, Stuttgart 1958, p. 173.

14. Detailed reports on the risings in the summer of 1918 are to be found in *Voprosy Istorii*, No. 4/1965, p. 1210 ff. They include a statement that in proceedings against members of the Right Socialist Revolutionaries in 1922 it was proved that the French Consul-General in Moscow, René Marchand, took part in the organization of this rising. The chief organizer of the risings, Boris Savinkov, was arrested by the security organs by means of a trick and condemned to death. During the trial he admitted that about two million roubles had been put at his disposal by the French Government, but that the promised landing at Archangel had not taken place. 'We found ourselves in the position', said Savinkov, 'of men betrayed by the foreigners.'

15. There are precise descriptions in Soviet literature of the liquidation of the Left-Wing Socialist Revolutionaries. See for instance P. G. Sofinov, *Ocherki Istorii VECHEKA*. For Popov's fate see N. Zubov, op. cit., p. 108.

16. Quoted from E. J. Scott, *The Czeka* (see Note 10).

17. In our description of the development of the VECHEKA organization the above-mentioned work by P. G. Zofinov has been freely used.

18. P. G. Sofinov gives a full account of the diplomats' conspiracy, and George F. Kennan (op. cit.) has some interesting documentary material on this episode.

19. V. I. Lenin, Works (Russian edition), Vol. 28, p. 150.

20. M. Y. Latsis, *Chrezvychaynaya Komissiya po Bor'bie s Kontrerevolutsiyey* (Extraordinary Commission for the War against Counter-Revolution), Moscow 1920, p. 15 ff.

21. In this connection see V. Z. Tikunov, 'Sotsialisticheskaya Zakonnost' v Deyatel'nosti Organov Gosbezopasnosti' (Socialist legality in the activity of the security organs), in *Sovetskoye Gosudarstvo i Pravo*, No. 8/1959. Also V. S. Tadevosyan, 'V. I. Lenin o Sotsialisticheskoy Sakonnosti' (Lenin on Socialist legality), in *Sovetskoye Gosudarstvo i Pravo*, May 1960.

22. V. I. Lenin, Works (German edition), Vol. 50, p. 318.

23. Quoted from E. J. Scott, *The Czeka* (see Note 10).

24. *Malaya Sovetskaya Entsiklopediya*, Moscow 1932, Vol. I, p. 360, and Raphael R. Abramovich, *Die Sowjetrevolution*, published by Dietz Nachfolger, Hanover 1963, p. 184 f.

25. Material on this subject appeared for the first time in *Istorichesky Arkhiv*, No. 55, September/October 1957, p. 182 ff, published by the Academy of Sciences of the USSR, Moscow.

26. *Malaya Sovetskaya Entsiklopediya*, Moscow 1930, Vol. 7, p. 231.

27. Quoted from Vladimir Gsovsky, 'Vorbeugungshaft und Inhaftierung durch die Exekutive in der Sowjetunion, (preventive detention and arrest by the executive in the Soviet Union), in the *Journal der Internationalen Juristen-Kommission*, Geneva 1961, Vol. III, No. 1, p. 152.

28. Details of the ever-worsening relations between the sick Lenin and Stalin are to be found in Lev Trotsky's *Stalin: Eine Biographie*, published by

Kiepenheuer & Witsch, Cologne and Berlin 1952, and also in D. Shub, op. cit·
The text of Lenin's testament was first published in full after Stalin's death.

29 P. G. Sofinov, op. cit., p. 136 ff. Note that the author, although he had
ample material at his disposal, sees every event through the spectacles of a
confirmed Stalinist.

30. N. Zubov, op. cit., p. 272.

31. Certain documents of Lenin's, which show the hostility and ever-worsening relations between him and Dzerzhinsky, were published in various periodicals
after Stalin's death. They are also printed in the omnibus volume *V. I. Lenin o
Sovetskom Stroitel'stve*, p. 634 ff.

32. Trotsky, op. cit., p. 462 ff.

33. For the resolution concerning Sultan Galiyev see *KPSS v Revolutsiyakh
i Resheniyakh S'ezdov, Konferentsiy i Plenumov TSK*, Vol. I, Moscow 1954,
p. 759 ff. Sultan Galiyev, b. 1892, Party member since 1917, was from 1919 the
Commissar for Muslim Affairs in Central Russia. He was expelled from the
Party in 1927, arrested, and later, in 1939, liquidated. He was one of the most
important leaders of the Soviet Orient and throughout the East, and left a series
of theoretical works on the Communist movement in the Orient.

34. Trotsky, op. cit., p. 532 f.

35. V. Fomin, *Zapiski Starogo Chekista* (notes of an old Chekist), Moscow
1962.

36. In the Western countries there is a rich and well-documented literature
about the concentration camps. Among the works consulted for this book are
David J. Dallin and Boris Nikolayevsky, *Arbeiter oder Ausgebeutete? Das
System der Arbeitslager in Sowjet-Russland*, published by Die Neue Zeitung,
Munich 1948, and the works of Polish writers, of special importance for their
documentation: P. Zwierniak and S. Mora, *Sprawiedliwosc Sowiecka* (Soviet
legality), Italy 1943.

37. *Politichesky Slovar'*, State Publishing House for Political Literature,
Moscow 1940, p. 54.

38. This instruction was published in *Istoriya SSSR*, Moscow 1963, p. 610.

39. *Sotsialistichesky Vestnik*, the central organ of the Russian Social Democratic Workers' Party (Menshevik), published in New York. The article mentioned, by Wollin, appeared in the February/March 1955 number.

40. P. G. Chernopitsky, *Na Velikom Perelome* (The great turning point),
published by the University of Rostov 1965, p. 24.

41. *Voprosy Istorii KPSS*, No. 2/1964, p. 45.

42. *Ocherki Istorii Kollektivizatsii Selskovo Khozyaystva v Soyuznykh
Respublikakh* (outline of the history of the collectivization of agriculture in the
Union Republics), State Publishing House for Political Literature, Moscow
1963, p. 57.

43. The Shakhty case was reported at the time by the Soviet daily press, and
in detail by the Communist press throughout the world. Compare also the
Comintern organ, *Internationale Presse-Korrespondenz*, Nos. 28-60, 1928.

44. Alexander Orlov, *Kremlgeheimnisse* (Kremlin secrets), published by
Marienburg-Verlag, Würzburg 1953, p. 324.

45. According to *Internationale Presse-Korrespondenz*, No. 85, 1928.

46. *Sotsialistichesky Vestnik*, Nos. 7-8, July-August 1956.

47. Organ of the Trotskyists in exile, *Byulleteny Oppozitsii*, No. 11, March
1930.

48. Valuable details about events in the Comintern are to be found in

Günther Nollau's *Die Internationale: Wurzeln und Erscheinungsformen des Proletarischen Internationalismus*, Cologne 1939.

49. The poisoning of Menzhinsky by the Trotskyists is actually asserted in Vol. 27 of the *Bolshaya Sovetskaya Entsiklopediya*, p. 148, published in 1955, i.e. after Stalin's death.

50. Orlov, op. cit., p. 300 f.

51. There are various references to this in a work by Prof. Reinhart Maurach, *Handbuch der Sowjetverfassung*, Isar Verlag, Munich 1955.

52. D. S. Karev, op. cit., p. 170.

53. *Istoriya Kommunisticheskoy Partii Sovetskogo Soyusa*, Moscow 1962, p. 486.

54. Giuseppe Boffa, *Dopo Krusciov*, Einaudi, Turin 1965, p. 152 ff.

55. A correct account of Kirov's murder was published at the time in *Byulleteny Oppozitsii*, and Orlov, op. cit., adds some important details. For the Stalinist interpretation of the murder see *Geschichte der KPdSU (B)*, *Kurzer Lehrgang*, Verlag Neuer Weg, Berlin 1945, p. 395 ff.

56. Orlov, op. cit.

57. More precise information concerning Ignats Reiss (cover-name Ludwig) is to be found in *Byulleteny Oppozitsii*, Nos. 68/69 (1938) and 79/80 (1939).

58. Beria, L., *Zur Geschichte der Bolschewistischen Organisationen in Transkaukasien*, a lecture given on 21 and 22 July 1935 to an assembly of activists in the Party organization of Tbilisi, published by Dietz Verlag, East Berlin 1950, p. 220.

59. The People's Commissariat of Justice of the USSR published a shorthand transcript of this trial in 1937, and a German translation is available.

60. *XXII S'ezd Kommunisticheskoy Sovetzkogo Soyusa* (shorthand transcript), Vol. 2, Moscow 1962, p. 587.

61. G. Margenyan, *Postyshev*, Moscow 1965, p. 291.

62. Y. P. Petrov, *Partiynoye Stroitel'stvo v Sovetskoy Armii i Flote 1918-1961*, Moscow 1964, p. 299.

63. After the text of Khrushchev's speech at the 20th Communist Party Congress in 1956, published by the *America Service*, 13 June 1956, p. 16.

64. Ibid., p. 14.

65. More precise details in the foreword to M. N. Tukhachevsky's *Izbrannye Proizvedeniya* (select works), Vol. 1, Moscow 1964.

66. See, e.g., the *Bolshaya Sovetskaya Entsiklopediya*, p. 696, Vol. 1, Berlin 1952.

67. Leonty Rakovsky in his essay on Tukhachevsky in *Neva*, No. 4/1966.

68. More precise details in Y. P. Petrov, op. cit.

69. A good account of this act of 'provocation' is given in an article by Adam Ciolkosz entitled 'Tajemnica Tuchaczews-Kiego' (the secret of the Tukhachevsky case), in *Polemiki*, London, Vol. 1, autumn 1963, pp. 103-41.

70. Quoted from Lev Nikulin, 'Die Affäre Tuchatschewskij', in *Geköpfte Armee*, Berlin, p. 92.

71. A complete list of the liquidated military theoreticians, with an exact account of their services, will be found in *Voprosy Strategii i Operativnogo Iskustva v Sovetskikh Voyennykh Trudakh 1917-1940* (questions of strategy and operational art in Soviet military studies), Moscow 1965, p. 736 f.

72. More precise details in L. P. Borisov's 'OSOVIAKHIM, Stranitsky Istorii 1927-1941 Goda', in *Voprosy Istorii*, No. 6/1965, p. 45 ff.

73. *Vsesoyuznoye Soveshchaniye Istorikov* (Union Congress of historians), Moscow 1964, p. 75.

74. Ibid., p. 89.

75. See the biography in *Ukrainska Radyanska Entsyklopediya*, Vol. 16, Kiev, p. 606. Further information obtained from the victim's family living in the West.

76. Arvo Tuominen, *Le campane di Cremlino*, Stockholm 1958, pp. 203-7.

77. See *Novy Mir*, No. 4/1966, p. 213 ff.

78. For more detailed information see the *Prozessbericht über die Strafsache des Antisowjetischen Blocks der Rechten und Trotzkisten*, heard before the Military Board of the Supreme Court of Justice of the USSR, 2-13 March 1938, Moscow 1938.

79. Robert Vincent Daniels, *Das Gewissen der Revolution*, Kiepenheuer & Witsch, Cologne 1962, p. 448.

80. Quoted from Theo Pirker, *Die Moskauer Schauprozesse 1936-1938*, p. 73.

81. N. R. Mironov, 'Vosstanovleniye i Razvitiye Leninskikh Printsipov Sotsialisticheskoy Zakonnosti, (restoration and development of the Lenin principles of Socialist legality), in *Voprosy Istorii KPSS*, No. 2/1964, pp. 17-29.

82. Ibid.

83. *Visti Tsentral'noho Vykonavchoho Komitetu USSR* of 25 June 1938, No. 144.

84. Quoted from *America Service* for 13 June 1956, p. 18.

85. Y. P. Petrov, op. cit., p. 303.

86. For the text of this resolution see *KPSS v Rezolutziyakh i Resheniyakh S'ezdov, Konferentsiy Plenumov TsK*, Vol. 3, Moscow 1954, p. 306 ff.

87. *Geschichte der Kommunistischen Partei der Sowjetunion*, Berlin 1960, p. 638.

88. *Ocherki Istorii Kommunisticheskoy Partii Turkestana*, Ashkhabad 1965, p. 500.

89. The official biography of Beria in the Stalin period is contained in the *Bolshaya Sovetskaya Entsiklopediya*, Vol. 4, Moscow 1950, p. 22 f. It includes several details mentioned by S. Danilov in the periodical *Na Rubezhe*, Nos. 3 and 4, Paris 1952.

90. For a highly informative report on the development of the security organs under Yezhov and Beria see Boris Meissner, *Russland im Umbruch*, Verlag für Geschichte und Politik, Frankfurt-am-Main 1951, p. 31.

91. *Krasnaya Zvezdafor*, 13 November 1964.

92. Quoted from *Dr. Sorge Funkt aus Tokyo*, by Julius Mader, Gerhard Stuchlik, and Horst Pehnert, Deutscher Militärverlag, East Berlin 1966, p. 154.

93. Ibid., p. 187.

94. A good survey of these events is in a brochure by Wladyslaw Wiehlhorski, *Trzy Pytania i Trzy Odpowiedzi* (three questions and three answers), London 1964.

95. Margarete Buber-Neumann, *Als Gefangene bei Stalin und Hitler* (prisoner of Stalin and of Hitler), Verlag der Zwölf, Munich 1949.

96. *Lykho s Roamu* (understanding causes suffering), Paris 1967, p. 147 ff. The documents were also published in English under the title of *The Chernovil Papers* (McGraw Hill, New York, Toronto, London, etc., 1968).

97. H. Greiner, *Die Oberste Wehrmachtführing 1939-1943*, Wiesbaden 1951, p. 326, based on *Voprosy Istorii*, No. 5, 1965, p. 25.

98. XXX 'Sovetskiye Organy Gozudarstvennoy Bezopasnosti v Gody Velikov Otechestvennoy Voyny' (the Soviet State security organs during the years of the Great Patriotic War), in *Voprosy Istorii*, No. 5, May 1965.

99. *Istoriya SSR*, Moscow 1963, p. 678.

100. See the article by A. Yeremenko in *Krasnaya Zvezda* of 24 October 1963: 'Pravda o Gibeli Generala V. Kachalova' (the truth about the fate of General V. Kachalov).

101. Mykola Selesj, 'Jak Dijutj Stalinski Agentury ?', in *Vpered*, No. 2, 1959.

102. According to the account of Tz.K., an *émigré* from the Soviet Ukraine.

103. The problem of the deportation of peoples in the Soviet Union under Stalin, and the later rehabilitation, is treated in most detail by R. Conquest in *The Soviet Deportation of Nationalities*, Macmillan, London 1960.

104. G. Kargaskov, 'Polki Mobilizovanniye Gulagom', in *Na Rubezhe*, November 1951, Paris.

105. Josef Swiatlo's statements were broadcast by Radio Free Europe from Munich in several languages.

106. N. Sinevirsky, *SMERSH*, Verlag Grani, Limburg 1948.

107. *Voprosy Istorii*, No. 5, 1965, p. 34.

108. *Pravda*, 7 May 1965.

109. Lieutenant-General V. Petrov, head of the KGB in the Ministerial Council of the Belorussian SSR, gave a series of reports on these events in *Sovetskaya Belorussiya*, May 1965.

110. Ibid.

111. This is at any rate the thesis of the Kremlinologist B. Nikolayevski (now in the USA), which he has expounded in several articles in *Sotsialistichesky Vestnik* and *The New Leader*.

112. At the time the case aroused much discussion, especially in the Ukrainian exiles' press, after certain UPA partisans had brought to the West an original copy of the leaflet concerning Anosov's death.

113. *Entsyklopediya Ukrainoznavstva*, Vol. 3, Paris and New York, 1960, p. 1117 f.

114. *Istoriya KPSS*, State Publishing House for Political Literature, Moscow 1950, p. 602.

115. The most detailed of the many biographies of Voznesensky are in *Voprosy Istorii KPSS*, No. 6, 1963, and *Ukrainsky Istorychny Zhurnal*, No. 6, 1963.

116. There are several references in *Istoriya SSSR, Epokha Sotsializma*, State Publishing House for Political Literature, Moscow 1958, p. 638, and in Khrushchev's speech in the closed session of the 20th Party Congress.

117. A shattering article on the subject appeared in the *Folksstimme*, the organ of the Polish Jews (Warsaw, 4 April 1956). Other details in the brochure *The Fate of Soviet Jewry*, Jewish Labor Committee, New York.

118. Among the author's papers is a brochure *A Decade of Destruction: Jewish Culture in the USSR 1948-1958*, published by the Congress for Jewish Culture, New York.

119. Details of the 'Mingrelian Affair' are to be found in Khrushchev's speech in the closed session of the 20th Party Congress and in *Istoriya SSSR, Epokha Sotsializma*, Moscow 1958, p. 683 f.

120. A good survey of these events is contained in three reports by Wlodzimierz Sznarbachowski in the weekly *Ostatnie Wiadomosci* (Mannheim), 11 and 25 May and 1 June 1951.

121. Franz Borkenau wrote a series of articles on this subject in the *Rheinischer Merkur* between January and May 1953.

122. *Ocherki Istorii Kommunisticheskoy Partii Gruzii*, Vol. 2, Tbilisi 1963, p. 243.

123. For further details see Borys Lewytzkyj, *Die Sowjetukraine 1944 bis 1963*, Cologne 1964, p. 87.

124. Quoted from the literary journal *Dnipro*, No. 12, 1962, Kiev.

125. Based on the statements of N. Khokhlov, published by him immediately after his removal to the West. See also his *Recht auf Gewissen*, Deutsche Verlags-Anstalt, Stuttgart 1960.

126. This was never officially acknowledged. The statement is based on press reports from leading Western journalists in Moscow.

127. The circumstances of Beria's liquidation are graphically described by Wolfgang Leonhard in his *Kreml ohne Stalin*, Verlag für Politik und Wirtschaft, Cologne 1959, pp. 106-15.

128. *Bakinsky Rabochy*, 23 March 1956.

129. B. Nikolayevsky, *Rastrel Ryumina* (the shooting of Ryumin), in the *Sotsialistichesky Vestnik*, 1956, p. 154, 1958.

130. For the official biography of Serov see *Bolshaya Sovetskaya Entsiklopediya*, Vol. 51, Moscow 1958, p. 268.

131. D. S. Karev, op. cit., p. 100, a summary of the measures taken to restore 'Socialist legality'. See also the Party organ *Partiynaya Zhizn'*, No. 4, February 1957, pp. 66-71.

132. Brigitte Gerland, *Die Hölle ist ganz anders* (Vorkuta concentration camp), Steingruben Verlag, Stuttgart; and Josef Schomer, *Die Toten kehren zurück* (the report of a Vorkuta doctor), Verlag Kiepenheuer & Witsch, Cologne 1954.

133. A more precise account of these events is given by Wanda Bronska-Pampuch (Alfred Brumeister), *Der Aufstand von Kingir*, in the 'Aus Politik und Zeitgeschichte' supplement of the weekly *Das Parlament*, 30 May 1956.

134. The titles of these three brochures, published by Nabat, are *Delo Parashutistov: Delo NTS; Delo NTS i Delo Trukhnovicha;* and *Delo Myullera: Delo NTS*.

135. After the report *Quadrat B-52*, published by Molodaya Gvardiya, Moscow 1956.

136. After reports that appeared in various Soviet newspapers in 1917.

137. *Poymany s Polichnym* (caught in the act), Moscow 1962.

138. Klaus Westen, 'Recht und Rechtsprechung in der Sowjetunion', in *Osteuropa*, Nos. 7/8, July/August 1965.

139. A comparatively good analysis of this dangerous 'national crime' is to be found in M. V. Turetsky's *Osobo Opasnye Gosudarstvenniye Prestupleniya*, published by the Moscow State University. Our account is taken from p. 19.

140. Reinhart Maurach, 'Todesstrafe in der UdSSR', in *Osteuropa*, Nos. 11/12, November/December 1963, p. 745 ff.

141. 'Die UdSSR und die Todesstrafe', in the *Bulletin der Internationalen Juristen-Kommission*, No. 12, Geneva 1961, p. 69.

142. *Vedomosti Verkhovnogo Soveta SSSR*, No. 17, 1947.

143. See *Die Zeit* (the Hamburg weekly), Nos. 26/27 of 26 June and 3 July 1964. Also in *Kultura* Nos. 7 and 8, 1962, *Poetzya Przed Zadem v Leningradzie*, pp. 3-28. A selection of Brodsky's poems, translated into German by Heinrich Ost and edited with a foreword by Alexander Kaempfe, was published in *Ausgewählte Gedichte* by Berchtle, Munich, in 1966.

144. For more details compare the work of the American writers David Wise and Thomas B. Rose, *Die Unsichtbare Regierung*, Scheffler, Frankfurt-am-Main 1966, p. 121 ff.

145. German edition: Oleg Penkovsky, *Geheime Aufzeichnungen*, Droemersche Verlagsanstalt, Munich 1966.

146. See, e.g., Erich F. Pruck's commentary in *Osteuropa*, No. 4, April 1966.

147. See, e.g., *Suchasnist'*, a monthly published in Munich, No. 8, 1965, p. 124.

148. *Golos Rodiny*, Berlin, No. 91, November 1960.

149. For a well-documented but one-sided account of the murder of Rebet and Bandera see Karl Anders, *Mord auf Befehl: Der Fall Stashynsky*, published by Fritz Schlichtenmayer, Tübingen 1963.

150. Quoted from *Programme and Statute of the Communist Party of the Soviet Union*, approved by the 22nd Congress of the Party in October 1961, Dietz Verlag, East Berlin, p. 100.

151. Quoted from *Die Kunst gehört dem Volke: Reden zur Kulturpolitik*, Dietz Verlag, East Berlin 1963, p. 114 f.

152. Ibid., p. 122.

153. Published in *Nedelya* (the Sunday edition of *Izvestiya*), No. 35, November 1965.

154. According to *Sovetskaya Yustitsiya*, No. 6, March 1966.

155. *Izvestiya*, 13 January 1966. See also the *Bulletin der Internationalen Juristen-Kommission*, No. 26, June 1966, Geneva, p. 37 ff.

156. Ibid., p. 39 ff.

157. *L'Humanité*, 1 February 1966.

158. *Bulletin der Internationalen Juristen-Kommission*, No. 26, June 1966, Geneva, p. 48.

159. Vasyl Symonenko, *Bereh Chekan'* (shore of expectation), Verlag Prolog, New York and Munich 1965.

160. Quoted from N. Zubov, op. cit., p. 276.

161. *Pravda*, 31 May 1966.

162. Ibid., 1 April 1966.

163. Ibid., 30 May 1966.

164. Theo Pirker, *Die Moskauer Schauprozesse 1936-1938*, Munich 1963.

165. *Die Sozialistische Gezetzlichkeit im Urteil des XXII. Kongresses der KPdSU*, in the *Bulletin der Internationalen Juristen-Kommission*, No. 13, 1962, p. 42.

Bibliography

AGABEKOV, G., *OGPU; The Russian Terror*, New York 1931
ALEKSANDROV, N., 'Ukreplenie Sotsialisticheskoy Sakonnosti, Vazhnoe Us-
lovie Razvitiya Sotsialisticheskogo Stroja' (the strengthening of Socialist
legality, an important precondition for the development of the Socialist
system), in *Kommunist*, No. 1/1957
ANDERS, KARL, *Mord auf Befehl*, Verlag Fritz Schlichtenmayer, Tübingen
1963
ARTEMYEV, V., *Labour Camps and Colonies: Studies on the Soviet Union*, In-
stitute for the Study of the USSR, Munich, No. 4/1962
AVTORKHANOV, A., *Tekhnologiya Vlasti* (technology of power), Verlag ZOPE,
Munich 1959
——, *The Communist Party Apparatus*, New York 1966
BAILEY, G., *La Guerre des Services Secrets Soviétiques*, Paris 1962
BALTICUS, S., 'The Russian Mystery: Behind the Tukhachevsky Pact', in
Foreign Affairs, October 1937
BARNES, J., 'The Great Bolshevik Cleansing', in *Foreign Affairs*, April 1939
BARTON, P., 'An End to Concentration Camps ?', in *Problems of Communism*,
Washington, Vol. XI, March 1962
BECK, F., and GODIN, W., *Russian Purge, and the Extraction of Confessions*,
New York 1951
BERMAN, H., *Justice in Russia: an Interpretation of Soviet Law*, Cambridge,
Mass., 1963.
——, 'Soviet Law Reform: Dateline Moscow 1957', in *Yale Law Journal*, July
1957
——, and KERNER, M., *Documents on Soviet Military Law and Administration*,
Cambridge, Mass., 1963
BERNAUT, E., and LEITES, N., *Ritual of Liquidation*, Glencoe 1954
BERSHEDA, R. V., *Zakhody Zomunistychnoi Partii i Radyanskoho Uryadu po
Zmitsnennyu Sotsialistychnoi Zakonnosti* (measures of the Communist Party
and the Soviet Government for the strengthening of Socialist legality), Kiev
1956
BILYNSKY, A., and HOLUBNYCHY, V., 'Kontsentratsiyni Tabory' (concen-
tration camps), from the *Entsyklopediya Ukrainoznavstva*, Vol. III, Paris/
New York 1960
BLIT, LUCIAN, *The Case of Henryk Erlich and Viktor Alter*, London 1943
BOURGART, J. R. D., *L'Espionnage Soviétique*, Paris 1962

332 BIBLIOGRAPHY

BRZEZINSKI, Z., *Political Control in the Soviet Army*, New York 1954
——, *The Permanent Purge: Politics in Soviet Totalitarianism*, Cambridge, Mass., 1957
BUBER, M., *Als Gefangene bei Stalin und Hitler*, Verlag der Zwölf, Munich 1949 (*Under Two Dictators*, trans. E. Fitzgerald, Gollancz 1949)
BURGANOVA, D. A., and SARKIN, V. G., *Na Strazhe Leninskogo Edinstva i Chistoty Partiynykh Ryadov* (on the watch for Leninist unity and the purity of the Party cadres), Kazan University Press 1965
BUSHUEV, I. A., *Ispravitel'nye Raboty*, Moscow 1959
CHERNYAVSKY, V., and PETROV, L., 'Razvedka SShA: Vliyanie na Vneshnyuyu Politiku' (USA news service: influence on foreign affairs), in *Mezhdunarodnaya Zhizn*, No. 10/1964
CHISTYAKOV, N. F., 'Sotsialisticheskaya Zakonnost' i Syazi s Sovetskoy Obshchestvennostyu—Osnovye Printsipy Deyatel'nosti Sledsvennogo Apparata Organov Gosudararstvennoy Bezopasnosti' (Socialist legality and its connection with Soviet society – the main principles of the organs of State security), in *Sovetskoe Gosudarstvo i Pravo*, No. 11/1960
CILIGA, A., *The Russian Enigma*, London 1940
CISZEK, W. J., *L'Espion du Vatican*, Paris 1966
COHEN, S. F., and TUCKER, ROBERT (editors), *The Great Purge Trial*, New York, 1965
COLLARD, D., *Soviet Justice and the Trial of Radek and Others*, London 1937
CONQUEST, R., *Power and Policy in the USSR*, New York 1966
——, 'De-Stalinization and the Heritage of Terror', in A. Dallin and A. F. Westin's *Politics in the Soviet Union*, New York 1966
CZAPSKI, J., *Terre Inhumaine*, Paris 1949
DALLIN, D. J., and NIKOLAEVSKY, B. I., *Forced Labour in Soviet Russia*, New Haven 1947
DANIELS, R. V., *The Conscience of the Revolution: Communist Opposition in Soviet Russia*, Cambridge, Mass., 1960
DANISZEWSKI, T., *Feliks Dzierzynski, Jego i Zycie, Praca i Walka*, Warsaw 1948
DEUTSCHER, I., *Stalin: A Political Biography*, London 1949
——, *The Prophet Outcast: Trotsky 1919-1940*, London 1963
DEWEY, J., et al., *Not Guilty*: Report of the Commission of Inquiry into the Charges Made against Leon Trotsky in the Moscow Trials, New York 1963
DULLES, ALLAN, *The Craft of Intelligence*, New York 1963
DUNNE, K., and EDWARDS, B., *A Study of a Master Spy*, London 1961
DZERZHINSKY, F., *Izbrannye Stat'i i Rechi*, Moscow 1947
DZIEWANOWSKI, M. K., *The Communist Party of Poland: an Outline of History*, Cambridge, Mass. 1959
EDELMAN, MAURICE, *GPU Justice*, London 1938
EHRENFELD, B. K., 'Delo Malinovskogo' (the Malinowsky case), in *Voprosy Istorii*, No. 7/1965
EPOPKIN, M. I., *Upravlenie v Oblasti Okhrany Obshchestvennogo Poryadka* (administration in the department of the maintenance of public order), Moscow 1965
FAINSOD, M., *How Russia is Ruled*, Cambridge, Mass., 1953
——, *Smolensk under Soviet Rule*, Cambridge, Mass., 1958
FARAGO, L., *The Way of War: the Anatomy of Espionage and Intelligence*, New York 1954

FEDENKO, P., 'The Principle of Selective Rehabilitation', in *Bulletin of the Institute for the Study of the USSR*, Munich April 1962

——, *Pislya Protessu Sohdana Stashynskoho* (after the proceedings against Bogdan Stashinsky), Munich 1963

FEIFER, G., *Justice in Moscow*, New York 1964

FISCHER, RUTH, *Stalin and German Communism*, Cambridge, Mass., 1948

FOMIN, F., *Zapiski Starogo Chekista* (notes by a former Chekist), Moscow 1962

GLICHSMAN, J., *Tell the West*, New York 1948

——, *Police-State Methods in the Soviet Union*, Boston 1953

GOLINKO, V. K. L., 'Pervos Dela VECHEKA' (the 'first case' of the VECHEKA), in *Istoriya SSSR*, No. 4/1965

GONZALEZ, G., and GORKIN, J., *El Campesino: Life and Death in Soviet Russia*, New York 1952

GORNY, O. G., 'O Roli Sotsialisticheskoy Zakonnosti v Stroitel' stve i Ukreplenii Sovetskikh Vooruzhennykh Sil' (on the role of Socialist legality in the build-up and strengthening of the Soviet armed forces), in *Sovetskoye Gosudarstvo i Pravo*, No. 4/1963

GRZYBOWSKI, K., *Soviet Legal Institutions: Doctrines and Social Functions*, Ann Arbor, Mich., 1962

GSOVSKI, W., *Soviet Civil Law*, Ann Arbor, Mich., 1948

GSOVSKY, WLADIMIR, 'New Trends in Soviet Justice', in *Problems of Communism*, No. 1/1956

HAGEN, WALTER, *Die Geheime Front*, Nibelungen-Verlag, Linz/Vienna 1950 (W. Hoehl, *The Secret Front*, trans. R. H. Stevens, Weidenfeld and Nicolson, 1953)

HAZARD, J. N. (ed.), *Soviet Legal Philosophy*, Cambridge, Mass. 1941

——, *The Soviet System of Government*, Chicago 1957

——, 'Social Control through Law', in A. Dallin and A. F. Westin's (editors) *Politics in the Soviet Union*, New York 1966

HEALEY, DENIS (ed.), *The Curtain Falls: the Story of the Socialists in Eastern Europe*, London 1951

HEILBRUNN, OTTO, *Der Sowjetische Geheimdienst*, Verlag für Wehrwesen Bernard & Graefe, Frankfurt am Main 1956 (*The Soviet Secret Services*, Allen and Unwin 1956)

HEISLER, F., *The First Two Moscow Trials*, Chicago 1937

HERLING, A. K., *The Soviet Slave Empire*, New York 1951

HERLING, G., *A World Apart*, New York 1952

HINKLE, L. E., Jun., and H. G. WOLFF, 'Communist Interrogation and Indoctrination of Enemies of the People,' in *Archives of Neurology and Psychiatry*, Vol. 76/1956

HLYBINNY, U., *Vierzig Jahre Weissruthenischer Kultur unter den Sowjets*, Munich 1959

HOLUBNYCHY, V., 'Outline History of the Communist Party of Ukraine', in *Ukrainian Review*, Munich, No. 6/1958

——, 'History of the Ukrainian Soviet Socialist Republic', in *Ukraine: a Concise Encyclopedia*, Toronto 1965

HUNTER, E., *Brainwashing, from Pavlov to Powers*, New York 1960

IGNOTUS, P., *Political Prisoner*, Routledge, London 1959

JASNY, N., 'Labour and Output in Soviet Concentration Camps', in *Journal of Political Economy*, October 1952

KANAY, Y., 'Yak Zgynuly v SSSR providnyky Bundu' (how the Bund leaders in the Soviet Union died), in *Vpered*, No. 1/2, Munich 1951 (Ukrainian)

KAREV, D. S., 'Soviet Criminal Law Reform', in *Harvard Law Record* for 1 May 1958

KELSEN, H., *The Communist Theory of Law*, New York 1955

KENNAN, GEORGE F., *Soviet-American Relations 1917-20*, Faber and Faber 1956

KHOKHLOV, N. E., *In the Name of Conscience*, London 1960

KONDRATIEV, N., *Marshal Blyukher*, Moscow 1965

KOROL'KOV, Y., *Chelovek Dlya Kotorogo ne Bylo Tayn* (Richard Sorge, the man for whom there were no secrets), Moscow 1966

KOSTIUK, H., *Stalinist Rule in the Ukraine*, New York 1960

KRAKHMALNYK, L. G., 'Pravovoe Regulirovanie Ispravitel'nykh Rabot' (law regulation in corrective works), in *Uchenye Zapiski Vsesoyuznogo Nauchno-issledovatel'skogo Instituta Sovetskogo Zakonodatel'stva*, Vypusk 7, Moscow 1966

KRIVITSKY, W. G., *Ich war in Stalins Dienst!*, Albert de Lange, Amsterdam 1940 (*I was Stalin's Agent*, Hamish Hamilton 1939)

KUDRYAVTSEV, P. I., 'Vazhny Etap v Razvitii Sovetskogo Zakonodatel'stva i v Ukreplenii Sotsialisticheskoy Sakonnosti' (an important stage in the development of Soviet legislation and the strengthening of Socialist legality), in *Sovetskoe Gosudarstvo i Pravo*, No. 2/1959

KULBERG, Y. M., *Prestupleniya Protiv Pravosudiya* (crimes against justice), Moscow 1962

LASKY, M. J., 'Why Kremlin Extorts Confessions', in *Commentary*, January 1952

LEONHARD, SUSANNE, *Gestohlenes Leben*, Frankfurt am Main 1956

LEONHARD, WOLFGANG, 'Terror in the Soviet System: Trends and Portents', in *Problems of Communism*, March/April 1958

——, *Kreml ohne Stalin*, Verlag für Politik und Wirtschaft, Cologne 1959 (*The Kremlin since Stalin*, trans. Elizabeth Wiskemann, O.U.P./1962)

LIPPER, E., *Eleven Years in Soviet Prison Camps*, Chicago 1951

LIPSON, LEON, 'Socialist Legality: the Mountain has Labored', in *Problems of Communism*, March/April 1959

LOEBER, DIETRICH, 'Sowjetische Gesetzlichkeit im Zeichen des XX. Parteikongresses der KPdSU', in *Osteuropa-Recht*, Stuttgart, October 1956

MADER (JULIUS), STUCHLIK (GERHARD), and PEHNERT (HORST), Dr. *Sorge Funkt aus Tokyo*, Deutscher Militärverlag, East Berlin 1965

MAURACH, REINHART, *Handbuch der Sowjetverfassung*, Isar Verlag, Munich 1955

MAXIMOFF, G. P., *The Guillotine at Work*, Chicago 1940

MCCLOSKY, H., and TURNER, J. E., *One of the Fifteen Million*, Boston 1952

MEISSNER, BORIS, *Russland im Umbruch*: der Wandel in der Herrschafts-ordnung und Socialen Struktur der Sowjetunion, Verlag für Geschichte und Politik, Frankfurt am Main 1951

——, *Russland unter Chruschtschow*, R. Oldenbourg, Munich 1960

MINAYEV, *Taynoe Stanovitsya Yavnym* (the secret is revealed), Voyenisdat, Moscow 1961

MIRONOV, N. R., 'O Sochetanii Ubezhdeniya i Prinuzhdeniya v Bor'be s Antiobshchestvennymi Yavleniyami' (on the combination of persuasion and force in the struggle against anti-social phenomena), in *Kommunist*, No. 3/1961

——, 'Vosstanovlenie i Razvitie Leninskikh Printsipov Sotsialisticheskoy

Zakonnosti, 1953-1963' (restoration and development of Leninist principles of Socialist legality), in *Voprosy Istorii KPSS*, No. 2/1964

MOORE, B., 'The Recent Purge in the USSR', in *Review of Politics*, January 1947

——, *Soviet Politics: the Dilemma of Power*, Cambridge, Mass., 1950

——, *Terror and Progress, USSR*, Cambridge, Mass., 1954

MORA, S., and ZWIERNIAK, P., *Sprawiedliwose Sowiecka*, Rome 1945

MORGAN, G. G., *Soviet Administrative Legality: the Role of the Attorney General's Office*, Stanford, Cal., 1962

MOSELY, P., 'Recent Soviet Trials and Politicians', in *Yale Review*, June 1938

MURASHOV, S. V., and SOLOPANOV, Y. V., 'Sovetskaya Militsiya kak Organ Okhreny Obshchestvennago Poryadka' (the Soviet militia as an organ for the maintenance of public order), in *Sovetskoe Gosudarstvo i Pravo*, No. 12/1962

NICOLAEVSKY, B. I., and DALLIN, D. J., *Forced Labour in Soviet Russia*, New Haven 1947

NIKOLAEV, V., 'Preodolenie Nepravil'nykh Teorly v Ugolovom Prave: Vazhnoe Uslovie Ukrepleniya Sotsialisticheskoy Zakonnosti' (the overthrowing of false theories in criminal law: an important precondition for the strengthening of Socialist legality), in *Kommunist*, No. 14/1956

NIKULIN, LEV, *Tukhachevsky*, Voenizdat, Moscow 1964

NOBLE, J. H., *I was a Slave in Russia*, New York 1958

ORACH, E. M., 'Ponyatta Sotsialistychnoi Spravedlyvosti' (the meaning of Socialist legality), in *Viznyk*, Kiev 1966

ORLOV, ALEXANDER, *Kremlgeheimnisse*, Marienburg-Verlag, Würzburg 1953

OURALOW, A., *Staline au Pouvoir*, Paris 1952

PAMPUCH-BRONSKA, WANDA, 'Predsmertnaya Chistka Kominterna' (the purging of the Comintern before its abolition), in *Sotsialistichesky Vestnik*, June/July 1952

——, 'Zhenshciny na Kolyme' (women in Kolyma), in *Sotsialistichesky Vestnik*, October 1952

——, 'Ikh Deti: Vstrcha Novogo Goda 1938' (your children, New Year's Eve 1938), in *Sotsialistichesky Vestnik*, January/February 1953

——, 'Kolyma va Vremya i Posie Voyny' (Kolyma during and after the war), in *Sotsialistichesky Vestnik*, March 1953

PANKOV, D. V., *Komkor Eideman*, Voenizdat, Moscow 1965

PARVILAHTI, UNTO, *In Berijas Garten: 10 Jahre Gefangener in Russland und Sibirien*, Verlag Das Bergland-Buch, Salzburg 1960 (*Beria's Gardens: 10 Years' Captivity in Russia and Siberia*, trans. Alan Blair, 1959)

PASCHNER, GÜNTHER, *Im Teufelskreis des Terrors*, Harald Boldt, Boppard, 1964

PESKOV, E., 'Sotsiologiya Razvedki i Shpionazha' (sociology of the information service and espionage), in *Kommunist*, No. 11/1960

PETROV, L. P., and CHERNYAVSKY, V., 'Razvedka SShA: Vliyanie na Vneshnyuyu Politiku' (information service of the USA: its influence on foreign affairs), in *Mezhdunarodnaya Zhizn'*, No. 10/1964

PETROV, V., *Soviet Gold: My Life as a Slave Laborer in the Siberian Mines*, New York 1949

PETROV, Y. P., *Partiynoe Stroitel'stvo v Sovetskoy Armii i Flote 1918-1961* (the Party structure in the Soviet army and fleet), Voenizdat, Moscow 1964

PIRKER, THEO, *Die Moskauer Schauprozesses 1936-1938*, Deutscher Taschenbuchverlag, Munich 1963

——, *Utopie und Mythos der Weltrevolution*, Deutscher Taschenbuchverlag, Munich 1964

336 BIBLIOGRAPHY

PISTRAK, L., 'Khrushchev and the Purges', in *Problems of Communism*, Washington, Vol. XI, January 1962

PRUCK, ERICH, 'Die Sowjetischen Streitkräfte in Politischer Sicht', in *Zeitschrift für Politik*, No. 4/1957

——, 'Die Geheimpolizei im Totalitären Regime', in *Politische Studien*, No. 109/1959

——, *Der Rote Soldat*, Günter Olzog, Munich 1961

RACZYNSKI, EDWARD, *Wsojuszniczym Londynie 1939-1945* (in allied London), Polish Research Centre, London 1960

ROSENTHAL, G., *Mémoire pour la Réhabilitation de Zinoviev: L'Affaire Kirov*, Paris 1962

ROSS, THOMAS B., and WISE, DAVID, *Die Unsichtbare Regierung*, Heinrich Scheffler, Frankfurt am Main 1966

RUDENKO, R. A., 'O Zadachakh Dalneyshego Ikrepleniya Sotsialisticheskoy Zakonnosti v Svete Resheniy XXI, S8ezda KPSS' (concerning the further development of Socialist legality in the light of the resolutions of the 21st Congress of the Communist Party of the Soviet Union), in *Sovetskoe Gosudarstvo i Pravo*, No. 3/1960, pp. 1-12

SAVARIUS, V., *Freiwillige für den Galgen: die Geschichte eines Schauprozesses*, Verlag Wissenschaft und Politik, Cologne 1963

SAVITSKY, V. M., *Prokurorsky Nadzor za Doznaniem i Predvaritel'nym Sledstviem* (control of the state attorney's office in regard to confessions and preliminary investigations), Moscow 1919

SCHACHMAN, M., *Behind the Moscow Trial*, New York 1956

SCHANDORFF, WERNER, *Moskaus Permanente Säuberung*, Günter Olzog, Munich 1964

SCHAPIRO, L., *The Origin of the Communist Autocracy: Political Opposition in the Soviet State 1917-1922*, Cambridge, Mass., 1955

SCHATTEN, FRITZ, 'Renaissance der Tscheka: Chruschtschow und die Geheimpolizei', in *Die Politische Meinung*, October 1952

SCHLESINGER, R., *Soviet Legal Theory*, London 1945

SCHOLMER, J., *Vorkuta*, New York 1955

SCHULTZ, LOTHAR, 'Die Entwicklung der Rechtswissenschaft seit Stalins Tod', in *Osteuropa-Recht*, Stuttgart, December 1955

SCOTT, E. J., 'The Cheka', in *St Anthony's Papers: Soviet Affairs*, Chatto & Windus, London 1959, No. 1

SEDOV, L., *Livre Rouge sur le Procès de Moscou*, Paris 1936

SERGE, VICTOR, *From Lenin to Stalin*, New York 1937

SLOSSER, R. M., and WOLIN, S., *The Russian Secret Police*, New York 1957

SOFINOV, P. G., *Ocherki Istorii VECHEKA 1917-1922* (outline history of the VECHEKA), Moscow 1960

SOLZHENITSYN, A., *One Day in the Life of Ivan Denisovich*, New York 1963

STEVENS, J., 'The Russian Purge Seen from Below', in *New Republic*, 20 October 1937

STOIANOVICH, A., *La Philosophie du Droit en URSS*, Paris 1965

STROGOVICH, M. S., *Osnovnye Voprosy Sovetskoy Sotsialisticheskoy Zakonnosti* (the basic questions of Soviet Socialist legality), Moscow 1966

STYPULKOWSKI, Z., *Invitation to Moscow*, London 1951

SWIANIEWICZ, S., *Forced Labor and Economic Development*, New York 1965

SWIATLO, J., *Za Kulisami Bezpieki i Partii*, New York 1955

TADEVOSYAN, V. S., 'V. I. Lenin o Sotsialisticheskoy Zakonnosti' (Lenin and Socialist legality), in *Sovetskoe Gosudarstvo i Pravo*, No. 5/1960

TROTSKY, LEO, *Stalin: Eine Biographie*, Kiepenheuer & Witsch, Cologne & Berlin 1952 (*Stalin*, 1947)

TSCHERNAVIN, V. T., *I Speak for the Silent Prisoners of the Soviets*, Boston 1935

TURETSKY, M. V., *Osobo Opasnye Gosudarstvennye Prestuoleniya* (especially dangerous crimes against the state), Moscow 1965

VYSHINSKY, A. Y., *The Law of the Soviet State*, New York 1948

——, *Teoriya Sudebnykh, Dokazatel'stv v Sovetskom Prave* (the theory of legal evidence in Soviet law), Moscow 1950

WEISSBERG-CYBULSKI, ALEXANDER, *Hexensabbat*, Verlag der Frankfurter Heft, Frankfurt am Main 1951

WESTEN, KLAUS, 'Recht und Rechtsprechung in der Sowjetunion Heute', in *Osteuropa*, No. 7/8, 1865

WRAGA, RYSZARD, 'Trust' (Polish), in *Kultura*, No. 4/5, Paris 1949

YAKOVLEV, *Konsentratsionnye Lagerya SSSR* (concentration camps in the USSR), published by the Institut zur Erforschung der Geschichte und Kultur der UdSSR, Munich 1955

ZAWODNY, J. K., *Death in the Forest*, Notre Dame, Ind., 1962

ZELLWEGER, EDWARD, 'Das Prinzip der Sozialistischen Gesetzlichkeit', in *Journal der Internationalen Juristen-Kommission*, Vol. V, No. 2, winter 1964

American Federation of Labor in Russia, Washington 1949

Entsiklopedichesky Slovar' Pravovykh Znaniy (encyclopedic dictionary of jurisprudence), Moscow 1965

Kommunisticheskaya Partiya v Bor'be za Uprochnenie i Razvitie Sotsialisticheskogo Obshchestva, 1937 god—Iyun' 1941 goda (the Communist Party in the struggle for the establishment and development of the Socialist society, 1937 to June 1941), Moscow 1962

Kommunisticheskaya Partiya Uzbekistana v Tsifrakh (Sbornik Statistcheskikh Materialov) 1924-1964 gody (the Communist Party of Uzbekistan in figures, a statistical omnibus volume for 1924-1964), Tashkent 1964

Lazlo Rajk und Komplizen vor dem Volksgericht, Dietz Verlag, East Berlin, 1949

Lenin o Sotsialisticheskoy Zakonnosti, Moscow 1961

Lyudi Bud'te Bditel'ny! (men, be on the alert), Tallinn 1961

Marshal Tukhachevsky, Voenizdat, Moscow 1965

Methods of Forceful Indoctrination: Observations and Interviews, Group for the Advancement of Psychiatry, New York 1957

Penkovsky's Papers, New York 1965

Poymany a Polichnym (caught in the act), Kiev

Problemy Pravoznavstva, Kiev

Problemy Razvitiya Sovetskogo Ispravitel'no-Trudovogo Zakonodatel'stva (problems of the development of Soviet legality for corrective and labour camps), Saratov 1961

Radyanske Pravo, Kiev

Rech F. E. Dzerzhinskogo na Otkrytii IV Konferentsii Gubernskikh Chrezvychaynykh Komissiy. Vvodnaya stat'ya A. K. Goncharova/I. A. Doroshenko. (The Speech of F. E. Dzerzhinsky at the opening of the 4th Conference of the Government Cheka Commissions. Academy of Sciences of the USSR, Moscow 1917-1919)

Sotsialisticheskaya Zakonnost'

'Sovershenstvovanie Sledstvennoy Raboty: Vashnoe Uslovie dal' neyshego Ukrepleniya Sotsialisticheskoy Zakonnosti' (perfection of the interrogation system: an important precondition for the firmer establishment of Socialist legality), in *Sovetskoe Gosudarstvo i Pravo*, No. 11/1964

Sovetskaya Kriminologia, published by the Institute for the Study of the Causes of Crime and Measures for its Prevention, Moscow 1966

Sovetskaya Yustitsiya

'Sovetskie Organy Gosudarstvennoy Bezopasnosti v gody Velikoy Otechestvennoy Voyny' (Soviet security organs during the Great Patriotic War), in *Voprosy Istorii*, No. 5/1965

Sudebnaya Praktika Verkhovnogo Suda SSSR (the judicial procedure of the Supreme Court of the USSR)

The Dark Side of the Moon, New York 1947

Uchenye Trudy Vsesoyuznogo Instituta Yuridicheskikh Nauk (studies of the Union institute of juristic science)

Uchenye Zapiski Vsesoyuznogo Nauchne-Issledovatel'skogo Instituta Sovetskogo Zakonodatel'stva (studies of the scientific Union research institute of Soviet jurisprudence)

United Nations, International Labour Office, Report of the Ad Hoc Committee on Forced Labour, No. 36, Geneva 1953

United States Department of State Information Service, Forced Labour in the Soviet Union, Publication No. 4716, Washington 1952

Vestnik Moskovskogo Universiteta, 12th Series, *Law*

Zbirnyk na Poshanu Ukrainskykh Uchenykh Znyshchenykh Bol'shevytskoyu Moskvoyu. Zapysky Naukovogo Tovarystva im. Shevchenka. (Omnibus volume in honour of the Ukrainian intelligentsia liquidated by Bolshevist Moscow. Drawings by the scientific Shevchenko Institute.) Vol. CLXXIII, Paris 1962

Valuable references and documents concerning the activities of the Soviet security organs will be found in the following journals.

Byulleten' Oppozitsii, the organ of the Trotskyists in exile (for the years 1929–1941; discontinued)

Sotsialistichesky Vestnik, the organ of the Russian Mensheviks, published in New York

Ostprobleme, published in Bonn

Osteuropa, published in Stuttgart

Bulletin der Internationalen Juristen-Kommission and *Journal der Internationalen Juristen-Kommission*, both published in Geneva

Index of Persons

Index of Persons